LOCAL GOVERNANCE IN INDIA

Local Governance in India
Decentralization and Beyond

edited by
NIRAJA GOPAL JAYAL
AMIT PRAKASH
PRADEEP K. SHARMA

OXFORD
UNIVERSITY PRESS

OXFORD

UNIVERSITY PRESS

Oxford University Press is a department of the University of Oxford.
It furthers the University's objective of excellence in research, scholarship,
and education by publishing worldwide. Oxford is a registered trademark of
Oxford University Press in the UK and in certain other countries

Published in India by
Oxford University Press
22 Workspace, 2nd Floor, 1/22 Asaf Ali Road, New Delhi 110002, India

First Edition published in 2006
Oxford India Paperbacks 2007
Sixth impression 2015
Digitally Printed in 2024

ISBN-13: 978-0-19-569296-9
ISBN-10: 0-19-569296-9

Typeset in Bembo 10.5/12.5
by Sai Graphic Design, New Delhi 110 055
Printed at Manipal Technologies Limited, Manipal

Contents

Tables, Figures, and Boxes

TABLES

FIGURES

BOXES

Preface

In September 2000, world leaders agreed, on the Millennium Development Goals (MDGs), which are an ambitious agenda for reducing poverty and improving lives, at the Millennium Summit. The MDGs are time-bound and quantified goals and targets for addressing extreme poverty in its many dimensions. Eradicating extreme poverty and hunger, along with other goals such as achieving universal primary education, promoting gender equality and empowering women, reducing child mortality, improving maternal health, combating HIV/AIDS, malaria and other diseases, and ensuring environmental sustainability, provides the overarching framework for development action by all concerned. The attainment of the MDGs hinges not only on sound pro-poor macro-economic policies but also on how well the institutions of governance are structured and how well they function, especially at the local level. Increasingly, more and more countries are beginning to realize the importance of strengthening local governance to achieve development goals.

If designed and executed properly, decentralization promotes efficiency and equity in service delivery, inclusiveness in local governance through representation and participation, and accountability. A development strategy based on decentralized decision-making has great potential for combating poverty.

In India, though panchayati raj has been around for a long time, it was not until the passage of the 73rd and 74th constitutional amendments that it acquired a legally mandated status and thus paved the way for direct democracy at local levels, both in rural and urban areas. Over a decade of constitutionally mandated panchayati raj has led to the emergence of a large number of locally elected leaders, including for the first time over one million women. 'The world's largest experiment in local democracy' is how Mark Malloch Brown, a former UNDP Administrator and now Chef de Cabinet to UN Secretary General, described India's panchayati raj on one of his visits to India.

Panchayati raj offers tremendous potential to make a difference to the pace and pattern of local development. How this potential will be realized depends a great deal on how well the panchayats are empowered with funds, functions, and functionaries. Panchayats have been playing a major role in the implementation of anti-poverty programmes. The recently launched National Rural Employment Guarantee Scheme (NREGS) also envisages a key role for panchayats in the identification of works, employment planning, and conducting social audit. NREGS is different from previous employment schemes as it recognizes employment as a legal right whose realization depends a great deal on the effectiveness of the local governance.

UNDP has been an active partner of national governments the world over in promoting decentralized governance. In India, the UN System has adopted the United Nations Development Assistance Framework (UNDAF) with strengthening decentralization as one of the two key priorities, with the other being promotion of gender equality. Decentralization is thus the underlying strategy for all UN agencies in India.

In order to learn from others' experience in how local action can bring about human development and social transformation, it is important that there is a place for governments, civil society organizations, local bodies, academia, and other stakeholders to share what works and, even more importantly, what does not. The United Nations remains committed to the sharing of such experience widely throughout the country. To this end, the UN Country Team has recently initiated a knowledge management initiative, Solution Exchange, to facilitate knowledge networks in thematic areas that are key to achieving the MDGs particularly as they relate to India's development goals and targets. One such network of Solution Exchange is the Community of Practice for Decentralization, which we believe will serve as a robust platform for the continued pursuit of the way forward in strengthening decentralization as a major strategy for human development.

This volume contains select papers that were presented at a Workshop on Local Governance organized by the Centre for the Study of Law and Governance at the Jawaharlal Nehru University, in collaboration with the UNDP and UN-Habitat in April 2002. UNDP's support to that workshop was a part of our continuous endeavour to interact with eminent researchers, scholars and on-the-ground practitioners. The papers in this volume examine a range of issues surrounding decentralization. The subtitle of the volume is indicative of the need to go beyond decentralization and look at aspects of local political dynamics and structure of local governance. I thank the Centre for the Study of Law and Governance and UN-Habitat for this important collaborative effort.

Partnership with UN-Habitat brought a special urban flavour to the workshop and I am happy that a section in this volume has papers that examine decentralization in an urban context.Another distinctive feature of this book is an examination of traditional local institutions and their interface with more formal local institutions.

I hope this book will contribute to the expansion of knowledge on decentralization in India and will provide fresh insights into the issues around deepening democracy for poverty eradication.

Maxine Olson
UNDP Resident Representative and
UN Resident Coordinator

Acknowledgements

This volume brings together a selection of essays on local governance that were presented at a Workshop on Local Governance organized by the Centre for the Study of Law and Governance, Jawaharlal Nehru University, in collaboration with the United Nations Development Programme (UNDP) and the United Nations Human Settlements Programme (UN-Habitat) on 11–12 April 2002. The workshop was supported by the Ford Foundation project grant to the Centre for the Study of Law and Governance, and by the UNDP and UN-Habitat. The editors would like to express their gratitude to these institutions.

The Workshop on Local Governance was a part of a series of conferences, workshops and seminars organized by the Centre for the Study of Law and Governance, JNU with the support of a project grant from the Ford Foundation. This grant has enabled the Centre to develop a variety of activities relevant to its academic mandate, including visiting fellowships and conferences, for which the Centre is truly grateful. Apart from the Workshop from which the present volume has emerged, conferences—national and international—have also been organized on a wide variety of themes, including governance, globalization and democracy; sustainable reforms in Indian administration; regulation; law, economics, and development; and the social and political dimensions of globalization. A series of volumes, based on the proceedings of these conferences, has already begun to emerge, the first of which—*Administrative Reforms: Towards Sustainable Practices*, edited by Amita Singh—has already been published, while three others are in various stages of publication.

The editors would like to thank all the contributors to this volume not only for their initial contributions but also for revising and updating their papers for inclusion in this volume. We are also thankful to Professor Kuldeep Mathur for his continued encouragement and support.

The views expressed in all the papers are the individual views of their respective authors, and do not necessarily represent the views of either the institutions to which they are affiliated or the agencies that supported the workshop.

Editors

1

Introduction

■ Niraja Gopal Jayal

The essays in this volume attempt to describe and analyse the complexity of local governance, both rural and urban, in contemporary India. The terms decentralization and local governance are often used interchangeably, but the subtitle of this volume alludes to the idea that, while decentralization must be the point of departure for any understanding of local governance in India, it by no means exhausts the subject of local governance, either as an empirical description of local reality or as a satisfactory analytical perspective on the subject. There is more to local governance today than a focus on decentralization alone allows us to apprehend.

There are at least three important reasons why a focus on decentralization in India can provide only a partial account of local governance. This is so because, first, decentralization—as mandated by the constitutional amendments, and enacted into law by the states—is minimalist in its conception and design. Given the rather narrow remit of decentralization, it would be risky to ignore or occlude from our vision the substantial areas left untouched by it. These are not empty spaces, but spaces that have institutional inhabitants and a political content that it is assuredly the business of the scholar to examine. Second, the achievement of an adequately robust form of decentralization remains a project beset with many difficulties, both institutional as well as social and political. Indeed, it is unclear whether this project is merely incomplete or unrealized at the present juncture, or whether it is, in its current form and design, incapable of accomplishment. A more comprehensive picture of local governance in all its complexity can arguably help us to explain at least some of the unfulfilled promises of decentralization, and point to the areas that need to be addressed for the objectives of decentralization to be more effectively realized. Finally, there are enormous regional variations in the way in which decentralization has been designed and implemented, and a comparison between, say, Kerala and Haryana might, to a first-time observer of Indian decentralization, even suggest that these states belong to two different countries! Variations across states in the practice of decentralization, and in the broader context of local governance, afford important comparative lessons.

To widen our vision beyond the design and implementation of the project of decentralization is to immediately perceive the fact that the revival of *panchayati raj* institutions (PRIs) has been paralleled by a proliferation in the number and variety of actors involved in governance at the local level. The local state is, in institutional terms, a constant, but in actual practice an entity whose relations with other emergent structures of governance merits investigation. Non-governmental organizations, for instance, are increasingly engaged in the delivery of public services; and user groups/committees are involved in the management of natural resources, sometimes in partnership with the state. The emergence of these, along with the constitutional institutions of local self-governance, suggests that there has occurred a transformation in the complex interrelationships that obtain at the local level: between panchayat institutions, the local state and bureaucracy, the non-governmental organizations, user committees, and self-help groups, among others. What are the implications of this proliferation of institutions of different types, whether they belong to the domain of the state or that of civil society, or even occupy an in-between space? Should their role be evaluated in terms of their functional efficacy or in terms of their contribution (or otherwise) to the project of local democracy? If description must precede evaluation, such descriptions are on the whole rather few and far between, and it is at least part of the purpose of this volume to make good this gap.

THE CASE FOR DECENTRALIZATION

Theoretically, the normative appeal of arguments for local democracy has resided in the belief that the quality of political participation, and therefore of public life itself, will be substantively transformed only when people foregather to collectively debate and deliberate on issues of common concern, and are provided with decision-making powers to give effect to their shared concerns. The most distinguished ancestor of this view was, of course, none other than John Stuart Mill who provided two important arguments for local democracy: first, that local political institutions are 'a school of political capacity', making citizens capable of genuine and informed participation; and, second, that such institutions would be more efficient if informed by local interests and local knowledge. Local democracy, thus, became a way of enabling both participation and deliberation, of effecting a form of direct democracy, and so imparting a richer and more immediate meaning to the democratic ideal than the rather minimal conception of it implied in the idea of elections.

Another argument for decentralization, weaker and more instrumentalist but also grounded in the democratic ideal, questions centralized patterns of decision-making because they are insensitive to the local problems and conditions that require attention, and that the people of the locality know best. The people, on this account, are the best judges of their needs and aspirations, and decentralization ensures that those who are likely to be affected by decisions participate in the making of them.[1] The idea that centralized decision-making can only provide inappropriately uniform solutions to diverse local problems is of course a particularly compelling argument in the context of large and heterogeneous societies like India's.

In the Indian context, the ideal of local democracy, as incorporated in the 73rd and 74th constitutional amendments, has been invested with these hopes and more.[2] Apart from the domestic political imperatives of this enactment, the global context also helps to explain why local democracy suddenly became the magic formula for all that is desirable—enhanced participation, greater public accountability, effective programmes of poverty alleviation, and even the mitigation of the cumulative effects of social and economic inequalities. The new currency acquired by the idea of decentralization, both in international agencies and in many countries across the world, was only partly a result of a revisiting of the idea of local democracy. It also reflected a strong disenchantment with centralized modes of governing.

Centralized governance had become substantially discredited in the post-Cold War world, with the collapse of the erstwhile socialist states on the one hand, and the whittling down of welfare state apparatuses on the other. In Western Europe and North America, decentralization was part of the institutional response to fiscal crisis and the growing restlessness with large and ineffectual public sector bureaucracies, paralleling the ideological shift from state to market. As the legitimacy of the public sector as a service provider was called into question, decentralization was often presented as a component of the strategy to manage the economic crisis by allowing for greater local diversity in public service delivery, and as part of the search for the appropriate 'institutional mix' for an effective state–society synergy. In the now vast literature on the new public management, decentralization is endorsed because it is seen to be furthering efficiency and economy. The contracting out of public service delivery to non-governmental and private agencies, or in partnership with these, has the same rationale.

In non-normative academic analysis, too, the idea of decentralization has been explored and endorsed in various ways. The literature on fiscal federalism in the 1970s (Oates 1972) had argued the importance of devolving powers of taxation to local authorities, the justification being that this would encourage greater fiscal responsibility, and raise the stakes of local authorities in the cost-effectiveness of public expenditure (Gaiha 2003: 141). Public choice approaches also advocated decentralization as a means of creating a market-like situation between citizens (as 'buyers') and local authorities (as 'sellers') on the assumption that the preferences of the buyers would be reflected in the offerings of the sellers (Manor 1999: 28).

The early work of Charles Tiebout (1956) had argued that, under conditions of greater knowledge for the 'consumer-voter', competition among multiple local jurisdictions and freedom of residential mobility, local public service provision would be more efficient and reflective of people's preferences. This was contested by the 'consolidationist' school, which argued that integrating multiple and overlapping jurisdictions was by far more conducive to efficiency and redistribution (Hooghe and Marks 2003: 235). More recently, writings on governance have recognized not just the importance of horizontal displacements of power, but also vertical displacements, as the power of the central governments is redistributed upwards, downwards, and sideways. In a globalizing world, this tendency towards the displacement of national power to supranational/global as well as sub-national (both regional and local) institutions of governance is unmistakable (Pierre and Peters 2000). Institutions of global and local governance have come to supplement the traditional understanding of governance as an activity that takes place primarily, if not exclusively, at the level of the national state. The world over, including in India, decentralization and devolution are perceived as of a piece, rather than at odds, with the emerging institutions of global governance.

While many of the arguments of efficiency and economy have acquired currency in donor discourse in India, it is important to remember that the imperative of the administrative reforms, including decentralization, of the 1980s and 1990s in the West was essentially administrative. In India, on the other hand, the imperative for decentralization was political rather than administrative, which may suggest why the administrative aspects have received less than the attention they perhaps deserved. The normative-political project of greater inclusion, and the representation of historically disadvantaged and marginalized groups constitutes the truly exciting part of the Indian experiment. Of course, the persistence of patriarchy, and of entrenched caste and class hierarchies, often militate against the success of the experiment, but there is also much evidence that affirms its worth.

The failures that have been observed are not altogether due to inherited social inequalities; many of them can be attributed to an absence of the required reform in law, or of a clear reworking of the relationship between local elected institutions and administrative structures. In some cases we even find that communities that have historically negotiated their social relationships through indigenously evolved, reasonably egalitarian, mechanisms become fractious and conflict ridden as decentralization brings with it development funds and new opportunities for the concentration of social power (Jayal 2004). The picture is complex and requires an understanding of the interpenetration of old and new institutions; of the changing rules of engagement between citizen and state; of politics and society on the one hand, and law and administrative structures on the other.

DECENTRALIZATION IN INDIA:
PRECEPT AND PRACTICE

There are arguably multiple criteria by which particular institutions of local governance can be evaluated and assessed. These may invoke and refer to an extremely wide range of presumed benefits of decentralization: equity through redistribution and enhanced social welfare; poverty alleviation; effective development through local voice in development planning and monitoring; greater state responsiveness; improved governance processes such as greater participation, transparency, and accountability; mitigation of inherited social inequalities such as caste and gender; women's empowerment; enhancement of capability for collective action; and so forth. Not all of these are the stated goals of decentralization in particular contexts, but combinations of them frequently are, though actual policy and political motivations may be rather different. Of the many theses offered to explain the introduction of decentralization, those of donor conditionality and fiscal crisis are least favoured in the literature on this subject (Manor 1999). There is, however, widespread agreement about the fact that the most recent wave of decentralization, to which over sixty countries worldwide succumbed, was on the whole a top-down affair, effected by the political leaderships of these countries.

In India a string of committee reports and recommendations had, since Independence, emphasized the importance of panchayats, mostly with a view to making development more effective through local participation.[3] Indeed, it would not be an exaggeration to state that earlier attempts at decentralization were driven by explicitly developmental and administrative considerations, rather than by concerns about democracy and representation. The enactment of the 73rd and 74th constitutional amendments in December 1992 sought to reverse this bias. It is worth noting that an earlier attempt, in 1989, to enact a similar amendment, had been defeated in Parliament, though the then prime minister, Rajiv Gandhi, had justified its necessity in the following terms:

A wide chasm separated the largest body of the electorate from a small number of its elected representatives. This gap has been occupied by the power brokers, the middlemen and vested interests. . . . With the passage of this Bill, the panchayats would emerge as a firm building block of administration and development . . . as an instrument in the consolidation of democracy at the grassroots.

(Rajiv Gandhi 1989)

Considering the wide range of expectations that the term 'decentralization' gives rise to, it is important to note the remit of the

Indian project of decentralization, in the amended Article 243-G of the Constitution:

The Legislature of a State may, by law, endow the panchayats with such powers and authority as may be necessary to enable them to function as institutions of self-government and such law may contain provisions for the devolution of powers and responsibilities . . . with respect to—
  (a) The preparation of plans for economic development and social justice.
  (b) The implementation of schemes for economic development and social justice as may be entrusted to them including those in relation to the matters listed in the Eleventh Schedule.

(Constitution of India)

Within the customary classification of decentralization models, the Indian model was apparently intended to conform to the model of democratic decentralization in which powers and funds are transferred from higher-level institutions to elected bodies at the local level. These may include powers of decision-making and also sometimes powers to raise revenues. Democratic decentralization is clearly different from, on the one hand, purely fiscal decentralization (which transfers only funds and/or revenue-raising powers, and not necessarily to elected bodies at the local level); and, on the other, from administrative decentralization or de-concentration, which envisages the transfer of administrative powers and personnel from higher levels in the political system to lower-level structures. Of these three types of decentralization, it is only democratic decentralization—sometimes also referred to as devolution—that devolves funds and powers to elected bodies at the local level, which also enjoy, therefore, a certain degree of autonomy of higher levels of government (Manor 1999: 5–6).

The amendments to the Indian Constitution clearly intended that panchayats should be institutions of self-government through which the people would participate in the process of planning for economic development and social justice, as also in the implementation of schemes for these purposes. The structures designed to facilitate these processes were panchayat institutions at three (in some cases two) levels: the *gram panchayat*, the *panchayat samiti* (at the block level), and the *zilla parishad* (the district level). The bedrock of this pyramidal structure would be the *gram sabha* (or village assembly), composed of all citizens eligible to vote, and so the foundation of local democracy and the ultimate forum of accountability. The establishment of these institutions was mandatory, as were the provisions relating to the reservation of one-third seats (at every level and among the chairpersons of these bodies) for women; and the reservation, in proportion to their percentage in the population of the area, for members of the Scheduled Castes and Scheduled Tribes. Though the amendment specified that the powers devolved to panchayats would be among those listed in the Eleventh Schedule of the Constitution,[4] it was left to the states to decide which of the subjects on that list they would devolve. The word 'may' in the phrase 'the Legislature of a State may' was interpreted by most states in a rather tight-fisted manner, suggesting that the amendment had failed to anticipate the well-known propensity of authority to resist shedding power.

However, by 1994 most states had completed the process of enacting conformity legislation and holding the first round of elections to the panchayats. In many states a second and in some a third round of elections has also been held. The most striking aspect of the experience has undoubtedly been the election of large numbers of women, and members of the Scheduled Castes and Tribes. The first round of elections saw the creation of

- 226,188 village panchayats, with 3,198,554 members;
- 5736 intermediate panchayats, with 151,412 members; and
- 467 district panchayats, with 17,935 members.

In terms of representation, it brought to the panchayats at all levels close to a million women, a large number of members of the Scheduled Castes and Scheduled Tribes, and in some states—which provided for such reservation in their conformity Acts—members of the OBC category as well. The holding of elections, and the creation of a guaranteed institutional space for panchayats in the structure of governance, were not meagre achievements. No less impressive an achievement was the representation of disadvantaged sections—women, Dalits, Adivasis—through their election to reserved positions, and despite various deficits in terms of actual ability to participate. Through elections, and the provision of a voice for the disadvantaged, the project of democracy was certainly advanced. It is less easy to be sanguine about the project of decentralization, which was circumscribed in many ways, most of all by the inadequate devolution of functions and finances.

The test of any programme of decentralization is arguably the actual powers and functions that are devolved to the institutions of local government and the autonomy they enjoy in the exercise of these. Are panchayats agents of the state government or do they actually have the power to determine their own developmental priorities? Few conformity acts—notable among them being West Bengal and Tripura—state that they aim to endow panchayats with powers and functions that can enable them to work as institutions of self-government. The Haryana Act explicitly states that the objective of panchayats is to *administer* rural areas better, and specifies the 'functions and duties' of the gram panchayat as follows:

It shall be the *duty* of the Gram Panchayat within the limits of the funds at its disposal, *to make arrangements for carrying out the requirements of sabha area* in respect of the following matters.... (emphases added) (Tekchandani et al. 1998: 358).

In many states, governments can omit, add, or amend any power by an executive order. There are many examples of functions being devolved, sometimes with great ceremony and fanfare, and then being quietly retracted in due course.[5] Indeed, many states have conveniently used delegated legislation in the form of rules and executive orders, rather than statute, to assign functions. In some cases an impressive list of functions is delineated, but there is provision for neither funds nor staff to discharge these functions. In most states, panchayats do not have an exclusive functional domain, as line departments continue to carry out developmental functions and are funded accordingly. With law and order, policing, and judicial powers in any case remaining in the hands of the state government, devolution is ultimately about implementing schemes conceived by the central or state governments rather than about self-government. Even in the restricted sphere of development, there exists a clear duality of control with elected bodies simply paralleling state structures.

The performance of even the few developmental functions that have been devolved is inhibited by the fact that panchayats are for the most part resourced by central government schemes (such as the Swarnajayanti Gram Swaraj Yojana or the Sampoorna Grameen Rozgar Yojana), providing 'tied' funds attached to centrally-planned programmes, and therefore unavailable for plans evolved at the local level. Tax-sharing arrangements yield little, and the power to levy taxes even less.[6] Expenditure by the state governments on panchayati raj institutions has been shown to be less than 10 per cent of the total expenditure of state governments. Karnataka and Kerala are notable exceptions to this trend, where this goes up to 30 and 40 per cent respectively. A study of 12 states has shown that, in nine of these, the tax revenue of the local bodies (both panchayats and urban local bodies) was less than 5 per cent of the total tax revenue of the state government (National Commission to Review the Working of the Constitution 2001: 29). The limited fiscal autonomy of panchayats renders them excessively dependent on the central and state governments.

The effects of this limited fiscal autonomy are further compounded by the Members of Parliament Local Area Development Scheme (MPLADS), by whose provisions Members of Parliament (MPs) are given an 'untied' fund of Rs 20 million annually to develop their constituencies. The scheme has been widely interpreted as a way of compensating the loss of patronage and local clout of MPs following the constitutional amendment, and the timing of its enactment— exactly a year after Parliament passed the 73rd and 74th amendments— gives credence to this interpretation. The works that MPs can take up are in precisely those 29 areas that are specified in the Eleventh Schedule, which obviously means an overlap with the panchayats' area of functioning. The fact that these works are on the whole implemented through the district collector and the district administration tends to undermine the panchayats by creating a parallel, and better funded, structure.

The planning process is similarly encumbered. The constitutional amendment had envisaged a multi-tiered and participatory planning process. Plans prepared at the gram panchayat are supposed to be consolidated at the panchayat samiti level, and these in turn consolidated and harmonized at the zilla parishad level. A District Planning Committee (DPC) was supposed to be constituted in every district to draft the development plan for the district as a whole, but there are only seven states in which it has been constituted in all districts, another two which have it in some districts, while in the remaining states DPCs have not yet been established (*Panchayati Raj Update*, April 2003: 5). In those states that have such committees, a fifth of the total number of members are nominated, leading to the domination of civil servants and higher-level politicians (such as the local MP and MLA). Being only partly elected, the committee is not accountable to the people, and can easily become a rival power centre. It is supposed to facilitate the use of the expertise and technical skill of officials in the preparation of plans, but it becomes difficult in practice to combine or balance the principles of expertise with those of democracy and accountability.

A related problem is that of the relationship of the panchayats with the local or district administration, and with the line departments. The constitutional amendment is silent on the question of the relationship between the three tiers, and a lack of coordination between them tends to weaken the structure as a whole. At each level there is the feeling that the higher level has more powers and resources, and there are no criteria specified for functional efficiency or economy to define more clearly the role of each tier in the planning and implementation of programmes. In some states, the control of the government over the two higher tiers has been strengthened by ordinance. In others there is a de facto dominance of the bureaucracy, which guides and directs the activities of the panchayats, a role that is submissively accepted by the latter. The confusion is compounded for the lower-level government functionaries attached to the panchayats, who are simultaneously accountable to the elected leaders of the panchayats as well as to their superiors in the government. For example, the secretary to the panchayat is recruited, trained, and controlled by the state government, though half his salary is paid by the panchayat; a staffer of the District Rural Development Agency may be attached to the zilla parishad, but expects to take orders from the district collector. Much the same applies to education officers, engineers, and others.

In sum, it could be argued that the purpose and design of decentralization in India was driven by two objectives: first, *democratization* through representation and voice for disadvantaged groups; and second, effective, because of more participatory, *development*. It could also be argued that while the first has been realized to a greater degree than the second, there remain serious constraints on the realization and institutionalization of both these goals. As has already been noted, insufficient devolution of functions, excessive dependence on state and central governments, and the dominance of mainstream administrative departments and functionaries are among the factors contributing to the poor performance of the panchayati raj institutions. Resource constraints exacerbate the dependence on state agencies and administrative structures, such that panchayats have neither the capacity to finance development programmes, nor the power to influence existing programmes. Elected members (especially if they also happen to be local notables) often behave like contractors, while the poor are excluded from participation. Indeed, it has been suggested that members of the zilla parishad and panchayat samiti tend to view the devolved funds as equivalent to the funds received by MPs and MLAs for constituency development. There is pressure to distribute the funds equally between all members, who decide which schemes to implement and to which contractor the work should be awarded. Unsurprisingly, the chosen schemes are the ones that offer the most opportunity for commissions and are the most difficult to monitor.

Panchayats are mostly busy implementing construction-oriented schemes, which promote contractor-wage labour relationship. These do not require participation of the poor as equals, on the other hand these foster dependency of the poor on the Sarpanch and block staff. In such a situation, panchayat activities get reduced to collusion between the Sarpanch and block engineers. Panchayats are not active in education, health, SHGs, watershed, pastures and forestry programmes, which require people to come together as equals and achieve consensus.

(Saxena 2004:4)

Additionally, there are many elements of institutional design that inhibit participation, including provisions such as the two-child norm, no-confidence motions, and quorum requirements to unseat chairpersons and deputy chairpersons who happen to belong to vulnerable groups. Indeed, social and economic inequalities have repeatedly proved to be stumbling blocks in the path of more effective performance by panchayats. Among the strategies used by upper-caste men to undermine women and lower-caste members are: threats and intimidation; physical violence; taking advantage of the unlettered; and tokenism and surrogate representation. Above all, the gram sabha—village assembly—has not evolved into the robust institution of direct local democracy it was meant to be. It is too large in size, meets infrequently, is generally poorly attended because its members are scattered over a number of villages and because the time and place of meetings are not always equally convenient for all. Added to this is the discouraging effect on the participation of women and lower-caste groups of the local power structure, as also the low awareness of the powers and role of this institution. Consequently, it is hardly surprising that the main achievement of the gram sabha is invariably the rather passive and perfunctory passing of the annual accounts; and at its most active, the selection of below-poverty-line beneficiaries for various centrally-sponsored schemes.

One of the more heartening aspects of the panchayati raj experiment has been the inclusion and participation of variously disadvantaged groups such as Dalits, Adivasis, and women. Despite the multiple constraints and exclusionary practices that prevent such participation from being realized in its fullest and most desirable form, it is unarguable that the provision of quotas has generated widespread awareness. Studies have shown that the developmental outcomes in panchayats headed by women are impressive, even if empowerment impacts have been rather slower in materializing. Even so, there is a documented recognition of powerlessness within the home and outside, and often a recognition of illiteracy as a formidable handicap in fighting it. Some of this recognition has translated into developmental gains, such as a new emphasis on education for the girl child. The long-term transformative potential of such trends is unmistakable (Jayal, forthcoming).

ISSUES IN LOCAL GOVERNANCE

Further complicating the picture of inadequate functions and finances on the one hand, and jurisdictional confusions on the other, is the recent proliferation of a large variety of bodies whose numbers have been increasing exponentially. Apart from a mushrooming of non-governmental organizations—active in both rural as well as urban local governance, through public–private partnerships in service delivery—new types of groups have also emerged. These include user groups for natural resource management, such as forests and water; stakeholder committees; and self-help groups (SHGs) for micro-credit and various other livelihood creation activities. It is important to note that donor agencies often prefer to route their assistance through NGOs, SHGs, and user committees, ignoring the fact that these are non-elected bodies paralleling the already existing panchayats, and the fact that they are equally vulnerable to elite capture. Indeed, it has often been seen that where the local elite have lost their erstwhile control over the panchayats—mostly due to reservations for women or lower-caste groups—they have retained their control over water and forests through their hold over user committees.

The generic term 'parallel bodies' is being increasingly used as a label for all such organizations. The convenience of a singular label, however, tends to obscure the diversity among them: of design, of purpose, and of implications for the panchayats. Many of these institutional innovations have been the creation of international donor agencies, and are often funded by these in addition to being supported by the state. The rationale for such bodies, in donor perceptions, is that such groups provide greater opportunities for ordinary citizens at the grass roots to influence decisions that affect them.

User committees are frequently single-purpose committees composed of all those who belong to a particular category or chosen by them. There are, of course, inherent biases, as when a water users' committee consists not of all consumers of water but of landowners who need water to irrigate their fields. There are essentially three types of problems with such parallel bodies: overlapping jurisdictions; lack of representativeness and considerations of inclusion; and participation and accountability. As far as *jurisdictional issues* are concerned, it is frequently the case that subjects such as minor irrigation, watershed development, and minor forest produce, which are under the purview of the panchayats as per the Eleventh Schedule, are in effect moved to these parallel structures. In Gujarat, for example, the Panchayat Act vests the power over minor forest produce in village panchayats, and provides for the income earned from the sale of such produce to go to the panchayat funds. However, the committees set up under the Joint Forest Management programme render meaningless the panchayats' control over minor forest produce. Likewise, the water users' groups formed under the Uttar Pradesh Sodic Lands Reclamation Project have been entrusted with the very functions—of formulating plans relating to irrigation management; the construction, maintenance, and management of link and main drains; and determining the rates of water charges—that fall within the purview of the Panchayats' Water Management Committee and Construction Committee (PRIA 2001: 10–11). This 'usurpation of roles and functions', as James Manor has called it, not only produces confusion but contributes to the weakening of panchayats as the user committees are better funded than the panchayats, which are virtually starved of resources.

The second important issue is that of the *representativeness* of these parallel bodies. James Manor (n.d.) has identified the three methods that are most commonly used to select members of such bodies: all (or most) members of a particular category; appointment by officials from line ministries of the government; and some form of democratic 'selection'. While appointment from the top is patently the least likely to give any real influence over decision-making to the poor, even the first and third methods—or any combination of them —are seen to be exclusionary. The poor are frequently excluded from such committees, and even where they are not they tend not to have 'voice' as a result of domination by those with wealth and status. Nor is there, as in panchayats, assured representation for women or for socially disadvantaged groups in society. Even in the case of elected committees, there is evidence to show that poorer voters are inhibited from expressing their true preferences, and that user committees are frequently manned by persons whom the lower-level officials find amenable (ibid.).

Finally, there is the question of *participation and accountability*. Clearly, the democratic deficit in the method of selection adversely affects the possibilities for participation. Beholden to government officials for their selection, members tend to lack assertiveness. On the whole, officials restrict their powers—such as the power to propose an agenda for a meeting—such that the committees are 'often generously funded, but not generously empowered' (ibid.: 11). Consequently, control over the design of the programmes or the power to influence imple-mentation is missing. As with the panchayats, the control of officials tends to undermine the participatory possibilities, especially in sectors where rent-seeking is possible: thus, government personnel are seen to take a greater interest in the forest sector than in the primary education sector. The lack of accountability is even more pronounced in situations where non-governmental organizations are engaged in service delivery.

An altogether distinct form of parallel bodies is the multi-purpose bodies that have been created by state governments themselves. The Janmabhoomi programme launched by former Andhra Pradesh chief minister Chandrababu Naidu is an example. The objectives of the Janmabhoomi programme were not markedly different from those of the panchayats, and encompassed primary education, primary health, community works, environment conservation, and responsive governance. The programme was implemented through a division of the state into micro-units called habitations, a distinct administrative structure, and resourced by diverting funds from centrally-sponsored schemes such the Jawahar Rozgar Yojana or the Rural Water Supply Scheme, which would normally have been administered by and through the panchayats. The only linkage with the panchayats was through the representation of the sarpanch in the Habitation Level Committee. Such bodies also usurp both the roles and the resources of the legitimately elected panchayats, which they effectively undermine.

Indeed, the presence of this multiplicity of bodies at the local level is symbolic of, on the one hand, the reluctance of elected representatives in state legislatures and Parliament to shed power and, on the other, the determination of local government functionaries to subvert the intent of the constitutional mandate. The denial of powers and resources to the panchayats signifies the former, while the involvement of the official hand in the creation of parallel bodies is clear evidence of the latter. Even at the level of the central government, the divergence of perceptions has been remarked. The guidelines of the Union Ministry of Environment and Forests for strengthening the Joint Forest Management (JFM) programme do not mention panchayats at all, indicating that there is no role for these institutions in JFM activities. On the other hand, the Union Ministry of Rural Development has recommended that all powers in relation to forest and water management should be vested in the three tiers of the panchayati raj institutions (Upadhyaya 2005: 15–16). In some states, such as Himachal Pradesh, attempts have been made to explore linkages between panchayati raj institutions on the one hand, and JFM committees on the other. Clearly, successful devolution is unlikely unless it is supported by the line departments of both the central and state governments.

THE VOLUME

The essays in this volume seek to illuminate some of the lesser-known aspects of the interface between panchayats and other institutions of local governance, whether district administration or parastatal agencies or civil society organizations. While these have been remarked and noted, even if relatively less analysed, one area that has largely escaped scholarly attention is that of customary or traditional institutions. It is, therefore, altogether appropriate that the first section of the volume is devoted to a consideration of the relationship between these institutions and panchayats. Traditional institutions of local governance are of particular importance in the context of the scheduled areas, and in the management of natural resources such as forests and water. Notwithstanding the rejection of the mythology of village republics in India—whether in the Henry Maine or the Karl Marx version—there is a distinguished tradition in Indian social anthropology of studying the village as the home of community and the site of culture. In recent times, this preoccupation has been echoed in accounts of natural resource management, which sometimes reify community by presenting it as inherently conservationist. Studies of local society, even of local power structures, have rarely engaged specifically with the issue of traditional institutions of self-governance, and the 29th Report of the Commissioner for Scheduled Castes and Scheduled Tribes which attempted to make good this shortcoming, signified a notable departure. Today, scholars are rediscovering traditional institutions—the *gaon ki* panchayat—and studying their relationship with the constitutionally-mandated institutions of local democracy—the *sarkari* panchayat (Krishna 2001). There is, it appears, nothing necessary or inevitable about the one being less and the other more inegalitarian or about the norms that they exemplify or about the extent of their legitimacy.

Kripa Ananth Pur's study of the interface between customary panchayats and the formal panchayats in rural Karnataka is instructive. Ananth Pur shows that despite the widespread assumption that the former are meant for dispute resolution and the latter for development implementation—two quite distinct activities that do not require an interface between them—customary panchayats do in fact influence the gram panchayat in a variety of ways. Before panchayat elections, the customary panchayats control nominations, by proposing their own candidates and persuading others to withdraw. They effectively play a gatekeeping role vis-à-vis prospective women candidates in the case of reserved seats. There is also frequently an overlap of leadership between the two sets of institutions, with the head of the customary panchayat getting elected as the head of the formal panchayat. After the election is complete, the customary panchayat continues to play a role by supporting the initiatives and activities of the gram panchayat, but more importantly in the selection of below-poverty-line beneficiaries for anti-poverty projects.

Another type of traditional institution is the *van* (forest) panchayats in Uttaranchal, which long enjoyed legal status, but were dependent on state agencies for a variety of permissions and sanctions. Ashok Kumar's study of this institution compares the old and new rules governing these panchayats, and shows that these actually strengthen the hold of the district administration as well as the forest department over the van panchayats. Bottom-up practices of forest management are being replaced by top-down interventions, and people's rights of access to forest resources have been severely curtailed. In this case, the interface between the van panchayat and the new PRIs is cordial enough; the problem lies in the interface with the bureaucracy.

Indeed, elected panchayats are frequently—even in the perception of their members—accountable to bureaucrats rather than to the electorate. This latter type of interface is the subject of the second section of the volume, on the new panchayati raj institutions and administrative structures in West Bengal and Uttar Pradesh. The essays in this section explore how the district administration has responded to the new challenges of governance in the form of participatory institutions. Dwaipayan Bhattacharyya's chapter argues, in the context of West Bengal, that decentralization, participatory democracy, and local governance are not always complementary. Inaugurated by the Left Front government in West Bengal in 1978, more than a decade before the constitutional amendments, decentralization was a strategy of de-bureaucratization, and a mechanism for land reform and welfare policies generally. Over the years, rural society in West Bengal has been completely reinvented as a territorialized locality with decentralized governance. There is some evidence of a gradual breakdown of ethnic and caste identities, as a new form of community has been produced. This is the village locality—administratively and electorally defined—reinvented and acting as a political unit. However, Bhattacharyya cautions, there are limits to the success of such a governmental production of the local, which ultimately fails to eliminate the reality of unequal power relations, as a variety of social identities— caste, class, gender, ethnicity—work through informal and non-governmental networks beyond the official domain of the panchayat.

Ravi Srivastava's chapter examines the interface of panchayats and bureaucracy in the context of poverty alleviation programmes in the state of Uttar Pradesh. He argues that devolution has increased contestation over the use of funds for local development, and there is, therefore, more at stake than was the case before in the elections to panchayats, especially to the post of the *pradhan*. While there is evidence of the propensity of the pradhans to self-enrichment, the chapter also shows that those pradhans who are committed to the public good are consistently obstructed by the local bureaucracy, which attempt to make the elected institutions subservient to and appendages of a corrupt state. However, despite the many ways in which the functioning of panchayats is affected by the bureaucracy and the dynamics of local society, the poor still favour greater devolution and perceive the impact of panchayats on rural development as largely positive. The chapter yields the important observation that where panchayats work well, the gains for the poor are the highest, and suggests some important hypotheses for further examination.

The third part of this volume addresses sectoral experiences in health and primary education, two areas in which decentralization has been invested with great hope. These are clearly critical areas that impinge on social citizenship, in terms of both the access of the poor to basic needs as well as the effectiveness of these institutions. Rama V. Baru and Meena Gopal examine the impact of decentralization on disease control programmes, through a case study of filariasis control programmes in three districts of Kerala, Andhra Pradesh, and Uttar Pradesh. The authors compare the levels of endemicity of the disease and the extent of risk in the people's perceptions; the accessibility and quality of health services; variations in the social composition of the local communities and the level of participation by different caste groups; and the role of health workers and health services. On the basis of this comparison, Baru and Gopal argue that mere decentralization of responsibilities to the community, without the necessary administrative and financial support structures at every level, is unlikely to yield positive outcomes. Such programmes must be differently planned, through a bottom-up process that addresses and balances the priorities of communities as they perceive them, with their lack of technical expertise and skills.

The essay by Vimala Ramachandran and Aarti Saihjee reports the results of a study of the District Primary Education Programme, arguably the most ambitious primary education initiative ever undertaken in India. The chapter draws attention to the 'hierarchies of access': even as enrolment at entry level is declining in government schools, and there is evidence of large numbers of children who are not in school, enrolment in private schools is rising. As children of better-off sections move to private schools, the pressure on government schools is considerably reduced. This has significant gender and equity impacts, as it is mainly the poor—including Scheduled Castes and Scheduled Tribes—who continue to need and access government schools. If, as is often the case, the institutions of local governance—not only panchayats, but also village education committees and school betterment committees—are controlled by those who do not need the government school system, there is little interest in ensuring that these schools function well or provide a decent quality of education. In the absence of sufficiently empowered stakeholders in the publicly provided primary education system, the latter ends up reproducing inequalities and disadvantage in the form of educational imbalances.

Jagpal Singh's case study of three Ambedkar villages in western Uttar Pradesh points in the same direction, of the manifest disinterest of those who matter: elected panchayat members, Members of the Legislative Assembly and Parliament, and educational bureaucrats. The villages studied by Singh have witnessed a dramatic increase in the number of unaided and unrecognized (UAUR) schools, which are, however, different from private schools in that they enrol children of all social classes. However, these institutions work through informal arrangements with government schools, which provide the formal enrolment that enables students to take the Board examinations. Inter-caste—and frequently even intra-caste—conflict is apparent in the schools studied. The contribution of the local panchayats is to reinforce the dominance of the stronger groups through various ways, including the low priority given to primary education, while the predictable—and for some profitable—construction of roads and electrification of villages is given much more importance. Ultimately, the task of improving the quality of primary education is left to civil society and community initiatives.

Issues of local governance are all too often defined in exclusively rural terms. The fourth section of the volume is on urban governance, and addresses the question of whether the institutions set up in accordance with the 74th Constitutional Amendment have in fact provided the urban poor with voice, with access and avenues of influence to decision-making. The relationship between urban local bodies and parastatals is explored, as also the all-important question of the devolution of funds from state governments to these bodies. The chapter by Solomon Benjamin, R. Bhuvaneswari, and Sanjiv Aundhe asks how the futures of the urban poor in two cities—Chennai and Bangalore—are shaped by the relationship between urban local bodies and parastatals. In both these cities, the urban space emerges as an arena of conflict, with the issue of land being central to urban poverty. Parastatals and specialized finance institutions are seen to increasingly shape decisions about urban development, as they form a part of alliances with big business on the one hand, and party elites on the other, the net result being a reduction in the political space available to the poor and for resistance to anti-poor policies. This chapter presents a very insightful account of how parastatals function as instruments of higher-level party politicians whose dependence on the local leadership is reduced by their control over land development, and whose power to influence the implementation of mega projects is enhanced through the parastatals.

The relationship between urban local bodies and the district administration is explored by K.P. Krishnan's case study of urban water supply in Karnataka. Krishnan questions the conventional wisdom of treating urban water supply as a local public good. He argues instead that while there are aspects of urban water supply (such as retail distribution) that are local, there are also other dimensions (such as the advantages of aggregation) that make it a regional, rather than a local, public good.[7] The legislative framework of decentralization mandates *political governance* with *administrative accountability*. Thus, the deputy commissioner of the district is not a part of the decision-making mechanism on urban water supply, and economic considerations relating to the provision of local public goods, or even economies of scale, are not part of the legislative framework. These are, however, relevant considerations, as indeed is the district as a regional unit for the delivery of certain public goods, and Krishnan makes a persuasive case for treating urban water supply as just such a good.

The chapter by Ajit Karnik, Abhay Pethe, and Dilip Karmarkar seeks to develop a quantitative framework that could be used to determine the appropriate level of devolution of funds to local bodies, and enunciates and justifies five cardinal principles for this purpose: political feasibility, equity, adequacy, computational transparency, and efficiency. On the basis of this methodology and the available data, the authors analyse the appropriate devolution to the districts of Maharashtra.

The first chapter in this section on governance is Marina Pinto's account of participatory urban governance and people-centred development in Mumbai. Her discussion of the 'new localism'—both vertical (Centre–state–local) and horizontal (state–civil, society–market)—presents evidence of local activism in the form of public–private partnerships and interventions by non-governmental organizations. The work of the Society for Promotion of Area Resource Centre (SPARC), in alliance with the National Slum Dwellers Federation and Railways Slum Dwellers Federation, was successful in rehabilitating and resettling large numbers of people by working together with the state government, the municipality, and the railways. Pinto also describes the work of the Annapurna Mahila Mandal in the empowerment of women rendered jobless by the textile strike of 1974 and of Pratham in pre-school education in the slum communities to argue that growing local activism and citizen awareness—in partnership with municipal authorities and the private sector—have the potential to bring about people-centred development.

The last two sections of the volume discuss issues of participation, transparency, and accountability. An important instrument of participation in the design of the new PRIs was intended to be the District Planning Committees which, as noted earlier, have been formed in very few states. The Madhya Pradesh government was one of the state governments that initiated the exercise of drafting an annual District Plan through the DPC. The chapter by Anwar Jafri and Vikas Singh assesses the extent to which women's participation has been actualized and women's issues incorporated in such planning. Their research was conducted in five villages each of three districts in Madhya

Pradesh, and the attempt was to understand the role played by women, especially women *panchs*, in planning at every level of the panchayats, including the gram sabha. Their findings were largely consistent with many other studies that have documented the enormous obstacles placed in the way of women's participation. Interestingly, the Madhya Pradesh conformity law, which was amended and renamed as the Madhya Pradesh Panchayati Raj Evam Gram Swaraj Act in 2001, provides for eight gram sabha committees, in all of which there is provision for reservation and the annual rotation of the presidency of the committee. The study shows that despite turnout for gram sabha meetings being generally low, women belonging to the Scheduled Castes and Scheduled Tribes tend to attend more frequently than those belonging to other groups. Nevertheless, the gram sabha committees cannot be said to have attained any degree of robustness in their functioning.

The issue of accountability in local governance is addressed in Amita Singh's comparative study of infrastructure development in two industrial townships of Haryana—Faridabad and Gurgaon. Her focus on multiple sectors of infrastructure, from land development and transport, to power and telecommunications, shows that despite the new focus on technology, little has changed on the ground. The future success of decentralization will depend upon further changes in consumer laws, the implementation of the Citizen's Charter, the attitude of the local bureaucracy, and above all corruption. V. Vijayalakshmi's chapter on local governance studies two districts of Karnataka and one in Kerala, both states having enacted a variety of measures for enhanced transparency and accountability. Once again, the bureaucracy emerges as a dominant and overbearing presence, often colluding with elected representatives in rent-seeking practices. The author arrives at the rather depressing conclusion that despite instituted legal, regulatory, and participatory measures for greater accountability—such as audits of accounts and of performance, the institution of the ombudsman, the right to information, beneficiary committees, and so on—the actual achievements are dismal. In Kerala, performance audit reports are not made public; information about official performance remains unavailable; the ombudsman takes inordinately long to act; and beneficiary committees formed to implement public works exist only in name and many of them are actually fictitious. However, publicity for these institutional methods has created a widespread citizen awareness about these issues. In Karnataka accountability mechanisms are at the level of the gram panchayat, rather than the higher two tiers. Elite capture of panchayats, the role of party elite, and the persistence of clientelism and corruption undermine the possibilities of accountability.

Rama Nath Jha argues that mere devolution of powers is an insufficient guarantee of good urban governance, the chief failure of which in India has been an inability to address urban poverty, with its attendant problems of slum settlements and informal markets. The acceptance of services provided by the urban poor but a denial of their legitimate claims to housing and other civic services on the grounds of their being outside the purview of the law cannot ensure sustainable governance. Jha identifies and discusses four elements that are critical to successful urban governance: the recognition of urban poverty as an issue that deserves policy attention, participation, transparency, and security.

The essays in this volume are fairly wide-ranging, empirically grounded in field-based research, and seek to illuminate many dimensions of local governance in contemporary India. A common thread running through most of the papers is the continued domination of the bureaucracy and party elite over elected local institutions. Another is the persistence of rent-seeking in development works, which has too easily contaminated the new panchayati raj institutions, often through the incorporation of the elected leaders in collusion with the local bureaucracy. As such, while inadequate functional and financial devolution remain important concerns, it is clear that addressing these legal and institutional issues alone will not strengthen the new institutions of local governance. These will need to be complemented by strategies that are effective in keeping both capture and corruption at bay.

NOTES

1. On the normative justifications for local democracy, see Phillips (1996) and Stoker (1996).
2. In India, the location of the idea of panchayats (as units of self-government) in the Directive Principles of State Policy suggested that neither the Gandhian vision of India—as a constellation of village republics, based on the principle of village self-sufficiency—nor the rival vision of Ambedkar of the Indian

village—as a 'sink of localism, den of ignorance and narrow-mindedness'—had been accepted by the framers of the Indian constitution. A recent study of this issue, from the perspective of economics, demonstrates that decentralized government is vulnerable to capture by vested interests in specific contexts and under particular conditions that need to be empirically assessed. Cf. Bardhan and Mookherjee (2000).

3. These include the Balwant Rai Mehta Committee Report, 1957; the Ashok Mehta Committee Report, 1978; and the L.M. Singhvi Committee Report, 1986.

4. These include: agriculture, land, forests, rural industries, health, education, women and child development, the social welfare of marginalized and disadvantaged groups, and many others.

5. In Madhya Pradesh, for instance, the state gave the responsibility for the maintenance of handpumps (for drinking water) to the gram panchayats, then shifted it back to the district panchayats and then again to the water supply department. While the first decision was announced with fanfare, the last understandably was not announced at all.

6. It has been suggested that agricultural land, which is currently not subject to income tax, should be made taxable by panchayats. This would augment the resources of panchayats and make them more autonomous in their pursuit of development in accordance with local preferences (Rajaraman 2003: 159).

7. This is in line with the argument of Wallace E. Oates that 'the proper goal of restructuring the public sector cannot simply be decentralization....The basic issue is one of aligning responsibilities and fiscal instruments with the proper levels of government' (1999: 1120).

REFERENCES

Bardhan, Pranab and Dilip Mookherjee, 'Capture and Governance at Local and National Levels', *American Economic Review,* 90 (2), 2000, pp. 135–9.

Gaiha, Raghav, 'Decentralization and Poverty Reduction', in Ernesto M. Pernia and Anil B. Deolalikar (eds), *Poverty, Growth and Institutions in Developing Asia,* Basingstoke: Palgrave Macmillan, for the Asian Development Bank, 2003.

Hooghe, Liesbet and Gary Marks, 'Unraveling the Central State, but How? Types of Multi-level Governance', *American Political Science Review,* 97 (2), 2003, pp. 233–43.

Jayal, Niraja Gopal, 'Democracy and Social Capital in the Central Himalaya: A Tale of Two Villages', in Dwaipayan Bhattacharya, Niraja Gopal Jayal, Bishnu N. Mohapatra, and Sudha Pai (eds), *Interrogating Social Capital: The Indian Experience,* New Delhi: Sage Publications, 2004.

———, 'Engendering Local Democracy: The Impact of Quotas for Women in India's *Panchayats*', in *Democratization,* London: Frank Cass, forthcoming.

Krishna, Anirudh, 'Global Truths and Local Realities: Traditional Institutions in a Modern World', Working Paper Series SAN01-02. Terry Sanford Institute of Public Police, Duke University, 2001.

Manor, James, *The Political Economy of Democratic Decentralization*, Washington, DC: World Bank, 1999.

———, 'User Committees: A Potentially Damaging Second Wave of Decentralization', Mimeo.

National Commission to Review the Working of the Constitution, 'Review of the Working of the Constitutional Provisions for Decentralization (Panchayats)', consultation paper, New Delhi, 2001.

Oates, Wallace, *Fiscal Federalism*, New York: Harcourt Brace Jovanovich, 1972.

———, 'An Essay on Fiscal Federalism', *Journal of Economic Literature*, 37(3), 1997, pp. 1120–49.

Panchayati Raj Update, April, 2003.

Phillips, Anne, 'Why Does Local Democracy Matter?' in Lawrence Pratchett and David Wilson (eds), *Local Democracy and Local Government*, Basingstoke: Macmillan, 1996.

Pierre, Jon and B. Guy Peters, *Governance, Politics and the State*, Basingstoke: Macmillan, 2000.

PRIA, *Parallel Bodies and Panchayati Raj Institutions: Experiences from the States*, New Delhi: Society for Participatory Research in Asia, 2001.

Rajaraman, Indira, *A Fiscal Domain for Panchayats*, New Delhi: Oxford University Press, 2003.

Saxena, N.C., 'Accountability through Decentralisation', keynote paper at the seminar on Decentralisation: Institutions and Politics in Rural India, Delhi, 2004.

Stoker, Gerry, 'Introduction: Normative Theories of Local Government and Democracy' in Desmond King and Gerry Stoker (eds), *Rethinking Local Democracy*, Basingstoke: Macmillan, 1996.

Tekchandani, Bharti, Kiran Jyoti, and Priti Sharma, *They Call Me Member Saab: Women in Haryana Panchayati Raj*, New Delhi: Multiple Action Research Group, 1998.

Tiebout, Charles M., 'A Pure Theory of Local Expenditures', *Journal of Political Economy*, 64 (5), 1956, pp. 416–26.

Upadhyaya, Videh, 'Beyond the Buzz: Panchayats, User Groups and Natural Resources in India', Working Paper, CSLG/WP/05–06. New Delhi: Centre for the Study of Law and Governance, Jawaharlal Nehru University, 2005.

2

Selection by Custom and Election by Statute
Interfaces in Local Governance in Karnataka*

■ Kripa Ananth Pur

PREAMBLE

Ideas about 'democratic decentralization' and 'participatory governance' are prominent in contemporary development discourse. It is now widely accepted that to be effective, governance should be pluralistic: authority should be spread across many levels and across 'multiple centers of authority' (Hooghe and Marks 2003). Decentralized forms of governance are believed to make the process of local democracy more inclusive by creating spaces for increased participation and wider representation by various citizen groups that have been traditionally marginalized and/or excluded from mainstream political processes.

A significant feature of the present-day world is the wide spread of democracy as the accepted system of governance. As Huntington (1991) observes, more than half the world's population now lives under elected governments. This follows from the 'third wave' of democratization in the 1980s and 1990s. Not only has the number of elected national governments increased over the past decade, but also advances have been made in a number of existing ones to deepen the degree of democracy. An important manifestation of this is the widespread movement towards democratic decentralization.

India figures prominently in the democracy map of the world. Despite adverse statistical odds—the fact that it is a very poor and highly diverse society—it has been a relatively stable and competitive electoral democracy. Initiatives aimed at deepening democracy at the grass roots in India include the process of democratic decentralization as well as positive discrimination in the form of quotas for SCs, STs, OBCs, and women in local government.

Decentralization has a fairly long history in India. Since Independence several attempts have been made to revitalize this system.

But important milestones in this process were the 73rd and 74th amendments to the Constitution of India in 1992. As a result, panchayati raj institutions (PRIs) gained constitutional status and came to be regarded as the third level of governance.

The 73rd Amendment to the Constitution envisages setting up of local governance structures with the intention of deepening democracy at the grass roots. This was to be achieved by bringing marginalized groups to the mainstream political process through affirmative action. Positive discrimination in the form of reservation of seats in the local governance structures resulted in spaces being created for better and increased participation by various politically marginalized groups.

Given that these formal structures such as gram panchayats (GPs) are newly created local-level institutions, it is logical to expect that there may exist customary institutions at the local level over which these new institutions have been superimposed. The most important among these are the customary panchayats (CPs), which are essentially dispute resolution bodies.

Not much effort has gone into understanding the role played by these customary institutions after the creation of formal local governance structures. The general assumption appears to be that customary panchayats are 'traditional' and shrinking in the face of competition from elected local bodies. In actual fact, traditional/customary governance structures and leadership are emerging as important variables in influencing the process of local governance. Researchers studying the process of decentralization in most developing countries are increasingly looking at the relationship between elected representatives and traditional leaders and institutions, and analysing their implications for participation. Examples of traditional leadership such as tribal chiefs in Africa,[1] powerful landowners in Latin America (Fox 1994), and biradari in Pakistan[2] putting up barriers for effective participation by citizens in local governance are numerous. While it is true that the local leaders are not the same as institutions, there is some evidence to indicate that the customary institutions influence the formal democratic institutions at the local level in two ways—either directly as an institutional intervention or through the leaders who constitute these institutions.

Despite the great interest that researchers have shown in the 'Indian village' over many decades, there are enormous gaps in our understanding of the contemporary realities of local-level authority and governance. There are several reasons why this large accumulated body of local-level research is less useful than one would expect: (a) much of the research was anthropological in orientation, with a limited focus on politics and governance; and (b) most was conducted before the 'intensification' of decentralized democracy after 1992 (Béteille 1971; Rudolph and Rudolph 1967; Srinivas 1987).

THE KARNATAKA CONTEXT

The state of Karnataka has a fairly impressive record in terms of decentralization. The first major landmark in recent times is the 1983 Act (the Karnataka Zilla Parishad, Taluk Panchayat Samiti, Mandal Panchayats and Nyaya Panchayat Act 1983). This Act, influenced by the Ashok Mehta Committee's recommendations (1978) at the national level, went further in some respects. It established a two-tier structure with the zilla parishad (ZP) and *mandal* panchayat (MP), both elected, and a *taluk* panchayat samiti which was ex-officio. A notable feature was 25 per cent reservation for women in ZPs and MPs even before this was mandated by the Constitution. Elections under this Act were held in 1987.

This Act was substituted by a new legislation in 1993 (the Karnataka Panchayat Raj Act, 1993). This was due partly to the need to accommodate the mandatory provisions brought in by the 73rd and 74th amendments to the Constitution. By virtue of these amendments, PRIs obtained a constitutional status. Further, a three-tier elected structure was also made mandatory (with a few exceptions). As a result, the 1993 Act provides for the following three-tier structure—zilla panchayat (district level), taluk panchayat (block level), and gram panchayat (village level).

Given this long history, extensive research has been conducted on the Karnataka decentralization model. However, research on local governments in Karnataka has not focused sufficiently on the interface between the customary institutions and formal structures of governance. The reasons for this are many. One is the assumption referred to above that customary panchayats are shrinking in the face of competition from formal structures, and that gram panchayats have filled the vacuum left by these shrinking customary institutions.

However, field research indicates otherwise. Contrary to popular belief, there has not been a unilinear displacement of customary panchayats by the formal structures of governance such as gram panchayats. Rather there is some evidence to suggest that customary institutions themselves both influence and adapt to the existence of formal governance structures.

This evidence raises a number of critical questions as to what happens to the existing informal institutions at the village level when formal governance structures are introduced, particularly to those that are part of village governance.

- Do they get subsumed by the newly created formal structures of governance?
- Do they continue to function as parallel bodies?
- Do they try to influence the formal structures?

This chapter attempts to look at the interface between the customary and gram panchayats in two districts in Karnataka and understand its implications for participatory governance. This is based on extensive research in eight villages (four in each district) in Mysore and Dharwad districts. The chapter is structured as follows: the first section looks at the institutional structure of the customary panchayat. The second part analyses the interface between the formal and customary institutions, and the third section includes conclusions as well as some possible areas of intervention.

CUSTOMARY PANCHAYATS

Traditional institutions are an integral part of rural India. There are numerous civil society organizations functioning at the village level. This chapter is concerned with the institution that deals principally with dispute resolution. The importance of this institution arises from the fact that it has a certain centrality in village governance. Given that this body is known by different names in different regions of Karnataka, a more generic term such as 'customary panchayat' is used here to describe this institution, which mainly deals with dispute resolution along with other social functions. It is also necessary to point out that this institution is distinct from caste panchayats that are restricted to a particular caste.

The CP is a forum consisting of all the senior caste leaders in a multi-caste village. Thus, it is essentially a council of elders (or leaders). The head of this panchayat is usually the senior caste leader of a higher/forward-caste group. Typically, a second junior leader is identified to take care of such tasks as informing the villagers regarding meetings and other petty chores. There is a clear difference in the composition of CPs between big and small villages. In a very large village, there are numerous centres of power and leadership. For example, every two or three streets (*onis*) in a village might have one or two individuals identified and accepted as local leaders. In such a situation, all the important leaders come together only if the matter concerns the entire village, for example, communal riots, village temple activities, etc. Otherwise they continue to operate as competing centres of power within the village. This relation is based mainly on a patron–client relationship and serves as a basis for building the support base of these individual leaders. This was observed in one village with a population of nearly 10,000 people. It was also observed that as the size of the village diminishes, the CP becomes more visible and important. Generally, in smaller villages, the customary panchayat operates more strongly and has a significant impact on citizens' lives compared to larger villages.

Nature of Leadership

The customary panchayat is essentially a council of leaders. Significant changes can be observed in the nature of leadership of this forum. In the villages studied, CPs were not controlled or dominated by a single leader. They were perceived more as forums of leaders where decisions are arrived at after deliberation and consensus. The head of the CP is almost always a person belonging to a dominant caste group such as the *lingayat*s or *vokkaliga*s. However, there is a perceptible change in the nature of leadership itself in some villages. Emergence of SC leadership is visible in villages where the SC population is substantial.

Another interesting phenomenon is the emergence of 'neo leadership', particularly in Dharwad district. Here along with the traditional caste leaders, a new leadership has emerged. While caste and traditional leaders continue to be an important part of the customary panchayat, it now includes a new set of leaders who are part of the process due to modern *influences*. Political linkages, education, mobility, contact with government functionaries, etc. seem to be the newer criteria for leadership. This has resulted in the emergence of a new set of leaders in the customary panchayat who otherwise would not have been part of the process. Emergence of new leadership is not a new phenomenon. Béteille (1965) has identified the emergence of a new set of leaders, independent of both caste and class to a certain extent, as also the shift in power from the traditional elite to these new leaders in villages of Tamil Nadu. Krishna (2002) in his study of Rajasthan and Madhya Pradesh villages identifies three sets of leaders, traditional village leaders, panchayat leaders, and *naya netas* (new leaders), but he observes them as three different streams with very little overlap of leadership. It is here that the experience from Karnataka differs. The emergent new leadership has become a part of the customary panchayat and plays an active role in dispute resolution along with traditional caste leaders.

In addition, there is a visible overlap of leadership between customary panchayats, gram panchayats, and to a certain extent (where present) with the new leaders. This is explained in detail later in the discussion.

FUNCTIONS OF CUSTOMARY PANCHAYATS

1. The principal task of the customary panchayat is 'dispute resolution' in the village. The types of disputes that come before it are varied and include petty disputes in the village, marital problems including spousal abuse, bigamy, and alcoholism. Land or property disputes between siblings or others might first come before the customary panchayat. Criminal cases are handed over to the police.

2. Another important task of the customary panchayat relates to the village temple. Temple activities usually referred to as '*devara karya*' involve organizing festivals and festival-related religious processions (*jathre*) and ritualistic activities, temple construction and maintenance, etc. This is an important task of the customary panchayat and assumes significant relevance as it relates to organizing a major social activity in the village and also networking with neighbouring villages.

3. This apart, the customary panchayat also acts as a support structure in specific situations. There are cases of it helping destitute or

widowed women to get their husbands' property and collecting funds from the villagers to help accident victims (generally poor families) of the village.

4. The customary panchayat also acts as a village corporate organization (VCO) to raise and manage funds that are used mostly for local economic activities—for example, irrigation management and a wide range of other development programmes (Wade 1988). In fact, the customary panchayats play a significant role in informal resource mobilization at the village level, which may be utilized for village development activities or for the maintenance of the local temple.

The customary panchayat is not a homogenous body. Since it is a forum consisting of a heterogeneous group of people in terms of caste and social status, the inherent social tensions of rural society are apparent in this institution as well. The veneer of cohesiveness projected by villages to outsiders is a contested issue. Does cohesiveness really exist? Who enforces it and at what cost? These matters have been the subject of much debate. Misra and Parthasarathy (1981) illustrate this effectively with the analysis of a case study of a dispute between vokkaligas and adikarnatakas (SCs) in a Mysore village. However, social conflicts and tensions within the villages are constantly negotiated and managed by the customary panchayats, and an appearance of cohesiveness is projected in its interface with statutory bodies.

CUSTOMARY PANCHAYAT–GRAM PANCHAYAT INTERFACE

Customary panchayats have a certain centrality in village governance as they provide an element of social security and local law and order. In the 1990s this centrality has gained from their role in influencing elections to gram panchayats. Customary and gram panchayats occupy different spaces, mainly state and non-state spaces. Yet there is considerable interaction between them. It is important to identify and analyse the areas where these two institutions intersect and interface with one another. These could be complementary as well as conflicting in nature.

At first glance these two institutions appear to operate at different levels and as such should have few points of intersection. The villagers by and large feel the same. The general opinion is that the customary panchayat is meant for dispute resolution within the village and gram panchayat for implementing development activities. Hence, there is hardly any interface between these two. In a way this implies that the customary panchayat is perceived as a social institution and the gram panchayat as a political structure, each with different sets of activities.

However, deeper inquiry reveals that the customary panchayat does influence the gram panchayat in various ways. This influence, is restricted to the village level and does not extend over the entire gram panchayat area. This may be analysed in two phases. The gram panchayat's election is chosen as a point of reference here, as customary panchayat's influence in shaping its composition is most visible during this phase. This is not to suggest that the interaction or influence of customary panchayats over gram panchayats is restricted to elections. Customary panchayats continue to influence and interact with gram panchayats in different ways even after the elections, and this is an ongoing process.

PRE-ELECTION PHASE

This is a significant phase as it is here that the customary panchayat has the potential to determine and influence the selection process of gram panchayat candidates.

Field experiences vary widely in this respect. A general assumption is that villagers are by and large quite free to contest elections at the local level. There have been reports pointing to the presence of political patronage by village elite in determining candidates for local elections (Inbanathan 2000). This is seen more as a consequence of individual/ elite power. The presence of an institutional influence (of customary panchayats) in controlling nominations to the gram panchayat elections has generally not been debated in the discourse on decentralization. Field experience indicates the presence of both, depending upon the context and the size of the village.

A common pattern seen in many villages is that wherever the customary panchayat's influence is strong, it plays a significant role in influencing the type of candidates that are represented in local governance. In six out of eight villages studied, the customary panchayat prepared a list of candidates to be selected for gram panchayat elections. But the way in which this is operationalized varies from village to village. This takes place either before nominations are filed or when they are being finalized. In some villages, the selection of candidates is done prior to filing of nominations to gram panchayat elections and in other cases the decision is taken at the time of finalizing the nominations.

Once the last date for withdrawing the nominations is announced, the customary panchayat meets and asks some candidates to withdraw in favour of its candidates. This has worked in many instances and the number of 'unanimous' elections has been quite significant in Karnataka (*Deccan Herald* 2000; *Hindu* 2000). In others where there have been contested elections, villagers admit that most of the candidates who were elected were those originally chosen by the customary panchayats.

In two villages in Mysore district. candidates withdrew their nomination papers because of the intervention of the customary panchayat. In another village, the customary panchayat leaders admitted that they had asked a woman candidate to withdraw her nomination. The reason given for this was that she came from a family of troublemakers and if she became a gram panchayat member, it would be difficult to get work done through her or her family.

Interestingly, customary panchayats' influence on gram panchayat elections has also been linked to informal resource mobilization. Where 'unopposed' elections have taken place, potential shortlisted candidates are asked to contribute to the village fund the equivalent of what their election campaign would cost. These candidates are then 'unanimously' elected. The money is usually utilized for village development or for maintaining the village temple (*Indian Express* 2000; *Times of India* 2000). In one village in Mysore district, Rs 25,000 was mobilized through 'unanimous' gram panchayat elections and the resource thus collected was utilized to purchase land to build living quarters for the local nurse.

But an area where the control over nominations to gram panchayats is becoming increasingly visible is in women's participation. Progressive legislation that reserves for women one-third of seats in elected local councils has been in place in India since 1993. It is widely known that, despite widespread formal compliance with this legislation, women representatives are rarely able to exercise much political influence. It is generally believed that the main reasons lie in the patriarchal biases against women that permeate Indian culture. However, research in Karnataka suggests a more direct and tangible institutional explanation:

the influence over local elections of customary panchayats. This is particularly visible in the number of women representatives re-elected to gram panchayats, which has been small enough to cause serious concern among researchers working in this area. This lack of continuity in office prevents women from building their political skills and constituencies, and limits their political careers. It also results in a new set of inexperienced women entering the political arena for the first time. Consequently women's political participation in local governance will continue to be less than impressive.

An important reason attributed for this is the pressure from the 'community' not to contest. Customary panchayats' influence in determining the candidates for women's seats in gram panchayats appears to be particularly strong. Paradoxically, most of these former women gram panchayat members were pressured by the 'community' to contest during the previous term. Objections to their entry into politics were faced at the family level. But during the subsequent elections, these women members who had undergone training and were keen to continue their political career were asked by the community not to contest. The justification for this was: 'We [the community] have given you an opportunity to participate in gram panchayat, now we should give the same opportunity to other women. One must not be greedy or selfish and deny other women this opportunity.' The community, on further probe, is none other than the village leaders and the institution of the customary panchayat. This institution's intervention in determining candidates for seats reserved for women in the gram panchayat seems to be more effective when compared to men. Women by and large tend to obey the dictates of the customary panchayat and do not go against the wishes of the community. Women have very few avenues or sources of support if they wish to defy the dictates of the customary panchayat. Consequently, the number of women candidates who have done so and contested elections has been insignificant. A couple of former women gram panchayat representatives (trained by an NGO) who went ahead and contested elections despite the lack of support from the customary panchayat were defeated.

Customary panchayat leaders tend to evade addressing this issue of controlling the nominations of women candidates. Generally they claim that they are keen to encourage women who are capable of getting work done for the village. According to the leaders, selection of women candidates for the gram panchayat is based on one of two criteria:

1. If a woman is educated and active in the village, she is selected as she might do good work in the village as gram panchayat member.
2. If a woman candidate is not active but her husband is, they might choose her as her husband would be capable of taking care of gram panchayat work on her behalf.

But even in cases where women candidates have performed well, they have either not been allowed to re-contest or if they did, they were not elected. This is serious cause for concern, as it does not allow women to build their political skills or further their political careers. Women candidates feel that they were asked to contest in the first place because they were ignorant and would listen to the dictates of the village elders. But once they developed political skills and started forming their own identities as leaders and began questioning the decisions of the leaders, they were perceived as a threat to the hegemony of the customary panchayat. Research on women's political participation in local governance has indicated a host of reasons and barriers affecting their political performance. But the existence and impact of this specific institutional barrier, in the form of customary panchayats in controlling women's access to political space, has not been sufficiently explored.

Overlap of Leadership

This leads to the issue of *overlap of leadership* between the two structures. In one village, an important customary panchayat leader from the village was also the president of the gram panchayat during the last term. In the same village, the following term the son of the village head was elected as a gram panchayat member. In a couple of villages, customary panchayat leaders have also been elected as gram panchayat members. The president of the gram panchayat in one village is also the wife of an important customary panchayat leader in the village. Since she is illiterate, her husband handles most of the panchayat activities. A former gram panchayat vice-president in one of the villages is the daughter-in-law of an important traditional leader of the village.

Overlap of leadership makes the interface between these two institutions intense and consequently requires deeper analysis to appreciate its importance.

Admittedly, there is evidence that traditional power structures tend to reproduce themselves in formal institutional structures. But an encouraging development is that reforms from above, such as, democratically contested elections and reservation of seats, create spaces to counter this process. Some of the examples given later illustrate this point quite clearly. In a village in Mysore district, the head of the customary panchayat and the dominant caste leaders in the village have very little interest in or impact on the gram panchayat candidates' selection process as all the three seats in this village are reserved for SCs and STs. In another village, the villagers admitted that although the caste leaders try to arrive at a list of candidates, it usually does not work, as a number of people in the village want to contest gram panchayat elections and usually there is a failure to reach a consensus. In yet another village, the head of the customary panchayat and the sister-in-law of one of the caste leaders in the village both contested gram panchayat elections during the last term and lost. This is encouraging in that although the customary panchayat tries to influence and shape the formal local governance structures, it does not always succeed. This suggests that increasing political awareness is the most important bulwark against formal institutions being exploited by the dominant sections

POST-ELECTION PHASE

The post-election phase brings to relief several facets of the interaction between customary panchayats and gram panchayats. There is evidence of negotiations, trade-offs, and other forms of interplay. This phase also reflects the ongoing interactions between these two institutions. What is striking is that the interaction is often subtle, invariably indirect, and influenced by the context or the issue under consideration. There is some evidence of the customary panchayat's influence over gram panchayats, which may not always be benign. Whatever the result of the interface, it supports the proposition made earlier, namely, that there is a noticeable nexus between the two. Principally, three forms of interplay can be distinguished:

1. where the customary panchayat functions as a support mechanism for local elected representatives in general and new entrants in particular by reinforcing whatever case they wish to present;
2. where the customary panchayat influences the gram panchayat to act for the well-being of the entire village; and
3. where the customary panchayat intervenes in the process of selection of beneficiaries for anti-poverty schemes.

Each of these forms of interaction is reviewed here and, finally, drawing upon this analysis, their impact on the gram panchayat and its participatory prospects are discussed.

The customary panchayat provides support to gram panchayat members in getting work done through it. In a village in Mysore district, the customary panchayat leaders along with a gram panchayat member approached the rest of the gram panchayat to get the broken water pump in the village repaired. The gram panchayat member was appreciative of the customary panchayat leaders' assistance as he felt that the matter could not have been resolved so quickly if he had tried to tackle it alone. In another situation the customary panchayat leaders along with a gram panchayat member managed to get some land donated from a villager in the neighbouring village for building a pre-school facility (*anganwadi*). Here, too, the gram panchayat member was ready to admit that this would not have been possible if the customary panchayat leaders had not taken an active part in the process. This reflects the positive role the customary panchayat can play in ensuring effective service delivery from the gram panchayat to the village.

As a support structure, the customary panchayat assists members in negotiating with the gram panchayat for benefits to the village. This could take the form of putting pressure on the grama panchayat members for development projects such as constructing or repairing school buildings and community halls, or providing drinking water, which benefit the entire community. There are a number of examples from the field illustrating this point. Gram panchayat members in most of the villages, studied have admitted to pressure from the customary panchayat with regard to provision of school buildings, bus services, etc. In some villages customary panchayat leaders directly pressurize the gram panchayat representatives to secure benefits to the village. In others there is a silent understanding that those supported by the customary panchayat will contribute something back to the village. In one village in Dharwad district, the customary panchayat leaders sit together with a male gram panchayat member prior to a gram panchayat meeting and brief him regarding the development needs of the village.

The most fundamental area of the interface has to do with decisions impacting directly on the poor. In some villages it was found that customary panchayat leaders played an important role in the selection of beneficiaries for various anti-poverty projects and schemes. The involvement of the customary panchayat in this process may make the selection process more transparent or it might result in customary panchayat leaders using their influence to strengthen their position in the village by bestowing favours on those who support them. The following illustrates this point. According to one customary panchayat leader, since they are well attuned to the village reality, they are better suited to select the beneficiaries. He admitted that since they know who the 'really needy' people are in the village; even if these beneficiaries do not put in an application for these benefits, the customary panchayat leaders suggest their names and ensure that they get the benefits.

Selection of beneficiaries apart, the location of facilities and services also has strong implications for the poor. In almost all the villages studied, the local gram panchayat representatives, especially those that are hand-picked by the customary panchayat, consult the latter's leaders in the implementation of development projects in the village. Often, customary panchayat leaders intervene in deciding the location of roads, street lights, water taps, or drainage. If these decisions are biased in favour of the village elite and/or are not pro-poor, then the intervention of customary panchayat in gram panchayat activities at the village level will have a negative impact. According to some of the gram panchayat representatives who were unanimously elected (by the customary panchayat pressurizing others to withdraw their nominations), they consult the customary panchayat leaders on implementation of development activities and their location as these leaders are well versed with the problems of the village. According to one gram panchayat representative, he does not take any decisions without consulting the customary panchayat leaders. 'Just because I'm a member of the gram panchayat, I cannot take decisions independently....That is not right. When elders are present in the village as a part of the villag : institution, we should take their views into consideration and seek their advice.' This suggests a feeling of obligation that these gram panchayat members might experience towards the customary panchayat leaders, thus making them susceptible to pressure in discharging their duties as gram panchayat members.

Local leaders generally play an important role in negotiating with the formal governance structures (for benefits to the village), even in the absence of such an institutional structure. But the intervention of the customary panchayat as an institution in the process of negotiations with formal structures assumes importance when issues related to common property resources or disputes with neighbouring villages occur.

There are interesting examples where the spheres of activities of the customary panchayat and gram panchayat have either been complementary or conflicting. In a village in Dharwad, a case of encroachment of a public road by a family in the village was pending as the customary panchayat had not been able to enforce its decision. But once some of the customary panchayat leaders became part of the gram panchayat, they decided to take up this issue. They briefed the customary panchayat leaders about their plan of action. The gram panchayat members got the fence removed and built an open drain. The other party has now gone to court claiming that the gram panchayat has encroached upon his land to build the road as well as the drain. But the gram panchayat has filed a counter-suit against him and is confident of winning. The gram panchayat members feel that because there was an understanding between the customary panchayat and gram panchayat, such swift action was possible. If they did not have the cooperation of the customary panchayat, the matter would not have been resolved. Here the interaction was complementary as the objectives of both these institutions converged.

In another village in Mysore district, there was some minor altercation between the customary panchayat and gram panchayat regarding the ownership of the village pond. Usually the customary panchayat leased the pond to the people for pisciculture. The money thus earned was to be used for temple activities. But the previous year the person who regularly leased the pond went to the gram panchayat instead of the customary panchayat and got a contract to use the pond for pisciculture even as the customary panchayat was planning on leasing it to another person. The customary panchayat leaders of the village complained to the gram panchayat secretary regarding this matter. They were told that the pond actually came under the jurisdiction of the zilla panchayat and neither the village nor the customary panchayat had any rights over it. The customary panchayat leaders decided to pursue this further. They met officials at the fisheries department in Mysore city and enquired about their situation. The officials reconfirmed the fact that the pond belonged to the ZP and the customary panchayat had no right to lease it. The fisheries department cited similar disputes elsewhere and told them that there was very little that the customary panchayat could do. This has been a disappointment to the leaders and the villagers as the pond was a good source of revenue for the village. The customary panchayat leaders are contemplating their options as they felt that they should have ownership rights over the pond that has always been considered to be the common property of the village.

It is arguable from the above that the complementary or conflicting nature of the interaction is largely contextual. But conflicts between customary and gram panchayats regarding the ownership and access of common property resources like ponds and forests are likely to occur more frequently as each of these institutions tries to reinforce its areas of influence and control access to them.

SUMMING UP

The strong presence of customary panchayats at the village level, and their ability to adapt and influence village governance, are becoming increasingly visible. The interface between the gram panchayat and customary panchayat is both subtle and obvious. For the process of democratic decentralization to be effective, the discourse on it should focus on the institutional interfaces between customary and democratically elected bodies.

Customary panchayats do play an important role in influencing the gram panchayat elections. Customary panchayats have been particularly damaging to those women in local governance interested in building their political skills and careers by denying them continuity. This is despite claims by customary panchayat leaders that it is essential to encourage 'good' and 'educated' women representatives. But the number of women representatives who were re-elected to gram panchayats in

Karnataka has been insignificant. According to some of the women representatives from the last term, they were either 'not allowed' or discouraged by the customary panchayats to re-contest. Those who did go ahead lost.

In fact, customary panchayats act to a certain extent as a 'gate-keeper' institution in controlling nominations to the gram panchayat elections. Conway (2001) has identified gatekeeper institutions as those that control or influence nomination of candidates (party leaders, funders, interest group leaders, etc.). This, she particularly notices, in the context of women's political participation in the US. Conway's basic point is that while reasons such as culture and patriarchy are important determinants in influencing women's political participation, sufficient attention has not been paid to the gatekeeper institutions, which play an important role. According to her, there is substantial evidence to suggest that gatekeepers play a much bigger role than has been understood in influencing the 'prior selection of office seeking' of women candidates in the US. She feels that this selection process has received very little attention by scholars even though it is a 'major contributor to women's limited access to elected office'. Interesting parallels can be drawn between these gatekeeper institutions and the customary panchayats. While the customary panchayats do play an important role as gatekeeper institutions in controlling nominations in general, their influence in determining which women may take advantage of the reservation to stand for election and/or re-contest is much stronger.

This raises questions regarding possible areas of intervention that can help women overcome this bias. Thus, an inquiry into the extent to which solidaristic action by women, such as, women's networks or *mahila mandals* (women's self-help groups), can overcome the institutional bias that arises from the power of male-run customary panchayats needs to be studied in greater detail. This has important implications for effective women's political participation.

However, a positive trend is that in most villages, the villagers have rebelled against the dictates of the customary panchayat and contested elections for at least one or two seats. In a village with six gram panchayat seats, the customary panchayat managed to select candidates for two seats, but consensus could not be reached among the villagers regarding the other four. Hence, elections were held for four seats.

This is encouraging as it indicates that customary panchayat does not always succeed in its interventions in influencing the composition of gram panchayats. Reforms from above such as democratic decentralization appear to give a fillip to citizen's participation even if institutional barriers exist in the form of customary panchayats.

Krishna's (2002) study of villages in Rajasthan, one of the few contemporary analyses of traditional institutions, reveals certain similarities as well as variations between traditional institutions dealing with dispute resolution in Rajasthan and customary panchayats in Karnataka. The structure and composition of this institution seem to be quite similar in both states, but a clear distinction is seen in the interface between the formal and informal governance structures. For example, Krishna identifies village councils (traditional institutions) and gram panchayats to be two separate, distinct institutions with very little interaction between them. Equally, there seems to be no overlap of leadership between these two institutions. This is interesting and surprising since the Karnataka experience points to a strong interface as well as a clear overlap of leadership.

An area that has remained largely unexplored in this context is the extent to which political affiliations play a role in influencing the choice of candidates by customary panchayats. In theory, gram panchayat elections are to be contested on a non-party basis in Karnataka. But in practice, political parties do play a significant role in determining the selection of candidates for gram panchayats. Hence, the extent to which political affiliations have influenced the choice of candidates has been difficult to discern.

The customary panchayat's interventions in village development activities cannot be construed as a wholly negative influence as these are beneficial to the entire community. But this intervention can have a negative impact when the customary panchayat starts influencing and interfering with decisions affecting the poor. This is an area that requires interventions in terms of strengthening and making gram sabhas (where selection of beneficiaries is expected to take place) more participatory.

Customary panchayats are an important local institution in rural areas. Since these institutions provide an element of both social security and local law and order, their importance at the village level assumes significance. There has been no unilinear process of displacement of customary institutions by formal governance structures such as gram panchayats. These two institutions continue to coexist and influence each other. The intervention of the customary panchayats in gram panchayat activities is not always negative. Customary panchayats do play a positive role in village governance and research efforts should concentrate on ways in which the negative influence of customary panchayats can be neutralized. This is particularly important if gram panchayats are to emerge as effective local political structures. A deeper understanding of the dynamics of this interaction would greatly increase the capacity of government agencies and social movements to intervene effectively to help promote the interests of the poor and disadvantaged.

NOTES

* This chapter is based on the research carried out in Mysore and Dharwad districts of Karnataka during 2000–1. Ford Foundation provided the financial support. Grateful thanks to Professor V.K. Natraj, MIDS, Dr Mark Robinson, Ford Foundation, Professor James Manor, Dr John Gaventa, and Professor Mick Moore, IDS, Sussex, for their inputs into the project.
1. Personal communication with Camilo Valderrama, D.Phil. student, IDS, Sussex.
2. Personal communication with Humera Mallik, a researcher from Pakistan.

REFERENCES

Béteille, André, *Caste, Class, and Power Changing Patterns of Stratification in a Tanjore village*, Berkeley, Los Angeles, London: University of California Press, 1965.

Conway, Margaret, 'Women and Political Participation', *PS: Political Science and Politics*, 34(2), 2001, 231–3.

Fox, Jonathan, 'Latin America's Emerging Politics', *Journal of Democracy*, 5(2), 1994, pp. 105–16.

Hooghe, L. and G. Marks, 'Unraveling the Central State, but How? Types of Multi-level Governance', *American Political Science Review*, 97 (2), 2003, pp. 233–43.

Huntington, Samuel P., *The Third Wave: Democratization in the Late Twentieth Century*, Norman and London: University of Oklahoma Press, 1991.

Inbanathan, Anand, 'Power, Patronage and Accountability in the Panchayats of Karnataka', Working Paper No. 68, Bangalore: Institute of Social and Economic Change, 2000.

Indian Express, 'GP Seats for Sale in Mandya', Bangalore, 4 February 2000.

Krishna, A., *Active Social Capital*, New York: Columbia University Press, 2002.

Misra, P.K. and J. Parthasarathy, 'Caste in Cohesion and Conflict in Village India', *Eastern Anthropologist*, 34(4), 1981, pp. 275–86.

Rudolph, Lloyd I. and Susanne H. Rudolph, *The Modernity of Tradition: Political Development in India*, Chicago: University of Chicago Press, 1967.

Srinivas, M.N., *The Dominant Caste and Other Essays*, New Delhi: Oxford University Press, 1987.

The *Deccan Herald*, 'GP Poll: No Contestants for 129 Seats', Bangalore, 16 February 2000.

The *Hindu*, 'Gram Panchayats Election Results Declared', Bangalore, 1 March 2000.

The *Times of India*, 'Democracy under the Hammer: GP Seats Auctioned', Bangalore, 22 February 2000.

Wade, Robert, *Village Republics*, Cambridge: Cambridge University Press, 1988.

3

Van Panchayats in Uttaranchal

■ ASHOK KUMAR

INTRODUCTION

The state of Uttaranchal was created on 9 November 2000 out of Uttar Pradesh, then the most populous state of India. Uttaranchal is predominantly a mountainous state, situated in the central zone of the Himalayas. The geographical boundary of the state touches Tibet in the north, Himachal Pradesh in west and north-west, the Gangetic plains of Uttar Pradesh in the south, and Nepal in the east. It is spread over an area of 53,119 sq. km. The total population of the state according to the 2001 Census was 84,97,562 which is 0.82 per cent of India's population (Government of India 2001).

This chapter presents an examination of van panchayats in the state of Uttaranchal. The chapter is divided into four sections. To set the discussion on van panchayats in an appropriate context, the next section provides an overview of rural local government in India and the state of Uttaranchal. Van panchayat, the institution itself, is introduced in the third section before presenting the current functioning, including the statutory provisions of van panchayats. Case studies based on fresh empirical research are presented in the third section. The chapter ends with some conclusions and policy recommendations.

THE STATE OF UTTARANCHAL

Uttaranchal state is divided into two divisions of Kumaon and Garhwal (see Figure 3.1), which have in all thirteen districts. Out of these, six districts—namely, Almora, Pithoragarh, Nainital, and the newly carved out districts of Bageshwar, Champawat, and Udhamsingh Nagar—constitute Kumaon division. The remaining seven districts of Uttarkashi, Chamoli, Dehradun, Pauri Garhwal, Tehri Garhwal, and the newly formed districts of Rudraprayag and Haridwar are components of Garhwal.

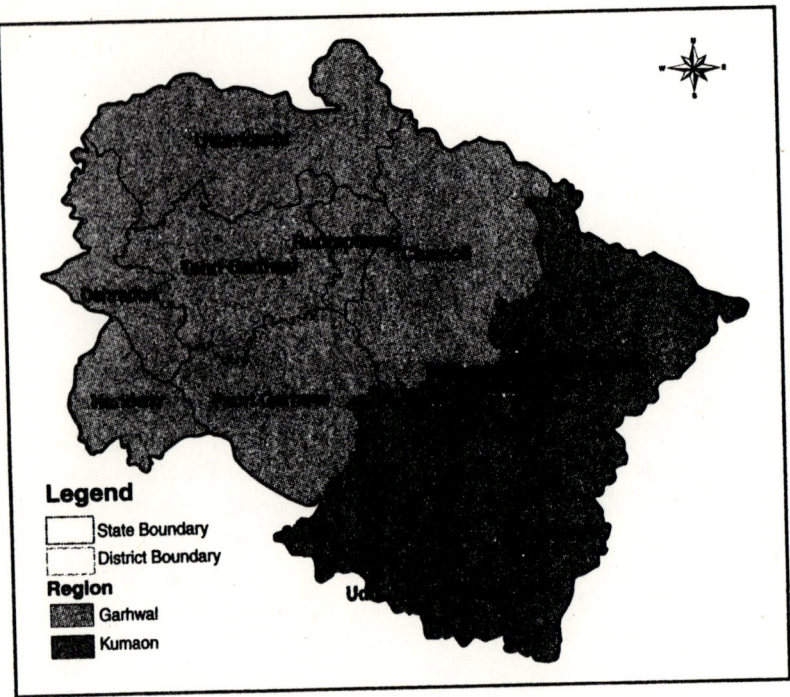

FIGURE 3.1: THE STATE OF UTTARANCHAL, 2000
Source: Forest Department, Uttaranchal (2000).

These 13 districts are further divided into 42 *tehsils*, 95 development blocks, and 15,669 inhabited villages. Larger settlements are mostly concentrated in the lower reaches of the Terai and foothills of Nainital, Dehradun, Haridwar, and Udhamsingh Nagar. The landscape in the upper reaches is dotted mostly with smaller settlements. Villages are usually small. The average population per village in the state according to 1991 Census was 391 (Government of India 1991).

More than 63 per cent of the total geographical area of Uttaranchal is under forest cover. In terms of relative ranking, Uttaranchal is the third most forested state in India after Mizoram and Manipur. However, the absolute forest area in Uttaranchal almost equals the total forest area of the top three forested states in the country.

Although agriculture is the predominant economic activity in the state, only about 12 per cent of the total geographical area is under agriculture. This amounts to about 0.08 hectare of agricultural area sown per person. Further, nearly three-fourths of the landholdings belong to the sub-marginal or marginal category, with an average size of 0.37 hectare. These can hardly be considered economically viable under the current pattern of technology usage and commercialization of the agricultural sector in the state. Levels of urbanization are extremely low in most districts of Uttaranchal, thus ruling out significant industrial or service activities at least for the present moment. It may, therefore, be fair to assume that large portions of the population remain dependent on forests for their economic sustenance.

Since Uttaranchal falls in the ecologically sensitive zone of the Himalayas, it appears prominently in the National Forest Policy of 1988 (Ministry of Environment and Forests 1999). As per the forest policy, at least 60 per cent of the Himalayan zone should be covered with forests. Although the recorded forest area of Uttaranchal is more than 63 per cent of its geographical area, the actual forest area as analysed from satellite imagery is only about 43 per cent. Forests with a crown density exceeding 40 per cent are about 17,849 sq. km, which is 33 per cent of the total geographical area and about half the recorded forest area (see Table 3.1). The distribution of forest area in Uttaranchal is shown in Table 3.2. The data for the new districts was not available separately and is accounted for in the corresponding old districts. The Garhwal division accounts for more than two-thirds of the forest area of the state.

Distribution of forest area in different districts of the state shows that the three most forested districts, namely, Uttarkashi, Chamoli (including Rudraprayag), and Pauri Garhwal, falling within the Garhwal division, account for nearly half the forest area of the state (see Table 3.2). More than two-thirds of the forest area falls under the jurisdiction of the Forest Department. Of the total recorded forest area of 34,000 sq. km, about 30,000, constituting 87 per cent, falls under the direct jurisdiction of the state government. Only about 4000 sq. km (about 12 per cent) is managed by the van panchayats. While the forest area in the Garhwal division is slightly more than double that in Kumaon division, the area managed by van panchayats in Kumaon is nearly 80 per cent more than that in Garhwal. Almost two-thirds of the forest area under van panchayats is located

TABLE 3.1: FOREST AREA BASED ON SATELLITE IMAGERY, 1999

District	Crown density more than 40%	Crown density between 10 and 40%	Total
Almora	2071	466	2537
Pithoragarh	2188	824	3012
Nainital	2920	649	3569
Garhwal	2198	978	3176
Chamoli	2530	622	3152
Dehradun	1239	331	1570
Tehri	1807	753	2560
Uttarkashi	2631	468	3099
Haridwar	265	320	585
Total	17,849	5411	23,260

Source: Forest Department Uttaranchal (2000: 12).
Note: Figures of Udhamsingh Nagar, Bageshwar, Champawat, and Rudraprayag are included in their parent districts. Figures in this table are based on the Forest Survey of India Report of 1999 (Ministry of Environment and Forests, 1999).

in the Kumaon division. Almora and Bageshwar districts in Kumaon together account for the highest proportion, that is, 31 per cent of area under van panchayats. In the Garhwal division, Pauri Garhwal district accounts for the maximum van panchayat area, constituting about 16 per cent of the total forest area.

Van panchayats really cover a small portion of the forest area of the state. In some districts, namely, Almora and Pithoragarh, van panchayats cover nearly 30 per cent of the total forest area. Practically, van panchayats are the only areas where local communities themselves directly get involved in managing forests despite a long history of a strong association of the people of the state with the forests. Thus, it is surprising to see that they are not equally strongly involved in managing and administering them, especially in the changing decentralization scenario over the last decade. It is in this context that the chapter aims to seek relevant answers. The following sections, therefore, analyse the condition of van panchayats in Uttaranchal in detail.

TABLE 3.2. FOREST AREA IN UTTARANCHAL, 2000 (figures in sq. km)

Districts	Forests under Forest Department	Forests under Revenue Department	Panchayati forest under van panchayats	Other forests	Total forest area	Total geographical area of district	Forest area to total geographical area (%)	Panchayati forest to total forest area (%)
Pauri Garhwal	2393.80	1450.87	651.53	10.94	4507.14	5440	82.9	14.5
Chamoli & Rudraprayag	3639.13	946.47	618.02	6.78	5210.40	9125	57.1	11.9
Uttarkashi	6800.41	70.09	77.80	0.00	6948.30	8016	86.7	1.1
Tehri Garhwal	2781.16	1261.36	16.38	0.00	4058.90	4421	91.8	0.4
Dehradun	1512.94	417.72	98.28	247.95	2276.89	3088	73.7	4.3
Haridwar	375.19	0.00		0.00	375.19	2360	15.9	0.0
Garhwal	17,503.00	4147.00	1462.00	266.00	23,377.00	32,450	72.0	6.3
Almora & Bageshwar	1471.97	1244.24	1204.75	23.30	3944.26	5385	73.2	30.5
Pithoragarh & Champawat	1377.98	831.47	1092.98	0.00	3302.43	8856	37.3	33.1
Nainital	2625.07	112.83	286.84	2.16	3026.90	6794	59.4	7.1
Udhamsingh Nagar	1011.11	0.00		0.00	1011.11	0		
Kumaon	6486.00	2189.00	2585.00	25.00	11285.00	21,035	53.6	22.9
Grand Total	23,989.00	6335.00	4047.00	291.00	34,662.00	53,485	64.8	11.7

Source: Uttaranchal Government (2000).

LOCAL GOVERNANCE IN INDIA

VAN PANCHAYATS IN UTTARANCHAL

In Uttaranchal 6777 van panchayats have been established. These van panchayats manage a forest area of about 4000 sq. km, forming about 12 per cent of the total forest area of the state. Figure 3.2 shows the number of van panchayats in the state. It may be observed that van panchayats are not present in Haridwar and Udhamsingh Nagar districts as both have very small areas under forests.

The maximum number of van panchayats is observed in the erstwhile Almora district, now divided into Almora and Bageshwar, numbering about 1900 (see Figure 3.3). The average forest area under a van panchayat is about 60 hectares. Uttarkashi has the largest average size of van panchayat forest, but it has a very small number of van panchayats. Tehri district has more than 90 per cent of its geographical area under forests, but has the least area under van panchayats. The average size of a van panchayat is also the smallest in Tehri district. It may also be observed that, in general, Kumaon division has both larger number and size of van panchayats. This may be due to the fact that the van panchayat movement actually started in the Kumaon

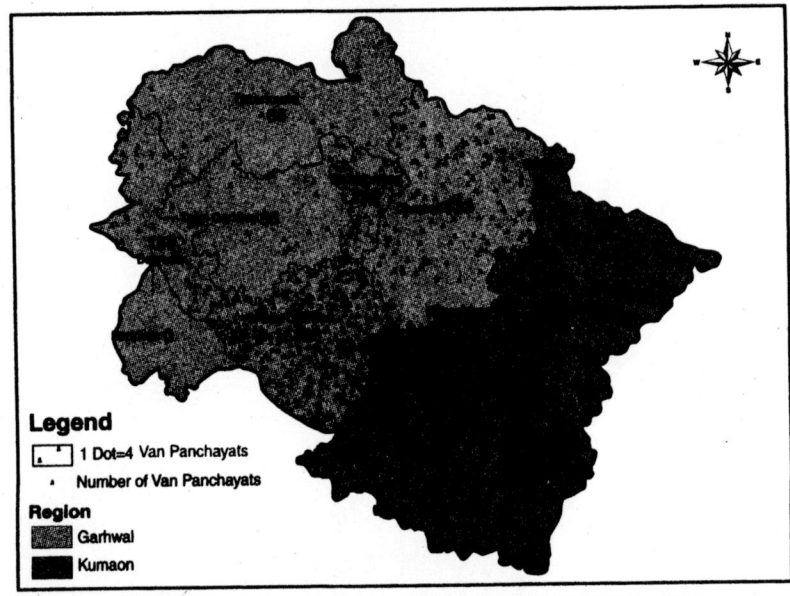

FIGURE 3.2: VAN PANCHAYATS IN UTTARANCHAL, 2000
Source: Forest Department, Uttaranchal (2000).

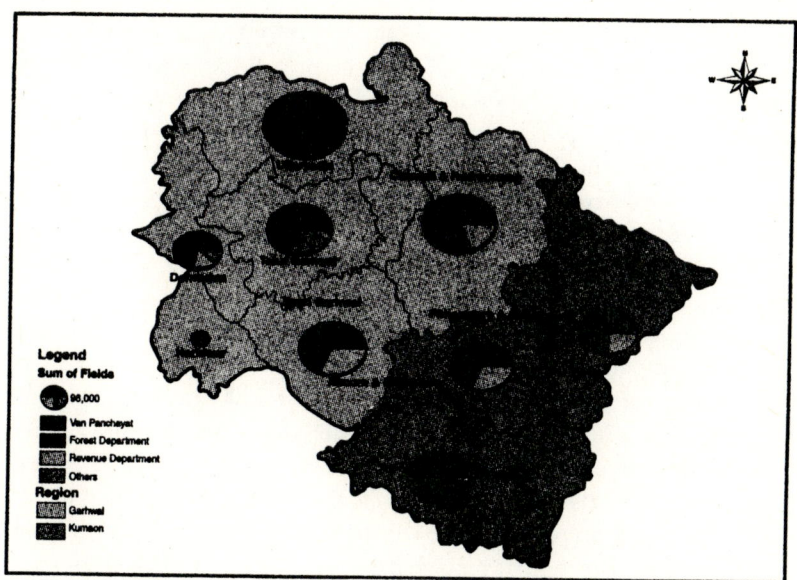

FIGURE 3.3: FOREST AREA IN UTTARANCHAL, 2000
Source: Forest Department, Uttaranchal (2000).

division. Original van panchayat rules were initially applicable to the Kumaon division only.

Thus, the five most important districts from the point of view of the importance of van panchayats are Almora, Pithoragarh, Pauri Garhwal, Chamoli, and Nainital. These are the districts with larger number of van panchayats and, as may be clear from Figure 3.3, have significant forest area being managed by them. In the next section we turn to the statutory position of van panchayats in the state of Uttaranchal.

STATUTORY POSITION OF VAN PANCHAYATS IN UTTARANCHAL

Under the chairmanship of P. Wyndham, the Uttar Pradesh government constituted a committee in 1921 known as the Kumaon Forests Grievances Committee. This committee recommended a reclassification of forests. According to the committee's recommendations, the Uttar Pradesh hill forests (now Uttaranchal) were divided into two categories: Class I and Class II. For Class I forests, provision to form van panchayats was made. Class II forests continued to remain under the direct control of the Forest Department. Subsequently, some van panchayats were also formed for Class II forests. These van panchayats could exercise the powers of a forest officer within the area notified under the Kumaon Panchayat Forest Rules, 1931. These rules have been amended from time to time. Major amendments were made in 1972, 1976, and 2001.

A van panchayat may cover five to six villages and consist of five to nine members, the number being decided by the subdivisional magistrate. A van panchayat is headed by a sarpanch and is responsible for panchayat forests, which is empowered to frame by-laws for the distribution of forest produce among right holders, regulation of grazing, cutting of grass, collection of fuel wood, and levying of fees to meet its administrative expenses. However, under the Uttaranchal Panchayati Forest Rules, 2001, any forest officer from the rank of range forest officer would have the power to inspect the panchayat forest, demand to see their records on forest maintenance, and forward these inspection notes to the deputy commissioner through the divisional forest officer.

At the present moment the formation and functioning of van panchayats in Uttaranchal are regulated by the Uttaranchal Panchayati Forest Rules, 2001. The Uttaranchal state government notified these rules on 3 July 2001 by making amendments to the Van Panchayat Rules of 1976. The Uttaranchal Panchayati Forest Rules, 2001, originate from Indian Forest Act, 1927. The constitution and composition, term, powers and duties, budget and accounts, and all other aspects related to functioning of the van panchayat are now entailed in the provisions of 2001 Rules. A brief examination of these provisions is attempted along with an analysis of 1976 Rules.

Constitution and Composition of Van Panchayats

Rule 3 of the 2001 Rules regulates the demarcation and formation of a van panchayat in a village. Under Rule 3, at least one-fifth of the adults residing in a village can apply to the subdivisional magistrate to formulate a van panchayat in their village. On receiving the application, a van panchayat is constituted under the supervision of the subdivisional magistrate under Rule 7.

Alternatively, the subdivisional magistrate is vested with powers under these rules to call upon the adult residents of a concerned village who could constitute a van panchayat for themselves. A van panchayat must have nine members and seats are reserved for women and underprivileged sections of the Indian society, such as the Scheduled Caste and Scheduled Tribe communities residing in the village. Division of seats is provided in the rules. Four seats, including one for members of Scheduled Caste or Scheduled Tribe communities, shall be reserved for women. One seat out of the balance five seats shall be reserved for a male member of the Scheduled Castes and the Scheduled Tribes. If the Scheduled Caste or the Tribe communities do not reside in a village, then the aforesaid seats shall be treated as unreserved.

Once the villagers have elected nine members, the members in turn elect a leader from amongst themselves, who is called the sarpanch of a van panchayat. Our empirical case studies show that this rule is violated in a majority of cases. A sarpanch is not eligible for election for more than two consecutive terms. Once a van panchayat is formally constituted, the subdivisional magistrate intimates its formation to the commissioner, conservator of forest, collector, and the divisional forest officer.

The panchayat van up-van *rajik* or the panchayat van *vid* (Deputy Forest Ranger) is a secretary of the van panchayat and any right holder of the panchayati forest selected by a van panchayat is the additional secretary. The term of a van panchayat, including a sarpanch and members, is five years. The subdivisional magistrate must initiate preparation for the election to a van panchayat at least six months before the expiry of its term.

The Uttaranchal Panchayati Rules, 2001 also provide for the constitution of a zilla panchayat van *paramarsh datri* samiti (District Panchayat Forest Advisory Committee) in every district. The composition of the samiti is shown in Table 3.3. The duties of a samiti include review of the working of van panchayats, issuing guidelines regarding improvement in panchayati forests, helping van panchayats to arrange funds from various sources, and assisting van panchayats in discharging their duties.

Plan-making Hierarchy

A hierarchy of plans has been introduced under the 2001 Rules (see Table 3.4), which was not the case under the 1976 Rules. It is obligatory on the part of a van panchayat to prepare a Micro Plan for

TABLE 3.3: COMPOSITION OF A ZILLA PANCHAYAT VAN DATRI
SAMITI

Member	Position
Adhyaksh zilla panchayat (Chairman, District Panchayat)	Chairman
Panchayat van vikas adhikari (Divisional Forest Officer)	Secretary
One male sarpanch nominated by the collector	Member
One female sarpanch nominated by the collector	Member
Divisional forest officer posted in the district	Member
District panchayat raj officer	Member
Block pramukh nominated by district magistrate (not more than two)	Member

Source: Uttaranchal Panchayati Forest Rules, 2001.

TABLE 3.4: HIERARCHY OF PLANS FOR FOREST MANAGEMENT
UNDER THE 2001 RULES

Plan	Approval/sanction	Perspective	In charge
Composite Management Plan	Conservator of forests	5 years	Panchayat van vikas adhikari
Micro Plan	Approval by a van panchayat and sanction by panchayat van vikas adhikari	5 years	Van panchayat to be assisted by Sahayak Panchayat Van Vikas Adhikari
Annual Implementation Plan	Approval by Sahayak panchayat van vikas adhikari	1 year	Van panchayat assisted by panchayat van vid (deputy forest ranger)

the management and protection of the panchayati forest for a period
of five years. The Micro Plan is prepared on the basis of the Composite
Management Plan prepared by the panchayat van vikas adhikari. This
Composite Management Plan is also prepared for five years. The
sahayak van vikas adhikari (Assistant Forest Development Officer)
assists the van panchayat in the preparation of the Micro Plan. The
right holders then approve the Micro Plan before the panchayat van
vikas adhikari sanctions it. Once the Micro Plan is approved and
sanctioned, the van panchayat is also required to prepare an Annual
Implementation Plan for the development and management of forests.

Here again the panchayat van vid (Deputy Forest Ranger) assists a van panchayat. This plan is to be approved by the sahayak panchayat vikas adhikari. A van panchayat can start implementation only after the approval and sanction of the Annual Implementation Plan.

It does not require a great deal of analysis to see that the planning system was much simpler under the 1976 Rules than 2001 Rules. While one plan is needed under the 1976 Rules, three plans are required under the 2001 Rules before a van panchayat may begin to implement its programmes. Tight bureaucratic control, however, remains in place under both the 1976 and 2001 Rules (also see Kapoor 1999).

Interactions: Meetings and Proceedings

Under the 2001 Rules, a van panchayat can hold a meeting at least once in every two months on a seven-day notice. Emergency meetings may be held by a sarpanch or at written requisition from more than one-half of the members on a day's notice. The proceedings of these meetings are required to be sent to the sahayak van vikas adhikari. Decisions in a van panchayat are taken on the basis of majority vote of the members present and voting. Government officials like the *patwari* (official maintaining land records in villages), van panchayat inspector, gram vikas adhikari (Village Development Officer), panchayat van up-van rajik, and panchayat van vid may attend meetings, but they are not entitled to vote.

A general meeting of all the right holders is required to be convened by every sarpanch once in a year. The right holders are apprised of the developmental works undertaken by a van panchayat, and the income and expenditure of a van panchayat. The right holders are required to intimate their demands of fuel wood and give their suggestions regarding development works that they want to be undertaken. The proceedings of these meetings should be sent to the panchayat van vikas adhikari.

Functions and Duties of Van Panchayats

As mentioned earlier, it is the duty of a van panchayat to prepare a five-year Micro Plan and Annual Implementation Plan for the management and protection of the panchayati forests. Apart from this, the duties of a van panchayat under the 2001 Rules include the following:

- To protect trees from damage and to use only those trees for silviculture that are marked for felling by the official nominated by the panchayat van vikas adhikari (divisional forest officer or DFO).
- To ensure that no land of the panchayati forest area is encroached upon.
- To fix boundary pillars, and to make boundary walls and to protect them.
- To abide by the directions and execute orders passed by the DFO regarding conservation and improvement of forests.
- To utilize the forest produce to the best advantage of the right holders, keeping in view silviculture health and sustainable resource management.
- To protect forests from illicit felling of trees, lopping, fire, and other damages, and to conserve them.
- To ensure that catchment areas of water sources are well wooded, with appropriate trees and vegetation species to maximize rainwater conservation.
- To promote natural regeneration through management of forest fires, controlling grazing by excluding one-fifth of panchayati forests from grazing annually by rotation.
- To ensure preservation of wildlife.

The powers of a van panchayat are detailed in Rule 20 of the Uttaranchal Panchayati Forest Rules, 2001. According to these rules, the status of a van panchayat is equivalent to a forest officer having following powers in his jurisdiction:

1. To compound fines for forest offences committed up to Rs 500 per offence depending upon the seriousness of the offence.
2. Provided if the offender is prepared to accept the offence, the forest panchayat shall realize the full market value of the property involved in the offence, as assessed by an officer not below the rank of a panchayat van vikas adhikari at the prescribed scheduled rate in addition to the compensation referred to in this rule.
3. To institute and defend suits and proceedings in respect of claims arising under these rules.
4. To regulate grazing and admission of the cattle into the panchayati forest.

5. To impound cattle trespassing into the panchayati forest in accordance with the Cattle Trespass Act, 1871.
6. To exclude from any or all privileges in the panchayati forest any person whom the forest panchayat may for sufficient grounds consider being responsible for fire or damage to the forest area, or who does not obey orders issued by the forest panchayat in the exercise of powers conferred on it.
7. To seize all tools or weapons used in committing forest offences within the area of forest panchayat.
8. To make local sale of forest produce without detriment to forests, and to issue permits and charge fees for grazing or cutting grass or collection of fallen twigs or trees for fuel if considered necessary, provided such an exploitation has the prior approval of the panchayat van vikas adhikari, and made for the bona fide use of the right holders; provided further that the permission of the panchayat van vikas adhikari will not be necessary for allowing grazing or cutting of grass or collection of fallen trees.
9. To extract and sell resin in accordance with the provisions of the Uttar Pradesh Resin and Other Forest Produce (Regulation of Trade) Act, 1976.

Powers of Van Panchayats: A Comparative View

The duties and powers of van panchayats have been compared under the 1976 and 2001 Rules. Increasingly, under the 2001 Rules, van panchayats have become merely implementing agencies of forest policies on behalf of the state government. While earlier, under the 1976 Rules, van panchayats could sell a tree to a right holder after passing a resolution, prior approval of the van vikas adhikari is needed under the 2001 Rules. Under the 1976 Rules, van panchayats could also lease some forest land for commercial purposes, which is not possible now under the 2001 Rules.

In addition to these, a van panchayat has the power to frame by-laws for the distribution of forest produce among eligible persons, regulate grazing, cutting of grass, and collection of fuel wood; and levy fees for its administrative expenditure and for any other purpose consistent with the rules. The panchayat van vikas adhikari, however, must approve these bye-laws. If required, a van panchayat can also appoint paid personnel for the protection and management of the forest.

Revenue and Expenditure

Each van panchayat must prepare an annual budget and allocate funds out of its income to discharge its duties. The budget of a van panchayat has to be approved by the van vikas adhikari. The sarpanch is responsible for keeping the accounts of all the income and expenditure in the form of a panchayati fund. The chief audit officer of the Government Cooperative Societies and Panchayats, Uttaranchal, does the audit of accounts of a van panchayat. The panchayat up–van vikas adhikari has been given the power to nominate three right holders to carry out summary interval audits every financial year.

The panchayati forest fund under Rule 28 is created for a van panchayat, and the income from the sale of proceeds of forest produce, government grants, any other source of revenue, and money being the share of a van panchayat lying unutilized with the collectors are to be deposited in this fund (see Table 3.5). The panchayati forest fund is managed by a van panchayat under the overall control of the panchayat van vikas adhikari. The account is operated by a sarpanch. All the withdrawals are made by cheque, which is countersigned by the secretary of the forest panchayat. Financial powers are largely same under both the 1976 and 2001 Rules, that is precarious and unsustainable.

Comparison between the Van Panchayat Rules 1976 and 2001

A comparative examination of the 1976 and 2001 Rules reveals that bureaucratic control over van panchayats has increased. However, the change from three consecutive terms for a sarpanch to two is more participatory. But a tall hierarchy of plans has no link with an equally tall hierarchy of plans to be pursued by rural local bodies created by the state government after the 73rd Amendment to the Constitution of India. In both cases approval is to be taken from a bureaucrat.

The 1976 and 2001 Rules manifest similarities as well as differences on many counts. While the 1976 Rules covered certain parts of Uttar Pradesh state, the 2001 Rules cover the same areas, which now make the entire state of Uttaranchal. Both the 1976 and 2001 Rules provide for similar procedures for the formation of van panchayats. Formation of van panchayat for a particular village remains optional under both sets of rules. Both rules even provide for a similar number, that is, one-third of residents, for opposing the formation of a van panchayat (see Table 3.6).

TABLE 3.5: PANCHAYATI FOREST FUND: THE 2001 RULES

Rule 28
A panchayati forest fund shall be created for every forest panchayat and the income from the following sources shall be deposited in it:

- The sale of proceeds of forest produce
- government grants
- any other source of revenue
- money being the share of van panchayat lying unutilized with the collectors

Rule 29
The forest panchayat under the overall control of the panchayat van vikas adhikari shall manage the panchayati forest fund.

The sarpanch shall operate the account; all the withdrawals shall be made by cheque, which shall be countersigned by the secretary of the forest panchayat.

Rule 30
The net income from the sale of resin and other forest produce shall be determined as follows:

- the forest department shall take all actual expenditure incurred in resin tapping and the state government may determine such overheads from time to time;
- as regards the other forest produce, the forest department shall charge 10 per cent of sale proceeds as administrative expenditure.

Distribution and utilization of the panchayati fund shall be done in the following manner:

- 20 per cent to zilla panchayat for implementation of development projects of public utility;
- 80 per cent of balance amount shall be for implementation of development purposes;
- Not less than 50 per cent of the amount shall be incurred for maintenance and development of panchayati forest; and
- forest panchayat shall incur not more than 50 per cent of the amount on implementation of projects of local utility.

Rule 31
The annual budget shall be submitted by 31 December of the preceding year and the panchayat van vikas adhikari shall accord his sanction by the following 31 March.

Rule 33
A proper account of all income and expenditure of the panchayati forest fund shall be maintained by the sarpanch.

Rule 34
The audit of the accounts of every forest panchayat shall be done under the orders of the chief audit officer to the Government Cooperative Societies and Panchayats, Uttaranchal, at such intervals and in such manner as the state government may direct.

TABLE 3.6: SIMILARITIES BETWEEN VAN PANCHAYAT RULES OF
1976 AND 2001

Subject	Van Panchayat Rules, 1976	Van Panchayat Rules, 2001
Extent	*Rule 1 (2)* Nainital, Almora, Pithoragarh, Garhwal, Chamoli, Uttarkashi, and Tehri districts; Chakrata tehsil in Dehradun district; any other area as notified by state government from time to time.	*Rule 1 (II)* Almora, Bageshwar, Champawat, Pithoragarh, Chamoli, Rudraprayag, Uttarkashi, Tehri, Pauri Garhwal districts; Nainital tehsil in Nainital district; hilly regions and Chakrata tehsil in Dehradun district; any other area as notified by the state government from time to time.

Opposing
formation of a
panchayati van
	Rule 5
	• Any area will not be
	   declared as panchayati
	   van if one-third or more
	   of the residents object to
	   the proposal.
	• Application should
	   include the location of
	   the area and its
	   boundaries.
		Rule 3
		• Any area will not be declared
		   as panchayati van if one-third
		   or more of the residents
		   object to the proposal.
		• Application should include
		   the location of the area and its
		   boundaries.

Constitution
of a van
panchayat
	Rule 9
	• A bureaucrat, i.e., deputy
	   commissioner could call
	   the residents of the
	   village at a convenient
	   place and time to
	   constitute a van
	   panchayat.
	• Any person who is a
	   government servant or
	   official of any local body
	   or any person who has
	   dues to pay to van
	   panchayat or any person
	   who is proved guilty of
	   moral turpitude is
		Rule 7
		• The district magistrate shall
		   call upon the residents of the
		   village at a convenient place
		   and time to constitute a van
		   panchayat.
		• Any person who is a
		   government servant or official
		   of any local body or official of
		   van panchayat or any person
		   who has dues to pay to van
		   panchayat or any person who
		   is proved guilty of moral
		   turpitude is debarred from
		   becoming a member or
		   sarpanch.

(Table 3.6 contd)

(*Table 3.6 contd*)

	debarred from becoming a member or sarpanch.	
Information about the panchayati forest and van panchayat	*Rule 13* After the constitution of the van panchayat, the deputy commissioner shall inform the conservator and divisional forest officer.	*Rule 9* After the constitution of the van panchayat, the subdivisional magistrate shall intimate the commissioner, the conservator of forest, the collector, and the divisional forest officer concerned.
Term of van panchayat members	*Rule 14* The term of members and sarpanch of a van panchayat is five years subject to extension by the state government.	*Rule 15* The term of members and sarpanch of van panchayat is five years.
Removal of a member by van panchayat	*Rule 15* • If a majority of van panchayat members feel it necessary to remove a member, then the sarpanch brings it to the notice of deputy commissioner, who will visit the village and take the views of persons having voting rights and work accordingly. • If the member is removed, then the deputy commissioner shall ask the voters to elect a new member for the remaining duration.	*Rule 17* • If a majority of van panchayat members feel it necessary to remove a member, then the sarpanch brings it to the notice of subdivisional magistrate, who will visit the village and take the views of persons having voting rights and work accordingly. • If the member is removed then the deputy commissioner shall ask the voters to elect a new member for the remaining duration.
Appointment of officials	*Rule 17* Subject to the availability of funds, the forest panchayat may appoint such number of paid personnel as may be considered necessary.	*Rule 22* Subject to the availability of funds, the forest panchayat may appoint such number of paid personnel as may be considered necessary.

The first major difference between the 1976 Rules and 2001 Rules is that the latter have introduced more bureaucratic control over the functioning of van panchayats (see Table 3.7). For example, even determining charges for grazing or cutting grass or issuing permits for the collection of fallen trees needs prior approval from the panchayat van vikas adhikari. Second, van panchayats are further restricted in using the panchayati forest fund, as the panchayat van vikas adhikari will strictly control the use of money out of it. While the 1976 Rules provided for only one special officer for the supervision of van panchayats, the 2001 Rules have created a hierarchy of bureaucrats. The 2001 Rules are thus obstructive in this sense, as more government does not necessarily mean good government.

The 2001 Rules have reduced the number of people from one-third to one-fifth for deciding whether a van panchayat should be formed in the first place. This point is important because now fewer people from a village can decide whether to have a van panchayat. While making this point, one does not make any value judgment in favour or against the existence of the institution of van panchayat *per se*. However, I believe that wider participation would yield more representative results and is likely to include the interests of a majority of the residents in the decision-making process.

The 2001 Rules are likely to better protect the interests of the weaker sections, including the Scheduled Castes or Scheduled Tribes, and women. In the 1976 Rules, a bureaucrat was empowered to nominate a member from the Scheduled Castes or Scheduled Tribes, which in the 2001 Rules has been made mandatory through the process of election.

Management of van panchayats was much simpler under Rule 11 of the 1976 Rules. It has been completely bureaucratized under Rules 11 and 12 of the 2001 Rules through the introduction of a hierarchy of plans to be prepared by a people's institution, but approved and sanctioned by an appointed bureaucrat.

While no provisions were made in the 1976 Rules, the zilla panchayat van paramarsh datri samiti is constituted under Rule 52 of the 2001 Rules. This committee consists of all nominated members, including the *adhyaksh zilla panchayat* (Chairman District Panchayat), panchayat van vikas adhikari of the district, one male and one female sarpanch nominated by the collector, divisional forest officers posted

TABLE 3.7: MAJOR DIFFERENCES BETWEEN VAN PANCHAYAT
RULES OF 1976 AND 2001

Subject	Van Panchayat Rules, 1976	Van Panchayat Rules, 2001
Appointment of special officer	*Rule 4* State government may, for the management and supervision of van panchayats constituted under these Rules, appoint an officer in van panchayat who shall be called special officer. Such an officer will function under the control of the commissioner, but under these Rules he will exercise the powers of a deputy commissioner.	*Rule 2 (j)* Panchayat van vikas adhikari, up panchayat van vikas adhikari, sahayak panchayat van vikas adhikari, panchayat van up-van rajik, and panchayat van vid shall mean, respectively, divisional forest officer, assistant conservator of forests, forest ranger, deputy forest ranger, and forester, specially deputed by the state government for performing duties under these rules.
Constitution of panchayati van	*Rule 5* Minimum of one-third adult residents of the village who have resided in the village for the past ten years prior to date of application can apply to the district magistrate.	*Rule 3* Minimum of one-fifth adult residents of the village who must have resided in the village for past ten years prior to the date of application, or if a resolution is passed by the area panchayat, can apply to the district magistrate.
Constitution of van panchayat	*Rule 9* The deputy commissioner shall call upon residents above the age of 21 at a convenient place and time to constitute a van panchayat. The people will elect five to nine members from amongst themselves. The elected members will elect a sarpanch from amongst themselves. The sarpanch will be responsible	*Rule 7* The district magistrate shall call upon the residents of the village at a convenient place and time to constitute a van panchayat. Notice of this will also be issued to the patwari and the pradhan of the village. There will be nine members in a van panchayat. Four seats are reserved for women of whom one is reserved for Scheduled Caste or Scheduled Tribe woman. Of the

(Table 3.7 contd)

(*Table 3.7 contd*)

Subject	Van Panchayat Rules, 1976	Van Panchayat Rules, 2001
	for the proper management of the forest. A sarpanch cannot be elected for three consecutive terms. *Rule 12* The deputy commissioner can, if he thinks necessary, nominate a person living in that village as member of the van panchayat. If there is no representation of Scheduled Castes or Scheduled Tribes in the van panchayat, then the person nominated should be from Scheduled Caste or Scheduled Tribe community.	remaining five seats, one is reserved for a male belonging to Scheduled Caste or Scheduled Tribe community. If there is no Scheduled Caste or Scheduled Tribe in the village then the seats will be treated as unreserved. Elected members will elect a sarpanch from amongst themselves. A sarpanch cannot be elected for two consecutive terms. If in any van panchayat the seat for Scheduled Castes or Scheduled Tribes or women is left vacant, then the van panchayat can pass a resolution and get the seats filled from amongst the persons belonging to that category residing in the village.
Management of panchayati forest	*Rule 11* Once a van panchayat is constituted, then the deputy commissioner will ask the van panchayat for a draft working plan for the management of forest and forward it to the commissioner for his approval.	*Rules 11 and 12* The panchayat van vikas adhikari shall prepare a Composite Management Plan for all panchayati forests under his control for a period of five years. It shall be obligatory for a forest panchayat to prepare a Micro Plan based on the guiding principles given in the Composite Management Plan and protection of the panchayati forest for a period of five years with assistance of the sahayak panchayat van vikas adhikari. The Micro Plan has to be passed by a general meeting of all right

(*Table 3.7 contd*)

(*Table 3.7 contd*)

Subject	Van Panchayat Rules, 1976	Van Panchayat Rules, 2001
		holders before being finally approved by the panchayat van vikas adhikari. It shall be the duty of the van panchayat to follow the Micro Plan strictly.
Auction	*Rule 22* After consulting the conservator and the DFO, the deputy commissioner can order for auction of forest produce, provided the valuation of the forest produce to be auctioned is done by the van panchayat and verified by the DFO. If the value of the forest produce to be auctioned is less than Rs 5000, then the auction will be done under the supervision of the sarpanch of the van panchayat. If the value of the forest produce is more than Rs 5000, then the DFO will supervise the proceedings.	*Rule 18* If the van panchayat feels that it has exploitable trees or other forest produce for commercial sale within its forests, it shall apply to the sahayak panchayat van vikas adhikari who shall forward the application after preparing an estimate of its value to the panchayat van vikas adhikari to sell it by public auction.

in the district, district panchayat raj officer, and block *pramukh* nominated by the district magistrate (not more than two).

Control over Van Panchayats

Van panchayats must work under the watchful eye of bureaucrats, as if people's institutions are to be trusted only to a minimal extent (see Table 3.8).

Both the 1976 and 2001 Rules provide sensible controls in the form of financial audits by bureaucrats. Rule 46 of the 2001 Rules provides that it shall be obligatory on the part of the collector to

TABLE 3.8: CONTROLS ON VAN PANCHAYATS, 1976 AND 2001 RULES

Subject	Van Panchayat Rules, 1976	Van Panchayat Rules, 2001
Administration of panchayats and assets	*Rule 26* The management of panchayati forest assets shall rest with the van panchayat under the control of deputy commissioner or any officer appointed by him. Proper accounts shall be maintained for all income and expenditure of the van panchayat and be closed every month. The same have to be reviewed and passed in the next month's meeting of the van panchayat.	*Rule 7* The management of panchayati forest assets shall rest with the van panchayat under the control of subdivisional magistrate or any officer appointed by him. *Rule 51* The Members of the Legislative Assembly, adhyaksh zilla panchayat, and pramukh of the kshetra panchayat shall be entitled to inspect any panchayat and its forests within the area they represent.
Removal of a sarpanch	*Rule 28* The deputy commissioner can remove a van panchayat sarpanch if a no-confidence resolution is placed by one-third members of the van panchayat and is passed by two-thirds majority.	*Rule 17* Van panchayat sarpanch can be removed by the subdivisional magistrate if a no-confidence resolution is placed by one-third members of the van panchayat and is passed by two-thirds majority.
Inspection of van panchayats' functioning by officers	*Rule 33* Forest officers are required to inspect a van panchayat during its tenure at least once in three years to assess its functioning. Their report has to be submitted to the conservator who in turn will file a report to the chief conservator with copies to the concerned commissioner and deputy commissioner. In addition to these, different forest officials are required to inspect van panchayats in their jurisdiction as per standards specified in the rules.	*Rule 24* The forest panchayat shall submit to the panchayat van vikas adhikari before the fifteenth day of April each year, an annual report of the working during the previous financial year, who will submit a compiled report of his region to the collector.

reconstitute a new forest panchayat within a period of six months from the date of supersession or dissolution of one. No such provision existed under the 1976 Rules. This is a step in the right direction. But at the same time, the collector has been given more discretionary powers for the removal of a sarpanch or van panchayat members.

The Uttaranchal Panchayati Forest Rules, 2001, propose strict administrative control over van panchayats. They are guided and controlled by the district administration right from the demarcation of the forest boundary to its day-to-day functioning. In the district the deputy commissioner exercises control over van panchayats through the subdivisional magistrate. The van panchayat inspector is the link between the administration and van panchayats. Due permission is required to be taken from the district authorities for carrying out any development work in the panchayati forest.

VAN PANCHAYATS: SOME CASES

In order to get a realistic picture of the current functioning of van panchayats, primary surveys were organized. Case study districts were selected from amongst the five identified to have significant van panchayat activity. Further, based on functional considerations of regional representation, van panchayat activity, and practical aspects like time and weather, two districts, namely Pauri and Nainital, were selected from the Garhwal and Kumaon regions respectively. Unlike the villages in the plains, those in the hills are smaller in size. There are about 150 to 200 households in each (except Bhaisodha and Srikot, which have fewer households). Therefore, the conflicts are correspondingly small in number, and often of minor nature (see Tables 3.9 and 3.10).

A total of six van panchayats were selected from Pauri Garhwal and Nainital districts for primary surveys: three in Pauri and three in Nainital. However, secondary data was collected for preparing a profile of the van panchayats in the two districts. Figures 3.4 and 3.5 show the growth of van panchayats. In Nainital, a significant number of van panchayats were formed, initially during the 1950s and 1960s, and then during the 1990s. It may be interesting to note that more than half the number of van panchayats was established during the period 1998–2000. The reason for such a sudden and fast increase in the number of van panchayats in these districts is attributed to a

TABLE 3.9: SELECTED VAN PANCHAYATS, 2002

	Van Panchayat					
	Dhanaculi	Parbara	Thapliya Meharagaon	Bhaisodha	Siku	Srikot
District	Nainital	Nainital	Nainital	Pauri Garhwal	Pauri Garhwal	Pauri Garhwal
Block	Dhari	Dhari	Bhimtal	Pabo	Pabo	Pabo
Establishment year	1932	1932	1950	1965	1954	2001
Van panchayat area	350	285	380	52	39	N.A.
Population	3000	1000	1300	400	725	400
Number of households	460	165	250	88	108	86

Source: Primary survey (January 2002).

TABLE 3.10: SOCIAL COMPOSITION OF SELECTED VAN PANCHAYATS, 2002

Community	Dhanachuli	Parbara	Thapliya Meharagaon	Bhaisodha	Siku	Srikot
	Number of Households					
Thakur	400	115	55	70	92	66
Brahmin	0	0	150	0	0	0
SC and ST	60	30	45	8	16	20
Others	0	0	0	10	0	0

Source: Primary survey (January 2002).

huge inflow of World Bank money for implementation of the Joint Forest Management programme in the state, as claimed by some local NGOs and van panchayat representatives.

The scenario in Pauri district seems slightly different. This is due to the fact that the detailed data for the district is only available till the year 1993, showing 895 van panchayats. The existing number of van panchayats in the district is 1633 in 2000. In Pauri district it has taken about seven years to double the number of van panchayats, while in Nainital district it took only two years.

The average area under a van panchayat is about 44 and 40 hectares in Nainital and Pauri districts respectively. Tables 3.11 and 3.12 show block-wise number and area of van panchayats in Nainital and Pauri districts respectively. A wide variation in the average sizes is observed within each district, though more so in Pauri. The smallest size in terms of area (15 hectare) of a van panchayat is observed in Pabo

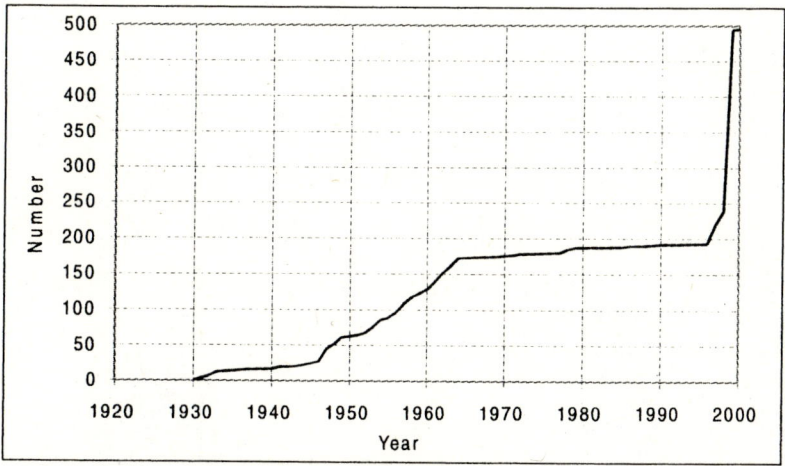

FIGURE 3.4: GROWTH OF VAN PANCHAYATS IN NAINITAL DISTRICT, 1920–2000

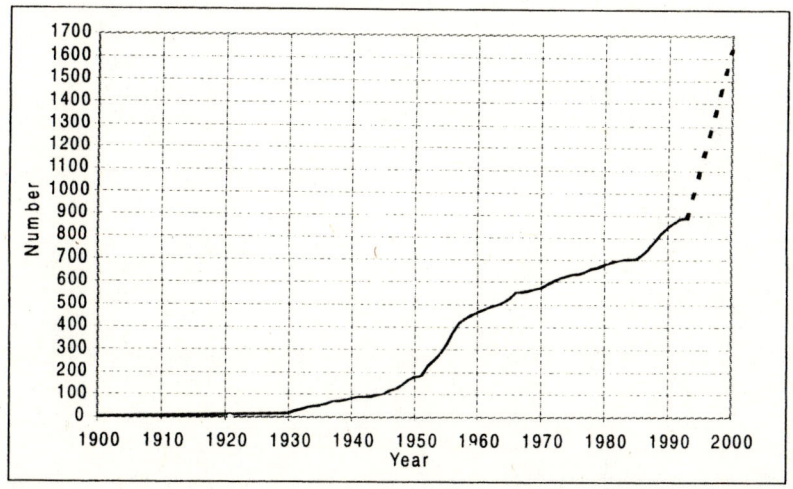

FIGURE 3.5: GROWTH OF VAN PANCHAYATS IN PAURI DISTRICT, 1900–2000

TABLE 3.11: AREA OF VAN PANCHAYATS IN NAINITAL DISTRICT, 2000

Block	Number of VP	Area of VP (ha)	Average area of VP (ha)
Betalghat	131	4044.02	30.87
Bhimtal	89	3824.18	42.97
Dhari	51	1034.74	20.29
Kotabagh	41	2052.02	50.05
Okhalkanda	95	8377.80	88.19
Ramgarh	88	2242.59	25.48
Total	495	21575.34	43.59

Source: Government of Uttaranchal (2000).

TABLE 3.12: AREA AND INCOME OF VAN PANCHAYATS IN PAURI DISTRICT, 1999

Block	No. of VP	Area of VP (ha)	Agricultural area (ha)	Agricultural area as % of VP area	Annual income of VP (Rs)	Average annual income of VP	Average area of VP (ha)
Bironkhal	62	2287.70	277	12.11	36368	587	36.90
Dugadda	69	2704.09	470	17.38	14,7119	2132	39.19
Dwarikhal	48	145.94	193	13.26	79209	1650	30.33
Ekeshwar	64	1546.73	346	22.37	37972	593	24.17
Jaiharikhal	65	2682.37	150	5.59	12,2545	1885	41.27
Kaljikhal	43	1009.85	180	17.82	1697	39	23.48
Khirsu	25	1812.04	65	3.59	12334	493	72.48
Kot	40	627.30	122	19.45	5127	128	15.68
Nainitanda	126	4507.32	356	7.90	17,5046	1389	35.77
Pabo	27	405.25	49	12.09	5930	220	15.01
Pauri	54	1511.05	102	6.75	81839	1516	27.98
Pokhada	50	919.94	85	9.24	23083	462	18.40
Rekhnikhal	88	6765.94	579	8.56	10,4428	1187	76.89
Thalisian	87	6110.31	165	2.70	10,6348	1222	70.23
Yamkeshwar	47	1733.54	409	23.59	16812	358	36.88
Total	895	36,079.37	3548	9.83	95,5857	1068	40.31

Source: Government of Uttar Pradesh (1999).
Note: VP = van panchayat.

block in Pauri district, while the largest is about 88 hectare in Okhalkanda block in Nainital district.

Information regarding the income of van panchayats is available only for the Pauri district. Table 3.12 shows a block-wise profile of van panchayats in the district. The average annual income of van panchayats in Pauri district in the year 1999 was a paltry Rs 1068. The lowest income observed, in block Kaljikhal, was Rs 39, while the highest was in block Dugadda, Rs 2132. Annual income of van panchayats in Pauri district is extremely low. The average annual income in blocks was found to be less than Rs 40. Apart from Bironkhal block, the average income of van panchayats in other blocks remains less than Rs 2000. These unimpressive financial figures clearly establish that an extreme resource constraint due to the limited financial base has been experienced by van panchayats.

The remainder of this section takes up cases of a few selected villages and explores the role and functions of van panchayats. It also seeks to assess the relevance of van panchayats in the protection of forests and the lives of rural folk.

VILLAGE DHANACHULI

The village of Dhanachuli is situated in Dhari block of Nainital district. Dhanachuli van panchayat was formed on 23 October 1932 as a sanyukt van panchayat, covering four villages, namely, Dhanachuli, Agheria, Majhela, and Dheri. In 1957 the sanyukt van panchayat was split into respective village van panchayats. At present, Dhanachuli van panchayat exercises control over Dhanachuli panchayat's forests. The population of the village is about 3000. There are 460 households, of which 400 households belong to the Thakur community and the rest to Scheduled Caste communities. Dongar Singh, the sarpanch, belongs to the Thakur community. He was the first person interviewed for his views on the functioning and relevance of van panchayat to his village, particularly the forests.

There is no secure source of income in this van panchayat. Generally, each household pays Rs 70 per annum. The annual revenue of the van panchayat was found to be about Rs 12,000 in 2001. The van panchayat has also appointed two watchmen for forest protection. They are paid Rs 600 each per month. The present income is not adequate to meet basic needs. The accounts are maintained by the sarpanch of the van panchayat. Passes are issued to individuals from neighbouring villages to take forest produce. These also do not add much to the revenue of the van panchayat as the passes are for merely Rs 5 or Rs 10, valid for a month or so.

There is no common member between the van panchayat and gram panchayat. The gram panchayat is responsible for the development and welfare of the village as a whole. The forests are looked after by the van panchayat. The two institutions function independently. The gram panchayat is invited to the meetings of the van panchayat. The van panchayat has no say in the decisions of the gram panchayat and vice versa. But since both the panchayats are formed by the same group of people of the village, both consider each other's views in the decision-making processes.

Dhanachuli van panchayat is under the direct control of the district magistrate. The subdivisional magistrate is the mukhya van adhikari (Chief Forest Officer). The SDM exercises the administrative powers on behalf of the district magistrate. The van panchayat inspector is the link between the district administration and the van panchayat. The van panchayat has to take permission from the district magistrate for cutting any tree in its area. No financial assistance is provided by the district administration. Management of the forest is handled by the van panchayat with the support of villagers.

Since the Joint Forest Management programme is not being implemented in the village, there is no direct relationship between the van panchayat and the Forest Department. However, the van panchayat is aware of the World Bank project. They know that a van panchayat has to prepare a Micro Plan with the assistance of the Forest Department, which will be implemented through the Joint Forest Management programme. The van panchayat is also aware of the fact that on implementation of the Joint Forest Management programme, 80 per cent of the project cost is borne by the World Bank and the remaining 20 per cent is given by the village either in monetary form or in the form of *shram daan* (free labour).

Lal Singh, who was earlier the pradhan of the gram panchayat, was interviewed because of the non-availability of the present pradhan. According to him, gram panchayat meetings are held once in a month to discuss the welfare and development of the village. A general meeting of the van panchayat is held once in six months, which all the villagers are required to attend. This is the time when the gram panchayat members also put forward their views. The issues discussed by the gram panchayat and van panchayat include illegal cutting of trees, construction of check dams in the forest area, etc.

Gram and van panchayat roles are defined and hence they rarely interfere in each other's work. However, gram panchayat decisions overrule van panchayat decisions. This could be probably due to the statutory nature and good financial health of the gram panchayat. There has been no incidence of conflict between the two in the past few years. The reasons for good relationship between the two are that the functional domain and administrative boundary of the van panchayat are clearly demarcated.

A group of local residents was also interviewed. All of them were aware of the existence of the van panchayat in the village. However, none had ever held any position in the van panchayat, nor had they attended any meetings. All the members of the van panchayat come from the village and often discuss issues relating to the forest. So there is no enthusiasm to attend van panchayat meetings. They had never been in conflict with the van panchayat. According to them, the van panchayat exercises transparency in its working. All sections of the society are treated equally, though women's representation is low.

Elections are not held for the van panchayat. The villagers nominate the members. The term of the van panchayat is five years. The members or the sarpanch of this van panchayat have never acted in a manner for which they needed to be punished. Objections are raised in the general meetings of the gram sabha and resolved there.

Permission is not required to take resources from the forest. People generally collect dry leaves and sticks from the area. For this each household pays Rs 70 per annum to the van panchayat. This is not a fixed amount and depends on the paying capacity of individuals. People are, however, never stopped from entering the forest area, except for cutting young branches, trees, and green leaves. This suggests that this van panchayat has been successful in implementing the vital provisions of the 2001 Rules.

Earlier, the van panchayat and the gram panchayat used to interfere and resolve conflicts between individuals. But now the parties themselves settle matters. The forest produce is sufficient for villagers and forest quality has improved over the years. The van panchayat, however, occasionally plants trees in the forest area.

VILLAGE PARBARA

Parbara village is also situated in Dhari block of Nainital district. The Parbara van panchayat was formed on 22 October 1932, and exercises control over Parbara panchayat's forests. The population of the village is about 1000. There are about 750 Thakurs and the remaining 250 persons belong to the Scheduled Caste communities.

Chandan Singh, who is a member of the van panchayat, belongs to the dominant Thakur community. He was interviewed to ascertain the response of the van panchayat in respect of its functioning and relevance to the people's lives. The details of the interview are given in the following paragraphs.

The van panchayat does not have any secure source of income. Generally, each household pays about Rs 60 per annum to the van panchayat. The van panchayat has also appointed two watchmen for the forest, who are paid Rs 400 each per month. During the Joint Forest Management programme, the watchmen were paid Rs 1200 per month. The salary of the watchmen was included in the Micro Plan and paid by the Forest Department. The present income of the van panchayat is not adequate. The sarpanch of the van panchayat maintains the accounts. Passes are also issued to individuals from neighbouring villages to take forest produce, which also gets this van panchayat some funds.

There is no common member between the van panchayat and gram panchayat. The forests are looked after by the van panchayat. These two bodies function independently. Sometimes the gram panchayat gives money from the development fund to the van panchayat for tree plantation. However, the van panchayat has no say in the decisions of the gram panchayat, and similarly gram panchayat cannot influence van panchayat decisions. But each panchayat considers the other's view in decision–making. No conflict between the gram panchayat and van panchayat has been reported.

The van panchayat is under the direct control of the district magistrate. The subdivisional magistrate is the mukhya van adhikari. The subdivisional magistrate exercises administrative powers on behalf of the district magistrate. A van panchayat inspector is the link between the district administration and the van panchayat. The van panchayat has to take permission from the district magistrate for cutting any tree in their area. The district administration provides no financial assistance. Day-to-day management of the forest is carried out by the van panchayat with the support of the villagers.

Since the Joint Forest Management lasted for only three years, at present there is no direct relationship between the van panchayat and the Forest Department. The pradhan of the Parbara gram panchayat, Gopal Singh, was interviewed for understanding the relationship between the gram and van panchayats and the former's views on the latter.

Gram panchayat meetings are held once in a month to discuss the welfare and development of the village. A general meeting is held once in six months, which all the villagers are required to attend. This is the time when the van panchayat members also put forward their views. Issues discussed by the gram panchayat and van panchayat include illegal cutting of trees, construction of check dam in the forest area, etc.

Gram panchayat and van panchayat roles are defined and they rarely interfere with each other. There has been no incidence of conflict between the two in the past few years. The boundary of the van panchayat is clearly demarcated and hence there is no conflict over jurisdiction.

Some local residents were also interviewed in the village. They were aware of the existence of the van panchayat in the village, but had never held any position there. Nor had they attended any meetings of the van panchayat. The people of this village have never been in conflict with the van panchayat. According to them, it manifests transparency in its working. However, women's representation is low on this van panchayat.

Elections are not held for this van panchayat either, and the villagers nominate members. The term of the van panchayat is five years in accordance with the 2001 Rules. This van panchayat is one year old, and its members and sarpanch have never given cause for complaint. Objections, if any, are raised in the general meeting of the gram sabha and resolved there.

No permission is required for taking benefits from the forest. People generally collect dry leaves and sticks from the area. The Rs 60 per annum paid to the van panchayat is not a fixed amount and depends on the paying capacity of individual households. They are never stopped from entering the forest area. The only restriction is on cutting young branches, trees, and green leaves.

The forest produce is sufficient for villagers. Forest quality has improved over the years. This van panchayat occasionally plants trees in the forest area.

VILLAGE THAPLIYA MEHARAGAON

Thapliya Meharagaon village is situated in Bhimtal block of Nainital district. The van panchayat for the village was formed on 17 January 1950. Two villages come under the jurisdiction of this van panchayat: Thapliya Meharagaon and Amia. The population of Thapliya Meharagaon is about 800 and that of Amia is about 500. There are about 150 households in Thapliya Meharagaon and about 100 households in Amia. In Thapliya Meharagaon there are about 25 households of Scheduled Caste communities, 20 of Thakurs, and the rest of Brahmins.

A member of the van panchayat, Vishnu Singh, belonging to the Thakur community, is from Thapliya Meharagaon village. He was interviewed to obtain his views on the functioning and relevance of this van panchayat for people and the forests.

Sources of finance for the van panchayat include minor fines from defaulters and charges for issuing passes to the villagers. Apart from this, the Joint Forest Management programme is being implemented in the village. The van panchayat area covered under the programme is 240 hectares. The programme has been implemented as part of the current Micro Plan prepared by the van panchayat in association with the Forest Department. Under the Joint Forest Management programme, the van panchayat has spent on average Rs 300,000 annually, so far totalling Rs 1,196,050. Activities undertaken and those to be undertaken in the Micro Plan include:

- protection of 240 ha of forest area;
- forestation on 30 ha of forest area;
- densification of old forest area in 20 ha;
- fifty check dams for soil conservation; and
- boundary wall for 210 ha of forest area.

The accounts are maintained by the sarpanch of the van panchayat. Different members sit on the bodies of van panchayat and gram panchayat. There is no member who is common to both. The van panchayat sarpanch and members are respected in the village, and their views are considered while decisions are made by the gram panchayat. No conflict has been reported between the two.

Administrative control over the van panchayat is exercised by the district magistrate through the subdivisional magistrate (mukhya van adhikari). The van panchayat inspector is the link between the district administration and the van panchayat. Management of the forest is carried out by the van panchayat with the support of the villagers.

The pradhan of the gram panchayat, Bishan Singh Pokharia, is a Brahmin from Thapliya Meharagaon village. He answered the survey on behalf of the gram panchayat. Their meetings are held once in a month. The general meeting is held once in six months when all the villagers are required to attend. Members of the van panchayat do attend the meetings of gram panchayat. Issues relating to forests are also discussed at these meetings. Gram panchayat and van panchayat roles are defined and they rarely interfere in each other's work. There has been no incidence of conflict between the two.

A group of local residents was interviewed who told us that they were aware of the existence of the van panchayat in their village. But none of them had ever held any position in it, nor attended any meeting. The main reason cited for this was that most of the time they were not aware of the van panchayat meetings, indicating that van panchayat meetings are not well publicized. They, however, have never been in conflict with the van panchayat.

Members and the sarpanch are generally nominated for the van panchayat by the villagers. The term of the van panchayat is five years. However, the last van panchayat sarpanch held the post for seven years. It seems all sections of the society are treated equally and there is fair representation of women.

No permission is required for taking benefits from the forest. Generally, people collect dry leaves and sticks from the area. Passes are also issued for Rs 10. In this village also people are never stopped from entering the forest area except for cutting young branches, trees, and green leaves. At times, the sarpanch and members behave in a partisan manner in giving permission to the people to cut trees. It was found that people of depressed classes were stopped from entering the forests though the forest produce is sufficient for villagers. People perceive that the forest quality has improved over the years.

Basing his arguments on the views of the villagers, the security guard, and a worker of an NGO called Central Himalayan Rural

Action Group (CHIRAG), Rakesh Agrawal (n.d.) argues that people of the village have clearly benefited from the Joint Forest Management programme in the following ways:

1. The workload on women has been reduced considerably as there are fewer animals to look after and one does not have to walk a long distance to collect fuel wood and fodder.
2. The forest's lost glory has been restored. Large hillsides around the village look vibrant with vegetation that was clearly not there a decade ago. Due to plantation, the variety of species has also increased and today broadleaf species predominate.
3. People have an additional source of income, thanks to the money given to them for raising nurseries and paid labour for plantation.
4. In this van panchayat, agricultural output coupled with fruit production has increased. The villagers are able to sell fruits in the nearby fruit market at Bhowali.
5. CHIRAG workers who have installed hand pumps near water sources confirmed an increased availability of water.

VILLAGE BHAISODHA

Bhaisodha is situated in Pabo block of Pauri Garhwal district. Bhaisodha van panchayat was formed in 1965. The population of Bhaisodha is about 400, with about 88 households. There are seven households of the Scheduled Caste communities, ten of minorities, that is, Christians, and the rest belong to the general communities.

Two members of the van panchayat, Harsh Singh Negi and Sunder Singh Negi, responded to the survey questionnaire. The only source of finance for the van panchayat is minor fines from defaulters. Apart from this, the Joint Forest Management programme is being implemented in the village, under which the following works have been undertaken through the Micro Plan.

- twelve check dams in the year 2000–1 have been constructed;
- ten check dams for the year 2001–2 have been planned;
- construction of two *chabutras*, that is, social congregation spaces, have been planned.
- a water channel for cattle has been planned;
- forestry on five hectares of forest area has been planned;

- development of a *pokhar* or tank is under way. Rs 25,000 have been sanctioned by the Forest Department for its development.

According to the members and the pradhan of gram panchayat, the amount at their disposal is not sufficient. It would be appropriate if an additional amount of Rs 50,000 is sanctioned.

There is no member who is common to both the van panchayat and gram panchayat. Since van panchayat is part of the village, its members also attend the general meetings called by the gram panchayat. There is no conflict between the gram panchayat and van panchayat.

Administrative control is exercised by the district magistrate through the subdivisional magistrate (mukhya van adhikari). The van panchayat inspector is the link between the district administration and the van panchayat. As the Joint Forest Management programme is being implemented in the village, the van panchayat works in close coordination with the Forest Department, which also pays the watchman Rs 1200 per month.

The gram pradhan, Balwant Singh Negi, responded to the survey on behalf of the gram panchayat. Generally gram panchayat meetings are held once a month. The general meeting is held once in six months, and is attended by all the villagers. Roles of the gram panchayat and van panchayat are defined clearly, and they rarely interfere in each other's work. There has been no incidence of conflict between the two.

Local residents were aware of the existence of the van panchayat in their village. However, none could be found who had held any position in the van panchayat. People usually attend the meetings of van panchayat. They have never been in conflict with the van panchayat. Elections to the van panchayat are normally not held, and villagers nominate the members. The term of the van panchayat is five years. Earlier there was no fixed term for the van panchayat, but after introduction of the Joint Forest Management programme, the term has been fixed.

Permission is not required for extracting forest produce of certain kind. Generally people collect dry leaves and sticks from the area. They are never stopped from entering the forest area except for cutting young branches, trees, and green leaves. The forest produce is sufficient for the villagers.

VILLAGE SIKU

Siku is located in Pabo block of Pauri Garhwal district. The Siku van panchayat was first formed in 1954, with three villages under its jurisdiction. They are Siku, Mangli, and Bera Jagat. The population of Siku is around 625, with 92 households. There are ten households of the Scheduled Castes and the rest belong to the general communities. The other two villages are small in size. Their combined population is 100. All these villages are covered under Siku gram sabha.

A member of the van panchayat, Goverdhan, explained to surveyors the functioning and relevance of the van panchayat in the context of their village and the forests. The van panchayat's only source of finance is minor fines from the defaulters. According to the members of van panchayat and pradhan of the gram panchayat, the Joint Forest Management programme is not being implemented in the village. But a Micro Plan has been prepared, a copy of which has been placed in the divisional forest officer's office.

There is no common member in the van panchayat and gram panchayat, and no conflict between the bodies has been reported.

All administrative powers are vested in the district magistrate. The subdivisional magistrate is the mukhya van adhikari. The van panchayat is aware of the Joint Forest Management programme and that the technical support is provided by the Forest Department.

The gram pradhan, Sukhdev Singh, responded on behalf of the gram panchayat to the queries relating to the functioning of the gram panchayat and van panchayat, and the relationship between the two bodies. Gram panchayat meetings are held once in a month. The general meeting is held once in six months and attended by all villagers. General welfare issues are discussed in the meetings. The gram panchayat generally does not interfere in the functioning of the van panchayat. There is no conflict between the two institutions.

Local residents are largely aware of the van panchayat in the village. Many of them have not held any position in the van panchayat and never have attended any meetings. But people we met had never been in conflict with the van panchayat. The villagers nominate the members to the van panchayat. The term of the van panchayat is five years. All sections of society are apparently treated equally.

Permission is not required for taking benefits from the forest. Generally, people collect dry leaves and sticks. They are never stopped from entering the forest area except for cutting young branches, trees, and green leaves. The forest produce is sufficient for villagers and forest quality has improved over the years.

VILLAGE SRIKOT

Srikot village is situated in Pabo block of Pauri Garhwal district. The Srikot van panchayat was formed in 2001 after the Uttaranchal Van Panchayat Rules, 2001. The population of Srikot is about 400 with about 86 households. Twenty households belong to the Scheduled Castes and the rest belong to other communities. The sarpanch of this van panchayat, Meena Devi, responded on behalf of the van panchayat. In our survey, this is the only van panchayat chaired by a woman (see Table 3.13).

At present, the van panchayat has not been able to identify sources of finance to pursue its legal functions. There is no common member between the van panchayat and gram panchayat. Since the van panchayat is officially formed only on paper, it is not functional. Hence, there is no conflict with the gram panchayat. The only time the district administration interacted with the van panchayat was during its formation. Since then there has been no communication from the administration. This is in complete violation of the 2001 Rules. This van panchayat knows about the Joint Forest Management, but neither have they approached the Forest Department, nor has the Forest Department approached the van panchayat. The gram pradhan, Balwant Singh, responded on behalf of the gram panchayat. He said that generally gram panchayat meetings are held once in a

TABLE 3.13: GENDER AND SOCIAL REPRESENTATION, 2002

	Dhanachuli	Parbara	Thapliya Meharagaon	Bhaisodha	Siku	Srikot
Gender of sarpanch	Male	Male	Male	Male	Male	Female
Total members of van panchayat	9	9	9	10	8	10
Women members	Nil	1	2	6	1	10
Scheduled Caste or Scheduled Tribe members	1	1	3	2	1	2

month, with a general meeting every six months, which is attended by all the villagers. Since the van panchayat is not functional, issues relating to the forest are also taken up by the gram panchayat. The van panchayat is only a year old and there is no conflict between the two organizations. A local resident was also interviewed who seem to be aware of the van panchayat in the village. However, he has not held any position in the van panchayat. No meeting of the van panchayat has taken place so far, nor has he ever been in conflict with the van panchayat. All the members are women, which is very good because mostly women are involved in getting forest produce and it is they who can manage the forest best.

The van panchayat has not taken any decisions till now. In this village, a mahila raksha samiti has been formed, which maintains and protects the forest. The members and sarpanch of the van panchayat are also part of this samiti. They generally collect small amounts of money from the villagers for their activities. For an overview of all six van panchayats in respect of their functions, finance, interactions, and relationship with other organizations, see Tables 3.14 and 3.15.

CONCLUSIONS AND POLICY ISSUES

CONCLUSIONS

Statutory Position of Van Panchayats

- The British created an administrative set-up known as the Forest Department for the industrial and commercial exploitation of forests. Van panchayats came into existence as a reaction to the exploitative policies of the then British government of India. Van panchayats have become even more important now as the state government tightens bureaucratic control over people's institutions.
- Van panchayats came into existence after a number of rebellions against the control of forests by the British. A committee under the chairmanship of P. Wyndham known as Kumaon Forests Grievances Committee was constituted in 1921. The committee recommended classification of forests and the forests were divided into Class I and Class II categories.
- Van panchayats have now existed since the last 75 years as an institution for the management of forests by the people. The first

TABLE 3.14: FUNCTIONS, FINANCE, AND INTERACTIONS OF SELECTED VAN PANCHAYATS, 2002

	Dhanachuli	Parbara	Thapliya Meharagaon	Bhaisodha	Siku	Srikot
Functions	Protection and management of van panchayat forests	Protection and management of van panchayat forests	Protection and management of van panchayat forests	Protection and management of van panchayat forests	Protection and management of van panchayat forests	Not aware but they manage and protect their village forest in the traditional manner with the support of the gram panchayat
Finance	Minor fines from defaulters; villagers contribute Rs 70 from each household annually	Minor fines from the defaulters; villagers contribute Rs 60 from each household annually	Minor fines from defaulters; passes issued	Minor fines from defaulters	Minor fines from defaulters	No source of income
Meetings	Once a month	25th of every month	Once a month	Once in two months	Once a month	None held so far

TABLE 3.15: RELATIONSHIP OF OTHER AGENCIES, 2002

	Dhanachuli	Parbara	Thapliya Meharagaon	Bhaisodha	Siku	Srikot
Relationship with the gram panchayat	Cordial	Cordial	Cordial	Cordial	Cordial	Cordial
Joint Forest Management programme	Not being implemented	Not implemented during the term of previous van panchayat; the programme has been discontinued after 3 years of implementation	Being implemented; total amount sanctioned is about Rs 1.2 million	Being implemented	Not being implemented	Not being implemented
Relationship with the administration	District magistrate exercises powers through the subdivisional magistrate; district administration gives no assistance	District magistrate exercises powers through the subdivisional magistrate; district administration gives no assistance	District magistrate exercises powers through the subdivisional magistrate; district administration gives no assistance	District magistrate exercises powers through the subdivisional magistrate; district administration gives no assistance	District magistrate exercises powers through the subdivisional magistrate; district administration gives no assistance	District magistrate: There has been no interaction with the district administration since the formulation of this van panchayat
Relationship with the forest department	Muted as JFM not being implemented	Muted	Regular interaction	Regular interaction	Muted	Muted

set of rules was published in 1931, which gave some powers to local people for the protection and regulated use of forest resources. Under these rules, van panchayats could be primarily formed for Class I forests.

- The 1976 Rules provided further powers to the people for electing their own representatives to manage panchayat forests. A minimum of one-third adult residents of a village could come together and apply to the district magistrate for the formation of a van panchayat. The deputy commissioner primarily regulated the functioning of van panchayats.

- The Uttaranchal Panchayati Forest Rules, 2001, have now replaced the 1976 Rules. In comparison to the 1976 Rules, the 2001 Rules are more interventionist in that control of bureaucracy has been broadened and deepened. A hierarchy of plans including the Composite Management Plan, Micro Plan, and the Annual Implementation Plan have been introduced. Before a plan can be implemented, bureaucratic approval has been made mandatory.

- While the Uttaranchal Panchayati Forest Rules, 2001, provide for election of van panchayats, our case studies have revealed that in all cases, members and the sarpanch are nominated to van panchayats rather than elected through the due process.

- The National Forest Policy of 1988 of the Ministry of Environment and Forests has stipulated that the Himalayan zone, which also includes the state of Uttaranchal, must have at least 60 per cent area under forests.

- Forests are largely owned by the state through its Forest Department or Revenue Department. Some forests may be owned by the private sector. As far as the forests under the control of van panchayat are concerned, the competent authority of the state could entrust these forests to such van panchayat by taking such forests from the Forest Department or Revenue Department. If the forests are located on village common land entrusted to a gram panchayat by the Revenue Department, such forests may also be handed over to a van panchayat on a written request by one-fifth adult residents to the magistrate during the demarcation and formation of a van panchayat.

Bureaucratic Control over Van Panchayats

- The Uttaranchal Panchayati Forest Rules, 2001, are also restrictive in the sense that only one-fifth adult residents of the village are now required to make a proposal to the district magistrate for the formation of a van panchayat. However, a negative provision of one-third adult residents opposing the initial proposal has been added. In any case, this is likely to result in a democratic deficit because popular participation has been stalled in the initial stages. Most important of all, unlike gram panchayats, the formation of van panchayats remains optional.
- Van panchayats hardly have any autonomous function or powers. As per the 2001 Rules, right from their formation to their day-to-day decision-making, they have to heavily depend on either the Forest Department or district administration.
- The Uttaranchal Panchayati Forest Rules, 2001, strengthen the control of the district administration and the Forest Department over the van panchayats. Powers given to the van panchayats under these rules are largely superficial, as they have to take the approval of either the district administration or the Forest Department to perform even basic functions. Bottom-up practices of van panchayats are being replaced by joint forestry projects, which are essentially top-down in nature. The subdivisional magistrate controls the process of van panchayat formation and functioning.
- The rights of the people in respect of the use of forest resources have been severely curtailed. Composite Management Plans are based on the principles of silviculture rather than the needs of the people. Persons whose rights are not recorded in the van panchayats cannot have access to any of the forest resources. By-laws pertaining even to the elementary use of resources by a van panchayat need approval from a government officer.
- According to Rule 43 of the Uttaranchal Panchayati Forest Rules, 2001, the collector can suspend, supersede, and dissolve any van panchayat. These are extensive coercive powers possessed by the bureaucracy. To review the working of van panchayats, Rule 52 provides for the constitution of a zilla panchayat van *paramarsh datri* samiti. But this samiti consists of all nominated members. Even van panchayat finances are kept under the overall control of panchayat van vikas adhikari (divisional forest officer), who shall countersign all cheques signed by a sarpanch.

- The up panchayat van vikas adhikari (deputy forest development officer) has been given the power to nominate three right holders to carry out a summary interval audit every financial year. This could have negative as well as positive implications.
- Either the panchayat van up-van rajik (deputy forest ranger) or the panchayat van vid (forester) is the secretary of a van panchayat, and any right holder of the panchayati forest as selected by a van panchayat as the additional secretary. It is highly likely that the bureaucratic burden is going to increase in the working of van panchayats. Even the proceedings of the meetings are to be sent to the sahayak van vikas adhikari for approval.
- Each van panchayat is required to prepare a Micro Plan for a period of five years for the development and management of forests. The Micro Plan has to be approved by the right holders, which will then to be sanctioned by the panchayat van vikas adhikari. Once the Micro Plan is sanctioned, the Annual Implementation Plan will be prepared by a van panchayat, which has to be approved by the sahayak panchayat vikas adhikari (forest ranger). In all this, the Forest Department officials assist a van panchayat. It does not take much time for such assistance to become control.
- A van panchayat can use only those trees that have been marked for silvicultural felling by the official nominated by the panchayat van vikas adhikari. Van panchayats must also abide by the directions and execute orders passed by the van vikas adhikari regarding conservation and improvement of forests.
- Van panchayats must take prior approval from the panchayat van adhikari before selling the forest produce. Even the by-laws prepared by a van panchayat are required to be approved by the van vikas adhikari. Similarly, the budget has to be approved by him. Overall, it seems van panchayats are being used as agents by the state government and Forest Department to further their own objectives, which may or may not conform to the objectives of van panchayats.

Financial Sustainability of Van Panchayats

- Finances of van panchayats are precarious, on average not exceeding a few hundred rupees annually. Van panchayats are largely dependent upon government grants, as they have no sustained source of income to fund even basic functions such as the hiring of watchmen for the protection of forests. On the one hand, the Uttaranchal Panchayati Forest Rules, 2001, provides for restrictive use of forest resources. But on the other hand, forest produce is listed as the primary source of income for van panchayats. This has made the funding of van panchayat activities exceedingly implausible.

- The financial position of those van panchayats where the Joint Forest Management programme is being implemented has improved considerably in comparison with those where this programme is not being implemented: Finances are particularly lacking for employing and keeping credible watchers or chowkidars.

- The panchayati forest fund is managed by van panchayats under the overall control of the panchayat van vikas adhikari. A sarpanch may operate the accounts, but all the withdrawals are to be made by cheque, which is required to be countersigned by the secretary of the van panchayat who is a bureaucrat.

Present Status of Van Panchayats: Distribution and Extent

- Uttaranchal is known for its forest resources. Of the total forest area of 34,000 sq. km, about 30,000 sq. km, constituting 87 per cent of the area falls under the direct control of the state government. Only about 4000 sq. km, that is, 12 per cent, is managed by the van panchayats.

- Over 60 per cent of the total geographical area is under forests. However, according to data obtained from satellite images, only 43 per cent of the geographical area of Uttaranchal is covered with forests. But most important of all, the intensity of forest cover has been reduced due to over exploitation. Forests with a crown density exceeding 40 per cent are about 17,849 sq. km, which is 33 per cent of the total geographical area and about half of the recorded forest area. This scenario presents a grim situation of an ecologically sensitive habitat.

- While the forest area in Garhwal division is slightly more than double that of the area in the Kumaon division, the area managed by van panchayats in Kumaon is nearly 80 per cent more than that in Garhwal.

- Most of the forest area falls in the Garhwal division. Only about one-third forest area is in the Kumaon division. Among the districts of Uttarkashi, Chamoli and Rudraprayag have 34 per cent of the total forest area of the state. The districts of Pauri Garhwal, Tehri Garhwal, Almora and Bageshwar, Pithoragarh, and Champawat all have more than 10 per cent each of the state's forest area. Apart from Chamoli, Rudraprayag, Pauri Garhwal, and Tehri Garhwal, all other districts fall in the Kumaon division.

- At the present moment, forests are controlled by various agencies: the Forest Department, the Revenue Department, and the van panchayats. The Forest Department controls about 70 per cent and the Revenue Department about 18 per cent of the total forest area in the state. Van panchayats merely look after about 12 per cent of the total forest area. Almost two-thirds of the forest area under van panchayats is located in the Kumaon region.
- Almora and Bageshwar, and Pithoragarh and Champawat account for 57 per cent of the total van panchayat forests. All these districts are located in the Kumaon division. Pauri Garhwal, Chamoli, and Rudraprayag account for over 31 per cent of the total van panchayat forests. These districts are located in Garhwal division.
- Over 30 per cent of the panchayat forest area is located in Almora and Bageshwar, and the same is true of Pithoragarh and Champawat. These districts are located in the Kumaon division.

Context of Van Panchayats

- The relationship of van panchayats with gram panchayats has been found to be cordial. In our case studies, no instances of conflict between van panchayats and gram panchayats were reported. There is no overlap in terms of functions and members. The sarpanch of a van panchayat generally attends the annual meeting of a gram panchayat and raises issues pertaining to the welfare of a village.
- The relationship between van panchayats and the bureaucracy has been muted. Many respondents have reported that officials simply do not visit van panchayats. But when a van panchayat decides to take up certain issues, the bureaucratic machinery creates statutory and non-statutory hurdles. The subdivisional magistrate possesses extensive powers over the formation and funding of van panchayats.
- A Composite Management Plan, Micro Plan, and Annual Implementation Plan are prepared and implemented under the Uttaranchal Panchayati Forest Rules, 2001. Neither in local government Acts nor in the Uttaranchal Panchayati Forest Rules, 2001, is it

made clear how these plans relate to another hierarchy of plans prepared for a village, block, or district under the United Provinces Panchayati Raj Act, 1947, and the Uttar Pradesh Kshetra Panchayat and Zilla Parishad Adhiniyam, 1961, as per the 73rd Constitutional Amendment. This creates a highly problematic and confusing situation as far as the governing of the van panchayats is concerned. The prime minister has already written to the state governments to address issues of duplicity and repetition in respect of tiers of government.

The Joint Forest Management Programme

- After the Uttaranchal Panchayati Forest Rules, 2001, the state government hastily formed a number of van panchayats to secure and use the World Bank funds under the Joint Forest Management programme. In one of the case studies, Srikot in Pauri Garhwal, the patwari lured the villagers to form a van panchayat. However, the villagers are not even aware of its functioning. The mahila raksha samiti along with the gram panchayat still manages and protects the village forests.

- Field surveys show that Micro Plans are being prepared by van panchayats with the assistance of the Forest Department. These are now being implemented as part of the Joint Forest Management programme. The Uttaranchal Panchayati Forest Rules, 2001, require that a Micro Plan along with the Composite Management Plan and Annual Implementation Plan must be prepared by all van panchayats. However, this study has revealed that Micro Plans are prepared only by those few van panchayats where the Joint Forest Management programme is being implemented. Field surveys have also revealed that Micro Plans have been used as a bureaucratic control mechanism over van panchayats.

- Until recently van panchayats were purely local initiatives created out of the genuine concern of the people to protect their forests, which culturally is their provider and protector. However, a recent spur in the creation of van panchayats, coinciding with the inflow of vast funds in the state through the Joint Forest Management programme, is a result of more than just a genuine concern for the forests.

- Therefore, the growing numbers of van panchayats are no indicator of greater forest protection. As observed in the example of village Srikot in Pauri district, the women of the village had for a long time formed a mahila raksha samiti (Women Defence Committee), which was functioning well for the protection of forests. However, recently the village patwari lured them into forming a van panchayat by promising large amounts of money. Now the village has a van panchayat but no one actually knows how to make this institution functional.
- Implementation of a Micro Plan under the Joint Forest Management programme in a van panchayat could complicate its functioning. For example, Bhaisodha van panchayat in Pauri Garhwal district mostly undertook construction work, which is not the central activity of a van panchayat. Minor efforts were made by this van panchayat to enhance area under forests.

Likelihood of Conflicts among Various Organizations

- In Anarpa in Dhari block, Nainital, the van panchayat used to cover four revenue villages. In 2001, however, the new policy provided for a separate van panchayat for each revenue village. The patwari divided one van panchayat into four despite strong objections by the villagers. Whereas some villagers now have a larger area or all the broadleaf part of the forest, the others are left with only pine or a fraction of the original forest area. Acute conflicts have erupted between the villages when there were none before.
- Forests and forest management now fall under the jurisdiction of both the gram panchayat and the van panchayat. In fact, Section 16 (a) of the Uttar Pradesh Panchayati Raj Act, 1947, lists the 'management and maintenance of forests situated in a panchayat area' to be one of the functions of a gram panchayat. Although at the present moment, no conflicts are observed, these statutory provisions may lead to a situation of conflicts of interest and jurisdiction over a period of time.
- In Parbara van panchayat (Dhari block, Nainital), acute conflict has broken out within the village over the implementation of the Joint Forest Management programme, which is now before the Supreme Court of India.

Accountability of Van Panchayats

• Both the van panchayat and gram panchayat are accountable to the people. However, it was observed that while people do participate in the proceedings of the gram panchayat, only a few had any direct involvement in the van panchayat. This comparative democratic deficit of van panchayats need to be reduced. In any case, the van panchayat is representative as it is generally selected by the gram sabha, though through a process of nomination rather than by actual elections.

Women's Participation

• 'Lack of women's participation in van panchayats is noticeable. Women are responsible for carrying fuel wood and fodder from forests and they know the forest better than men. Yet their participation in van panchayats and its decision-making process is negligible.

PROPOSALS

• Having examined the functioning of van panchayats in the state of Uttaranchal, it is recommended that people's institutions such as van panchayats must be strengthened in terms of larger participation of village residents as well as more autonomous functioning of sarpanches and members of van panchayats.

• Optional formation of van panchayats under Rule 3 of the Uttaranchal Panchayati Forest Rules, 2001, should be scrapped and replaced by mandatory formation of van panchayats for all forest settlements. This recommendation is made in the hope that participatory decision-making processes will result in the better use of forest resources. People will own up the decisions that they make and it is highly likely that those decisions will be carried forward and implemented.

• Women-centred raksha samities should be encouraged to develop in all van panchayats as our case studies have shown that women can better protect and regenerate forests.

• The Uttaranchal Panchayati Forest Rules, 2001, should be also amended to allow use of forest resources on the basis of people's needs rather than silviculture principles because people's basic needs are paramount under any environmental conditions.

- Excessive approval seeking and hierarchical plan preparation regimes should be discarded and replaced with single approval of an annual van panchayat development plan similar to what was provided under the 1976 Rules. This annual plan could be prepared and integrated with the village development plan, which would eventually become part of the district development plan. This is important not only for coordination and integration with other plans, but also for securing assured funds through the State Finance Commission.
- Administratively, van panchayats may continue to be governed under the amended Uttaranchal Panchayati Forest Rules, 2001. But in order to improve the financial health of van panchayats, they could be made part of the work of the State Finance Commission. The position of van panchayats requires to be strengthened by giving van panchayats financial status equivalent to gram panchayats. The State Finance Commission would then, among other things, work out fund allocation for van panchayats along with gram panchayats. This is particularly important since van panchayats have a weak financial base and cannot raise taxes locally due to small size of villages and forest resources.
- Notwithstanding the problems associated with the implementation of the Joint Forest Management programme in van panchayats, continuation and introduction of the programme are recommended. The prime reason for this is that the programme can further ensure the financial sustainability of van panchayats for carrying out their basic functions, including protection of forests.
- As more and more funds begin to flow into the van panchayat, exchequer's conflicts between various stakeholders are likely to increase. Our case studies have conclusively established that when funds through the Joint Forest Management programme were received by van panchayats, they tended to have conflicts either with their own people or with the associated gram panchayats.

REFERENCES

Agrawal, R. Thapliya, 'Meharagaon Van Panchayat: From Waste to Wealth', *Environment* [online], http://www.india-syndicate.com/sci/rkagg2 (undated).

Bhatt, M. and M. Chakraborty, *Techniques for Conflict Resolution*, New Delhi: Research, Advocacy, and Communication in Himalayan Areas, 1998.

Forest Department, Uttaranchal, *Uttaranchal State Forest Statistics*, Nainital: Forest Department, 2000.

Government of India, *Census of India*, New Delhi: Government of India, 1991.

_____, *Census of India*, New Delhi: Government of India, 2001.

Government of Uttaranchal, *Van Panchayat Directory 2000*, Dehradun: Uttaranchal Government, 2000.

Government of Uttar Pradesh, *Van Panchayat Directory 1999*, Pauri Garhwal: Uttar Pradesh Government, 1999. Jain, A., 'Van Panchayats', Dehradun: Rural Litigation and Entitlement Kendra, *An Unpublished Study*, 2002.

Jain, A., 'An Unpublished Study: Van Panchayats', Dehradun: Rural Litigation and Entitlement Kendra, 2002.

Kapoor, A., 'Need to Re-write UP Forest Rules', the *Times of India*, 18 October 1999.

Ministry of Environment and Forests, *National Forestry Action Programme*, vol. I, New Delhi: Ministry of Environment and Forests, 1999.

Sivaramakrishnan, K.C., *Power to the People, The Politics and Progress of Decentralization*, New Delhi: Konark Publishers, 2000.

Tewari, R.T., R. Mujoo, and B. Tewari, *Uttaranchal: Infrastructure and Economic Development*, New Delhi: APH Publishing Corporation, 2001.

Uttar Pradesh Government, *Van Panchayat Rules, 1976*, Uttar Pradesh Government, Lucknow, 1976.

Uttaranchal Government, *Uttaranchal Panchayati Forest Rules, 2001*, Uttaranchal Government, Dehradun, 2001.

4

Writers' Buildings and the Reality of Decentraiized Rural Power
Some Paradoxes and Reversals in West Bengal

■ DWAIPAYAN BHATTACHARYYA

This chapter has a narrow focus: it traces the stages of decentralization in West Bengal against the backdrop of a wider debate on decentralization in the country as a whole. In a broader perspective, however, the chapter seeks to discuss how decentralization has been used in the recent times by the Indian states as an instrument for achieving certain objectives of governance. In West Bengal such activities have yielded fairly positive results although pockets of absolute failure also persist. It is argued, that the ruling coalition of the Left Front has remained in power for a record period due to its successful implementation of certain policies, which include the policy of carrying out administrative functions in the rural areas through a three-tier system of elected local governments at the village, block, and district levels. The coalition has retained its popularity by obtaining around half of popular votes in almost all elections in the state since 1977.

West Bengal, however, lags behind many other states in terms of several key human development indices, and in some important areas such as education and health, the state can best be described as middle-ranking in the context of other states in the country (GoWB 2004a). Such a long tenure for the Left Front could not have been possible if popular mandate was directly a reflection of only the performance of the government. An area of strategic politics, in effect, opens up the possibilities of various kinds of correlation between electoral choice and the conduct of governance. I will argue in this chapter that decentralization has much to do with the making of such strategic politics in West Bengal.

Though often used in one breath most of the time, decentralization does not necessarily reinforce either local governance or participatory democracy. A dictatorial regime can initiate decentralization (as indeed President Musharraf did a couple of years ago in Pakistan) to bolster local government institutions, but going by all available evidence it had little positive effect on either popular participation or democracy. Local governments below the level of the regional states always formally existed in independent India but—due to lack of any serious devolution of power from the national and regional state capitals until the early 1990s, and due also to selection rather than election as their principal mode of composition—they were of little democratic significance. Similarly, local democracy is known to have elicited vigorous participation in electoral processes, but failed to offer key governmental functions for deliberation and planning at the local level. Finally, it is possible to have extensive decentralization as well as robust local government in a society where the hierarchies of local status and power make democratic participation difficult. It is important, therefore, not to obfuscate the analytical distinction between these three closely linked categories.[1]

In this chapter we refer to decentralization specifically as the creation of legally protected bodies of local government especially in the rural areas, ensuring periodic renewal of such bodies, following certain institutional norms in the transaction of their business, and making them suitably responsible for administering policies pertaining in particular to the population and resources of their respective jurisdictions. This in West Bengal is aligned both chronologically and strategically with two other politically significant processes: implementation of substantial reforms in agrarian relations and expansion of the Left-wing political parties—mainly the CPI(M)—in the countryside. Indeed, the land reform policies, based on distributive principles of equity, created a democratic potential for decentralization by removing local oligarchies. The CPI(M)'s incursion as a fairly centralized and disciplined organization, however, produced an entire range of unanticipated—and as yet unexplored—consequences.[2]

DEBATING DECENTRALIZATION

Political thinking on decentralization in India took several turns in the last six decades. I would argue that the principal strands of such thinking can be framed within a developmental–integrationist discourse that involved two mutually contradictory positions, of

Ambedkar and of Nehru. Even the mainstream Left can be located within the terms of the debate though it sought to maintain a critical distance from both the positions. Gandhi offered the only alternative vision, but much of its relevance failed to touch even his avowed disciples. And most of the ideals that Gandhi so cherished were subsequently found unworkable for the purpose of laying the foundations of a modern nation-state.

In the course of the debate on the draft Constitution, the problem of decentralization was treated as the challenge of 'designing' a truly federal as well as a just polity. This is also true of the various committees formed in the subsequent decades for recommending 'fair' power sharing between the Centre and the local bodies. It was consistently maintained that among the main obstacle for decentralization was the absence of adequate legal recognition (and subsequently, protection) of the local government institutions. Ambedkar's idea of the village as 'a sink of localism, a den of ignorance, narrow-mindedness and communalism' (CAD 1948: 38–9) and his call for holding the individual (not the 'village') as the unit of India's future polity drew severe criticism. It is of little surprise that someone fighting the cause of the 'depressed classes' found a stable, strong, centrist, and intervening modern state as a far better guarantee of social justice than decentralized governance which, he reckoned, would keep the myriad pockets of locally nourished caste tyranny virtually unaltered.

Indeed the main pro-decentralization arguments in the debate produced a discourse framed by the deployment of a series of oppositions, namely, tradition versus modernity, urban versus rural, and colonial versus national. The modern Constitution could not afford to be oblivious of 'our great Indian culture', the values of which were thought to be the exclusive preserves of the 'immutable' village communities. It was now the task of the new ruling elite to modernize the village by taking down the light of knowledge 'like the Russian village soviets' (CAD 1948:285). Ambedkar's attitude allegedly reflected the most insidious tendencies of 'an urban highbrow' that modern India should better do without (CAD 1948:219–21). Now the project was seen as one of linking the rural with the urban, urbanizing the rural, and of expanding the facilities of industry and infrastructure into backward economies (CAD 1948:286-7). Nationalist mobilization, it was believed, had created the groundwork for an energized rural economy by assimilating the villages into the political mainstream (CAD 1948:257–8).

Although those who fought Ambedkar and his 'centrism' did so by using 'the Father of the Nation' on their side, their arguments had little in common with those of Gandhi. Gandhi's thinking on the village as a unit of decentralized governance often changed tracks— and it is not possible to make a summary here; yet we can highlight a few of his core values to draw the contrast. Gandhi's village, in ideal terms, is based upon the premise of a self-sustaining unit capable of reconciling without any outside interference the tension between internal autonomy and external necessities, and between individual freedom and community ethics. Nowhere in his scheme are those tensions resolved by a contract or an authorization by the state, or by an ideology of development as a framing concern behind the drive for administrative decentralization. This was no less than a conception of 'a republic of every village in India' (Gandhi 1959:8–12).

Such glorified ideas of the village as a self-fulfilling community of people are, of course, open to criticism for being unrealistic, romantic, tautological, or ethically utopian. More important, Gandhi frequently uses the 'oceanic circle' as a metaphor to clarify his position. By definition, every circle has to have a centre, but in an 'oceanic circle', the centre is identifiable only in its perpetual displacement and self-denial. Talking about his idea of India after Independence Gandhi says:

Independence must begin at the bottom.... Life will not be a pyramid with the apex sustained by the bottom. But it will be individual always ready to perish for the village, the latter ready to perish for the circle of the villages, till at last the whole becomes one life composed of individuals, never aggressive in their arrogance but ever humble, sharing the majesty of the oceanic circle of which they are integral units... (Gandhi 1959:8–9).

A dispersed, non-linear, and mutative notion of power had little practical significance in independent India's planning initiatives that made attempts to uplift the villages from their alleged 'backwardness'.

Turning to governmental practices, serious thinking on institution-alising decentralization set in after the Emergency (1975–7), which had witnessed the limits of centralization of the executive powers of the Indian state. The defeat of Indira Gandhi following the Emergency was widely viewed as a victory of the Indian electorate against the autocratic and unitary tendencies of the Congress. The victorious Janata government, a coalition of various political outfits, considered itself an heir to what it claimed was a Gandhian upsurge led by Jayaprakash Narayan. Consequently the new regime was obligated to set up the Ashok Mehta Committee in December 1977 for looking into the shortcomings of democratic decentralization including 'the Panchayati Raj institutions' and suggest measures for improvements.[3] For our purpose, the importance of the Committee lies also in the fact that the veteran CPI(M) leader E.M.S. Namboodiripad was one of its members, and when the Committee submitted its Report, Namboodiripad attached a note expressing his differences with some key suggestions made in it.

The 'Approach and Recommendations' of the Report give the impression that the Committee was driven by a genuine urge to federalize the polity through the building of largely autonomous institutions below regional states. While making recommendations for a two-tier system of local governance (the district and the mandal levels) the Committee explained why the existence of local oligarchies cannot be made an excuse (as Ambedkar had argued) for not conducting decentralization: oligarchies are everywhere. The Committee also systematically linked up decentralization with local development and created the impression of a serious devolution bypassing—and at times undermining—the bureaucracy's authority. In addition, the Committee strongly favoured special provisions for what it called 'the weaker sections' (an aphorism for the Scheduled Castes, Scheduled Tribes, and Other Backward Classes) of the rural society.

While concurring with the Committee on most counts, EMS raised a few queries of which the most interesting are the ones with policy implications for his party. EMS criticized the Committee for its alleged failure to value the importance of 'political will' without which no decentralization can ever be effective. In his definition of the 'weaker sections', EMS included an economic (or class) criterion in addition to the social dimension (this eventually informed the CPI(M)'s attitude to the Mandal debate a decade or so later). He argued against co-option and nomination of members at any level of the panchayat, and favoured a proportional system of voting that would make electoral reservations based on caste virtually redundant.

He also tried to explain why it was important not only to decentralize the administration's development-oriented functions, but also necessary to decentralize the regulatory functions of the state. Finally, he maintained that decentralization would be partial without a review of the federal relation between the Centre and the states within the polity as a whole.

What is important to note, in this context, is that EMS did not have any fundamental differences with the general views expressed by the Committee; he suggested rather some fine-tuning of the administrative and electoral processes involved. The Committee treated decentralization as a project of 'democratic development management' (Kashyap 1989: para 8, 181) and EMS concurred with that. The Committee described decentralization, by contrast to Gandhi's 'oceanic circles', 'not in the usual point-by-point way but rather in *concentric circles*', circles with a single, determinate, and sovereign centre (quoted from Kashayap, 1989:179, emphasis added). EMS had no problem with that either. EMS rather sought to underscore the need to acknowledge decentralization as a *political* problem, rather than one of a simple administrative relocation of resources. He also put the Marxist idea of class upfront in dealing with the issues of social exploitation, and urged for proportional representation in constituting the local bodies. In recent times, however, the CPI(M) has accepted reservation of seats in the panchayat on the grounds of caste rather than class, and also revised its position on proportional representation. Lastly, as the West Bengal experience has shown that attempts to decentralize the regulatory mechanisms of the state runs into massive controversies.[4] In addition, the advent of neo-liberal economic regimes and the opening of the market to wider domestic and global exchanges have made the demand for restructuring Centre-state relations largely redundant. It is in this context that the mainstream Left found itself increasingly in agreement with the developmental–integrationist model of decentralization that emerged as the democratic answer to the autocratic tendencies of the Indian state in the 1980s and the 1990s. The Left Front-initiated decentralization in West Bengal, which surely is one of the front-runners in the country in this respect, can properly be understood if we keep this broader perspective in mind. We now turn to more specific elements of administrative and political rationale for decentralization in the state.

DECENTRALIZATION IN WEST BENGAL

After the Left Front was elected to power in 1977, a substantial campaign for agrarian reform was launched that significantly altered the relations of power in the rural areas. The new government distributed ceiling-surplus land among agricultural workers and made laws to protect the sharecroppers from unlawful eviction by the landlords. The Left—which was increasingly achieving an expanded and coordinated network in the countryside—had to counter resistance from the vested interests in the lower rungs of bureaucracy and from the dominant rural classes. An intricate mechanism of vigilance and public pressure was found necessary to counter such force at the local level. Hence, the panchayat proved to be instrumental from the perspective of administering land reforms.

Panchayats also carried an important political relevance. In the late 1960s the CPI(M) underwent a split in its ranks as it failed to decide which path to choose: a radical line of peasant mobilization to immediately address the outstanding agrarian issues or a moderate approach of slow institutional reform without disturbing the existing order of governance in any major way. In the midst of such confusion, the coalition of left-of-centre parties—the United Front—failed to offer a stable government on two consecutive occasions. That proved costly for the CPI(M). Through the early 1970s, the Congress targeted the Left of all hues, both physically and politically, the process reaching its peak during the Emergency. In 1977, when voted to power, and that too with an overwhelming majority in which the CPI(M) itself carried more than half seats in the legislature, the Left Front had only one objective—consolidation of its governance. Leaders of the mainstream Left, who devoted much of their energy in the 1960s and the 1970s to strengthen their respective organizations at the grass roots level, felt that the durability and popularity of the new government would largely depend on its ability to energize the official set-up that often acted as a wall between the policy-makers and the population, the targets of such policies. Panchayats were thus taken as a key component of a larger political campaign to narrow the gap between the governmental agencies and the rural population.

In the 1950s and 1960s, the panchayat was indeed in discussion within the domain of governance in West Bengal, as it was in the rest of the country. But there is a crucial difference between the structure of the panchayat that was presented in this period and the one that the Left Front finally adopted in the 1970s. In 1957 the first Panchayat Act was passed, in 1963 the Zilla Parishad Act, instituting a four-tier system following the recommendations of the Balwant Rai Mehta Study Team. There was no provision for direct election except in the lowest tier at the village level. The lowest was also the least powerful stratum, with no autonomy, and—more importantly—with no legal provision for periodic elections. Consequently, instead of strengthening democracy, such decentralized administration helped to consolidate the dominant rural classes by offering them governmental leverage.

The United Front genuinely wanted to stop this farce. It circulated a document called 'Basic Ideas about the Reorganization of Panchayats in West Bengal' and, eventually, brought a Panchayat Bill in 1969. There were significant anomalies between the two; and the government failed to explain in the face of criticism from the Opposition why the Bill proposed a four-tier system, one more than in the aforesaid document (GoWB 1969:4–5; see Jainal Abedin's speech). The debate that followed on the floor of the House was instructive for two reasons: first, some members argued that the MLAs should have additional membership of the panchayat at the block and district levels (surely a sign of insecurity due to the prospect of losing some share of institutional control), and secondly, Congress members opposed partisan contest for panchayat berths on the ground that it would disturb the 'peace' by introducing 'politics' in the countryside. The government, however, was toppled before the Bill could be passed. In 1973, the Congress regime passed a largely progressive West Bengal Panchayat Act, which seemingly it never meant to implement. Eventually, the Left Front put the Act to practice in 1978 with the intentions that we have already mentioned.

Several amendments to the Act were brought since 1978, which can be classified in four phases. In the first phase (1978 to mid-1980s), the panchayat bodies were expected primarily to implement plans under the tutelage of either the party or the bureaucracy. This period witnessed a sweeping implementation of land reform policies with the active involvement of the panchayats especially in gathering information on land-use and tenurial transactions at the local level. This was the period when the CPI(M) succeeded in positioning itself as the central figure of West Bengal's rural society by way of using the panchayat as an instrument for spreading its presence. Echeverri-Gent observed that the rural middle classes had a definitive sway within the party apparatus making any form of popular participation almost impossible without either its direct involvement or approval. So the rise of the panchayat was coeval to the rise of the party within the rural society that diminished the possibility of an unmediated popular initiative, especially by the rural poor difficult: 'Our study has shown that elevating the role of the *panchayats* has given political parties, especially the CPI(M), a prominent role in guiding development' (Echeverri-Gent 1992:1414).

In what can be marked as the second phase (mid-1980s to early-1990s), attempts were made to equip the panchayats with the specialized authority for dealing with sectoral allocation of resources, both internal as well as received, with some degree of autonomy. Standing Committees at district (zilla parishad) and block (panchayat samiti) levels were activated to draw participation of the elected members in area planning (Webster 1992:35). In West Bengal, unlike in Kerala, for reasons discussed below, this had only limited effects. In early 1990s, the third phase (early-1990s to 2000) was initiated, when the West Bengal Panchayat Act, 1992 introduced a new level called 'gram sabha' constituted at each electoral constituency and convened twice a year. In tune with the requirement of the 73rd Amendment (1993) of the Indian Constitution, the gram sabha was later substituted by 'gram sansad' (a body that included the entire population within an electoral booth area). Representation of the socially and economically backward sections at all levels of the panchayat in proportion to their share in the population of the district was made mandatory and one-third of seats were reserved for women.

Since 2001–2 two major steps were taken to make the panchayats functionally more accountable as well as inclusive. The government launched the 'Participatory Gram Panchayat Planning under Convergent Community Action' in 2001 with the aim of involving the lowest level of panchayat administration in the planning process (Midnapore Planning and Development Society 2002). Eventually in 2003, the government proposed the formation of *Gram Unnayan Samitis* or Village Development Councils for each gram sansad area comprising not only of the pradhan, the up-pradhan, and the representatives of the booth area, but also the nearest defeated contestant, in addition to five other villagers elected by the electorate in the booth (sansad) area (GoWB 2004b: Section 16A[6]).

Some significant tendencies are apparent in these legislative moves by the Left Front. First, there was an attempt to take the apparatus of local governance further down the line, from the gram panchayat to the booth level. Second, to make the local bodies more active in drawing up plans and managing resource, rather than latching on to the directives from above. Third, to enlarge the scope of popular participation by offering the opposition a designated place in the structure of local governance. This had become necessary particularly in view of the massive dominance of the Left in general and the CPI(M) in particular in these bodies, and also due to the corresponding public apathy and non-involvement, except in times of elections.

The membership profile of the panchayat bodies clearly illustrates the dominance of the Left. The Front has never polled votes less than around 60 per cent (in 1998, the highest 73 per cent in 1988) in gram panchayat, 66 per cent (in 1983, the highest 79 per cent in 1988) in panchayat samiti, and 74 per cent (in 1983, the highest 92 per cent in 1978) in zilla parishad elections. In the 2003 election, the Left Front's share of total seats stood at 65.75, 74.05, and 86.82 per cent in the gram panchayat, panchayat samiti, and the zilla parishad respectively (CPI(M) 2004). As far as the social composition is concerned, women are represented to the extent of around 36 per cent in the gram panchayat, 35 per cent in the panchayat samiti, and 34 per cent in the zilla parishad. The Scheduled Castes and Scheduled Tribes hover around 17 per cent and 7 per cent respectively at all levels. It is difficult to comment on the class composition of the panchayat, and its variation at different levels, in the absence of any systematic survey.[5]

In 1980, the Evaluation Team of the state government conducted a survey of 100 gram panchayats with 1466 members spread over 1143 *maujas* (GoWB 1980). Both Left Front leaders and independent scholars have frequently referred to this survey as a vindication of the claim that the bulk of gram panchayat members are poor and marginal farmers or agricultural workers. The survey suggested that the composition of the gram panchayat was overwhelmingly male, more than half between 25 and 39 years of age, around half were owner–cultivators, 14 per cent teachers, 7.5 per cent unemployed, less than 5 per cent agricultural workers. Of the owner–cultivators, a substantial section (around 43 per cent) owned below two acres, and more than a quarter (around 28 per cent) owned between two and five acres. That is, more than 70 per cent of the owner–cultivators had below five acres and, therefore, were poor and marginal peasants. When looked against all occupations, members belonging to this category were only 36 per cent, a more moderate figure than what is usually claimed.[6] Two points worth noting are: 14 per cent of teacher members were pradhans (the highest pradhan-member ratio) and the presence of sharecroppers was indeed negligible (1.7 per cent).

It is rather obvious that the Left forces—thanks to their concerted campaign, pro-poor reforms, and organizational efficacy—were the main beneficiaries of the local elections even as early as 1978. Among them, the CPI(M) had the maximum gain not just in absolute but, more importantly, in relative terms. For instance, in 1988 the Left parties contested against each other in many village panchayat constituencies displaying their relative capacities to draw votes, an opportunity that is normally unavailable for these parties for elections at higher levels. In this election, the CPI(M) contested in 44,803 gram panchayat seats and won 33,834, its degree of success being 75.51 per cent, much higher than the Congress(I) (28.46 per cent), Revolutionary Socialist Party (25.60 per cent), Forward Bloc (18.16 per cent), and CPI (54.34 per cent) (GoWB 1988:6). In 1998, the Left Front partners had an internal contest in 10.96 per cent seats, in 2003 this happened in 14.02 per cent seats. In both the elections, despite which the rate of success (the ratio between candidates contested and elected) of the CPI(M) exceeded that of its major coalition partners (CPI(M) 2004).

DEMOCRATIC PARTICIPATION IN WEST BENGAL

By democratic participation we mean here such capacities of the people that enable them to determine on just and equal terms the institutional policies that affect their everyday lives. In this sense, therefore, democratic participation is broader in scope than mere election; it involves an urge and an ability to know, comprehend, deliberate, and act upon the policy issues of governance. The central issues associated with democratic participation in West Bengal underwent certain changes during the Left Front period primarily in response to various phases of decentralization. Below we catalogue some obvious implications of these changes in four broad spheres, assertion of dignity by the poor, formats of institutional management, forms of local public action, and the salience of local knowledge.

In the first phase, the problem was one of sensitizing the bureaucracy so that enough pressure could be generated at the ground level against the subversive activities of the large landowning classes that were adversely hit by the reform policies of the state government. Therefore, a series of 'reorientation camps' were organized by the panchayat and the kisan sabhas to enable the government officials to interact with the rural poor bypassing the propertied sections. Dramatic and sentimental descriptions of such meetings abound in the files of the Department of Land and Land Reforms at the Writers' Building in Calcutta (Bhattacharyya 1993, ch. 2). These meetings turned also into occasions for many poor peasants and agricultural labourers to muster the courage to actually present themselves to the 'sahibs' without any feeling of humiliation or indignity as the local leaders of the panchayat and the kisan sabha; while hundreds of others like them, stood by, and the venue was not the courtyard of the village landlord (where the land settlement contracts were usually authorized), but the local school building, or the porch of the village temple, or some other such 'neutral' premises. Atul Kohli commended such a turn rather over-enthusiastically: 'From this perspective, it may not be an exaggeration to argue that the politics of West Bengal is undergoing a fundamental structural change' (Kohli 1987:113). The main implication of democratic participation in this phase was, therefore, an assertion of dignity—however limited—for Bengal's rural poor.

Since the mid-1980s the panchayat was expected not only to identify beneficiaries and implement state policies, but also to shoulder some key planning functions. A drawback detected now was that the village panchayat had no role in planning, they could only send lists of their requirements to the block level planning committee that, in turn, was severely restricted by bureaucratic formalities. While important 'first steps' in local participation were indeed taken, 'there are very few indications that the Left Front parties give priority to furthering this process' (Westergaard 1987: 110). Doubts were raised also on how far the panchayat, where the middle peasants and the school teachers continued to play a dominant role, was a representative body. Members of the Scheduled Tribes and especially women were found grossly under-represented, and the leading players were almost invariably drawn from relatively middle ranking families with higher social status (Webster 1992: 118–21). It was quite obvious by now that for the left-wing parties in the state the aim to consolidate the gains achieved so far was getting the better of a strident mobillization of the poor. From radical assertion, the mood now turned toward 'institutional management' (Lieten 1996: 63).

It was felt by the early 1990s that to raise the efficacy of the management of rural development, it was necessary to move below the gram panchayat. For providing better representation of the villages within the gram panchayat, an institutional format at the booth level was conceived. Such bodies were thought to be more effective as well as desirable—since they would be better placed for dealing with the problems at the village level than the gram panchayat. The gram sansads were devised. These were to meet twice a year (May and November) to discuss on important issues including financial outlay, beneficiary lists for various employment schemes, and helping in the preparation of the below-poverty-line list, etc. Early reports of the number of gram sansad meetings, and their attendance rates, were highly discouraging. As the then minister of panchayats himself acknowledged, only 8.9 per cent such meetings could be held in a year drawing less than 20 per cent of the population (Mishra 1998:73). The state government claims that the number of such meetings went up to 89 per cent in 1997, and 99 per cent in 1999, though the rate of attendance hovered around a dismal 20 per cent (Datta 2001:48). There is no doubt that such low enthusiasm for local public action requires explanation that we will attempt later.

To turn gram sansad from a mere deliberative to a planning body, a new initiative—known as 'Participatory Gram Panchayat Planning under Convergent Community Action'—was launched in 2000. In the first leg, only four panchayat samities in four different districts were chosen as a pilot project. Among the most vital aspects of this programme was the making of a village register, with detailed information on social, economic, religious, and other characteristics of each household. Since such registers were prepared on the basis of deliberations within the '*para*' (neighbourhood), chances of omission or misreporting were minimal (Midnapore Planning and Development Society 2002). In addition a manual in Bengali was circulated by the Department of Panchayat and Rural Development that contained detailed explanations of the methodology of local level planning. Special emphasis was placed on agricultural, small-industry, and infrastructural planning (GoWB 2002). The Village Development Council, as we mentioned before, was another such instrument for activating local knowledge to draw up plans for the benefit of the entire population of the village. The Council was supposed to include the opposition elements of the gram panchayat as well so that the panchayat could function above narrow party interests.

LOCAL GOVERNANCE IN WEST BENGAL

Local governance in a democratic set-up can be viewed as a culmination of two different processes: of taking governmental institutions to the local level so that administration can be made more responsive as well as accountable to the local people, and of turning a locality—about which little can be known from the seat of the central power—into a governmental entity by acquiring detailed knowledge of its characteristics, by assimilating and classifying such details, and making them locally available for the formulation of good public policies (Crook and Manor 1998).

It is important to highlight a few of the key changes that followed the introduction of local governance in West Bengal. It indeed signified a departure from previous (that is pre-Left Front) forms of governmental practices, which were administered primarily through bureaucratic agencies. The rural population now got access to governmental instruments at the village, even the booth, levels. Politics in rural areas always carried a certain visibility, its actors were familiar and the issues immediate; panchayat (at least potentially) aligned it to the procedures of planning and disbursement along the principles of rational administration (Williams 1999: 229–52). As a result, local governance got largely demystified and turned into a sphere of intimate interaction, changing such complex issues of rights and entitlements, bureaucracy and law, and corruption and malpractice from obscure and unreachable areas of 'high' politics to subjects of candid discussion and everyday scrutiny. It had two immediate effects.

On the one hand, it gave the rural population a sense of being 'counted', making them less vulnerable than before to the manipulation of the powerful classes. On the other hand, rather paradoxically, local governance in West Bengal broke the wall between the formal and the informal worlds of politics as the personal and the political got entangled at the institutional level within and around the panchayat. Relationship between families and individuals in a rural setting (where people live in close proximity, and where there is little option other than relying on collectively generated support mechanisms) constitutes the substance of politics in a rather intricate and enduring manner that often overlaps with partisan and sectional divisions. It is not unusual, therefore, that such informal, familial, community ties and differences would have a more prominent role in the functioning of the so-called formal structures of politics such as the panchayat or the local units of various political parties than are usually taken to have in more anonymous urban milieux. We will have occasions to talk more on this. For the time being, let us only note that the process of local governance does not only entail an extension of the apparatuses of governance into the localities, it also involves an obvious localization of governance or, what may be called, government of the locality.

If local governance indeed helps the production of localized forms of governmental instruments and exchanges, one wonders why in West Bengal one such mode of interaction, the gram sansad meetings, proved to be somewhat lacklustre in popular appeal. A recent study argues that the affluent do not go to such meetings since they have little to gain from anti-poverty programmes that they deliberate on; political minorities do not go since they know that their opinion carries little weight, the backward groups do not since their representation in the Left-wing leadership is insufficient; and women do not for reasons associated with obvious gender discrimination (Ghatak and Ghatak 2002: 50–1). These are important reasons, no doubt, but they do not explain why, say, a sizeable section of even the upper caste males from the poorer families who support the ruling party keep away from such meetings. True, as the minister himself has pointed out, efforts should be made to make these meetings more meaningful and democratic for enlisting larger support and greater participation at the local level (Mishra 1998); and attempts to create capacities for local planning and the engagement of the gram unnayan samiti are surely steps in that direction. However, an explanation for widespread popular indifference can perhaps be found not entirely within these institutions; but in other informal practices that make up the body of local governance work in a rural situation. Not attending a meeting can well be a sign of protest, of either non-cooperation or an attempt not to conform to the interests of the ruling clique. It could also be that people do not attend meetings because they do not have to; in order to get anything done they can easily make use of other channels that are available to them in the informal sphere of rural politics.

Any fieldworker in the rural areas can give several illustrations of the daily *adda* (extended session of conversation with friends and acquaintances) in the tea-stall by the arterial road, the bazaar, on the porch of the village temple or mosque, even in the informal gathering of the peasants where they exchange information relating to the techniques of cultivation or inputs such as seeds and fertilizers. These exchanges are significant not only because they are germane to the self-organization of the village, but also because they often take up problems and practices, suggest solutions, seek linkages, and use leverages that *cannot* be brought into the formal–legal sphere of governance. When a survey asked the respondents whom they turn to in moments of crisis, only half of over one thousand respondents spread all over rural Bengal said that they go to the panchayat (which is significant by itself), while a vast majority of the remaining half go either to any local important person, or to the office of any political party, or to the local club (West Bengal part of National Election Survey, 2004, conducted jointly by the Centre for the Study of Developing Societies, Delhi, and the Centre for Studies in Social Sciences, Kolkata). Clearly, channels of governance for providing security and well-being to the rural population in West Bengal spread well beyond the formal institutions such as the panchayat.

It is not uncommon for the peasants to take refuge in informal arrangements even where the production processes are involved. One of the first political moves of the Left Front was to formalize agricultural practices to put an end to various oppressive rituals and transactions. For instance, laws were made and implemented to register sharecroppers so that their risky dependence on the informal commitments of the landlord could be minimized. Yet, as research on tenurial transactions shows, informal arrangements do continue to exist in the form of *sanjha* whereby the landowner gets fixed payment in produce from the cultivator for the *boro* (summer) crop without making any investment on land. In official nomenclature, sanjha either exists no more, or occurs as a form of *barga* which it clearly is not (Gupta 1996:160–7). Cases of reverse tenancy or selling of *patta* land are also not rare as forms of extra-legal measures to cope with escalating labour costs and falling crop prices (Chakraborti 2002). Another example of informal practices is shown by Ruud's study. In his enquiry into how governance works at the local level, the people are observed to be making an extensive use of kinship ties to undermine the humiliating relationship of domination in the formal sphere of power (Ruud 2000). Rogaly has also shown that familial, ethnic or religious considerations frequently supersede political or economic rationality in the employment of labourers (Rogaly 1998:2734).[7]

So the village has a pattern of self-rule, and that often does not appear to coincide with the formal legal priorities of the state in which the 'citizen' appears as the universally recognizable unit. This 'self', however, is autonomous only in a relative sense, constantly mutating through its interaction with the governmental agencies at the local and supra-local levels. Such interaction is possible, and productive, only when the local society has a repository of skill, education, and some degree of expertise to establish and sustain linkages with the outside world. In the absence of such qualities, the locality fails to draw any sustenance from the institutions of local governance causing apathy and inaction on the part of the panchayat bodies in the midst of excruciating poverty. Certain areas inhabited mainly by the tribal population in the western and southern regions of the state (mainly in Purulia, Bankura, and West Midnapore) have already witnessed hunger related deaths in recent times where governance, as such a mode of transaction, appears to have collapsed completely.

Formal institutions of governance can, therefore, become truly democratic and enlist participation when they can strike a mutuality of interests with the self-organization of a locality in a region. There are, however, various kinds of self-organization of the local communities, producing different kinds of results. Comparing the cases of planning and of the delivery of public goods in West Bengal

and Kerala may illustrate this point. Kerala is noted for a steady
devolution of financial resources to the local level and quite a
significant initial spurt of participation in the village-based institutions
of local governance (Das 2000; Isaac and Franke 2000). It is also
recognized that Kerala has implemented public policies on basic
education, health care, social security and nutritional support etc. more
effectively than any other state (Dreze and Sen 2002). There obviously
cannot be an easy explanation for Kerala's achievements, but a possible
lead can be traced in the recent history of how social reforms and
local public action related to each other in that state as compared to
West Bengal.

Caste offered in Kerala the primary associative form 'in which the
peasant masses rose in struggle against feudalism', and the locally
articulated caste demands could be translated into class reforms for a
wider delivery of public goods (such as facilities for education and
health care) (Namboodiripad 1952:102, also see Ramachandran 1997).
In Bengal, by contrast, both at the state level and in the popular
imagination, caste discrimination never did become a major public
issue (Ghosh 2001:50). When the initiative came from within the
peasant castes, such that of the *Mahishya*s and the *Namasudra*s, the
aim was not to conduct structural reform *within* the communities for
eliminating traditional indignities, or to radically eliminate the method
of deprivation, but to get a slice of the governmental pie, which the
bhadralok had enjoyed for decades.[8] Paradoxically, however, when the
initiatives for reform came from outside, such as that of the bhadralok
communists in the *Tebhaga* agitation (1940s), 'class' was found an
insufficient category for expressing locally specific forms of peasant
solidarity (Chatterjee 1984:207–9; Guha 1997:169–71).

Though there is not much room here for a detailed discussion, it
can perhaps be stated that the lack of an organic movement from
below in West Bengal can partly be explained by the peculiar location
of its cultural elite—the middle class intelligentsia of Calcutta or the
bhadralok. Historians of social reform in Bengal have shown that this
section did not make a 'fundamental class' organically linked to an
advanced mode of production in the nineteenth century (Sen 1977).
As internal to the civic institutions of the colonial metropolis, this
class, therefore, had a problematic relation with the 'national-popular'
(Chatterjee 1985:70–89; Poddar 1977; Sarkar 1973:504–34).[9] This
was further complicated by the imperial economic interests which

distorted 'the organic connection between the literate and rustic levels of Bengali society' (Ray 1984:11–13). The near complete collapse of zamindari rights around early 1930s, and the migration following the partition of Bengal in the late 1940s, largely 'delinked' the urban cultural milieu from the rural population.

Consequently, two trends of rural transformation emerged in Bengal. The bhadralok communists had to source 'reform' from the discursive field of the urban public sphere external to the informal 'self' of the local/rural.[10] Second, the success of such reforms, in turn, depended to a large extent on the reformer's capacity to make use of the 'symbolic capital' internal to the informal sphere of the local/rural society. This produced two complex tendencies, by no means mutually exclusive. First, there was no coordinated demand for social transformation from within rural society, which could have induced greater governmental action for public provision such as health care and education enhancing the capabilities of the population. Second, that did not mean that the peasants were completely lacking in social and political skills and were entirely vulnerable to elite manipulation. As an anthropological account has pointed out, a village leader in West Bengal cannot hope to 'buy' votes: 'Even after the introduction of panchayati raj and mass mobilization, villages retained a large degree of internal self-rule' (Ruud 1995:286–7). Nevertheless, to put it schematically, while in Kerala the demands for public provision were thrown up as a result of social reforms from below, in West Bengal the availability of these services depended largely on the political will of the governing elite at the top.

To sum up, we can argue that it is futile to measure the efficacy of local governance or rural public action through the formal governmental structure alone as much of the action takes place outside its fold. Local governance in West Bengal, mainly for contextual reasons, makes it imperative to analytically focus on the perpetual interface between the formal and the informal spheres of popular and political activism. Given this, it has now become increasingly necessary to appreciate that local governance also mean dealing with specific governmental rationalities at the local level, not just 'managing the locality' after an imposing institutional design. Equally, where local society for reasons of historical disadvantage and lack of mobility fails to properly connect to the formal agencies of governance, the service delivery system of the local government collapses.

RECENT TRENDS

Studies on decentralization have gained momentum in recent times both in India and elsewhere. Most of them are empirically grounded, and many have shown the need to refine our existing understanding of the processes. A number of recent works on West Bengal, as we note in this section, have offered some striking observations. Pranab Bardhan and Dilip Mookherjee have studied 89 villages across 15 districts, the preliminary results of which were published recently (Bardhan and Mookherjee 2004). Williams, Veron, Corbridge, and Srivastava (2003) and Crook and Sverisson (2001) have studied West Bengal's decentralization in comparison with other states and countries. The Centre for Studies in Social Sciences, Kolkata has also under-taken a detailed survey of the households and the functionaries of around 150 gram panchayats in all districts (except Kolkata and Darjeeling); and the results of the first round are being tabulated at the time of this writing.[11]

Williams *et al.*, have looked into the problems of popular participation in West Bengal. While the state government recorded a better targeting of employment schemes to the poor than some of its neighbours, this was not related to the participation of the poor in local government institutions in any direct manner. In fact, participation for the proper disbursement of government projects was found to be 'sometimes marginal to the interests of the poor, and always mediated by the local power brokers' (Williams *et al.* 2003: 171). In Debra block of Midnapore district, where they conducted their study, such mediations often took place in the form of informal *baithaks* with the locally dominant CPI(M) leaders prior to attending any governing institutions. Though 'in theory' participatory development is supposed to challenge existing unequal political and social relationships, the authors found the opposite happening here. The poor people considered 'that political intermediaries played a valued role, and many recognized that party activists had forms of knowledge and social contacts that they did not have time to acquire' (Williams *et al.* 2003: 177). So neither the informality of any interaction nor the extent of attendance in the meetings of formal institutions (gram sabha meetings attracted 80 per cent here) could hide the fact that the poor could get an access to governmental schemes and programmes only through the mediation of the party as a power broker.

Bardhan and Mookherjee (2004) have argued in their study that decentralization by itself is no guarantee for generating or maintaining an effective service delivery system geared specifically to the needs of the poor. They have focused their attention rather on the social and political condition of the local settings. Some of their findings based on an impressive sample-set surely dislodge many of our commonsensical views on the role of the Left organizations in rural West Bengal. The delivery systems of the panchayat failed to cater to the poorer sections if a village happened to have a highly unequal distribution of literacy, economic assets, and social status, and if it lacked genuine political contestation or popular participation in formal institutions of governance. In fact, anti-poverty programmes yielded bad results in conditions of absolute poverty; poor cultivators with some land received higher benefits from the programmes than landless agricultural labourers. Similarly, a village dominated by agricultural labourers was less likely to receive support than a village dominated by small peasants. Literacy was a key leverage for the poor to make the agencies of governance work for them and, most strikingly, the programmes and other land reform measures were more beneficial to the poor when there was a high level of political competition and the Left was less certain about its re-election.

We need to look into this last factor more closely. The survey shows that land reforms were less successful in gram panchayats where the control of the Left was the maximum. In other words, land reforms were, rather paradoxically, taken up with less stridency where the local society was highly hierarchical, the poor were vastly illiterate, yet the Left had near monopolistic control over the gram panchayat. It would, however, be simplistic to hold the Left responsible for the lack of either land reform or the poor performance of the service delivery mechanism. Here the argument is that if the political parties are evenly poised in a village locality, they compete with each other to enlist electoral support and, therefore, try to deliver. By contrast when any party is singularly dominant, and when it faces no serious threat to its supremacy, it tends to lack any initiative to deliver. In the latter situation, the poor suffer the most, in absence of any leverage within the local society by which they could possibly have made their claims. Especially when the poor are additionally disadvantaged by the lack of literacy, and the existence of steep social and economic hierarchies, the service delivery systems scarcely take their needs into consideration. As in West Bengal, the organizations of the Left parties are more likely to be in a monopolistic power position than the non-Left parties, the chances of their coexistence with non-performing gram panchayats is statistically higher in any set of samples.

Our numerous visits to the districts and villages while carrying out our own survey on decentralization helped us to locate a few bottlenecks of decentralization in West Bengal. First, we found that there is a serious paucity of skills and personnel in running the day-to-day activities of the gram panchayat. A large number of these bodies do not have adequate infrastructure for the maintenance of accounts or for carrying out local planning, and their reporting to higher bodies at the block and the district levels is found to be irregular and, in many cases, improperly executed. Second, the functionaries of the panchayat, the elected representatives and officials, as well as some Block Development Officers, continue to treat the information of the panchayat as a special preserve of the panchayat itself. The lack of transparency is telling in many places. It is not difficult to explain why, in the midst of the apathy of the local population, the panchayat in some areas continues to act as a branch of local bureaucracy typical of a centralized administrative order. Third, the mediation of the political parties, mainly the CPI(M), has a double effect. On the one hand, the flow of information regarding various schemes and programmes is found to be smoother, covering wider ground in places where the Left organizations are active. As a BDO put it to us, 'the Left offers a *thashbunot* (tightly-knit) politics' that leaves practically no one unaffected. On the other hand, partisan solidarity of the Left means the political and, not uncommonly, social exclusion of individuals and sections within the villages which do not fall 'within the fold'. The most frequently made complaint in this regard came from the poor who alleged that they could not include their names in the Below Poverty Line (BPL) lists because of their 'wrong' political affiliation. Fourth, the message of resource mobilization at the local level by way of collecting taxes and fines has simply not sunk in. In most cases, the pradhan of the gram panchayat considered such taxation as unpopular measures, and therefore unworkable. Especially in a situation where the mechanism of local planning does not show any signs of taking off, the benefits of untied resources collected from the local sources are not adequately appreciated. Fifth, the Village Development Council has not worked in any significant way so far. Where any one party or coalition of parties holds sway, the opposition enjoys little voice, and in places marked by acute contestations, the public nature of the constitution of the Council (the adult population of the entire village can vote) often generate violent clashes. Pointing to these difficulties in the way of decentralization in West Bengal does not, however, mean ignoring the positive benefits that the state has received from its almost three decades of panchayat governance. Indeed, in a very large comparative frame, West Bengal stood out in the country (and among cases of decentralization in other developing countries) with respect to popular participation, representation, and responsiveness (Crook and Sverrison 2001: 49).

So West Bengal stands somewhat differently as far as decentralization in the rural areas is concerned, but this 'success' is not without its own problems. Such decentralization has been partial to the extent that the gram panchayats failed to take up the functions of local planning in any significant way. It is the mobilized force of the party, mainly the CPI(M), which acted as the backbone of decentralization in the state. While it ensured an evenly extended grip of the panchayat institutions, it also created conditions for political exclusion especially in places where the opposition is either weak or barely existent. Moreover, as West Bengal's decentralization is modelled on a top-down format of reform, some key public services such as education and health facilities have been poor almost everywhere in the state, and in the regions marked by the complete marginality of its population—such as those blocks that have heavy Scheduled Tribe populations—even the basic delivery mechanism of the panchayat system has collapsed. With the shifts in the economy in a so-called neo-liberal direction, the local government institutions are increasingly expected to weather the storm of production uncertainties and withdrawal of social support from the state. Will the panchayat in West Bengal be able to adapt to the new economic and political exigencies, or will the relative peace and social stasis that we obtain today be pierced by the prospects of violence? That remains the most important issue at the time of writing this article.[12]

NOTES

1. James Manor (1999) has discussed what he called 'many meanings' of decentralization: deconcentration or administrative decentralization, fiscal decentralization, and devolution or democratic decentralization. 'Each of them can occur in isolation, but any two (or all) of them can occur simultaneously'.

2. For an account of the Left-wing spread in rural West Bengal in the 1970s and the 1980s, as well as the debates and controversies that were associated with this spread, see Bhattacharyya 1999.

3. All references in this paper pertaining to this report may be found in Kashyap 1989. The book includes a chapter entitled 'Approach and Recommend-ations' from the original report in its Appendix D.

4. The West Bengal Block Level Pre-litigation Conciliation Board Bill, which is popularly known as the Salishi Bill, proposed by the Left Front with the intention of empowering the panchayat with some form of judicial functions has run into rough weather as it is opposed not only by the Opposition in the Legislative Assembly, but also the Bar Council of the Calcutta High Court. The CPI(M)-dominated Democratic Lawyers' Association has also sent ambiguous signals. It is apprehended that a body made of the political representatives cannot discharge judicial functions impartially especially where the organized Left has such a dominant presence. The government has also decided to go slow on the Bill for the moment in its efforts to garner consensual support from all concerned. See the *Telegraph*, Kolkata, Sunday, 3 July 2005.

5. The State Institute of Panchayat and Rural Development, Government of West Bengal, has recently conducted surveys of panchayat functionaries at the district level. Though several districts have been covered in these surveys, an all-West Bengal survey is yet to be conducted which alone can provide us with an overall idea of the character of representation in these grass roots bodies.

6. A Left Front minister claimed: 'The survey conducted by the Development and Planning Deptt of Govt. of WB (in 1978–79) covering 100 Gram Panchayats had revealed that more than 71 per cent of the representatives were small and marginal farmers (having landholding less than 2 acres 42.9 per cent, 2–5 acres 28.2 per cent)...' GoWB 1991:19. Benoy Chowdhury made a similar claim in 1988: 'It has been found by analysing the results of the 1978 election to the panchayat that among the members elected 85 per cent did not either have any land at all, or had land below 5 acres' CPI(M) 1988a:7.

7. 'The CPI(M)'s identity... shifts as it is used differently at the local level by particular jatis and classes...[W]orkers identify much more easily with somebody from a jati associated with wage work, and even better if he belongs to the class of wage workers'.

8   The Mahishya movement was that of the *Kaivartas*, a numerically significant middle-caste group in south-western Bengal, who in 1897–8 began to organize around various religious and educational issues for social uplift and, crucially, demanded enumeration of *chasi* (agricultural, as distinct from *jalia* or fishing) Kaivartas as Mahishyas, supposedly a 'cleaner' caste, in the census of 1901. The movement successfully retained its solidity and, thanks to the combined efforts of the rural *jotedars* (landlords, owning land above ceiling) and urban professionals, the Mahishyas were able to govern their identity by 1920. The Namasudras, a caste of 'untouchables', were mostly concentrated in eastern Bengal district of Faridpur and their agitation under the auspices of the Scheduled Caste Federation to eliminate higher caste oppression was led by a few educated professionals that the group had produced. Their struggle for proportionate representation in administration, and subsequently for education, invited severe wrath from the caste Hindu groups.

9. This, according to a number of Marxist historians, accounted for the dual nature of the so-called 'renaissance', as well as for the problematic connections between modernity and nationality in Bengal.

10. The name of the most popular reform measure of the Left Front (which formalized the rights of the share tenants on leased-in holdings) is 'Operation Barga' (barga=sharecropper). Why 'Operation'? Because 'Operation' stands for, in the minds of millions, an objective therapeutic treatment of the subject, possibly vivisectional, an action undeniably scientific, merciless (disregards particular pain for greater good), decisive (along a premeditated plan), and sufficiently alien (belonging to a body of knowledge that has its source outside the village).

11. The study team is headed by Partha Chatterjee. Other members are Surajit Mukhopadhyaya (coordinator), Pranab Das, Dhrubajyoti Ghosh, Manabi Majumdar, and myself. Subsequently, a report entitled, 'Strengthening Rural Development Programme: Design of Pupose-Level Indicators and Baseline Measurements in West Bengal District', was submitted to the Government of West Bengal.

12. Within months after the publication of this article, violence indeed broke out primarily in two places of southern West Bengal—Singur and Nandigram. In both places, the state government sought to bypass the local panchayats in its bid to acquire land for setting up, respectively, a car factory and a chemical hub.

REFERENCES

Bardhan, Pranab and Dilip Mookherjee, 'Poverty Alleviation Efforts of West Bengal panchayats', *Economical and Political Weekly*, 39(9), 2004, pp. 965-74.

Bhattacharyya, Dwaipayan, 'Agrarian Reforms and the Politics of the Left in West Bengal (1977-1990)', Ph.D. dissertation, Cambridge: University of Cambridge, 1993.

———, 'Politics of Middleness: The Changing Character of the Communist Party of India (Marxist) in rural West Bengal (1977-90)', in Ben Rogaly, Barbara Harriss-White and Sugata Bose (eds), *Sonar Bangla? Agricultural Growth and Agrarian Change in West Bengal and Bangladesh*, New Delhi: Sage Publications, pp. 279–300.

Chakraborti, Anil K., *Beneficiaries of Land Reforms: The West Bengal Scenario*, State Institute of Panchayat and Rural Development. Kalyani: Spandan, 2002.

Chatterjee, Partha, *Bengal 1920-1947: The Land Question*, Calcutta: K.P. Bagchi and Company, 1984.

———, 'The Fruits of Macaulay's Poison Tree', in Ashok Mitra (ed.), *The Truth Unites: Essays in Tribute to Samar Sen*, Calcutta: Subarnarekha, 1985, pp. 70–89.

Constituent Assembly Debates (CAD), Volume VII, Delhi: Manager of Publications, 1948.

CPI(M), *Poshchimbongo Shoshtho Panchayat Nirbachon: Tathya o Shomiksha*, Kolkata: West Bengal State Committee, 2004.

CPI(M), *Poshchimbonge Tristar Panchayat Nirbachan* [*Three-tier Panchayat Elections in West Bengal*] (28 February, 1988): *Janaganer Proti Abedan* [*An Appeal to the People*] (Poshchim Bongo Rajyo Committee) [West Bengal State Committe], 1988.

Crook, Richard C. and James Manor, *Democracy and Decentralization in South Asia and West Africa*. Cambridge: Cambridge University Press, 1998.

Crook, Richard C. and Alan Sturla Sverisson, 'Decentralization and Poverty-Alleviation in Developing Countries: A Comparative Analysis or, is West Bengal Unique?', *IDS Working Paper 130*, Sussex: Institute of Development Studies, 2001.

Das, M.K., 'Kerala's Decentralization Planning: Floundering Experiment', *Economic and Political Weekly*, 35(9), 2000, pp. 4300–3.

Datta, Prabhat, *Panchayats, Rural Development and Local Autonomy: The West Bengal Experience*, Kolkata: Dasgupta and Company Pvt. Ltd, 2001.

Dreze, Jean and Amartya Sen, *India: Development and Participation*, New Delhi: Oxford University Press, 2002.

Echeverri-Gent, J., 'Public Participation and Poverty Alleviation: The Experience of Reform Communists in West Bengal', *World Development*, 20, 10, 1992, pp. 1401–22.

Gandhi, M.K., *Panchayati Raj* (compiled by R.K. Prabhu). Ahmedabad: Navajivan Publishing House, 1959.

Ghatak, Maitreesh and Maitreya Ghatak, 'Recent Reforms in Panchayat System in West Bengal: Toward Greater Participatory Governance?', *Economic and Political Weekly*, 37(1), 2002, 45–58.

Ghosh, Anjan, 'Cast(e) out in West Bengal', *Seminar*, 508, 2001, 47–50.

GoWB (Government of West Bengal), *Debates on the West Bengal Panchayat Bill* (Extracts from the 'Proceedings of the Meeting of the West Bengal Legislative Assembly' held on 9 September 1969) Calcutta.

———, 'The Gram Panchayats in West Bengal and Their Activities' (mimeographed, Survey and Evaluation, Economic Planning Stream, Town and Country Planning Department, July 1980).

———, *Panchayati Raj*, vol. 17, nos 6–8, June–August 1988.

———, *An Alternative Approach to Development: Land Reforms and Panchayats* (by Surya Kanta Mishra, Minister of Panchayat and Rural Development). Calcutta: Information and Cultural Affairs Department), 1991.

———, 'Grambasider dara gram porikolpona (somonwito jono udyog sohobhagi porikolpona): nirdeshnama' (Village Planning by the Villagers), Kolkata: Department of Panchayat and Rural Development, 2002.

———, *West Bengal Human Development Report*, Kolkata: Development and Planning Department, 2004a.

———, *The West Bengal Panchayat Act, 1973: as modified up to 31st January, 2004*, Kolkata: Law Department, 2004b.

Guha, Ranajit, *Elementary Aspects of Peasant Insurgency in Colonial India*. Delhi: Oxford University Press (first edn 1983), 1997.

Gupta, Jayoti, 'Changing Land Relations in Midnapur District, 1960–88: A Case Study'. Ph.D. dissertation, University of Delhi, Delhi, 1996.

Isaac, T.M. Thomas and Richard W. Franke, *Local Democracy and Development: People's Campaign for Decentralised Planning in Kerala*, New Delhi: LeftWord Books, 2000.

Kashyap, Anirban, *Panchayati Raj: Views of the Founding Fathers and Recommendations of Different Committees*. New Delhi: Lancers Books, 1989.

Khilnani, Sunil, 'The Development of Civil Society', in Sudipta Kaviraj and Sunil Khilnani (eds), *Civil Society: History and Possibilities*, Cambridge: Cambridge University Press, 2001, pp. 11–32.

Kohli, Atul, *The State and Poverty in India: The Politics of Reform*, Cambridge: Cambridge University Press, 1987.

Lieten, G.K., *Development, Devolution and Democracy: Village Discourse in West Bengal*. New Delhi: Sage Publications, 1996.

Manor, James, *The Political Economy of Democratic Decentralization*. Washington D.C.: The World Bank, 1999.

Midnapore Planning and Development Society, 'Participatory Gram Panchayat Planning Under Convergent Community Action: Salboni Pilot Project', Kalyani: State Institute of Panchayat and Rural Development, 2002.

Mishra, Surjakanta, *Sreni Drishtibhongite Panchayat*. (Panchayat, Looking through the Perspective of Class), Calcutta: National Book Agency, 1998.

Namboodiripad, E.M.S., *National Question in Kerala*, Bombay: 102, 1952.

Poddar, Arabinda, *Renaissance in Bengal: Search for Identity*. Simla: IIAS, 1977.

Ramachandran, V.K., 'On Kerala's Development Achievements', in Jean Dreze and Amartya Sen (eds), *Indian Development: Selected Regional Perspectives*, New Delhi:Oxford University Press, 1997, pp. 205–356.

Ray, Rajat Kanta, *Social Conflict and Political Unrest in Bengal 1857-1927*, New Delhi: Oxford University Press, 1984.

Rogaly, Ben, 'Containing Conflict and Reaping Votes: Management of Rural Labour Relations in West Bengal', *Economic and Political Weekly*, 33(42–3), 1998: 2729–39.

Ruud, Arild Engelsen, 'Socio-Cultural Changes in Rural West Bengal', Ph.D. dissertation, London School of Economics and Political Science, London, 1995.

Ruud, Arild E., 'Talking Dirty about Politics: A View from a Bengali Village', in C. J. Fuller and Veronique Benei (eds), *The Everyday State and Society in Modern India*, New Delhi: Social Science Press, 2000, pp. 115–36.

Sarkar, Sumit, 'The Complexities of Young Bengal', *Nineteenth Century Studies*, 1(4), 1973: 504–34.

Sen, Asok, *Iswar Chandra Vidyasagar and his Elusive Milestones*. Calcutta: Riddhi, 1977.

Thomas Isaac, T.M. and Richard W. Frankel, *Local Democracy and Development: People's Campaign for Decentralized Planning in Kerala*, Delhi: LeftWord, 2000.

Webster, Neil, *Panchayati Raj and the Decentralization of Development Planning in West Bengal*. Calcutta: K.P. Bagchi and Company, 1992.

Westergaard, Kirsten, 'Marxist Government and Rural Development:The Case of West Bengal', *Journal of Social Studies*, 38, 1987:95–113.

Williams, Glyn, 'Panchayati raj and the changing micro-politics of West Bengal', in Ben Rogaly, Barbara Harriss-White and Sugata Bose (eds), *Sonar Bangla? Agricultural Growth and Agrarian Change in West Bengal and Bangladesh*, New Delhi: Sage Publications, 1999, pp. 229–52.

Williams, Glyn, Rene Veron, Stuart Corbride, and Manoj Srivastava, 'Participation and Power: Poor People's Engagement With India's Employment Assurance Scheme', *Development and Change*, 34(1), 2003: 163–92.

5

Panchayats, Bureaucracy, and Poverty Alleviation in Uttar Pradesh

■ RAVI S. SRIVASTAVA

INTRODUCTION

Decentralization at the level of communities, as something more than a mere delegation of power to lower levels of government, ordinarily implies a greater role for these communities in the provision of public goods and services. Such a role can make the provision cheaper and more efficient under certain conditions since it can lower transaction costs, take better account of local preferences, be based on improved information, and the providers can be made directly accountable to the local stakeholders. Locally elected officials may also have better incentive to use locally generated information. On the other hand, considerations of equity (between, and even within, local units) and economies of scale in production and information may dictate a more important role for higher levels of government (Prud'homme 1995). Higher levels of government may also be able to screen better talent to carry out tasks and, as Bird (1995) has argued, information asymmetry may work in both directions: the central government may not know *what* to do and the local government may not know *how* to do it.

However, another set of important issues relates to the proneness of local institutions as well as higher-level institutions to capture by vested interests (Bardhan and Mookherjee 2000). If it is argued that local institutions are more easily prone to such capture compared to higher levels of government, then the evaluation of their role will undergo a change on two main counts. First, local government institutions may then be more corrupt and hence less efficient than higher levels of government (Bardhan 1997; Shleifer and Vishny 1993). Second, and more specifically, their ability to provide goods and services for poor and minority households can easily be called into question. Such capture is naturally more likely in situations of prevailing inequality in which there is a 'dominant' local elite (Bardhan 1996).

It is, therefore, hardly surprising that the debate on rural decentralization in India echoes two strands: one which is favourable to decentralization and is based on a communitarian vision of a mutually interdependent and self-sufficient rural society, and the other less favourable to decentralization, based on a clear perception of deep-rooted socio-economic inequalities (Lieten and Srivastava 1999).

Theory, however, does not provide clear-cut support to such a neat divide. First, under certain situations, collective action may be a distinct possibility even with prevailing inequality (Olson 1965). Second, the implications of capture at the local level may be context specific and may depend, among other things, upon local political and electoral behaviour and rules (Bardhan 1997). Third, the functioning of higher levels of government at the local levels may have, over a period of time, become less accountable and more corrupt due to, for example, reinforcement of a perverse incentive structure so that usual comparisons between central and local corruptions may not have remained valid.

Another important issue (on which we also focus in this chapter) is that the usual distinction between local (decentralized) and higher-level (centralized) decision-making may not be altogether valid because of overlapping levels of authority, incomplete devolution, and interference of functionaries recruited at higher levels of government and elected political functionaries at these levels (Srivastava 1998b, 2001; Bardhan 1996). This may both obfuscate and complicate the accountability structure at the local level.

There are very few studies in India that examine the performance of the recent phase of rural decentralization in the light of the above. This chapter analyses the performance of anti-poverty programmes in Uttar Pradesh in the context of the post-73rd Amendment of the Constitution relating to rural decentralization. It is based on a field study of 20 village panchayats drawn from ten districts in the pre-bifurcation state and arises out of a larger study carried out for the Planning Commission (Srivastava 2002). The fieldwork was done during 2000–1, during and after the completion of the second post-73rd Amendment panchayat elections in UP. It was, therefore, in the unique position of evaluating the first tenure of the PRIs (1995–2000) in this phase. The survey used a number of instruments, including a census questionnaire for all households, a detailed questionnaire for over a thousand 'beneficiary' sample households, interviews with elected officials and bureaucrats, detailed case studies, and focus group discussions.

Anti-poverty programmes constitute a special class of programmes whose outcomes, by their very nature, are biased heavily in favour of the rural 'poor'. The rural rich may be interested in diverting these programmes away from the poor, either because of the funds that they draw, or because of the nature of goods associated with them, or simply because of the distributional implications of the goods/income/services that they provide to the poor. However, even if the rich do not overwhelmingly dominate decision-making in the local institutions, corruption and/or inefficiency may still reduce the gains for the poor.

CONTOURS OF DECENTRALIZATION IN UP IN THE CONTEXT OF ANTI-POVERTY PROGRAMMES

Following the Constitution (73rd) Amendment Act, 1992, the UP Panchayat Raj Act, 1947, and the UP Kshetra Samiti and Zila Parishad Adhiniyam, 1961, were amended and came into force in April 1994. The Conformity Legislation extends the spirit of the 73rd Amendment by providing for reservation for Scheduled Castes, Other Backward Classes, and women at all levels of the three-tier panchayati raj structure.

The institution that has been an integral part of the panchayat system, at its lowest level, is the gram sabha, the village assembly or meeting. The village assembly is expected to meet and to make recommendations and suggestions on development programmes, finances, community welfare programmes, identification of beneficiaries of government programmes, and other such issues. The gram panchayat (the executive committee) is supposed to give 'due consideration' to these recommendations.

The gram panchayat is chaired by the pradhan and, in his/her absence by the up-pradhan. Whereas the latter is elected by the panchayat (council) members, the pradhan in UP is elected directly by the electorate. The panchayat, which comprises a village or a group of villages having a population of around 1000, is divided into a number of territorial constituencies (wards) from which the members are elected. These constituencies also are rotated in order to comply with the gender and caste reservation.

Following the 73rd Amendment, the functions of the gram panchayat have been substituted under the 1994 State Amendment by a list of items included in the Eleventh Schedule of the Constitution. However, these functions have been further elaborated (as assistance to the state government; promotional; implementation of existing programmes; maintenance or directly developmental functions); and include interventions in the agrarian economy (agricultural extension, land consolidation, land reforms, soil conservation, water management, animal husbandry, social forestry, fisheries, etc.) and other functions ranging from rural housing, education, electricity, electrification, village roads, sanitation, social welfare, public distribution system, and poverty alleviation programmes. Under the new legislation, the panchayats are expected to constitute the following committees to assist in the performance of their duties: the *vikas samiti* (agriculture, rural industry, and development schemes), the *shiksha samiti* (education), the *lokhita samiti* (public health, public works), and the *samata samiti* (welfare of women and children, and the interests of SCs/STs and Backward Classes, and protection of these groups from 'social injustice and exploitation in any form'). The Act also now provides that: 'A Gram Panchayat shall prepare every year a development plan for the Panchayat area and submit it to the *Kshettra Panchayat* (intermediate tier local body) concerned before such date and in such form as may be prescribed.'

The 73rd Constitutional Amendment, and following that the 1994 State Amendment, considerably enhance the *responsibilities* of the panchayat institutions to areas mentioned in the Eleventh (and for the urban areas the Twelfth) Schedule, while their *functions*, and steps for enhancing their *powers and capacity* have slowly followed. It took nearly five years after the amended state legislation for 32 government departments to issue instructions for devolving powers and functions to PRIs. But almost in all cases, the administrative control of the officers concerned still remains by and large with the line departments.

Following significant devolution in neighbouring Madhya Pradesh, Uttar Pradesh decided to accelerate the speed of devolution in 1999 (Srivastava 2001). A new high-powered committee (referred to as the Bajaj Committee, after the name of its chairperson) was formed and recommended a number of steps to increase the speed of devolution to the rural local bodies. These steps included implementation of the First State Finance Commission recommendations for devolution of finances (4 per cent of net state tax revenue for rural PRIs) with some modifications.

Many of the measures taken up for introduction by the UP government aimed at increasing the powers and administrative capacity of the panchayat unit at the smallest level—the gram panchayat. These measures include a merger of village level posts of eight government departments in order to make available at least one government functionary to assist in the affairs of every village panchayat (a step recommended by the Bajaj Committee, though in a different form); transfer of assets from some departments to the village panchayats (primary schools, anganwadi centres, public tube wells); placement of some village-level functionaries such as anganwadi workers and primary school teachers under the partial administrative control of the village panchayats or its committees, giving the gaon panchayats powers to finalize beneficiaries of some schemes such as school scholarships and transfer of funds for such schemes to the panchayats; and giving the power to panchayats to recruit additional school teachers and panchayat assistants locally, subject to guidelines of the state government.

These devolution measures undoubtedly increased the administrative capacity and the powers of the gram panchayats (although there was a subsequent rollback) giving them a much greater role in the delivery of important social services such as primary schools and pre-school childcare and nutrition programmes such as the ICDS, social security programmes, and rural development/anti-poverty programmes (the last having been within the purview of the village panchayats, at least in principle, even before the 73rd Constitutional Amendment).

The rural development process in the state has had an extremely tenuous link with the PRIs in the past. The District Rural Development Agency (DRDA) (which is the nodal agency for all centrally-sponsored poverty alleviation schemes) remained a separate entity from the zilla parishad (ZP) (which has constitutionally mandated responsibilities for poverty alleviation). But in the changes made in 1999, however, the ZP chairperson has also been made chairperson of the DRDA.

State resources for districts are channelled through the District Plan. Changes have been made in the constitution of the District Planning Committee, in accordance with the 74th Amendment of the Constitution, which has provided a mandate for a new District Planning Committee, four-fifths of whose members shall be members elected to the district and municipal bodies. However, meetings of the District Planning Committee, which bring together the district heads of sector departments and elected representatives to finalize schemes to be executed under the District Plan, are chaired by a minister and not by the ZP chairperson, who shall be the deputy chairperson.

Even though large amounts of financial resources have been committed by the Union Finance Commission (UFC) and the State Finance Commission (SFC), the flow of funds to the PRIs has been tardy. In the case of the SFC amount, in the absence of clear-cut norms regarding expenditure, devolution only took effect in 1998– 9. But even since then, due to financial stringency, the transfer, which has been broken down into monthly instalments, is often subject to delays and procedural problems. In the case of the Tenth Finance Commission, the state government/local bodies found it difficult to meet their obligation of matching contributions resulting in delayed release of the grant (the grant for 1998–9 was released only in late 1999).

Apart from UFC and SFC grants, the PRIs have access to grants from the central and state governments for implementing designated programmes and schemes. In fact, financial resources transferred for employment generation and other programmes of the Department of Rural Development are still the largest source of funds for the panchayats. In 1999–2000, of the estimated Rs 11,000 million expected to be transferred from the Union and state governments, the Department of Rural Development was expected to account for Rs 5830 million, while the Tenth Finance Commission (TFC) and the SFC grants were expected to account for Rs 3280 million and Rs 1290 million respectively.

Even though in per capita terms, the amounts transferred to panchayats (which form the bulk of their financial resources) are still only about Rs 100, which is the amount estimated by the Tenth Finance Commission as the resources available to panchayats in 1971 (in current prices) as an all-India average, in the case of UP, as we have noted, the financial resources of the panchayats were very meagre and were continuously declining right up to 1989. Hence, this does represent a fairly significant increase in the quantum of resources available to them. Moreover, according to the government estimates presented earlier, this amounted to nearly Rs 100,000 per panchayat annually.

Thus, since the 73rd Constitutional Amendment a change has been engineered in the democratic rules governing panchayats which now have greater powers and resources to design and implement anti-poverty programmes. Since the 73rd Amendment envisages a shift of the planning and implementation of anti-poverty programmes from the bureaucracy to a local democratic institution, in which the local community, including the poor, can have greater say, the impact of this change has to be watched with great interest. Moreover, this study has been able to observe the first five years of PRIs after the 73rd Amendment as well as the transition to the second elected period. As such, our conclusions should be of some interest to all those concerned with the role of democratic institutions in anti-poverty interventions.

What do the above changes mean for design and implementation of anti-poverty strategies? What accounts for the variation, if any, in the performance of the panchayats? In the following section we document some of our observations on gram panchayats in the study areas.

VARIATIONS IN THE PERFORMANCE OF VILLAGE PANCHAYATS

Going by the assessments made by beneficiaries of anti-poverty programmes, opinions of the development functionaries, and our own observations, it is apparent that the gram panchayats have done poorly on a number of counts. But it would, of course, not be fair to prejudge the issue and conclude that all panchayats have fared poorly. In fact, our study demonstrates a range of experiences and dynamics, although it also highlights some of the general constraints. We use these variations to analyse some of the general features underlying the performance of panchayats in relation to anti-poverty programmes.

Establishing and characterizing the variations is, however, problematic because of multiple, and often, conflicting, dimensions of the issue. In one of the cases, for example, we observed a low level of corruption because the concerned pradhan simply chose to remain inactive. A low level of corruption, therefore, coexisted with absence of any meetings and a low delivery of programmes.

In order to examine this issue more closely, the study evolved some criteria for assessing performance variation by ranking the panchayats. Scores were given to panchayats along three dimensions—democratic functioning, transparency, and efficiency. The aggregate scores obtained by each panchayat were used to rank each of the panchayats. The criteria used are summarized in Table 5.1.

In a sense, both 'democratic functioning' and 'transparency' are process variables, which are linked to the quality of the implementation (outcome). There are two main reasons why these dimensions have

TABLE 5.1: CRITERIA USED IN THE RANKING OF PANCHAYATS

Dimension	Scale
Participation	
Regularity of gram panchayat meetings	Regular 03; Irregular 02; Not held 01
Participation in gram panchayat meetings	All sections 05; Some sections 03; On paper/nil 01
Regularity of gram sabha meetings	Regular 05; Irregular 03; Not held 01
Participation in gram sabha meetings	All sections 05; Some sections 03; On paper/nil 01
Transparency	
Selection of beneficiaries	Open meeting 05; Open meeting but tampered 03; Outside meeting 01
Selection of schemes	Open meeting 05; Open meeting but tampered 03; Outside meeting 01
Publicity of funds and expenditure	Well advertised 05; Selectively known 03; Not known to anyone 01
Implementation	
Level of activity	Active 03; Less active 02; Inactive 01
Supervision of works	Collective involvement 03; Pradhan or relative 02; Contractor 01
Quality of works	Good 05; Medium 03; Poor/very poor 01
Corruption	Honest 05; Relatively honest 03; Very corrupt 01

Grades for panchayats: Very good 40–49; Good 30–39; Unsatisfactory 21–29; Very unsatisfactory 11–20

been treated independently. First, the ramifications of these dimensions go beyond what is immediately observable in the implementation process. Second, not all relevant outcome variables are easy to summarize and the 'process' variables bridge this gap.

Not surprisingly, most of the study panchayats (75 per cent) rank in the 'Unsatisfactory' (12) or 'Very unsatisfactory' (3) categories. But two achieve a 'Good' rank while three achieve a 'Very good' rank (Table 5.2).

Of the five well-functioning panchayats, two were in the hill region, and one each was in the western, central, and eastern regions. Notably, two of the best functioning panchayats in the sample (Pithoragarh-A and Unnao-A) were headed by women pradhans from the upper castes. These two successful pradhans had significantly different profiles, yet they performed reasonably well as leaders of their respective panchayats. In the fourth well-functioning panchayat (Meerut-B), the pradhan was again a woman, but in this case all her duties were performed by her husband, a teacher. The fifth panchayat, which was a borderline case, was headed by an upper-caste male.

Some of the factors underlying the general performance of panchayats as well as those related to the variations in inter-village performance are discussed in the following sections.

DEMOCRATIC FUNCTIONING OF GRAM PANCHAYATS

It may be expected that the nature of democratic functioning of the panchayats and the participation of poor households in this process would have very important implications for the degree to which decisions are aligned to local preferences and the needs of the poor (Crook and Manor 1994; Srivastava 1998a). Provided that the poor participate effectively, this would also have implications for the 'capture' of local institutions by the dominant classes.

As discussed earlier, the fieldwork took place immediately preceding, and in the aftermath of, the second panchayat elections (after the 73rd Constitutional Amendment) in UP in 2000. It could, therefore, collect evidence on the functioning of the first post-Amendment panchayat and closely observe the transition to the second (including the electoral process that led to it).

The broadening of the base of the formal panchayat leadership that has occurred is the most striking change in post-73rd Amendment

TABLE 5.2: RANKING OF STUDY PANCHAYATS

District & village	Region	P1	P2	P3	P4	T1	T2	T3	I1	I2	I3	I4	Total	Rank
Aligarh-A	Western	1	1	1	1	1	1	1	2	2	1	1	13	V. Poor
Aligarh-B	Western	1	1	1	1	1	1	1	1	2	1	1	12	V. Poor
Meerut-A	Western	1	1	1	1	1	1	3	2	2	3	1	17	V. Poor
Meerut-B	Western	2	3	3	3	3	3	5	3	2	3	3	33	Good
Bareilly-A	Western	1	1	1	1	1	1	5	3	2	1	1	18	V. Poor
Bareilly-B	Western	1	1	1	1	1	1	3	1	2	1	1	14	V. Poor
Unnao-A	Central	2	5	3	5	5	5	5	3	3	3	5	44	V. Good
Unnao-B	Central	1	1	1	1	1	1	1	3	2	2	1	15	V. Poor
Fatehpur-A	Central	1	1	1	1	1	1	1	2	2	3	1	15	V. Poor
Fatehpur-B	Central	2	3	3	3	3	1	1	1	2	1	3	23	Poor
Hamirpur-A	Bundelkhand	2	3	3	3	3	1	1	2	2	1	1	20	V. Poor
Hamirpur-B	Bundelkhand	2	3	3	3	3	3	1	2	2	1	1	24	Poor
Pithoragarh-A	Hills	3	5	5	5	5	5	5	3	3	3	5	47	V. Good
Pithoragarh-B	Hills	3	5	5	5	5	5	5	3	3	3	3	45	V. Good
Allahabad-A	Eastern	1	1	1	1	1	1	1	3	1	1	1	13	V. Poor
Allahabad-B	Eastern	2	5	3	5	3	3	1	1	2	1	3	29	Poor
Jaunpur-A	Eastern	1	1	1	1	1	1	1	3	2	1	1	14	V. Poor
Jaunpur-B	Eastern	2	3	3	3	3	3	1	3	3	3	3	30	Good
Deoria-A	Eastern	1	1	1	1	1	1	1	3	1	1	1	13	V. Poor
Deoria-B	Eastern	1	1	1	1	1	1	1	2	3	1	1	14	V. Poor

scenario. A high proportion of the elected leadership is from the lower castes and from among women. The lower level of educational attainment of the pradhans is an important problem, although the proportion of illiterates is lower than the population at large. The problem is also more acute among OBCs and lower castes. There seems to be very little shift between the first and second rounds in the extent of the elected leadership's educational attainment (Table 5.3 and 5.4).

It can be observed that the proportion of illiterates among pradhans in both rounds was small (in relation to prevailing levels of adult illiteracy in the state), although their proportions were larger among female pradhans. Among male pradhans only one out of fourteen was illiterate in the second round, while in the first round, none was. However, among women, 40 per cent in the first round and one-third in the second round were illiterate, consequently posing severe constraints on their capacity to function in their post. But low levels of educational attainment are a major problem, with 45 per cent of pradhans in the first round and 35 per cent in the second round not having completed even the elementary school cycle.

Due the prevailing socio-economic milieu and ingrained patriarchy, there is a strong tendency to set up proxy candidates among the lower castes and women. These proxy candidates are quite often

TABLE 5.3: SOCIAL AND EDUCATIONAL PROFILE OF
SITTING PRADHANS

Caste group	Sex	Total	Illiterate	Primary	Middle	Secondary	BA or higher
				Educational attainment			
Upper-caste	Male	4		1	1	1	1
	Female	2		1			1
OBC	Male	4	1		2		1
	Female	4	2	1		1	
SC/ST	Male	6		1	3	2	
	Female	0	0				
Total	Male	14	1	2	6	3	2
	Female	6	2	2	0	1	1

Source: Srivastava (2002).

TABLE 5.4: SOCIAL AND EDUCATIONAL PROFILE OF
PREVIOUS PRADHANS

| Caste group | Sex | Total | Educational attainment | | | | |
			Illiterate	Primary	Middle	Secondary	BA or higher
Upper-caste	Male	6		1	1	2	1
	Female	2		1			1
OBC	Male	8		2	3	2	1
	Female	2	1	1			
SC/ST	Male	2		2			
	Female	1	1				
Total	Male	15		5	4	4	2
	Female	5	2	2			1

Source: Srivastava (2002).

illiterate or economically dependent on the powerful groups. This leads to a lack of autonomy on the part of elected formal leadership. Unfortunately, this is also a trend tacitly encouraged by the bureaucracy, which feels comfortable in dealing with the established dominant and male leadership.

The democratic process is also vitiated by the electoral practices (N. Srivastava 2001). In the elections observed by us, candidates spent anything between Rs 5000 and Rs 100,000. Several of them were known to have used muscle power to succeed in the electoral battle, and at least in three or four cases, such candidates had succeeded in cowing down the opposition.

However, there are countervailing forces and trends that can also be witnessed. There is a distinct trend among the lower-castes, especially the Scheduled Castes, to back a strong and capable leadership, and even among women some of those whom we observed emerged as strong and favoured leaders.

Gram sabha meetings are the formal vehicles of people's participation in the affairs of the panchayat once elections have taken place. Even though the UP government has, from time to time, emphasized that the gram sabhas meet at least twice every year to transact their business, regular meetings have not taken place in most of our study panchayats. A few meetings are reported to have taken place in six of the study panchayats, including both in the hills. In Jasrapur (Unnao) where the pradhan is a woman, a few meetings were held initially but participation was scanty. However, after the murder of the pradhan's husband, gram sabha meetings have become irregular, but gram panchayat meetings were reported to have been held more or less regularly.

The participation of women and poor households in gram sabha meetings is generally thin. In Jaunpur-A, a few meetings have been held to discuss the selection of the *kotedar* (public distribution system (PDS) shopkeeper) and to discuss educational problems and scholarships for students. A few members among SCs also participated in these meetings and offered their opinions. In Allahabad-A panchayat, three meetings were initially held, but these quickly turned acrimonious. In one of these, a woman member raised the issue of a drain, but was ignored. When the issue was pressed by another member (belonging to the boatman caste), he was thrashed. In some other panchayats an initial general meeting is reported to have taken place, but in others formalities have been completed only on paper and signatures have been obtained. The participation of women members was higher in two of the panchayats in which the pradhans were active women. By and large, the democratic record of the panchayats headed by Scheduled Caste members was also quite lacklustre, except in Meerut-B.

On the whole, interviews with over 1000 beneficiaries of anti-poverty programmes in the villages revealed that only 11 per cent males and 3 per cent females from these households had participated in any gram sabha meeting in the last one year. More than 85 per cent of our beneficiaries had no clear idea about these meetings, and what was discussed there. Nearly 89 per cent of those who attended these meetings indicated that they had only heard the proceedings and had not participated actively in the meetings.

Meetings of the gram panchayat, which is the next-rung democratic body, have also not fared much better. Though meetings have been held in a number of panchayats, the requirement of monthly meetings has not been met anywhere. Several meetings of the gram panchayat are reported to have been held in the Jaunpur-A, Allahabad-B, Unnao-A, Allahabad-A, Fatehpur-B, Meerut-B, Deoria-B, and Pithoragarh A and B panchayats, but no meetings are reported to have been held in Deoria-B, Fatehpur-A, Jaunpur-B, or Deoria-A, and signatures or thumb impressions of the members were obtained for the purposes of record.

In a number of cases where meetings have been held, a small number of members, usually the supporters of the pradhan, have participated actively. In a few cases where members have dissented strongly with decisions taken they have been beaten up. Women members have participated in the meetings only in Unnao-A, where the pradhan is also a woman, and in the two hill panchayats. A lower-caste female member reported that she initially participated in the meetings in Allahabad-A, but her interest waned when she found that she had no say in the decisions. In all other cases, the thumb impressions of female members have been obtained after the meetings.

By and large, the two hill panchayats have been the most democratically active, followed by Meerut-B and Unnao-A panchayats.

IDENTIFICATION OF BENEFICIARIES AND SCHEMES FOR DEVELOPMENT

Identification of beneficiaries and schemes/public works to be undertaken are two of the more important functions of gram panchayats, and decisions in this regard should be taken in the gram sabhas. But the overall weakness in the democratic process that we have observed earlier provides room in a number of cases for the pradhan and the bureaucracy to manipulate the names of beneficiaries and to select schemes of their choice. In some of the study villages (Fatehpur-A, Unnao-A, Pithoragarh-A and B, and Allahabad-A and B), an initial list of beneficiaries was prepared in gram sabha meetings. In most other cases, an initial list was prepared by the pradhan and his supporters, and in almost all the study villages, the pradhan and/ or the village-level government functionaries, other bureaucrats, and various other middlemen decided the final list and were the ultimate arbiters of who the beneficiaries would be.

Reportedly, one meeting was held in Allahabad-B to select beneficiaries for Indira Awas Yojana (IAY) and Integrated Rural Development Programme (IRDP), and a list was made but later modified. A middleman in this village was known to be in touch with bank and block officials and got names included in beneficiary lists on payment of bribe. In Fatehpur-B a meeting was held to identify beneficiaries, but some people selected in the open meeting had their names removed because they could not pay any money for inclusion in the final list. Similarly, in Jaunpur-B a list was prepared for land (patta distribution) by the pradhan, who included the names of those who approached him, but only names of those who were able to pay bribes to the *lekhpal* (land record keeper) figured in the final list. Almost in all other cases, the names of beneficiaries have been finalized by the pradhan, his henchmen, and ultimately by the village- and block-level functionaries, without even going through the formality of discussion in gram sabha meetings and, with a few exceptions (such as in village Unnao-A), beneficiaries had to pay for inclusion in these lists. What is alarming is that there is an institution of quasi-professional middlemen who keep a close liaison with the PRIs, banks, and developmental bureaucracy and mediate between them and the potential beneficiaries in a number of villages (Allahabad-B, Deoria-B, and Unnao-A).

Thus, except in four or five panchayats, names rarely found place on the list of beneficiaries of the IRDP, IAY, or land distribution programmes unless the potential beneficiary happened to be exceptionally close to one of them or money had changed hands.

Similarly, schemes to be taken up under the Jawahar Rozgar Yojana (JRY) or other programmes were rarely finalized in the gram sabha meetings, and exceptions to this were few and far between. A meeting was reportedly held in Unnao-B to decide the site for the panchayat building. Similarly, in Fatehpur-B the issue of what kind of public work should be taken up was discussed in a gram sabha meeting. The two Pithoragarh panchayats were again democratically active on this count as well. Generally, however, these decisions are taken by the pradhan, in informal consultation with his/her supporters and the village functionaries.

Thus, the two main functions of the gram sabhas (selection of beneficiaries and schemes) to be undertaken through democratic consent were subverted in a majority of the study panchayats by the pradhan and his supporters and/or the development bureaucracy at the village/block level, often in collusion with professional middlemen.

TRANSPARENCY IN BUDGETARY TRANSACTIONS OF THE PANCHAYATS

Transparency in budgetary transactions is potentially an important feature of accountability of local institutions. A number of government orders prescribe procedures to maintain budgetary transparency.

Panchayat receipts and expenditure, which are supposed to be boldly displayed on banners/hoardings by the gram panchayats, were generally shrouded in secrecy. Panchayat accounts were discussed in gram panchayat meetings in five panchayats (Pithoragarh-A and B, Meerut-B, Bareilly-A, and Unnao-A) and we came across a few villagers who were broadly aware of the panchayat's receipts and expenditures. In some panchayats issues relating to receipts and expenditure on schemes had been briefly raised in the gram panchayat meetings and there were some individuals who were aware of the broad details. We came across a few villagers in panchayats in Allahabad and elsewhere who were generally aware of the panchayat's budgetary details. But there was hardly any respondent in the other study villages, including some gram panchayat members, who could accurately report on this. In some cases (for example, in village Unnao-B) the pradhan claimed that even he was not aware of the details as the records and accounts were fully managed by the panchayat secretary.

In the early part of the fieldwork, in the immediate aftermath of the panchayat elections, records of panchayats were not available at the village level for scrutiny by the field staff. However, in the later part, records from the panchayats in Jaunpur and Fatehpur were scrutinized. Where available, these consisted of attendance registers, muster rolls, and expenditure details. Records pertaining to minutes of meetings and decisions taken were not maintained. In any case, the emphasis of the state government on transparency in the functioning of the PRIs has not percolated down, either through its own apparatus or through the elected bodies. In one case (Fatehpur-A) the pradhan invited the field staff to scrutinize the economic register late at night, when he could be assured that other villagers would not be privy to them. In any case, the pradhan of this village has a record of silencing any opposition to him through force if necessary, and the secrecy seemed to be added caution.

IMPLEMENTATION OF ANTI-POVERTY PROGRAMMES

Once the name of the beneficiary has been finalized (without payment of bribe in a minority of cases, as reported earlier), papers have to be processed and the loan/grant/pension is released through the bank in the case of the Swarnajyanti Gram Swarozgar Yojana (SGSY) or IAY or the post office. The final release was almost always subject to a hefty deduction by one or more of the various intermediaries—the pradhan, bank officials, block functionaries, or professional middlemen. The general modus operandi is for the middleman or the pradhan or the village functionary to accompany the beneficiary to the bank and take the amount from him as soon as the money was withdrawn. Middlemen negotiate the price of following through with the transaction, and even the price of the eventual loan default. In the case of pensions, the postal clerk will deduct an amount (if the pension account is in the post office).

It is true that not all pradhans are corrupt and some stay away from the entire exercise. Since the sanction and release of the assistance require at least one or two other agencies, bribes may have to be paid, and deductions made even if local elected functionaries are honest. But in other cases, pradhans justify taking a share of the deduction or at least 'kharcha' (expenses) to cover their expenses of travelling to and from the block office. The deductions could range from a paltry Rs 100 in case of pensions to Rs 6000 or more in the case of IAY/IRDP or even land pattas.

In the case of public works executed under JRY or similar schemes, pradhans or the panchayat secretaries have been almost invariably responsible for overseeing their execution. The solitary exception was a Pithoragarh village where a ward committee has been set up to supervise the public works.

As discussed earlier, the material used is often of poor quality, and labour is either not employed or is underpaid. It is difficult to estimate the leakage on these counts. As reported in the preceding sections, several pradhans candidly told us that the block functionaries have to be paid a minimum of 20 per cent of the amount defrayed. This was reported to be the case even of some of the best functioning panchayats in the hills. In some panchayats, for example, in one of the Hamirpur study village, almost 40 per cent of the funds were said to be paid to the block officials.

Other pradhans told us that they have to cover their own expenses and the expenses that they have to incur on visits by block and other officials from the JRY funds. The circumstances in which the pradhans work and the reactions of the community towards them vary, but it is clear that only a few of them have stayed away from making large amounts from the JRY.

However, the corruption and ineptitude of the panchayats (pradhans) should not be overemphasized. In the two hill panchayats, the pradhans provided effective leadership over a democratic village body, but faced constraints from the development bureaucracy. In Unnao-A the woman pradhan was able to inspire confidence among a large section of the village community and push forward a limited development agenda.

THE DEVELOPMENTAL BUREAUCRACY IN THE NEW DISPENSATION

It is quite clear that despite the limited devolution that has occurred, the block functionaries continue to have the upper hand. While names of individual beneficiaries can be suggested by the panchayat/pradhan, these are still finalized by the block functionaries who are not obliged to state reasons for their refusal. In fact, at all stages, inclusion in these lists is subject to the discretion of the officials—whether elected or not.

In the case of employment programmes, while these can be chosen at the village level, the appraisal of the works and the expenditure is carried out by the block functionaries and these must meet their 'satisfaction'. All in all, they continue to retain significant powers in the post-73rd Constitutional Amendment scenario.

Even the lowest village functionaries (the gram panchayat officer, the village development officer, and the lekhpal) are not accountable to the elected functionaries and are not responsible for the implementation of programmes, except in very limited (though important) roles. The 1999 reforms introduced an important change by merging the village-level cadres of eight departments into a village-level panchayat functionary—a move partially reversed in 2004. But these functionaries were still accountable to their line departments and are not regularly available in the panchayats. The study teams, which were resident in the study villages for several days continuously, found it difficult to contact the functionaries. Those who had been posted from the other departments had not acquired the competence to maintain records, and in one case the panchayat secretary paid another employee to maintain village records for him.

Since panchayat funds were widely believed to have been mismanaged, we considered it important to find out whether people considered it better that these funds were managed by the block officials, as was previously the case. In fact, most respondents were in favour of devolution of funds to the panchayats, but supported joint management (by the pradhan and block development committee member [BDC]; by the pradhan and the panchayat members, etc.). In all, 90 per cent of the respondents favoured devolution of funds to the panchayats and only 7 per cent favoured their retention by the block. This is a telling commentary on how, despite fairly unsatisfactory panchayat performance, the former mode of bureaucratic dispensation is still perceived by the largely poor respondents in the study villages.

As we shall see later, despite a disappointing beginning, poor households do see devolution as being, on the whole, favourable to the implementation of an anti-poverty strategy, and support it.

WHAT HAS DEVOLUTION MEANT FOR ANTI-POVERTY PROGRAMMES?

At the planning and implementation level, anti-poverty programmes now envisage a shift from the bureaucracy to local democratic institutions. Greater devolution was expected to improve the effectiveness of anti-poverty programmes.

From our preliminary observations in the field, it appears that devolution has brought increased contestation and debate over the use of funds for local development into the forefront at the local level. Expectations of what these resources are expected to do are high, often unrealistically. Reputations of pradhans are now made or marred on the basis of their performance in office.

At the same time, for those who seek election to become pradhan, there is more at stake now than previously was, not least because the financial resources at the disposal of the gram panchayat have steadily increased. The pradhan's goals vary, and not all are in the business of self-enrichment (although in our sample, 75 per cent who had completed a full term had acquired significant new assets in the form of houses, tractors, or motorcycles). By and large, their view of the village community is quite functional—they rely on local participation only to the extent necessary and, not surprisingly, the weaker pradhans are less autocratic and rely more on community support than those who are powerful.

There is some evidence from these field studies that the quality of local leadership has improved in the second round of elections and that some among the new leadership are more committed to a larger good. But on the other hand there is also a negative side, and our observations on the recent elections showed that money power (along with muscle power) had also become a very important instrument for garnering votes.

But even among pradhans fairly committed to a 'clean' and democratic functioning, both the extent of 'public good' that they can achieve and their autonomy are severely circumscribed, on the one hand, by the objectives and functions of the development bureaucracy, which seeks to reduce local democratic institutions into subservient appendages and the pradhan into the local linchpin of a corrupt and inefficient delivery system; and, on the other, by the nature of local society and its dynamics.

Among the poor beneficiaries, the increased role of the panchayats in the anti-poverty programmes is well recognized (63 per cent of the beneficiaries recognized this to be the case) and what is surprising is that despite the poor functioning of many of the panchayats, 68.5 per cent of the beneficiaries still favoured greater devolution and a larger role in the programmes, and 59.6 per cent saw the impact of the panchayats on rural development as being 'good'.

Thus, despite the negative images of the devolution that one collects through field observations, which are strongly reinforced by discussions with the development bureaucracy, the poor do not favour a roll back of devolution; in fact, the predominant view that emerges from all aspects of the study is that they advocate greater devolution, more democratic control, and greater accountability.

EXPLAINING PANCHAYAT PERFORMANCE:
SOME TENTATIVE CONCLUSIONS

In the beginning we had shown that the capture of panchayats by the dominant groups could seriously jeopardize the anticipated benefits of decentralization, especially in the context of anti-poverty programmes. Our results indicate that local democratic institutions are still prone to capture by the village elite and are generally too weak to influence the individualistic styles of functioning of elected officials.

Our analysis also shows that the bureaucracy still maintains the upper hand in expenditure disbursements. Moreover, it retains supervisory and regulatory functions over the village panchayats. Both these functions are used to bring elected officials in line.

Moreover, while PRIs have been given greater roles, and rules have been framed to ensure transparency in their functioning and to facilitate the new representatives from the weaker sections in performing their roles, the bureaucracy has not shown any interest in encouraging nascent institutions in gaining strength. One example of this is the lack of gender sensitivity shown by the bureaucracy in their manner of dealing with the women representatives and the 'pradhan patis' (husband of the (woman) pradhan acting as the de facto pradhan).

On the other hand, despite all the limitations, we have seen that there are places where panchayats as institutions have worked admirably well and where the development machinery has also been facilitative. In these areas, the gains for the poor (often under other adverse economic circumstances) are the highest.

Why have some of these institutions worked well? A full answer is outside the scope of this study. But our analysis suggests some tentative conclusions that can be treated as hypotheses in a more in-depth study.

First, a lesser degree of social and economic inequality, such as that prevailing in the two hill panchayats and in Meerut-B, appears to facilitate democratic functioning and collective action. On the other hand, a high degree of inequality and strong dominance were generally associated with the poorest performances.

Second, a higher degree of literacy and educational attainment (again the highest in the three panchayats mentioned above) also appear to play a similar role.

Third, the *quality* of elected leadership can play an important independent role in improving the performance of local institutions, *even in the presence of inequality*. One can cite here the case of Unnao-A, with its upper-caste woman pradhan. The village had one of the highest prevailing levels of inequality and poverty among the study panchayats. The case of Jaunpur-B panchayat with its less active but relatively benevolent Thakur pradhan is another example. In some of the panchayats, as in Unnao-A, political competition may have spurred the incumbent into good performance, although one can easily visualize political competition/factionalism having a reverse implication.

Fourth, the quality of government more generally, and specifically the nature of the development bureaucracy and its relationship with the elected functionaries are also vital. Bureaucratic functionaries tended to be less oppressive when confronted with a strong elected functionary and a democratic village body. Elected functionaries from poor backgrounds and low castes faced considerably greater constraints, both from within the rural community as well as from these functionaries. Because of this, very few were able to translate considerable degree of solidarity from their own caste/class into effective performance.

The strong performance of women panchayat leaders, even in the UP plains where patriarchal attitudes are strongly entrenched, demonstrates that women who have the capacity to function have been able to overcome gender-based constraints.

Some of the ingredients of successful panchayats mentioned earlier are amenable to broader dimensions of policy (promotion of education, land reform, gender and social equity, and so on) and need to be addressed.

These conclusions also imply that many other significant changes are still needed in shaping the nascent devolutionary process in order to make it more effective. Some steps that could facilitate the process are listed in the following paragraphs.

1. The electoral process in the panchayat elections in UP should be reformed to avoid excessive expenditure and other malpractices.
2. The state should amend the Panchayat Act to ensure that in case of no-confidence against the pradhan he/she is replaced by a member of the same community and gender.
3. There should be a provision for declaration of assets by the electoral contenders.
4. The rules of business of the gram panchayat and gram sabha meetings and the hamlet-wise quorum should be laid down.
5. Norms of identification of beneficiaries, scheme selection, supervision of projects, display of accounts, etc., should be strictly adhered to.
6. There is still ample scope for training and sensitizing both the elected leadership and the bureaucracy. Capacity building of the entire elected team should be a major focus of policy.

7. One of the important areas that needs to be considered is the nature of administrative and financial supervision that the panchayats require—both from above and below. Bureaucratic control over these institutions clearly has a significant negative value and should be replaced by independent watchdog bodies .

8. The panchayat functionary should be under the administrative control of the panchayat.

9. As with the SGSY, a small component of the other funds should be set aside to meet administrative expenditure with the approval of the gram sabha.

As stated in the beginning, devolution of anti-poverty programmes to PRIs has been treated with some scepticism in the light of prevailing rural inequalities. In the case of UP, the existing devolutionary process is also heavily circumscribed by the continuing role of the bureaucracy. It is, therefore, somewhat surprising that even with all the limitations and evidence of poor performance, the beneficiaries of anti-poverty programmes in the study villages and the other villagers still express qualified support for decentralization.

REFERENCES

Bardhan, Pranab and Dilip Mookherjee, 'Capture and Governance at Local and National Levels', *American Economic Review*, May 2000, pp. 135–9.

Bardhan, Pranab, 'Decentralized Development', *Indian Economic Review*, 31(2), 1996, pp. 139–56.

———, 'Corruption and Development: A Review of Issues', *Journal of Economic Literature*, 35 (3), September 1997, pp. 1320–46.

Bird, R.M., 'Decentralising Infrastructure: For Good or for Ill?', in A. Estache (ed.), *Decentralising Infrastructure: Advantages and Limitations*, (World Bank Discussion Papers 290), Washington, DC: World Bank, 1995.

Crook, R. and J. Manor, 'Enhancing Participation and Institutional Performance Democratic Decentralisation in South Asia and West Africa', Report to Overseas Development Administration, 1994.

Lieten, G.K. and Ravi Srivastava, *Unequal Partners: Power Relations, Devolution and Development in UP*, New Delhi: Sage Publications, 1999.

Olson, Mancur, *The Logic of Collective Action: Public Goods and the Theory of Groups*, Cambridge: MA Harvard University Press, 1965.

Prud'homme R., 'The Dangers of Decentralisation', *World Bank Research Observer*, August 1995.

Shleifer, Andrei and Robert Vishny, 'Corruption', *Quarterly Journal of Economics*, 108 (3), 1993, pp. 599–617.

Srivastava, Nisha, 'Social Security in U.P.: Moving Beyond Policy to Governance', in S. Mahendra, P. Antony, V. Gayathri, R.P. Mamgain (eds), *Social and Economic Security in India*, New Delhi: Institute for Human Development, 2001.

Srivastava, Ravi S., 'Devolution in India since the 73rd Amendment: Impact on Safety Nets and the Social Sector', Background Paper for the World Bank (Reducing Poverty in India: Options for More Effective Public Services, Report No. 17881-IN, Poverty Reduction and Economic Management Unit, South Asia Region) Washington, DC: World Bank, 1998a.

———, 'Programmes for Poverty Alleviation and Decentralisation in U.P.', Background Paper to the UP Economic and Fiscal Report, World Bank, 1998b.

———, 'Governance and Decentralisation in Uttar Pradesh', Background Paper to the Uttar Pradesh Human Development Report (draft), 2001.

———, 'Evaluation of Anti-poverty Programmes in Uttar Pradesh', Study Report, Planning Commission, New Delhi, 2002.

6

Decentralization and Disease Control Programmes
The Case of Filariasis*

■ RAMA V. BARU AND MEENA GOPAL

This chapter explores the feasibility and effectiveness of decentralization of disease control programmes with special reference to filariasis. In India, national disease control programmes are planned and designed at the central level and administered by the states. These programmes are conceptualized and administered as 'vertical programmes' with focus on a specific disease. During the 1990s, there was considerable debate on the need to decentralize health services through panchayati raj institutions. The primary motivation for this was to reduce the fiscal burden on the state and also to make them more responsive to the needs of the community. The experience of decentralization of health services has been varied and has very often not been priority for panchayats. The primary concerns of panchayats have been to invest in roads, education, water supply, sanitation, and the like. Health services have been brought under the control of panchayats in very few states. Even in these states, the devolution of financial and administrative control of these services to the panchayat is only partial (Nayar 2001). Given this scenario, two sets of issues arise when the concept of decentralization is applied to disease control programmes. Since these programmes are vertical in nature, the principles of decentralization are antithetical to their centralized approach. The second issue that is of importance is the concern that even if communities are given the responsibility for these programmes, will they be able and willing to assume responsibility for their planning, delivery, monitoring, and evaluation? Third, how willing are the personnel at different levels of the health services to devolve decisions to communities?

   This chapter draws upon a study that tried to evaluate the feasibility of a community and health services directed strategy for drug delivery as a part of the National Filariasis Control Programme, and highlights the possibilities and limitations of decentralization for this programme. The chapter is divided into three sections. The first is an introduction, which includes a background of the programme. The second section discusses the objectives, scope, and process of the study. The third section discusses the outcome of the two approaches adopted for drug delivery and analyses the reasons for the differences in coverage levels in the two approaches and its implications for decentralization.

INTRODUCTION

Even five decades after Independence, the major cause of death in India continues to be a host of communicable diseases. The government has initiated a number of programmes to control these diseases and they include programmes for the control of malaria, tuberculosis, and filariasis. These programmes have been largely centrally funded and implemented through the state government as vertical programmes (Banerji 1985).

The National Filariasis Control Programme was started in 1952 and it had two major components that included vector control, and detection and treatment of infectious cases through night blood smears. In the 1980s the programme initiated an annual mass administration of a drug, diethylcarbomazine (DEC), to the entire population for limiting the transmission of infection for a period of five years. This drug was administered to the entire population and excluded only the elderly, pregnant women, children below one year, and those suffering from serious illnesses. Since this drug had to be consumed by the entire community and required high coverage for interrupting transmission, a study was undertaken to assess the effectiveness of two strategies of drug administration, namely, one that involved delivery of the drug through the health services and the other the community through the panchayat. This chapter summarizes the process and results of a study that examined the feasibility and effectiveness of these two strategies for the control of filariasis. Filariasis manifests itself as two clinical conditions—elephantiasis, which is swelling of limbs due to the blocking of the lymphatic system, and hydrocele, which affects the scrotal sac.

OBJECTIVES, SCOPE, AND PROCESS OF THE STUDY

The objectives of the study were:

1. To assess the process and effectiveness of a delivery strategy of mass treatment with DEC by the regular health care system and to identify possible improvements.
2. To develop, implement, and assess the process and effectiveness of a system of Community Directed Treatment (ComDT) for control of filariasis, which includes health services at the level of implementation.
3. To compare the feasibility, effectiveness, and potential sustainability of the two approaches.

THE STUDY SITES AND DESIGN

For the purpose of this study, three districts representing different levels of development and endemicity were selected. These districts were Kozhikode from Kerala, Rajamundhry from Andhra Pradesh, and Varanasi from UP. Within each of these districts two blocks were selected to implement the drug distribution through the existing health services and in the others, the initiative was left to the community for the drug distribution. Finally, the feasibility and effectiveness of the community-directed treatment and the health services-directed treatment were evaluated and compared. The study was conducted in two phases. The first focused on understanding the community structure, decision-making processes through the panchayats at the village level, and the interaction between the community and the health services. The second was the implementation of the drug administration component of the programme through both the community and the health services. It also included an evaluation of coverage in these districts (NICD 1999 and 2000).

THE PROCESS

As mentioned earlier, this study was conducted in two phases. The first phase involved collecting information on the structure of the district, block, and village, health services organization, decision-making processes through the panchayat at the village level, and the participation of the different castes and religious groups in the decision-making process. In addition, information was elicited about past experiences of the communities with development programmes, their interaction and experiences with the health services system, and the community's perception, knowledge, and attitude towards filariasis.

STRUCTURE OF COMMUNITIES AND DECISION-MAKING PROCESSES

Across the three sites, the study population was rural and the major occupation was agriculture and allied activities. The majority of the population was Hindu, followed by Muslims and Christians. In Kozhikode Muslims constituted nearly 30 per cent of the population. As far as caste composition was concerned, 24.7 per cent belonged to upper-castes, 51.1 per cent to Backward Classes, and 24.1 per cent to Scheduled Castes. In Rajamundhry, 38.9 per cent belonged to the upper-castes, 38.6 per cent to Backward Classes, 21.5 per cent to Scheduled Castes, and 1.1 per cent to Scheduled Tribes. In Kozhikode, 17.1 per cent belonged to upper-castes, 70.1 per cent to Backward Classes, 12 per cent to Scheduled Castes, and 0.8 per cent to Scheduled Tribes (Tables 6.1 and 6.2).

In both Varanasi and Rajamundhry, the settlement pattern within the village was based on caste differences, with the Scheduled Castes and minorities living on the peripheries. In Kozhikode, the differences were not so apparent in the settlement pattern as in the other two. Across sites, the panchayat was the socio-political organization through which decisions were taken at the village.

TABLE 6.1: RELIGION OF RESPONDENTS

Religious Groups	Study site			Total
	Kozhikode	East Godavari	Varanasi	
Hindu	495	667	700	1,862
	(69.2%)	(92.9%)	(91.6%)	(84.8%)
Muslim	217	9	64	290
	(30.3%)	(1.3%)	(8.4%)	(13.2%)
Christian	3	42	0	45
	(0.4%)	(5.8%)	(0.0%)	(2.0%)
Total	715	718	764	2,197

Source: Field survey, 2000.

TABLE 6.2 DISTRIBUTION OF THE RESPONDENTS ACCORDING
TO CASTE

Religious group	Study site			Total
	Kozhikode	East Godavari	Varanasi	
Upper-castes	81	259	173	513
	(17.1%)	(38.9%)	(24.7%)	(27.9%)
Backward Classes	333	257	358	948
	(70.1%)	(38.6%)	(51.1%)	(51.5%)
Scheduled Castes	57	143	169	369
	(12.0%)	(21.5%)	(24.1%)	(20.0%)
Scheduled Tribes	4	7	0	11
	(0.8%)	(1.1%)	(0.0%)	(0.6%)
Total	475	666	700	1,841

Source: Field survey, 2000.

In Kozhikode, Rajamundhry, and Varanasi, the panchayats were functional and dominated by Backward Classes and upper-castes, while the minorities and Scheduled Castes were poorly represented. As a Dalit from one of the villages in Rajamundhry remarked: 'The panchayat is dominated by Backward Classes and upper-castes. Normally we do not have adequate representation on the panchayat. The decisions are benefiting mainly the upper castes.'Women belonging to the Dalit sections said: 'We have little say in the panchayat. There are no representatives from our *"peta"* [area] on the panchayat. We are on the edge of the village and totally cut off from the rest of the village. We have been telling the panchayat that our roads are in bad shape but nobody bothers. Every year they make promises at the time of elections and soon after forget about us.' In Varanasi the Dalits shared a similar perception. They said: 'The upper-caste people are reluctant to involve lower-caste people in the decision-making process. They do not invite us for meetings, nor do they ask for our opinion. At the end of the meeting they ask us for our signature and we sign. We are only labourers in the villages and it is the upper castes that take most of the decisions' (NICD 1999).

The minorities and Dalits in Kozhikode shared this kind of a perception: 'Now under the people's plan, it is the committees which decide everything, but there are a lot of shortcomings. Deserving persons do not get anything and the non-deserving get everything allotted to them.'

In Varanasi, the Dalits and minorities felt left out of the decision-making process and remarked that after decisions were taken they were conveyed to them. There was better representation of women in Rajamundhry and Kozhikode as compared to Varanasi. In Kozhikode, women participated actively in the panchayat compared to either Rajamundhry or Varanasi.

The decision-making process in the panchayat is effected through a meeting of its members. However, the structures were far more elaborate in Kerala as compared to the other two sites. At the neighbourhood level there were committees called 'ayalkootams' for every fifty households, with a convenor. The convenor initiated meetings at the ward level and included political representatives or club representatives. All decisions were made in these committees. For health-related matters there were working committees known as *karma samitis*, that consisted of medical officers, sanitary inspectors, panchayat members, and club and political representatives. The task of this committee was to prepare plans relating to institutions, manpower, and drug supplies. There were no such structures for decision-making in Rajamundhry and Varanasi. In both these sites the panchayat does not have any control over government health institutions. Here, the activities of the panchayat for health-related matters are restricted to chlorination of wells and digging ditches. (NICD 1999).

It is interesting to point out that across all three sites, the community has initiated religious and cultural activities, but when it comes to health and other development activities, they are restricted to assisting government programmes and national health programmes like Pulse Polio and Family Planning. A number of youth, women's groups, and NGOs were active across the three sites. In Kozhikode there were youth clubs which are involved in sports, literacy, and cultural activities. In Rajamundhry there were youth clubs, and the district women's credit groups are very active. These groups have played a significant role in assisting government programmes for maternal and child health.

In Kajaluru village in East Godavari district the health department trained members of the groups formed under the scheme for

Developmemt of Women and Children in Rural Areas (DWCRA) to prevent and treat diarrhoeal diseases. 'In Kajaluru we have given furoxone tablets and paracetamol tablets to some members of the DWCRA for treating fever and diarrhoea. We also have given them oral rehydration therapy (ORT) packets and informed the community that it is available with the DWCRA members. We have organized and trained interested members in this activity' (Group discussion with female health workers, Dugguduru Primary Health Centre, East Godavari). Similarly, in Kozhikode, volunteers were entlisted from the Mahila Swasth Sanghs (Women's Health Collectives) for the Pulse Polio programme. In addition, support was elicited from them to distribute oral rehydration solution (ORS) packets and manage Nirodh depots. However, the community as such has not used these volunteers. According to a medical officer in a primary health centre (PHC) in East Godavari district: 'These programmes have been discouraging because people do not go to community distributors but come to the health workers when they have a health problem' (NICD 1999).

Voluntary services by individuals or groups in the community as far as health programmes are concerned are no longer 'voluntary'. Volunteers are paid an incentive by these programmes, whether it is for motivating the community, participating in a training programme, or any other related activity by the government.

PERCEPTIONS AND FELT NEEDS OF THE COMMUNITY
REGARDING FILARIASIS

Across sites the awareness level regarding filariasis was high, but the perception of it being a risk to the individual and community was low. People were aware how the disease is transmitted and attributed it to the mosquito. The general awareness of filariasis was 97.3 per cent in Kozhikode, 89.7 per cent in East Godavari, and 91.6 per cent in Varanasi. However, the proportion of those who felt it was a problem for their community was lower, only 63 per cent felt it so for elephantiasis and 45 per cent for hydrocele. Even a smaller proportion perceived these two conditions as a threat to themselves or their families (21 per cent for elephantiasis and 14 per cent for hydrocele) (ibid.).

The experience of these communities with the health services also varied across the three sites. Varanasi had a weak health service structure in terms of accessability, availability, and responsiveness when compared to Rajamundhry and Kozhikode. Across the three sites the majority of the respondents reported that health workers only visited them once in a while, mostly for immunization and family planning activities. The major problems cited included non-availability of medicines, distance from the health centre, long waiting period, and the indifferent behaviour of the staff in all three sites. As a result, the utilization of public health services varied across the three sites. In Kozhikode people expressed satisfaction with the public services but people preferred to use the services of private practitioners for acute problems. Those who used PHCs did so for immunizations or if they did not have adequate money to pay for a private doctor. In Rajamundhry, people expressed satisfaction with the health services, but there were variations across caste and gender. Women from Scheduled Castes and minorities said that the health workers did not visit them as often as other parts of the village. The lack of medicines, long waiting periods, and indifferent behaviour of staff affected the Backward Classes and Scheduled Castes much more since they had to buy drugs from chemists when they went to public hospitals and they could not afford the cost of going to private practitioners. In Varanasi the majority of the respondents were not satisfied with the health services. The lower-castes felt they were discriminated against. Even when they called health workers for conducting deliveries, they had to be paid something (NICD 1999).

OUTCOME OF THE TWO STRATEGIES AND FACTORS INFLUENCING IT

The study shows that there are great variations in both coverage and effectiveness across the three sites and the two strategies. The treatment coverage was highest in Kerala through both the strategies. Compared to Kerala, the treatment coverage for both strategies was much lower in Varanasi and Rajamundhry. The performance of the community directed approach in both these districts was markedly poorer than through the health services (see Table 6.3).

Several factors have influenced for these variations in coverage and compliance.[1] Some of the key reasons are discussed.

TABLE 6.3: THE REPORTED AND OBSERVED TREATMENT
COVERAGE AND COMPLIANCE

Site districts	Reported coverage (%)	Observed coverage (survey) /compliance	
Kozhikode	79	75	/ 72
Rajahmundry	92	65	/ 62
Varanasi	78	51	/ 32

Source: Field Survey, 2000, cited in UNDP/World Bank/WHO-TDR (2001) *Drug Delivery Strategies for Lymphatic Filariasis Elimination in India*, Report of a Multicentre Study.

THE ENDEMICITY LEVELS OF THE DISEASE AND
PEOPLE'S PERCEPTIONS ABOUT IT

The levels of endemicity and the extent of 'risk' perceived by people is an important factor for compliance. It was observed that people did not perceive filariasis as a major threat as compared to other diseases. It must be pointed out that filariasis is not a 'killer' when compared to diarrhoea, pneumonia, or tuberculosis. This will definitely shape perceptions of people regarding the risk that this disease poses in their lives. Even as far as the priorities of the government are concerned, filariasis control is given a lower priority as compared to malaria, tuberculosis, and AIDS. This could explain why a 'campaign mode' for a filaria programme may not get the necessary visibility and support from the higher levels of the health service and political system, which is unlike the case for immunization or AIDS.

ACCESSIBILITY, AVAILABILITY, AND QUALITY OF HEALTH SERVICES

Accessibility, availability, and quality of services varied across the three sites and this had a bearing on coverage and compliance levels. While Kerala had better health services outreach, Rajamundhry was somewhere in the middle, but in Varanasi it was poor. The number of posts that were unfilled at all levels in the PHC and SCs was higher in Varanasi than Kerala or Rajamundhry. An additional factor that needs to be mentioned is that in Kerala, the health services were under the control of panchayats, whereas in the other two sites this was not the case. Health activities at the panchayat level in Varanasi and Rajamundhry were largely restricted to chlorination of wells or provision of water supply.

The data shows that the coverage levels were higher in the health services strategy in Kozhikode as compared to Rajamundhry and Varanasi (Table 6.3). One of the reasons for this is that the quality of the health service outreach is better in the former compared to the last two sites. The other important factor is that the state of health services has an influence on people's perceptions and experiences with the health service system. As discussed earlier, lack of drugs, distance of facililties, and indifferent behaviour of the health service staff contribute to lower levels of trust and therefore utilization of services. The issue of coverage is related to the state of health services, and in the community-directed arm it was influenced by the manner in which the drug was distributed. In some instances the panchayat leader and his family distributed drugs, while in others drug distributors were selected and trained. The study found that coverage levels were better when drug distributors were involved in the distribution.

Another important issue that came up in this study is that high or medium coverage did not result in compliance, that is, even if tablets were distributed to the households, it did not automatically mean that people consumed them. The gap between coverage and compliance can be related to a number of factors. First, the issue of whether people perceived the disease itself as a threat; second, they often were not convinced why healthy people should take the drug; and third, there was no perceived benefit after taking the drug. In addition, the side effects produced by the drug was an important reason for not complying. The last two became even more significant in the community-directed villages since 'non-health' personnel were administering the drug and they did not feel confident to manage them. Therefore, the experience of side effects of the drug became an important reason for non-compliance (NICD 2000).

VARIATIONS IN THE COMMUNITY-DIRECTED STRATEGY

In order to explain the variations in coverage across sites for the community-directed strategy, the structure of communities and caste composition of panchayats played a key role in the decision-making processes. During the first phase it was evident that Dalits and minorities felt that they were not involved in the decision-making process and often did not really gain as much from welfare inputs as did the other castes. This was expressed very forcefully in Varanasi as compared to Rajamundhry and Kerala. The decision-making process varied across the sites. In Kerala there were structures for decision making as discussed earlier. In the other two sites these structures were absent. Decision-making was, therefore, carried out by the panchayat when initiated by the sarpanch. Qualitative explorations regarding reasons for lower coverage in the community-directed strategy in Rajamundhry and Varanasi revealed that the selection of drug distributors was an important reason. In villages with better coverage, the drug distributors were selected from different strata of the community and there was better representation of different sections in the community. In villages with low coverage, either they did not have distributors or they were drawn from only the upper and middle strata, as a result of which the minorities and Dalits were 'left out'. The work patterns and migration of agricultural labourers also affected coverage since they were in the fields or had gone to work in nearby towns when the drug was distributed.

THE ROLE OF HEALTH WORKERS AND HEALTH SERVICES

In both approaches an important reason for low coverage included shortage of manpower, poor planning, and poor participation of vulnerable sections. The nature and quality of interaction between the health services and the community was also an important issue. In villages where health workers took the initiative to mobilize the community, it resulted in higher coverage. Much of it involved door to door canvassing, holding weekly meetings, and mobilizing through women's and youth groups, which required time and energy being spent by the health workers. In the community-directed approach, the attitude and willingness of the health personnel to devolve responsibility to the community did influence the coverage. A majority of the health personnel felt that the communities are incapable of carrying out the necessary tasks for such a programme. Some of the reasons cited by the health workers were that people have poor knowledge, there were caste differences, and the community had poor skills for organization, which had hampered the process. In their perception, communities must support their programmes, but should not be given the responsibility for implementation (NICD 2000).

MONITORING AND EVALUATION

Monitoring and evaluation is an essential component of any health programme for which records need to be maintained. In villages where the community was given responsibility for drug delivery, a small percentage of them maintained records. The health services, on the other hand, have a fairly elaborate system of record-keeping (NICD 2000). All health programmes require records for monitoring, evaluation, and future planning. Therefore, decentralization of programmes without back-up for data collection would impair programme planning. Disease control programmes require planning for large populations and therefore some amount of centralized planning is necessary.

CONCLUSION

The earlier analysis shows that decentralization of health programmes is programmatically and administratively a complex process. Merely handing over responsibilities to the community without financial and administrative back-up at different levels, namely, block, district, state, and Centre, results in poor outcomes. Ideally, a decentralized approach to disease control programmes must build in structures and processes that address the priorities of communities. This would then mean a 'bottom-up' approach to programme planning that has been talked about for decades. An additional issue that needs to be addressed, which was raised through this study, is the issue of how much responsibility communities are willing to take for health programmes. This study showed that across sites, the communities were willing to assist health personnel, but felt that they did not possess the expertise or skills to handle different aspects of the programme. While one may argue that health personnel do not want to give up their 'technical expertise', the community may also not have the necessary skills or be willing to direct a disease control programme that they perceive as the responsibility of the public health services. The experience of decentralization in this study can be best described as 'deconcentration' since all decisions regarding financing, technology, and implementation were centrally directed with the community only involved for the implementation of the programme. A number of valuable issues have been highlighted in this study that clearly underlines the complexities involved in decentralization of health programmes.

NOTES

*   The paper is based on a study entitled 'Drug Delivery Strategies for Lymphatic Filariasis Elimination in India', funded by the UNDP, World Bank, and WHO Special Programme for Research and Training in Tropical Diseases (TDR). We would like to thank all those who were a part of this study team. These include scientists from the National Institute of Communicable Diseases (NICD), Delhi, regional centres of the NICD at Rajamundhry, Varanasi, and Kozhikode, Jawaharlal Nehru University, New Delhi, SNDT Women's University, Mumbai, and the Tropical Disease Research division of WHO, Geneva.

1.   Coverage indicates the households that have been given the drug, and compliance refers to the actual consumption of the drug.

REFERENCES

Banerji, D., *Health and Family Planning Services in India: An Epidemiological, Socio-cultural and Political Analysis and a Perspective,* New Delhi: Lok Paksh, 1985.

National Institute of Communicable Diseases (NICD), *Community Directed Treatment of Lymphatic Filariasis in Kozhikode, East Godavari and Varanasi Districts of India,* Report of Phase I, New Delhi, 1999.

————, *Community Directed Treatment of Lymphatic Filariasis: Rajamundhry,* Draft Final Report, Rajamundhry, Andhra Pradesh, 2000.

————, *Community Directed Treatment of Lymphatic Filariasis: Kozhikode,* Draft Final Report, Kozhikode, Kerala, 2000.

Nayar, K.R., 'Politics of Decentralisation: Lessons from Kerala', in Imrana Qadeer, Kasturi Sen, and K.R. Nayar (eds), *Public Health and the Poverty of Reforms: The South Asian Predicament,* New Delhi: Sage Publications, 2001, pp. 363–78.

UNDP/World Bank/ WHO-TDR, *Drug Delivery Strategies for Lymphatic Filariasis Elimination in India,* Report of a Multi Centre Study, 2001.

7

The New Segregation in Primary Education
Implications for Local Governance*

■ VIMALA RAMACHANDRAN AND AARTI SAIHJEE

It is commonly believed that the decade of the 1990s was one of the most productive decades in primary education—a decade not only of tremendous churning, but also one where the country made a significant leap in literacy rates. While India still has a long way to go before we are able to ensure good quality basic education for all children up to the age of fourteen, even the worst of the sceptics will agree that the decade was one of optimism—the 2001 Census revealed that 65.4 per cent people (75.85 for men and 54.16 for women) are now literate, and that for the first time the absolute number of illiterates actually went down. It revealed a decadal jump of 11.8 per cent in the literacy rate among men and 15 per cent among women—Chhattisgarh recorded a jump of 24.87 per cent in literacy levels among women, Madhya Pradesh a 20.93 per cent jump in female literacy, and Rajasthan a jump 'of 21.47 (M) and 23.90 (F) per cent. A number of programmes were initiated during this period and the government mobilized considerable external funds for primary education.[1] While all this is indeed creditworthy, voices from below tell us that all is not well. Primary education is not only about formal access and literacy rates. It may be recalled that the National Policy of Education (NPE), 1986, stressed that the central issue was 'removal of disparities and to equalize educational opportunity by attending to the specific needs of those who have been denied equality so far'. The focus was both on education and social equality. The Programme of Action (POA) (Government of India 1992) correctly highlighted the intervening and empowering role of education in people's struggles for equality and justice. The question before us is whether the decade of the 1990s has made a difference to those who have been left out or pushed out of the education system.

This chapter, based on a recently completed study on the experience of the District Primary Education Programme (DPEP) titled

'Hierarchies of Access: Gender and Social Equity in Primary Education' (Ramachandran 2002) attempts to capture the impact of primary education programmes on the ground. The study started by acknowledging the historical baggage of social and economic inequalities that has reinforced educational disparities for over 50 years. Ploughing through data generated through the Censuses (1991 and 2001) and sample surveys on the one hand and education department statistics Educational Management Information System (EMIS and PMIS [Project Management Information System] of DPEP), we realized that most data fails to capture social and gender gaps. Our research team took on board the problems with relying on gross enrolment data, particularly from schools and the education department, since they are marked by a tendency for over-reporting. Instead, we tried to look at net enrolment, retention, transition, and average years of schooling data disaggregated by gender, social grouping, and type of school to assess the effectiveness of policies. We tried, wherever possible, to complement this data with information on dropouts and on those who have never attended school (Visaria and Ramachandran 2002). Our hunch about the inadequacy of existing data was confirmed—and we decided to supplement the desk review of DPEP data and project information with six qualitative studies. We examined if gender and equity issues had been 'mainstreamed', or whether they remained sporadic and localized. This led us to analyse if and how equity strategies were positioned in the programme and whether alternative schools and those under the Education Guarantee Scheme (EGS) are fast emerging as *the* vehicle to bridge the equity gap, especially with respect to children from disadvantaged communities and in scattered habitations. An important focus of our research related to a subtle but nevertheless discernible hierarchy of access in education resulting in a new form of segregation in primary schools. This chapter is based on our finding from the desk review and six qualitative studies.[2]

THE DISTRICT PRIMARY EDUCATION PROGRAMME

The District Primary Education Programme (DPEP) was initiated as a part of the larger Social Safety Net Credit Adjustment Loan under the Structural Adjustment Programme of the World Bank to India in 1991. Taking off from the policy guidelines in NPE 1986 and drawing upon the experience of a range of primary education programmes, the DPEP Guidelines of 1994 state that holistic planning and management are necessary to achieve universal primary education, and that it 'should incorporate a gender perspective in all aspects of the planning and implementation process'. It recognizes the importance of mainstreaming gender and making it an integral part of the DPEP, the need for gender focus in tackling the problem of access, retention, and achievement levels, and the importance of reaching out to children from the most disadvantaged groups/communities. Educationally backward districts with female literacy below the national average were taken as the priority districts. Equally, the project stressed education for socially disadvantaged groups. The goals set by the DPEP are:

1. reduce differences in enrolment, dropout, and learning achievements between gender and social groups to less than 5 per cent;
2. reduce overall primary dropout rates for all students to less than 10 per cent;
3. raise average achievement levels by at least 25 per cent over measured baseline levels by ensuring achievement of basic literacy and numeracy competencies, and a minimum of 40 per cent achievement levels in other competencies for all primary school children; and
4. provide access for all children to primary schooling or its equivalent non-formal education.

These goals bring out the programme's intent to increase coverage of girls, improve their academic achievements, and reduce gender disparities in respect of enrolment, retention, and learning achievements (DPEP et al. 2000a). Essentially, the DPEP adopted a two-pronged strategy to meet the gender and social equity goals:

1. Make the education system more responsive to the needs and constraints of girls and children from disadvantaged communities.
2. Create a community demand for girls' education and enabling conditions for greater participation.

In pursuance of these objectives, the DPEP created local structures for community participation and the involvement of local self-government institutions, namely, village education committees, school development and management committees, and mother–teacher associations. The panchayat pradhan was expected to play a crucial role in the functioning of these committees.

The DPEP is currently operational in eighteen states and 271 districts after taking into account recent bifurcations and trifurcations in districts and the carving out of three new states. Twenty-three districts of Gujarat, Orissa, and Rajasthan were included since April 2001.

OVERWHELMING FINDING

The overwhelming finding that emerged from the desk review of reports and data on education in the 1990s is that there has been a significant increase in overall literacy rates and school participation rates across the country. Gender and social disparities have declined with an overall increase in school attendance.[3] This is more than confirmed by the Census 2001 data and also the recent NFHS-II (1998–9) data. Perhaps the most significant change that has taken place in the 1990s is the increase in the demand for primary education across the country. Intensive campaigns, enrolment drives, and the changing social and economic situation contributed to an appreciable increase in the demand for schooling.

There has been a decline in the proportion of never enrolled children. Data also reveals an increase in the number of schools across the country—alternative schools (AS), Education Guarantee Scheme schools (EGS), and private aided and private unaided schools. The DPEP was initiated in low female literacy areas, and it is encouraging to note that very low female literacy districts have shown the maximum gains in literacy levels, especially in MP, Chhattisgarh, and Rajasthan (Census 2001). The share of girls to total enrolment in very low female literacy districts increased from 43.8 per cent in 1995–6 to 46.7 per cent in 1998–9 (Aggarwal 2000a, 2000b).

While this is indeed an encouraging trend, the data also indicates that we still have a long way to go before gender and social gaps are bridged. As Aggarwal (2000a) points out

While household enumeration has been conducted in many DPEP districts/ state to identify out-of-school children, the findings are not available in most of the cases....The NSS estimates (52nd round data, 1995–6) indicate that 31 per cent of children in the 6–11 age group were not attending school...

availability of schooling facility even within the habitation does not offer any guarantee that all children in the eligible age group attend school.

This observation is reinforced by Vaidyanathan and Nair (2001): 'While the narrowing of spatial disparities suggests that educationally poor areas have experienced, in general, relatively rapid improvements, scrutiny at a more disaggregated level (talukas and villages) reveals the existence of pockets of persistent educational backwardness.'

A large number of children belonging to disadvantaged communities, working children, and children with special needs have not yet been covered (coverage of AS and EGS schools are limited to some regions of the country). DPEP data reveals that this is particularly true of phase-II districts, where participation levels are still very low. Similarly, children living in urban slums and peripheral areas have largely remained outside the reach of the DPEP. Without addressing the concerns of urban out-of-school children, the goal of universalization of primary education (UPE) cannot be achieved in its entirety. Household surveys coordinated in 1997–8 by Vaidyanathan and Nair (ibid.) further confirm that 'literacy rate variations across space and between gender and caste groups are highly correlated; and that higher overall literacy goes with lower disparities between these groups'. Hence, the more educationally backward the region, the greater are social and gender inequalities (see Table 7.1).

However, we have yet to generate adequate data on educational access of disadvantaged groups. While the National Sample Survey (NSS), NFHS, and other sample survey data give us a macro picture, intra-regional and intra-community diversities as such are not captured in such surveys. Further, given the time lag in publication of detailed Census 2001 tables, most researchers are still relying on 1991 Census data, which is outdated, particularly in the light of preliminary 2001 data that reveals a significant jump in literacy levels. Some specific studies/data (mostly done before 1993) have addressed the issue of access and performance of marginal social groups. The National Council for Applied Economic Research (NCAER) data (Table 7.1) indicates the wide fluctuations between the literacy rates for men and women belonging to landless families, and Scheduled Tribe and Scheduled Caste households in selected states. For instance, in UP the overall literacy rates for men and women are 62 and 28 per cent respectively, and these figures sharply contrast correspondingly with

TABLE 7.1: EDUCATIONAL INDICATORS OF SELECT STATES (Percentage)

Indicator	Kerala	Tamil Nadu	Uttar Pradesh	Rajasthan	West Bengal	Maha-rashtra	Orissa	Haryana	Madhya Pradesh
Literacy rate (7+)									
Male	93.00	75.00	62.00	60.00	66.00	71.00	68.00	70.00	59.00
Female	87.00	53.00	28.00	19.00	50.00	47.00	41.00	38.00	27.00
Net enrolment rate (6–14)									
Male	99.00	91.00	73.00	78.00	67.00	88.00	79.00	84.00	69.00
Female	98.00	84.00	53.00	42.00	65.00	82.00	63.00	72.00	56.00
Discontinuation rate (6–14)									
Male	1.50	7.50	3.30	3.10	5.90	5.90	6.20	3.90	7.00
Female	2.00	14.80	5.60	6.60	6.90	8.40	9.30	4.60	9.00
Literacy rate of landless wage earners									
Male	86.50	60.50	38.20	44.00	43.60	54.60	43.00	52.50	40.10
Female	77.90	41.40	7.40	5.60	27.50	29.20	15.70	24.20	14.10
Literacy rate of medium-size landholders									
Male	98.40	89.30	80.50	63.70	83.80	70.10	85.90	72.50	64.20
Female	92.70	49.70	41.60	19.80	68.60	49.40	55.70	39.10	28.20
Literacy rate of large landholders									
Male	98.60	87.80	83.10	65.90	93.40	84.20	87.10	72.80	73.00
Female	100.00	61.10	53.80	21.40	84.30	51.40	64.20	45.30	37.60
Literacy rate of STs									
Male	—	—	—	39.10	—	52.90	40.70	—	42.80
Female	—	—	—	7.50	—	25.20	15.60	—	16.80

(Table 7.1 Contd)

(*Table 7.1 Contd*)

Indicator	Kerala	Tamil Nadu	Uttar Pradesh	Rajasthan	West Bengal	Maha-rashtra	Orissa	Haryana	Madhya Pradesh
Literacy rate of SCs									
Male	82.60	57.30	48.10	51.80	62.50	60.50	60.40	60.10	47.40
Female	72.20	37.40	13.80	9.10	46.00	34.40	29.80	28.90	17.50
Literacy rate of dominant minority									
Male	94.00	85.80	47.10	45.90	59.30	75.60	73.60	84.50	67.10
Female	89.40	67.90	20.20	7.80	44.40	52.10	41.50	59.70	30.30
Literacy rate of other Hindus									
Male	95.00	80.60	70.80	66.40	75.50	76.80	78.40	74.00	69.10
Female	87.40	57.90	35.60	23.90	58.80	51.50	52.40	43.10	34.50
Ever enrolment rate of landless wage earners									
Male	98.40	88.40	52.70	63.10	51.10	77.10	62.20	69.10	54.10
Female	100.00	76.80	25.80	15.20	45.50	72.50	32.20	50.00	39.30
Discontinuation rate of landless wage earners									
Male	1.70	9.50	5.20	4.10	3.50	6.00	11.40	4.60	9.20
Female	6.10	17.40	4.40	17.20	16.20	12.30	19.80	4.40	13.40

Source: Shariff and Sudarshan (1996).

38.20 and 7.40 per cent among landless families and 48.10 and 13.80 per cent among the Scheduled Castes.

Researchers have pointed out that 50 per cent of Dalit children who enter primary school leave by class V, with a majority dropping out before they reach class III (Nambissan 2001). According to the MODE/UNICEF report (1995):

The socio-economic profile appears to be a barrier to enrolment directly or indirectly. SC/ST families tend to live in colonies removed by a kilometre or more from the main village. A school in the village within walking distance for the families in the main village would still be at a distance to these children. Secondly, a feeling of alienation from the rest of the village and in turn fears (real or otherwise) of discrimination in school may keep these children away from school. At an indirect level, the high incidence of non-enrolment in SC/ST families almost 'legitimises' not going to school and makes it the norm rather that the exception in the community.

The learning environment, attitude of teachers, backstopping support from home/parents, and the sheer economics of school participation for extremely poor/landless families—all these factors tend to push children out of school.[4] Dominant perceptions about mental abilities of Dalit or tribal children, coupled with stereotypes about certain communities, lead to subtle and sometimes even blatant discrimination against some children.[5]

What about girls? We have made considerable progress with respect to girls' enrolment and, as revealed in the 2001 Census, in the more backward regions like Madhya Pradesh, Rajasthan, and Chhattisgarh, many more girls are in school than ever before. However, the situation of girls in poor households among disadvantaged groups remains a cause for concern. Education may be technically free, but it is not so in reality. Given the quality of government schools, parents also incur some expenditure on tuitions, even though this is more prevalent among children going to private unaided and aided schools. This has many implications for girls' participation (Bashir 2000; De et al. 2001). While gender is a determining factor at the time of decision-making by parents on whether and where to enrol, independent research studies and DPEP studies reveal that gender inequities and gender bias were not significant among enrolled girl children (De et al. 2001).

Administrators, educational researchers, and development practitioners agree that discrimination inside the school continues to be a major barrier in school participation for girls and other marginal groups (Madan 2002). Unfortunately, without the availability of adequate data, it is not possible to make generalizations on push-and-pull factors in the DPEP. With the exception of recent household survey data from Karnataka, the project has not generated any kind of textured micro data. This continues to be an important lacuna in the DPEP information system.

These extant issues of access and social equity in government formal schools are overwhelming and need to be given constant priority. Issues of equity in education seem to have taken on more complex overtones within the emergent context of declining enrolment in formal government schools, the growth of private schools across the nation, and the opening of state-sponsored alternative schools and education guarantee schemes in some parts of the country. This new development seems to be reinforcing the existing stratification evident in our educational system in rural areas (which so far has been a defining feature of urban areas). *Further, what is significant is that it is giving rise to a new trend of 'hierarchies of access', whereby, paradoxically, the democratization of access to schools seems to be accompanied by a reaffirmation of a child's caste, community, and gender in defining which school she or he attends.*

To add to the complexity, accumulating empirical evidence illustrates that while most teachers in private schools are untrained and work under adverse conditions, teachers in the extant government schools or the AS/EGS are ill equipped to address the needs of first-generation learners. In addition to concerns of quality and standards, what is disturbing is that there is no consistent policy vis-à-vis unrecognized schools. The remainder of this paper is devoted to exploring the variety of factors that frame these emerging dynamics of 'hierarchy of access' and their implications for issues of equity.

HIERARCHIES OF ACCESS: DEFINING THE PROBLEM

A significant revelation in recent years has been the documentation of a gradual decline in class I enrolment. As Aggarwal (2000a) points out:

Over the years, the enrolment in formal schools has shown declining trends.... It is observed that the states, which witnessed slower growth in formal school enrolment, registered faster increase if the enrolment of formal and alternative modes is combined. This is particularly true of Madhya Pradesh.... For the 1998–99 and 1999–2000 period, as many as 14 districts (out of a total of 40) showed a decline of more than 5 per cent in Grade I enrolment....The decline in enrolment of class I is more alarming for the educationally backward states like Orissa and Assam.... A pertinent question at this stage is, where are the children going?

Further, the DPEP data also reveals that after a spurt of enrolment in 1995–6 and 1996–7 in DPEP-I, class I enrolment is declining. At the national level, enrolment has remained steady at 110 million for some time now.

While enrolment in government schools has remained stagnant, there is growing evidence of a large number of out-of-school children on the one hand and growth of and enrolment in private schools on the other. This is indeed a disturbing trend, especially in educationally backward regions of the country. Table 7.2 documents that private schools constitute anywhere between 5 and 10 per cent of primary schools in Karnataka, Haryana, and UP (and the share increases with higher education) along with Andhra Pradesh (AP), MP, and Maharashtra as well. Research studies reveal that while there is a rising demand for primary education across the country and a sharp reduction in children who have never enrolled, there has been a steady growth in the number of private schools in both rural and urban areas[6] (Aggarwal 2000b; Bashir 1994 quoted in De *et al.* 2001; Krishnaji 2001; Srivastava 2001). Six per cent of rural children and 19 per cent of urban children at the primary stage are studying in private unaided schools; this proportion goes up when we include the 31 per cent children who are studying in private-aided schools (World Bank 2001).

Among the reasons for the growth of private schools is the reported decline in government school quality (poor infrastructure, shortage of teachers, lack of accountability of government schools leading to teacher absenteeism and negligence). This gives way to a positive preference for private schools even though they may have a relatively poor infrastructure, less qualified teachers, and are definitely more expensive (Aggarwal 2000a; De *et al.* 2001; PROBE 1999;Vaidyanathan and Nair 2001). DPEP studies reveal that parents are becoming disillusioned with the overcrowding and poor quality of instruction in government schools and are opting to send their children to private, fee-charging schools. Free education offered by government schools is no longer an attraction (DPEP 2000c). One of the reasons for

TABLE 7.2: DISTRIBUTION OF PRIMARY SCHOOLS BY
MANAGEMENT, 1998–9

State	Government			Private			
	Department of education	Tribal welfare	Local body	Aided	Unaided	Others	Data not available
Andhra Pradesh	8.37	78.11	4.42	8.69	0.04	0.02	0.36
Assam	96.44	0.87	1.15	0.20	0.13	0.26	0.95
Bihar	97.63	0.21	0.06	1.19	0.04	0.06	0.82
Gujarat	9.86	6.69	79.54	1.88	0.82	0.40	0.81
Haryana	90.83	0.65	0.39	1.27	3.60	0.21	3.05
Himachal Pradesh	97.98	0.28	0.14	0.07	0.07	0.57	0.89
Karnataka	87.05	0.47	1.16	3.43	6.30	0.15	1.44
Kerala	45.01	0.25	3.54	49.86	0.14	0.46	0.74
Madhya Pradesh	66.46	22.43	1.48	1.17	5.32	1.23	1.91
Maharashtra	0.93	1.85	78.53	14.57	3.58	0.13	0.41
Orissa	93.78	3.69	0.55	0.32	0.52	0.28	0.86
Tamil Nadu	13.78	4.36	71.27	10.00	0.16	0.12	0.30
Uttar Pradesh	92.08	0.38	1.23	1.90	2.79	0.57	1.04
West Bengal	8.24	0.23	90.42	0.18	0.03	0.09	0.81
DPEP states	62.43	10.34	19.06	3.96	2.65	0.43	1.14

Source: Aggarwal (2000a).

disenchantment with government schools is the indifferent attitude of the teachers towards teaching/learning and an uncaring approach to the social and economic hardships faced by students from poor and vulnerable families. These issues are relevant, as 30–40 per cent of the population in educationally backward areas are barely able to meet their survival needs (Aggarwal 2000a). Between 1986 and 1993 the enrolment in private unaided (recognized) schools increased at a compound growth rate of 9.5 per cent per annum. The corresponding increase in enrolment in government schools was 1.4 per cent per annum. While the contribution of private schools to universalization of elementary education (UEE) is significant, it raises a whole range of equity issues.

THE CHANGING COMPOSITION OF GOVERNMENT SCHOOLS

IMPLICATIONS FOR GENDER AND SOCIAL EQUITY

In the last ten years there has been growing evidence of a hierarchy of access to primary education—between states, between communities and groups, and between different types of schools. The DPEP focuses on improving the access and participation of children in the 6–10 age group so that all such children, irrespective of their place of origin or socio-economic background, are able to complete at least five years of reasonably good quality primary education. However, a few recent independent studies that have explored gender and equity questions (De *et al.* 2001; PROBE 1999; Vaidyanathan and Nair 2001) reveal a disturbing picture. Dysfunctional government schools continue to be an area of concern in the more underdeveloped regions of the country. Where children of the more powerful groups shift to private schools, the pressure on government schools declines sharply. While there is a growing demand for primary education, even in UP, Bihar, Orissa, and Rajasthan, the ability of the government schools to respond has not been demonstrated—as yet. With the exception of Madhya Pradesh and Andhra Pradesh, which have shown strong political will to ensure universal access to elementary education, the same cannot be said for other educationally backward states.

The most compelling evidence has been thrown up in reviews and research studies done under the aegis of the DPEP. Yash Aggarwal points out that while there was a rapid increase in enrolment in the formal system in the first two years of DPEP (phase-I districts), '*subsequently most of the increase in enrolment is accounted for in the alternative school system*'. Several states also report a gradual decline in class I enrolment—partly explained by a slowdown in population growth, improvement in the internal efficiency of the system, and the increasing preference for private schooling in some parts of the country. Despite the rapid growth of private and aided schools in many areas of the country, it has been noted that the proportion of girls is higher in government schools as compared to private schools. 'The proportion of girls in unrecognised schools was very low as compared to their share in the government schools. The gender bias in school choice by parents is quite evident. Many villagers report that girls are sent to government schools because they are entitled to various types of incentives' (Aggarwal 2000a). Researchers and administrators have also noted the prevalence of discrimination between girls and boys in the choice of schools (Sharma 1999).

As seen in Table 7.3, SC and ST populations are more concentrated in the low female literacy districts and the share of SC/ST enrolment to total enrolment has increased. However, Aggarwal (2000a) cautions: *'Taken together with evidence of increasing enrolment in private unaided (recognised) schools and increasing enrolment in AS/EGS schools, this increase in SC/ST enrolment may not be as encouraging as it seems.'* Evidence shows that it is the poor who access government schools—and SC and ST populations are amongst the poorest. Among the poor, it is the most disadvantaged and those living in remote habitations who opt for alternative schools. Given that the hardest to reach are most likely to enrol in government primary schools, and that the better off (at least in most parts of the country) opt for private schools, the raison de'être of a government programme should ideally be to respond to the educational needs of the poor. However, as Manabi Majumdar (2001) argues:

The recent phenomenon [of growing private schools] is obviously an outcome of unfulfilled educational demand of certain relatively affluent sections of society and their dissatisfaction with the low quality of instruction imparted in government and aided schools. *The question, therefore, is not about permitting*

TABLE 7.3: CHANGES IN THE SHARE OF SC/ST ENROLMENT BY LEVELS OF LITERACY

Category of district	Share of SC/ST enrolment to total enrolment by category (%)			
	SC		ST	
	1995–6	1998–9	1995–6	1998–9
Very low female literacy	15.80	16.70	20.30	23.90
Low female literacy	16.30	17.40	17.20	20.40
Moderate female literacy	22.30	22.90	9.30	11.70
High female literacy	8.90	7.60	3.80	3.00
Average for DPEP-I	18.60	19.40	13.40	15.90

Source: Aggarwal (2000a).

the private sector in education but about promoting it. Is there a case for encouraging the expansion of the private sector at the elementary level? (emphasis added).

Such expansion may further accentuate existing social divisions and reduce commitment towards quality improvement in government schools.[7]

The lack of a consistent policy towards private schooling and the proliferation of private schools in rural and urban areas—ostensibly imparting education in 'English medium'—have further widened the divide between social classes. For example, micro-studies done in Haryana, Karnataka, Tamil Nadu, and to a lesser extent in Chhattisgarh revealed that almost all the upper-castes and the economically well-off in the villages visited sent their children to private schools. Even children of school teachers and other government functionaries were studying in private schools— recognized and unrecognized. *Micro studies also point towards a trend among the better-off Dalit and tribal communities to send their children to private schools. Essentially, the bottomline seems to be that with economic security, parents pull their children out of government schools and send them to private schools.*

CONSEQUENCES FOR TEACHING AND LEARNING

The emerging dynamics of 'hierarchies of access' has important consequences for the process of teaching and learning in the classroom as it is also defined and created by the larger politics of teacher recruitment, appointment, and training, according to Aggarwal (2000a):

The large share of SC and ST population in DPEP II districts is also associated with low literacy rates in these districts. It was observed that out of a total of 30 districts in which the ST population was more than 5 per cent, as many as 11 districts showed less than 10 per cent female ST literacy (1991 Census).... In the 66 districts where share of SC population was more than 5 per cent, as many as 29 districts had female literacy varying between 10 and 25 per cent (1991 Census). *Thus most of the school-going children, especially the girls, in these districts will be first-generation learners* (emphasis added).

Thus, given that the proportion of government schools with a larger concentration of SC and ST students has been steadily increasing, such schools invariably have large numbers of first-generation learners and require more experienced teachers.

An overwhelming message emanating from DPEP studies and the Joint Review Mission (JRM) reports is that many states continue to

TABLE 6.4: DISTRIBUTION OF SCHOOLS BY SHARE OF SC/ ST
CHILDREN TO TOTAL ENROLMENT

	Phase I	
State	60–80% (1999–2000)	Above 80% (1999–2000)
Assam	8.10	30.00
Haryana	7.70	2.80
Karnataka	6.60	5.70
Madhya Pradesh	11.40	15.70
Maharashtra	12.30	14.10
Tamil Nadu	9.20	10.60

State	Phase II Above 80% (1999–2000)
Assam	42.70
Gujarat	28.90
Himachal Pradesh	15.80
Madhya Pradesh	15.40
Maharashtra	23.50
Orissa	23.00
West Bengal	15.70

Source: Aggarwal (2000a).

face a shortage of teachers. This is more than evident in data on the
proportion of single-teacher schools, especially in phase-II districts.
In DPEP phase-I districts, the overall share of single-teacher schools
has declined from 18.5 per cent in 1995–6 to 14.3 per cent in 1999–
2000. But in DPEP phase-II districts the proportion of single–teacher
schools increased from 14.3 per cent in 1995–6 to 19.1 per cent in
1999–2000 (Aggarwal 2000a).

If the shortage of teachers in general and the proportion of single-
teacher schools in particular are analysed in the context of teacher–
student ratio, the emerging picture does not augur well, especially in
educationally backward states. On the one hand, according to DPEP
data, Himachal Pradesh, Karnataka, Madhya Pradesh, and Orissa show
a high percentage of schools with less than 20 students per class (the
situation is different in multi-grade classrooms/single-teacher schools).

On the other hand, in states like West Bengal, Assam, and Uttar Pradesh, the share of schools with more than 90 students per classroom is high, at times with states like Assam having only one-room schools. According to Aggarwal (ibid.), 'There were about 25,553 schools with an estimated enrolment of 6.12 million students for which the Student Classroom Ratio (SCR) was more than 90.'[8] Another related issue that is integral to social equity is that most of the single-teacher schools, especially the AS/EGS category, are primarily frequented by children belonging to the SC and ST communities (see Ghosh 2002).

Among the strategies adopted by the DPEP to promote girls' participation is recruitment of female teachers. DPEP data reveals that one-third of the teachers are women (33 per cent or more in Gujarat, Haryana, HP, Karnataka, Kerala, and Tamil Nadu; 27 per cent in Maharashtra, 26 per cent in Assam and UP; 25 per cent in MP; 23 per cent in Orissa; 22 per cent in Bihar; 17 per cent in West Bengal; and 34 per cent in MP's DPEP districts). However, given the large number of single-teacher schools, the low distribution of women teachers in such schools is indeed worrisome; in addition, 72 per cent of two-teacher schools are without female teachers. For example, in Tamil Nadu, 86.8 per cent and 89.4 per cent single-teacher schools do not have any female teachers in phase-I and phase-II districts respectively. However, the picture seems to be slightly better in alternate schools, where reports indicate that Assam has 50 per cent, Bihar 100 per cent, Karnataka 10 per cent, Tamil Nadu 25 per cent, UP 62 per cent, and West Bengal 25 per cent single-teacher schools, where the teacher is female (DPEP 2000c). Though the presence of female teachers does have an impact on girls' participation, it emerges that functionality of schools is a far more critical factor for participation. Studies reveal that more than the gender of the teacher, dysfunctional schools and teacher absenteeism have a negative impact as parents are not happy about leaving their daughters unsupervised in school (Srivastava 2001).

IMPLICATION FOR LOCAL GOVERNANCE

The implication for local governance is indeed disturbing—a majority of the children in government schools come from poor and disempowered communities while local government institutions (panchayat, Village Education Committee, School Development and

Management Committee, etc.) are essentially in the hands of relatively well-off, whose children do not go to local government schools (be in municipality or panchayat). Therefore, people in influential positions have little interest in ensuring that government schools function well and provide good quality education.

Therefore, the need of the hour is to contain this trend, whereby the universalization of primary education is accompanied by the emergence of segregated schools based on caste and community identity. The initial evidence seems to indicate that 'hierarchies of access' are becoming an inevitable feature of UEE and this does not portend well for a democracy that is defined by multiple social identities and voices. The DPEP needs to keep this in mind and focus on steps that will strengthen the existing infrastructure as well as introduce new interventions that will make primary education truly democratic.

FUNCTIONING PRIMARY SCHOOLS: A KEY DETERMINANT

Essentially, research studies and reports on the DPEP during the last five years confirm increased demand for schooling among all sections of the population and also point to a significant increase in the supply of schools. Though gender inequalities have been shrinking and the prognosis for the future is positive, the persistence of regional, social, and economic inequalities, particularly with respect to access to *functioning schools* of a reasonable quality, remains an area of concern, more so in educationally backward districts of the country and especially for first-generation learners.

STAKEHOLDERS FOR GOVERNMENT SCHOOLS

Who has a stake in improving primary schools? The PROBE report and other studies of the late 1990s reveal that states like Himachal Pradesh, Tamil Nadu, and to a certain degree Kerala have achieved universal elementary education mainly through government schools and private-aided schools. In particular, children of almost all the important social and economic groups depend primarily on government schools. As a result, they have a stake not only in ensuring that schools function, but also improve in quality. It is rare to come across children in class V who cannot read or write. However, recent micro studies done in Uttar Pradesh (Srivastava 2001) and the micro study (see Note 2) done under this project in Chhattisgarh reveal that several children emerge from primary schools barely literate! Making sure that schools work (according to the stipulated timing and calendar) and that teachers teach has to become a non-negotiable agenda. While the DPEP Education Management Information System (EMIS) data from educationally backward districts suggests a sharp increase in enrolment, we still do not have any reliable information on functionality and quality.

We also have very little information on the functioning of village education committees/school betterment committees/parent–teacher associations. What we do have in the form of qualitative micro studies (see Note 2) is not very heartening. All the studies clearly indicate that strengthening mechanisms for community participation without ensuring the participation of parents is often counterproductive. Village leaders whose children do not go to government schools have no stake in it.

ELIMINATION OF SOCIAL BIASES

Elimination of gender, caste, and community biases inside the classroom, especially among teachers, remains a challenge. Biases persist and are reflected through:

1. attitudes of teachers and even educational administrators towards children from first-generation learner families;
2. stereotypes about tribal children (especially the more disadvantaged among tribal groups, for example, Pahadi Korba, Majhwar, Pando, and Kodaku in Chhattisgarh); and
3. students from disadvantaged Dalit communities (Valmiki, Rohit, Adi Dravida, and other communities which were part of erstwhile untouchable groups).

The indicators all point to a much deeper malaise in our society. These have been reflected in extensive reporting on the situation of Dalits by noted journalist P. Sainath (articles appearing in the *Hindu*) and reports of Dalit organizations struggling against the persistence of caste prejudices (World Conference against Racism, Racial Discrimination, Xenophobia and Related Intolerance in Durban,

South Africa in September 2001). While acknowledging that teachers are as much a part of this society as anyone else, it becomes more than evident that the government has to play a positive interventionist role to ensure a bias-free and a prejudice-free classroom. This unfortunately has not happened in the DPEP. While gender issues have been brought to the centre stage, the same cannot be said for caste, community, and other social prejudices.

A related issue is that there is a pressing need to critically interrogate generic social categories like SC, ST, and minorities, and further break them down into more region-specific subgroups in order to address their needs more effectively. The most glaring example comes from Chhattisgarh where there are vast differences among the Scheduled Tribes, with some being almost marginalized. The situation of Oraon or even Gond tribes is far better than that of the Pahadi Korba and Majhwars, among whom it is difficult to find even one literate adult. Recent press reports on starvation deaths among Pahadi Korba tribes and other marginalized subgroups among SC and ST communities further reinforce the issue that these need micro level and context-specific strategies since they remain the hardest to reach.

MOTIVATING AND TRAINING TEACHERS

DPEP studies and reports argue that the first and the most obvious implication of these hierarchies is for teacher training. Apart from social sensitization mentioned earlier, special training would be necessary for handling first-generation learners, especially from socially and economically vulnerable groups. The second implication is for more focused and ongoing support from block resource centres (BRC) and cluster resource centres (CRC), with respect to pedagogic renewal. Third, these schools need to be placed on a special watch list. Given that existing mechanisms for community involvement, including village education committees (VEC), are weak and strife-ridden, a far greater effort would be necessary on the part of the teachers to reach out. Teachers with commitment and aptitude would have to be posted in such schools. While the government has acknowledged the importance of this issue, specific strategies are yet to be developed to meet the changing composition of government schools. Similarly, the pedagogical implications of the changing composition of government schools are yet to be explored.

GROWING DEMAND FOR UPPER PRIMARY EDUCATION

Finally, there is unanimity among researchers and administrators about the need to increase children's access to upper primary and middle schools. The absence of post-primary educational opportunities continues to create greater inequalities in the system. Gender bias is more pronounced at this stage—many more girls drop out after the primary level because of lack of meaningful access to upper primary schools. Social inequalities in access are also more pronounced at the upper primary stage—with a smaller proportion of children from SC and ST families studying in private-aided and unaided schools. At this stage, it is the poor who depend more on government schools.

A recent World Bank report on the subject revealed that 72 per cent of the children in the 11–13 age group attend school; only 43 per cent of them attend upper primary, the rest are in primary school.[9] The NSSO 52nd Round, Sixth Educational Survey (1993), and other DPEP reports (DPEP 1998, 2000a, 2000b, 2001) reveal that the demand for upper primary education has been increasing exponentially in almost all areas, both rural and urban. Equally, given the wide variations in the quality of primary education, 61 per cent students (56 per cent girls) who enter class I complete the primary cycle. This national picture hides wide regional differences. However, what is encouraging is that most of the children who complete the primary cycle are eager to move on to the upper primary level. Micro studies done in this project also show that the presence of an upper primary and/or high school in the village is *the most* important factor affecting transition from primary to upper primary. This is particularly true for girls and for children from poor families.

SUMMING UP

No single programme or project, however extensive, can hope to correct decades of educational imbalances and inequalities. While acknowledging that the DPEP is perhaps the most ambitious primary education initiative in independent India, eight years is indeed a short time to bring about radical changes and turn the system upside down. This chapter acknowledges that the social and economic dynamics that frames educational access is not the creation of any programme, but a historical baggage—a product of over five decades of social development and educational planning. What, however, is disturbing is that we as a nation are becoming more insensitive as the years roll by. The two-glass system is not only confined to tea shops—it has permeated all social structures and institutions, including our schools, the real 'temples' of modern India.

A new kind of segregation is clearly discernible at different levels, and not all of it has been captured in the DPEP data and research studies. At one level children from clearly different social and economic groups attend different types of school—private unaided, private aided, government primary schools, EGS, alternate schools. Even within government primary schools, there is some evidence of sharp difference in quality—physical facilities, community participation, allocation of funds (Mazumdar 2001; Nambissan 2001; Ramachandran and Sethi 2001). Single-teacher schools, multi-grade situations (especially when the teachers are not trained to handle it), poorly trained para-teachers—all these have a greater impact on children from disadvantaged groups, as such children have no other options (private schools, tuitions) and their parents cannot support them at home.

General household characteristics like income, caste, occupation, and educational level of parents continue to determine access, attendance, completion, and learning achievements. Children from rural families with substantial land, non-agricultural occupations, and educational level have greater access than children from landless, agricultural wage-earning families, and migrating groups. In some regions of the country, for example Uttaranchal, researchers have found a strong positive correlation between distance of forest and water source and non-enrolment and dropout rate of girls, and even boys in specific age groups (Pande 2001). Children–women ratio was found to be an influencing factor in the enrolment and continuation of girls in school and the work participation rate influenced the enrolment of boys in Andhra Pradesh (Krishnaji 2001). Similarly, in many areas the number of animals to graze and manage also exerts influence on school participation, as parents cite grazing as an important reason for irregular attendance or non-enrolment. This is referred to as dependency ratio—'the larger the number of infants and old people in the household (i.e., the higher the "dependency burden" on the household), the smaller are the chances of children getting enrolled in school' (Vaidyanathan and Nair 2001). However, NGOs, especially those who are part of a nationwide campaign against child labour, argue that motivation of parents coupled with mobilization of working children to get back to school can overcome this challenge. Ravi Srivastava's (2001) study in UP reveals that the burden of dependency is generally borne by adult women and it is not necessarily passed on to small children. It may, however, be of greater significance at the upper primary and middle school level, particularly for girls.

Notwithstanding prevalent social and economic barriers to schooling, the overwhelming message emanating from DPEP schools is that the presence of a good quality government school, which functions regularly, can indeed surmount many obstacles. Special strategies would, however, be necessary to reach out to the hardcore —most of whom are people who not only belong to the most deprived subgroups of Scheduled Castes and Tribes; they are also the people with almost no voice in society.

The challenge is to reach out to this hardest-to-reach group with good quality education. We can no longer look at social and gender disparities in isolation—the intermeshing of geographic location, social status, economic position, gender, occupation, and displacement/ migration have resulted in new forms of disparities and disempowerment. Ensuring equal quality of access remains a big issue. Reaching out to the most deprived merits more resources, more human resource inputs, and a great deal of commitment from the government. Low-cost options will not do; they will merely accentuate existing cleavages in society.

Making local governance structures effective—especially in schools—involves careful thinking and strategizing on how people who have a stake in the schools are brought on board existing decision-making bodies. Among the questions that need to be explored are:

- How far has the community been involved/taken into confidence?
- Is there clarity on what constitutes the 'community'—parents of children in government schools or the larger community (regardless of their linkages with the school)?
- What are the parameters of active community involvement and ownership of the school system?

- How has participation of the community been ensured? How have structures such as SMC (School Management Committees), PTA (Parent-Teacher Association), MTA (Mother-Teacher Association),VEC (Village Education Committee), and other grass roots structures created and involved in the school, including clarity/differentiation of roles and their linkages with PRIs?
- Are local self-government institutions empowered to manage the school with appropriate representation from parents of the children?
- Is the community oriented/prepared for this role? And how are the 'groups' enabled to understand their role and develop a motivation towards it?
- How are teachers and school administration prepared for this process, including monitoring and support mechanisms, and enhancing the capacity of teachers?
- Is the role of community forum and structures limited to enrolment and attendance or do they encompass quality?

NOTES

* This chapter is based on a recently completed research study by Vimala Ramachandran (2002). The original version of the chapter was published (co-authored with Aarti Saihjee in 2002).
1. Discussing the spurt in elementary education spending in 1995–6, Sajita Bashir (2000) points out,

    After deducting the expenditure on these two programmes (DPEP and Lok Jumbish), real plan expenditure (domestic) for elementary education has grown at the rate of 22 per cent p.a., compared to 27 per cent p.a. when external funds are included. Thus, the increase in domestic funding has been the main factor in raising Plan expenditure on elementary education.

2. The micro studies discussed in this chapter are: Aarti Saihjee: 'Long live the alphabet! Reflections from Betul district, Madhya Pradesh'; Vidya Das: 'More Unequal than Others. Evidence from Surguja district, Chhattisgarh'; Vandana Mahajan: 'The Hidden Picture—A case study from Hisar district, Haryana';Vani Periodi: 'Second Generation Issues in Equity and Education. Learning from Kolar district, Karnataka'; Kameshwari Jandhyala: 'So close yet so far. Primary schooling in Warangal district, Andhra Pradesh'; and Aruna Ratnam: 'The Weft and the Warp of Public Education. A tale of two primary schools in Cuddalore district, Tamil Nadu'. All are published in Vimala Ramachandran (ed.) 2002.

3. 'Across states, districts and even villages, the literacy rates of females and Scheduled Castes and Tribes (SC/ST), though much below average, are highly

correlated with overall literacy rates. Also, inter-group disparities tend to decline as the average literacy rate increases. In other words, as we move up the scale of overall literacy, females and SC/STs are found to be more literate. Also gender gaps as well as the differences between socially disadvantaged and other caste groups become narrower' (Vaidyanathan and Nair 2001).

4. 'Schools in 46 districts in eight states were surveyed as part of the district primary education programme of the Ministry of Human Resources Development. The learning levels of over 50,000 students were assessed. It was found that in none of the 46 districts surveyed did primary school students achieve an average score of 80 per cent in the basic letter and word reading tests that were administered to assess their learning levels. In many districts students could barely read five to eight words correctly. Children also fared poorly in basic numerical skills.' (*Times of India,* 1994, quoted in Nambissan 2001).

5. P. Sainath, a noted journalist, has documented the situation of Dalits across the country from 1999 onwards. Articles appearing in the *Hindu* reveal persistent social discrimination inside the school. Certain specific groups among the Dalits, like Valmiki, Rohit, Thoti, and Chamar, and in tribal areas the non-dominant tribes and denotified tribes (classified as criminal tribes by the British) are not only discriminated against by the upper-castes, but by other Dalits, who consider them untouchable.

6. 'It is estimated that the enrolment in unrecognised schools is doubling every five years. *The proportion of girls in unrecognised schools was very low as compared to their share in the government schools. The gender bias in school choice by the parents is quite evident....*What we need is that the government schools should compete with private schools in terms of quality of access, efficiency and performance standards and both sectors supplement each other's effort to achieve the goal of universal primary education' (Aggarwal 2000a).

'Less than 10 per cent of poor families have their children in private schools as against nearly 30 per cent of middle¸income families and 45 per cent of well-to-do families' (Krishnaji, quoted in De *et al.* 2001).

Sajita Bashir's study in Tamil Nadu in 1994 revealed that pupils in private unaided schools came from relatively well-off backgrounds, with only 10 per cent being SC. In government schools, the proportion of SC children is 26 per cent in rural areas and 46 per cent in urban areas. She also discussed the educational status of parents from private unaided schools and aided schools as being very different, with more first-generation learners enrolled in government schools (Sajita Bashir, quoted in De *et al.* 2001).

7. 'This differentiation accentuates the precarious position of the disadvantaged groups in terms of access to basic education both quantitatively and qualitatively. This tendency, if allowed to continue, will further aggravate the already serious inequality in access to higher education, thus making a mockery of the notion that education is the most potent instrument for achieving greater equality of opportunity' (Vaidyanathan and Nair 2001).

8. 'West Bengal has recorded the lowest share of female teachers—merely 15.8 per cent as compared to 73.6 per cent in Kerala. As a first priority, the share of female teachers needs to be improved in single- and two-teacher schools.... Despite significant moves and gender sensitive recruitment policies, the position with respect to the availability and deployment of female teachers is less than satisfactory.... Serious concerns about deployment prevail, as the number of male-teacher schools is exceptionally large.... The trends indicate a stagnating share of SC/ST teachers in phase I' (Aggarwal 2000a: ch. 6).

9. ﹀'Across the total population aged 15 years and above in 1995–96, 32 per cent had completed at least an upper primary schooling. There were major differences by gender and income group. For urban males, the completion rate was 63.6 per cent and for rural females the rate was 14.6 per cent. While just over half of the members of the wealthiest 20 per cent of households had completed this level of schooling, the rate for the poorest 20 per cent was under 15 per cent' (World Bank 2001).

REFERENCES

Aggarwal, Yash, *An Assessment of Trends in Access and Retention*, New Delhi: National Institute of Educational Planning and Administration (NIEPA), 2000a.

———, *How Many Pupils Complete Primary Education in Five Years*, New Delhi: NIEPA, 2000b.

Bashir, Sajita, *Government Expenditure on Elementary Education in the Nineties*, New Delhi: European Commission, 2000.

De, Anuradha, Claire Noronha, and Meera Sampson,. *India: Primary Schools and Universal Elementary Education: India Education Team Report No. 3*, New Delhi: World Bank, 2001.

District Primary Education Programme (DPEP), *Observation and Analysis of EMIS Data 1997-98 from the Gender Perspective*, New Delhi: GOI and Gender Unit of Ed CIL, 1998.

———, *District Primary Education Programme, Parts 1 and 2, 11th Joint Review Mission*, New Delhi. Government of India, 2000a.

———, *District Primary Education Programme, Parts 1, 2 & 3, 12th Joint Review Mission*, New Delhi. Government of India, 2000b.

———, *Study of Declining Enrolment in Class I in Uttar Pradesh, Maharashtra and Tamil Nadu : A Synthesis Report*, New Delhi: Ministry of Human Resource Development (MHRD), Government of India, 2000c.

———, *District Primary Education Programme, Parts 1, 2 & 3 13th Joint Review Mission*, New Delhi: Government of India, 2001.

DPEP, MHRD, and GOI, *Bringing Girls Centrestage: Strategies and Interventions for Girls Education in DPEP*, New Delhi: DPEP, MHRD, and GOI, 2000.

Ghosh, Avik, 'Alternative Schools and Education Guarantee Scheme', in Vimala Ramachandran (ed.), *Hierarchies of Access: Gender and Social Equity in Primary Education*, New Delhi: European Commission, 2002.

Government of India, *National Policy on Education : Programme of Action*, New Delhi: GOI, 1992.

Krishnaji, N., 'Poverty, Gender and Schooling: A Study of Two Districts in Andhra Pradesh', in A. Vaidyanathan and P.R. Gopinathan Nair (ed.), *Elementary Education in Rural India: A Grassroots View*, New Delhi: Sage Publications, 2001.

Madan, Vandana, 'Inside the Classroom: Content Analysis of Classroom Processes Study done in Eight State', in Vimala Ramachandran (ed.), *Hierarchies of Access: Gender and Social Equity in Primary Education*, New Delhi: European Commission, 2002.

Mazumbar, Manabi, 'Educational Opportunities in Rajasthan and Tamil Nadu: Despair and Hope', in A. Vaidyanathan and P.R. Gopinathan Nair (eds), *Elementary Education in Rural India: A Grassroots View*, New Delhi: Sage Publications, 2001.

MODE/UNICEF, 'MODE Research: Attitudes Study on Elementary Education in India—A Consolidated Report', unpublished report, New Delhi, 1995.

Nambissan, Geeta, 'Identity, Exclusion and the Education of Tribal Communities' in Rekha Wazir (ed.), *The Gender Gap in Basic Education: NGOs as Change Agents*, New Delhi: Sage Publications, 2000.

————'Social Diversity and Regional Disparity in Schooling: A Study of Rural Rajasthan', in A. Vaidyanathan and P.R. Gopinathan Nair (eds), *Elementary Education in Rural India: A Grassroots View*, New Delhi: Sage Publications, 2001.

Pande, Anuradha, 'Uttar Pradesh', in A. Vaidyanathan and P.R. Gopinathan Nair (eds), *Elementary Education in Rural India: A Grassroots View*, New Delhi: Sage Publications, 2001.

PROBE, *Public Report on Basic Education in India*, New Delhi: Oxford University Press, 1999.

Ramachandran, Vimala (ed.), *Hierarchies of Access: Gender and Social Equity in Primary Education*; New Delhi: European Commission, 2002.

Ramachandran, Vimala and Aarti Saihjee, 'The New Segregation: Reflections on Gender and Equity in Primary Education', *Economic and Political Weekly*, 37, 2002, pp.

Ramachandran, Vimala and Harsh Sethi, *Rajasthan Shiksha Karmi Project: An Overall Appraisal*, Stockholm: Swedish International Development Cooperation Agency, 2001.

Shariff, Abusaleh and Ratna Sudarshan, 'Elementary Education and Health in Rural India: Some Indicators', in N. Rao, L. Rurup, and R. Sudarshan (eds), *Sites of Change: The Structural Context for Women's Empowerment in India*, New Delhi: FES and UNDP, 1996.

Sharma, Rashmi, 'What Manner of Teacher: Some Lessons from MP', *Economic and Political Weekly*, 9 June 1999.

Srivastava, Ravi, 'Access to Basic Education in Rural Uttar Pradesh', in A. Vaidyanathan and P.R. Gopinathan Nair (eds), *Elementary Education in Rural India: A Grassroots View*, New Delhi. Sage Publications, 2001.

Vaidyanathan, A. and P. R. Gopinathan Nair (eds), *Elementary Education in Rural India: A Grassroots View,* New Delhi: Sage Publications, 2001.

Visaria, Leela and Vimala Ramachandran, 'What DPEP and Other Data Sources Reveal', in Vimala Ramachandran (ed.), *Hierarchies of Access: Gender and Social Equity in Primary Education,* New Delhi: European Commission, 2002.

World Bank, *Expanding and Improving Upper Primary Education in India,* Washington, DC: World Bank, 2001.

8

Crisis of Governance and People's Alternatives
Schooling System in Some Villages of Western UP

■ JAGPAL SINGH

Local governance in Uttar Pradesh has been in crisis during the last quarter of a century in almost all major aspects—schooling system, health, law and order, and credit institutions. Lack of efficacy and transparency and the prevalence of rampant corruption on the part of the institutions of local governance have eroded people's trust in them. Dissatisfied with public institutions and unsure about receiving help from any quarter, people have attempted to find alternatives to public institutions on their own. They set up alternative schools to educate their children; they go to quacks and not qualified doctors; they depend on the community and on illegal/country-made arms rather than the police for security; they set up their own credit societies or turn to relatives rather than the public sector banks. Exclusively initiated and managed by the people, these alternatives are in no way aided or funded by the state.

This chapter deals with this crisis of governance with special reference to the schooling system in western UP; the failure of the government schools; and people's attempt to set up alternate schools. The chapter is divided into five sections. The first discusses the failure of the schooling system and people's initiatives for alternatives in the universe of study. The second section seeks to contextualize the governance of education. Section three is about the relationship between local governance and education. The last section reflects upon prescriptive measures to grapple with the crisis of governance in the schooling system.

The chapter purports to argue that it is not the state, nor the panchayati raj institutions, but the people/community/society themselves who have taken the initiative in the field of education. Both before and after the arrival of government schools, the initiative had been taken by the community. In comparison to the efforts of society, those of the state have been negligible. Before the establishment of government schools in villages, the community made informal arrangements for imparting education to their children. A teacher in such informal schools was neither a government employee nor did he hold any specific formal qualification. Somebody who knew the three Rs was invited by the villagers to teach their wards. The existence of the school depended on the will of the teacher in such informal arrangements. The teacher was paid in kind for his services. The attempts to set up an alternative schooling system show the continuation of a trend—which was disrupted for around two decades due to the state initiative to set up government schools—the predominant role of society, rather than the state, in imparting education. Within two decades of their existence, government schools have failed in their pursuit.

I

Since the mid-1970s, there has been an unprecedented growth of unaided and unrecognized (UAUR) schools from primary to secondary levels in the villages of Meerut. Managers of such schools make informal arrangements with recognized schools so as to show their students formally enrolled in the latter. When the students of such schools appear in the board examinations, they appear as the students of those recognized schools. Such an arrangement also helps in recognition of the certificates of these schools by the board.

Although the figures on UAUR schools are not available in official or unofficial records, I have observed during my fieldwork spreading over more than two decades in western UP, that the emergence of such schools has become too conspicuous to be ignored. In fact, it has been observed in some of the villages that parents are getting their wards' admissions cancelled in government schools in order to get them admitted to these alternative schools.

This paper captures certain trends in the primary schooling system in three villages—Maithana Inder Singh, Khanauda, and Uldypur, all located in a proximity of 10–15 km from Meerut city. These villages were identified as Ambedkar villages at different points of time.[1] The SCs, especially Chamars, form the majority households in these villages. At the time of first phase of survey conducted in 1995 (the second phase of survey was conducted in 2002), there were eight schools in these villages; three of these were government primary schools and five were UAUR schools. The latter were established between 1989 and 1995, whiie the government schools were set up in 1952 in one village and in 1965 in other two villages. Four UAUR schools went up to class VIII and one was up to class V. All government primary schools were up to class V.

It needs to be emphasized that contrary to general impression, UAUR or alternate schools are different from the private schools of the urban and semi-urban areas. Unlike the latter, where students generally come from more resourceful backgrounds, those from all social and economic groups study in UAUR schools. UAUR schools are private only in the sense of being managed privately, by non-state groups. The social and economic groups that used to educate their wards in government primary schools earlier now opt for UAUR schools. These schools are working as substitutes or parallel to government schools, which are sources of general public disappointment.

People feel that government schools have failed to impart 'good education', the attributes of which are discipline, etiquette, and moral values (respecting women and the elderly, helping others, and so on).[2] The teachers of government schools are considered to be mainly responsible for their decline. Being dissatisfied with the government schools, parents now have an alternate institution in UAUR schools for the education of their children. They feel that UAUR schools are doing what the government schools have failed to do; they are providing a good education to the children.

While the majority of the teachers of UAUR schools are drawn from the poor agrarian classes of wage labourers and small farmers, the managers of these schools belong to the Chamar and Rajput groups—the locally dominant groups.[3] The former are the largest of all castes and the most assertive among the weaker sections. The general perception that students of UAUR schools are better than those of the government schools does not comply with the comparative performance of students of both types of schools in the tests conducted by us for Hindi dictation and mathematics.

In all three villages of our study, developments that took place after the 1995 survey were a reflection of the general trends in the region. UAUR schools that started on a secular and apparently neutral note got embroiled in the politics of caste, crime, and dominance. Though symptoms of these trends were present since their foundation, in the later period these intensified and defeated the very purpose for which they were set up. It resulted in the closure of some schools and opening of others. Some teachers of these schools found alternative jobs, while others shuttled from one to another school. In one case a teacher changed his job from teaching to quackery and vice versa, along with cultivating his fields. The worst victims in this process have been the pupils. In the light of these developments, which led to the closure of the old schools and opening of the new ones, parents are forced to shunt their wards from one school to another. Meanwhile, another development has taken place in the area. A businessman has bought land in one of the villages not very far from our sample villages, where a school for studies in management courses is being constructed. It is, however, beyond the scope of this chapter to deal with this.

II

A considerable literature exists on the failure and causes of the schooling system in some states of India, including Uttar Pradesh (for a review of literature on this point, see Kingdon and Muzammil 2001; and Dreze and Gazdar 1997). But little effort has been made to contextualize the governance of education. In fact, public debate in India has been insensitive to basic education (Dreze and Sen 1995a). The belief system of the Indian elite is virtually opposed to the very idea of the children of poor parents getting an education. They fear that educating them would deprive the society of the working population (Weiner 1991). With the proposal of making elementary education a fundamental right and inclusion of education on the agenda of the village panchayats following the 73rd Constitutional Amendment, rhetoric has left performance far behind. While tall claims and declarations are made about providing education, the very people who matter in the formulation and implementation of the policies regarding education— MPs, MLAs, MLCs (Member of the Legislative Council), panchayat chiefs and members, education bureaucrats, and community leaders— do not consider education as a priority issue. Their agenda is different, whatever the cost; they are contributing more to the sectarianism of society than anything else.

The general milieu or the social context in Meerut, like in any other part of the state of Uttar Pradesh, has been marked by the criminalization of the society—breakdown of law and order and caste conflict. Many of those involved in these activities are also connected with the education system. As mentioned earlier, the erosion of trust in government schools is a reflection of the general trend in the research area. The local-level educational bureaucracy and government school teachers have behaved in such a way that the people have lost faith in them. Government school teachers have been involved in corrupt practices, including: *chauk chandani* (an annual ceremony in which pupils give gifts to the teachers; for details see Singh 1998), forced gifts and *inams* (reward to the teachers for being successful in the examination, inability to pay it resulting in the failure of students; for details, see ibid.) from the students, leakage of the question papers, and collusion in cheating; involvement in local politics; absenteeism; and misappropriation of money earmarked for various programmes meant for education by the educational bureaucray at the local level in collaboration with local vested interests (for absenteeism of teachers in eastern, central, and southern districts of UP, see Dreze and Saran 1995: 227). Besides, with the formalization of education, the traditional value system has been replaced. Though it was more feudal in outlook, the traditional value system accorded a high moral position to the school teacher. But with their turning into government salaried employees, the teachers did not feel responsible for education. Again, the involvement of teachers in non-teaching public activities like census enumeration or preparation of electoral rolls left him or her with no motivation to concentrate on the teaching duties.

Despite the grim situation, the education system has made a contribution to social change in the district. Though most of the students drop out by class X, in every caste and class group a section with some background of formal education has emerged. And those who were able to study beyond class X have entered various professions as lawyers, teachers, and government employees. This section is identified in local parlance as the 'intellectuals' of society. While these 'intellectuals' have mobilized villagers on secular issues like education—setting up UAUR schools (even though sectarian issues camouflaged these in due course), they have been mainly concerned with issues relating to their respective communities. This group plays a more significant role in sectarian activities—caste mobilization during inter-caste feuds or holding caste panchayats to decide the voting choice of their community.[4]

Education promotes 'human capabilities' (Dreze and Sen 1995b). But education devoid of the basic principles of morality and democratic values can also play a negative role. In our sample villages it has actually played a partisan and sectarian role. It seems to have become a tool of exploitation by those few who possess it. The latter use it to their advantage by cheating or misguiding people. Since the rural poor are not able to deal with the intricacies of the processes in government offices, especially courts and banks, they have had to depend on the educated people of the village. However, the Chamars of our sample villages no longer fall into the trap of the Jats or the dominant group, as they have become politically more assertive, and a large number of educated people—lawyers, activists, politicians, as well as organizations—have emerged among their caste in the district. The Most Backward Classes (MBCs) and Muslim backward classes have now become vulnerable in this context. However, it would be erroneous to generalize about the Chamars; their vulnerability or assertion varies in the context of time and space even within the same district. A Jat lawyer used his knowledge in one of the sample villages to usurp the land of these groups. He did not spare even the landless labourers (details are discussed elsewhere; Singh 2000).

III

The passage of the 73rd and 74th constitutional amendments in the 1990s placed education in the purview of local governance. The discourse on devolution generally points out that it is the dominant section of society that manipulates public institutions, policies, and their implementation (Jha and Mathur 1999; Lieten 1996; Lieten and Srivastava 1999).[5] The local state, including the police, is controlled and manipulated by the local Jat elite in several villages of Meerut district (Jeffrey 2000). The discourse on the functioning of local self-government usually considers the dominance in terms of control over resources and caste hierarchy. But, as mentioned earlier, irrespective of their social position, even the castes placed in the lower order of the social hierarchy may occupy a dominant position over other communities, including the ones who are dominant in a different time and space. In one of our sample villages, the dominance of one community has been replaced by that of another. A process of 'reverse dominance' or 'reverse discrimination' has set in. In both situations, the governance is sectarian. There are certain communities that remain vulnerable in both situations. They become the subject of discrimination by both erstwhile and new dominant groups. They do not have enough numerical strength, resources, and political patronage to affect electoral politics. These groups belong to the minority high castes, OBCs, and religious minorities. Agencies involved in governance—panchayats, dominant groups, and state institutions—in the sample villages discriminate against them (based on Singh 2000).

The role of panchayats in education in UP has largely remained a neglected subject in both academic discourse and public policies. The study of Dreze and Gazdar (1997:88), is an exception. But their discussion on the role of panchayats in education remains limited. The main focus of public policies regarding villages till the mid-1970s was on resourceful groups to whom the incentives were given through the Green Revolution or other measures in order to make the country self-sufficient in food production. No doubt, the Green Revolution added to the relative prosperity of every class in the villages.

The village panchayats, public institutions, and bureaucracy at the village level function in a partisan way; they protect the interests of the dominant groups, even as the interests of the politically and economically vulnerable are ignored. It was during the Emergency that poverty alleviation programmes were first introduced in the villages; these included means for self-employment like providing the rural poor with milch buffaloes or setting up of small shops. These measures were also made part of the policies of the Janata Party government during 1977–80 in the framework of Gandhian principles. Their inclusion in the Sixth Five Year Plan in 1980–5 and in the following period made these almost a permanent part of public policy.

Out of 37 programmes introduced in the Ambedkar villages during the regime of Mayawati, chief minister of UP, only one programme was related to education—the construction of school buildings and toilets. No attempts were made to restore the confidence or efficiency of government schools. Earlier attempts to provide incentives through the midday meal schemes also proved ineffective. Our study of the programmes introduced by the Mayawati-led government in one of these villages of our sample reveals the insensitive attitude of the panchayati raj institutions towards primary education. In the 1990s, the rural poor of Khanauda became the special target of welfare measures with its identification as an Ambedkar village. Apart from constructing a school building and toilets, the other main programmes included construction of a road linking the village to the main road; electrification of the village; construction of *khdanja* (brick road), *nali* (drainage), and free boring; IRDP; Indira Avas Yojana (Indira Housing Plan); potable water; construction of a *bhawan* (hall); and *kisan* (peasant)/old age pension and widow pension (see Advocate 2000: 39–40). With the exception of the Samajwadi Party, no political party campaigned on issues like education and health in the Legislative Assembly elections in UP in February 2002. In fact, for the Bahujan Samaj Party (BSP), education is not an issue. It is actually interested in social transformation, not in social change. (For the difference between the two concepts, see Singh 2002: 244–5.) While the programmes for the overall development of the village, like linking the village roads with the main roads and electrification, have been introduced, there has been a laxity in the implementation of policies meant for individuals (based on Singh 2000).

Introduction of welfare policies comes as a boon for vested interests—local bureaucrats, village level workers (VLWs), secretaries, patwaris/lekhpals, veterinary doctors, village pradhans and their agents, who form a nexus of the corrupt. It is in fact these who really benefit from the welfare measures; the actual target groups suffer more than they benefit.[6] In village Khanauda, the beneficiaries of welfare measures included those who were close to the husband of the pradhan (who used to be exclusively males before 1995) and those who enjoyed his patronage or paid a bribe to the pradhan and/ or local bureacrats.

It ought to be underlined that whoever bribed the VLW/secretary or the agent of pradhan was put in the category of the deserving beneficiary; there are examples of the better-off having availed of such government help. Some panchayat members also got themselves identified as belonging to the weaker sections, even though they were not so.[7] The aim of programme meant for the generation of self-employment was defeated when the grant received was utilized for purposes other than it was meant for. Some of these programmes, like widow pensions had to be discontinued in the face of malpractice. It was difficult to avail of help in certain programmes like maternity benefits, as the pregnant woman has to be taken to the block development office, which people usually do not prefer to do.[8]

There is a perception among the rural poor that the village panchayats and public institutions such as banks, police, local-level government functionaries, government schools, and political parties are not meant to serve them. Rather, they are via media through which the powerful get their interests served, who, unless bribed, do not care for the masses. The police and political parties or politicians are at the lowest order of public trust. The lack of trust in public institutions discourages people from relying on them. As mentioned earlier, people are searching for their own alternative means for solving their problems. But the alternative, in the form of cooperative societies or UAUR schools, are not recognized by the government, unlike NGOs. They do not get these registered precisely for two reasons: first, they do not possess the necessary resources for getting them registered as per the rules; second, they are wary of the formalities involved in the process of registration as they lack the necessary contacts and knowledge.

IV

In the light of the foregoing discussion, we are in a position to reflect on issues of educational governance at the local level and think of some prescriptive measures to meet the challenge. The crisis of the schooling system in the villages of our sample is a reflection of the crisis of governance in several areas in UP. There are four agencies involved in the schooling system in our sample villages—the state at the local level, including the education bureaucracy like the *basik shiksha adhikari*, and school inspectors; functionaries in the block development offices, panchayat members and leaders; and society including castes, communities, 'intellectuals', and private entrepreneurs. Among all these agencies it is the community that has played the leading role in taking an initiative in the education system. In fact, in comparison to the community, the role of the state has been rather negligible. No doubt, the intervention of the state has made a significant contribution to social change. But the very product of the system are also contributing to the sectarianism of the society. They are using education to their advantage at the cost of substantive democracy. There is clearly something wrong with the quality of education that has been imparted to them. Instead of the general interest of society, narrow political considerations seem to have impacted the education system. It seems to me that unless education with moral ingredients is imparted, real politik, caste, and other sectarian considerations are going to play a dominant role. By moral education, I do not mean religious or superstitious teaching, but an education system that inculcates the values of the general good or universal values of tolerance. But this is possible only when a suitable social context exists. It is at present hostile to the values of democracy and tolerance.

Notwithstanding the social context, however, policy makers as individuals, if placed in the vantage position, can play a decisive role in policy formulation (Mathur 2001). The state can introduce special measures to tap local resources. If the potential of the teachers of UAUR schools is channelled, either with the help of NGOs or through the incentive of the state, in collaboration with government schools and open learning institutions, the growing resentment against government schools can be neutralized and their credibility restored.

Two types of measures need to be devised to deal with UAUR schools: first, regarding those groups that start these schools with the purpose of making profit, and, second, regarding those educated and unemployed youth who establish such schools with the purpose of getting jobs. Restrictions need to be imposed on the first group to prevent them from extracting money from students and teachers. As far as the second group is concerned, the state needs to make special efforts to tap their energy. Though they meet all the expenses of UAUR schools from the fees collected from students, they do not have the requisite infrastructure, that is, land, buildings, furniture, etc., for getting the schools recognized and their jobs are uncertain. They can, therefore, be encouraged to set up NGOs. Their services can be utilized for the extension and spread of education by various policies of the state.

In order to enable NGOs to perform effectively, training camps, orientation, and refresher courses can be organized for them. Cultural troupes can be set up to impart moral education with democratic content. Ways to check corruption at the lower levels of bureaucracy need to be devised. Government schools need special consideration. Efforts can be made to ensure that whatever policy is meant for the schools is implemented properly, and funds utilized. The cooperation between government schools, NGOs, open learning centres, and other institutions can be established, and their services utilized in extending education to the rural areas, to tutors/counsels of open learning institutions.

NOTES

1. There is a false impression that the Ambedkar village development programme was started by Mayawati. Identified on the basis of the SC population being in the majority, Ambedkar villages were selected as such first in 1990–1 by the Mulayam Singh Yadav government in UP. The programme was continued by the Mayawati-led BSP–BJP governments. Under this plan, a village is identified as such only for one financial year. But the work once started in an Ambedkar village continues till its completion even after the period. Khanauda was one of around twenty villages identified as Ambedkar villages in Meerut district for the year 1990–1.

2. This is the general picture in several north Indian states (PROBE 1999). For the situation in the study area, see Singh (1995, 1998).

3. The concept of dominance needs to reconsider in the light of the context of time and space. It seems that the response of the state (its various levels, and especially the local state) and other agencies/institutions related to governance is dictated by the numerical strength of the communities, along with their level of politicization or consciousness, and of course their control over material resources. And this varies from context to context. In one place, one community could be a minority, but in another it could form a majority; it may be irrespective of the place of the community in the social hierarchy. In a particular context, even Chamars can form a dominant community. The state responds positively only to those groups/communities that can affect the electoral prospects of its managers; it does not care for those who cannot. My contention is that it is not always the economy and social hierarchy that show the real position of a community in democratic governance. It is a host of factors relevant in this context. Put together, these factors could be called social capital, and mainly include the network of the community, its sharing of norms and values, and the trust it reposes in its members and agencies with which it

interacts (Putnam 1993). There are problems with Putnam's popularization of the concept of social capital (for a critique of Putnam's concept of social capital, see Harriss 2001).

4. For the role of 'intelletucals of Saini society' who mobilized support for the BJP in an election, see Singh (1992: 187).

5. The experience of panchayats in primary education has not been encouraging in states like Rajasthan and West Bengal (see Acharya 2002; Narain 1972).

6. See Mendelsohn and Vicziany (1998; 162–3) and Singh (1992: 142–3). Lieten's (1996) study of seven panchayats in the neighbouring Muzaffarnagar district points out how they have become the preserve of the dominant village pradhans, even as other members are titular.

7. Even other studies (Dreze 1990; Lieten and Srivastava 1999) observe that the IRDP benefited a large number of better-off and 'ineligible' persons.

8. The case of *kanyadan* (gift to the girl at the time of her marriage) from the government in Haryana is the same. The Dalits were not able to avail of it, as it was mandatory to get an age certificate of the girl (she should be 18 years or above). In the absence of authentic records, the medical officer was supposed to certify the age of the girl. The amount given in kanyadan was Rs 5100. But for getting the age certificate, Rs 500 had to be spent on an X-ray and medical check-up, apart from the inconvenience caused and time spent. These are the findings of a survey conducted by the Guru Ravi Das Samaj Mahasabha (*Hindustan Times*, 17 May 2000).

REFERENCES

Acharya, Poromesh, 'Education: Panchayat and Decentralisation', *Economic and Political Weekly*, 37(8), 2002, pp. 788–96.

Advocate, Kumari Mayawati, *Bahujan Samaj Aur Uski Rajniti*, New Delhi: Bahujan Samaj Party, 2000.

Dreze, Jean, 'Poverty in India and the IRDP Delusion', *Economic and Political Weekly*, 25(39), 1990, pp. 95–104.

Dreze, Jean and Amartya Sen, 'Basic Education as Political Issue', *Journal of Educational Planning and Administration*, 9(1), 1995a, pp. 1–26.

———, *India Economic Development and Social Opportunity*, New Delhi: Oxford University Press, 1995b.

Dreze, Jean and H. Gazdar, 'Uttar Pradesh: The Burden of Inertia', in Jean Dreze and Amartya Sen (eds), *India Development: Selected Regional Perspectives*, London: Clarendon Press, 1997.

Dreze, Jean and Mrinalini Saran, 'Primary Education and Economic Development in China and India: Overview and Two Case Studies', in K. Basu, P. Pattanaik, and K. Suzumura (eds), *Choice, Welfare and Development: A Festschrift in Honour of Amartya Sen,* Oxford: Clarendon Press, 1995.

Harriss, John, 'Public Action and Dialectic of Decentralisation: Against the Myths of Social Capital as "the Missing Link in Development"', *Social Scientist*, 29 (11–12), 2001, pp. 23–40.

Jeffrey, Craig, 'Democratisation without Representation? The Power and Political Strategies of Rural Elites in North India', *Political Geography*, 19 (8), 2000, pp. 1013–36.

Jha, S.N. and P.C. Mathur (eds), *Decentralization and Local Politics*, New Delhi: Sage Publications, 1999.

Kingdon, Geeta Gandhi and Mohd. Muzammil, 'Political Economy of Education in India—I and II: The Case of UP', *Economic and Political Weekly of India*, 36 (32 and 33), 2001, pp. 352–63, 3178–85.

Lieten, G.K., 'Panchayats in Western Uttar Pradesh: "Namesake" Members', *Economic and Political Weekly*, 31(39), 1996, pp. 2700–7.

Lieten, G.K. and Ravi Srivastava, *Unequal Partners: Power Relations, Devolution and Development in Uttar Pradesh*, New Delhi: Sage Publications, 1999.

Mathur, Kuldeep, 'Does Performance Matter? Policy Struggle in Education', *Journal of Educational Planning and Administration*, 25(2), 2001, pp. 225–40.

Mendelsohn, Oliver and Marika Vicziany, *The Untouchables: Subordination, Poverty and the State in Modern India*, Cambridge: Cambridge University Press, 1998.

Narain, Iqbal, 'Rural Politics and Primary School Management', in S.H. Rudolph and L.I. Rudolph (eds), *Education and Politics in India: Organization, Society and Politics*, New Delhi: Oxford University Press, 1972.

PROBE, *Public Report on Basic Education in India*, New Delhi: Oxford University Press, 1999.

Putnam, Robert D., *Making Democracy Work: Civic Tradtions in Modern Italy*, Princeton: Princeton University Press, 1993.

Weiner, Myron, *The Child and the State in India: Child Labour and Education Policy in Comparative Perspective*, New Delhi: Oxford University Press, 1991.

Singh, Jagpal, *Capitalism and Dependence: Agrarian Politics in Meerut District of Western Uttar Pradesh 1951–1991*, Delhi: Manohar Publishers, 1992.

———, *Political Economy of Unaided and Unrecognised Schools: A Study of Meerut District of Western Uttar Pradesh* (project report), New Delhi: National Institute of Educational Planning and Administration (NIEPA), 1995.

———, 'In Search of Quality Education: Alternative Schooling in Meerut District of Western Uttar Pradesh', in Yash Aggarwal and Kusum K. Premi (eds), *Reforming School Education: Issues in Policy Planning and Implementation*, New Delhi: Vikas Publishing House, 1998.

———, 'Shifts in Patterns of Dominance: Agrarian Politics in Village Khanauda of North India', unpublished paper, 2000.

———, 'The Bahujan Samaj Party: Ideology, Social Basis of Support and Politics', in A.K. Jana and Bhupen Sarmah (eds), *Class, Ideology and Political Parties in India*, New Delhi: South Asian Publishers, 2002.

9

People-centred Development and Participatory Urban Governance
The Mumbai Experience

■ MARINA R. PINTO

Democracy and good governance are the buzzwords of today. But to have the one is not necessarily to have the other. A democratic state is undoubtedly all about people's governance, but it could represent the 'thinning of democracy' rather than the deepening of it, particularly when it is of the plebiscitary type. Democracy in India has been described as the playground of the corrupt, communal, and criminalized sectors of the polity and the economy. There is steady decline and decay of conventional mainstream politics and its institutional erosion. There is lack of people-centred development. The correctives have to be found in a vibrant civil society and local activism, defined as 'new localism' in the context of globalization. This chapter addresses these issues, highlighting developments with reference to Mumbai.

PEOPLE-CENTRED DEVELOPMENT

The thinking of the 1950s and early 1960s equated development with economic growth. The UN-declared first decade of development of the 1960s spoke of growth plus change. The emphasis was on investment, production, and growth, but the whole issue of distribution was absent. Before long, development was equated with modernization, taken to mean westernization. By the mid-1960s the modernization view was challenged for it was realized that the ills of developing societies were the result of colonialism and economic exploitation. Economic development was handicapped because of dependency on resources of foreign countries. While the first development decade considered the social and economic aspects of development separately, the second (1970–80) involved merging the two. The new paradigm formulated, emphasized the interaction of physical resources, technical processes, economic development, and social change. It was the 'unified approach' to development (UNRISD 1980: 16) that sought to integrate the economic and social components in the formulation of policies and programmes. The unified approach to development also looked for participative development as it wanted involvement of all sectors of the population in the development process, a focus on social equity, and high priority for development of the human potential.

The Conference on Employment, Income Distribution, and Social Progress organized by the ILO in 1976 offered another perspective, that is, the Basic Needs Approach (ILO 1977:7) which had the merit of having universal applicability while being at the same time country specific. The Dag Hammarskjold Foundation suggested in 1975 *Another Development*, which took into account the role of a country's own culture, societal values, and norms in gaining self-sufficiency and self-direction. In other words, 'endogenous and self-reliant growth' held the key to 'another development' (Dag Hammarskjold Foundation 1975). Taking it from there, the UNESCO promoted the concept of endogenous development that soon won acceptance. The third development decade of the 1980s, the decade of deregulation, demo-cratization, and decentralization, was also seen as the decade of debt and disillusionment. Many countries had to abandon or dismantle most of the earlier policies and devise their own development plans of action to grapple with their own unique problems. It was clear that the whole pursuit of development was very complex and there was a degree of global interdependence. Above all, in developing countries development had to be seen as a human enterprise.

What had happened was that conventional paradigms of develop-ment had failed. The *World Development Report* (World Bank 2000: 7), stated that 50 years of development experiment had clearly indicated that growth does not trickle down, and a more comprehensive approach to development is needed; that institutions do matter and that development should be sustainable and be rooted in processes that are socially inclusive and responsive to changing circumstances. The missing link in all the previous theories and strategies of development was the *people*, who ought to have been in the centre of development, both as the ends and the means of development. This was succinctly stated by the South Commission thus: 'The base for a nation's development must be its own resources, both human and material, fully used to meet its own needs ...Development has therefore to be an effort of, by and for the people. True development has to be people-centred' (South Commission 1990: 10–11).

People-centred development (PCD) is broadly seen as alternative development. 'Alternative' here generally refers to three spheres—agents, methods, and objectives or values of development. According to Nerfin (1977) alternative development is the terrain of the 'third system', or citizen politics, which becomes important because of the failure of developmental efforts of the government (first system) and economic power (second system). It is alternative in relation to the state and the market, and is essentially development from below. But in the 1980s, when the private sector came to be viewed as the leading sector of development, the scope of alternative development widened to include the state. Thus, Friedmann (1992) and others argued that a strong civil society and a strong state go together, with the state functioning as a change agent, a facilitator of people's self-development. So, 'step-by-step we have moved to a recognition that government, business, and voluntary organizations all have essential roles in development' (Korten 1990: 95).

Alternative development tends to be practice-oriented rather than theory-inclined. However, several alternative development thinkers merit attention. Korten (ibid.: 67), who sees development as a 'process by which the members of a society increase their personal and institutional capacities to mobilize and manage resources to produce sustainable and justly distributed improvements in their quality of life consistent with their own aspirations', is an NGO strategist. Rahman (1993) sees development as people's self-development, and people as creative forces of development. John Friedmann is primarily concerned with local and regional planning. Manfred Max-Neef and Hazel Henderson are alternative economists, the former engaged with local development and the latter with global alternatives.

Alternative development or PCD does not represent a paradigm break in development. There is no clear line of demarcation between mainstream development and alternative development. There can be overlap between the two. Forms of alternative development can become institutionalized as part of mainstream development, and, in fact, PCD is becoming a mainstream position (Nederveen Pieterse 2001: 94).

PCD has come to the centre stage since the 1990s. It sees development in a holistic fashion and gives vital importance to the role of the people in the developmental process, in decision-making, and in networking, thus enhancing their creativity and self-help capacity. The *World Development Report* recognizes the importance of the 'local' for raising levels of participation and providing people with greater ability to shape the context of their lives. It is here that the vertical structures of power get 'horizontalized and democratized and re-rooted locally in the political, social and economic organizations of the people themselves' (World Bank 1999: 173).

With PCD we need to redefine the role of the state and institutions of civil society. The state is an empowerment agent that facilitates greater participation of the needy and disadvantaged through organs of civil society. Scholars like Atul Kohli and L.C. Jain are of the opinion that the power of the state is itself to be determined by its ability to work with and through social actors. The new perspective is that of state-in-society, with partnerships viewed as 'instruments of governance' (Jon 1998: 20). When different actors with the development agendas in mind come together, there is a new form of 'synergy', a mutually reinforcing relation between governments and groups. It can make for the 'politics of restructuring and reconstitution or the shifting boundaries between the private and the public' (Brodie 1996: 396).

PCD, therefore, calls for 'basic' changes in the politico–administrative set-up in terms of attitudes and structures. The government has to provide the enabling policy environment, while non-governmental organizations and community-based organizations develop people's self-help capabilities and build networks. What PCD calls for is collaborative endeavours between public, private, and voluntary sectors.

CIVIL SOCIETY

Civil society is conceptualized as a space where people can pursue self-defined ends in an associational area of common concerns. It is critical to PCD in a democratic polity.

Democracy, as a viable form of governance, comprises representation, voice, due process, and accountability as its common features.
'Democracy ...therefore, does not merely imply creation and nurturing
of a political society ... Democracy requires nurturance and growth
of civil society ...This is the arena of grassroots democracy, this is the
space for citizen participation, this is the playground of civil society'
(Tandon 1997: 39). However, the pluralistic character of society neither
ensures democracy, nor implies a strengthening of the open domain
of public life. A vital civil society may sustain and be reinforced by a
viable constitutional democracy through institutionalized forms of
interaction and exchange that can prevent the monopolization of
power and resources. Democracy can be strengthened when citizens
engage in joint action while sharing a broad commitment to the
public sphere.

Any democratic polity, in order to ensure good governance, should
provide citizens with what Habermas (1990) describes as the 'public
sphere'. This public sphere is a pluralist civic space created away from
the state, in and out of civil society. The public sphere is not absorbed
into the state, but addresses the state and the 'sorts of public issues on
which state policy might bear'.

The concept of civil society has evolved over the years and has
meant different things at different times. Hegel subordinated civil
society to the state, while Marx reversed this by postulating the
primacy of civil society. While Gramsci emphasized the
interpenetration of state and society, Foucault conceptualized the
state as made up of bits of power located through society. Often,
much emphasis is put on the cultural dimension of civil society. It is
seen as a synonym for community (*gemeinschaft*) or mezzo-structures
between the micro level of family and macro level of the nation-
state.

Liberal thought emphasizes the role of individualism in civil society.
Authentic individualism, based on individual rights, provides the very
tapestry of associations. Individuals attach or detach themselves from
groups and associations and in this 'there is no sacrifice of will or
reason, rather will and reason are applied to bring success to a common
enterprise'.[1] Liberal thinking that upholds rights and dignity of the
individual identifies 'the central ideal of civil society as personal
independence and its central imperative as respect for persons'.[2]

Individuation and association are so interlinked that through associational activity one achieves liberty. In much of liberal theory, civil society is the sphere of rights and the rule of law that is guaranteed by the state. It exists because of the state. At the same time, liberal theorists like Alexis de Tocqueville have conceptualized civil society as a buffer that protects the individual against the state.

Civil society is best seen as that which is not government. It is distinct and different from the state. For most thinkers, civil society involves relationships that go beyond the family but are not within the realm of the state.

By and large, civil society here is taken in the liberal tradition. It alludes to the existence of organized public life and free associations beyond the tutelage of the state, yet oriented toward the public sphere and toward influencing public policies. It refers to the interlinking arena, where private interests meet public concerns and both are mutually structured in a public sphere with its own rules.

Civil society presupposes citizens' awareness. This leads to the formation of social capital that has to do with interpersonal trust, networks, and shared norms that enable people to act together more effectively to pursue shared objectives. Hence, social capital is intangible and is embodied in the *relations* among persons (Putnam 1993: 89).

There are several views on civil society in India. R. Kothari, A. Nandy, and D.L. Sheth are exponents of civil society as embodying customary and traditional ties. Ananta Kumar Giri wants civil society to have a spiritual dimension, namely, self and social transformation. D. Gupta would relate civil society to citizenship and emphasize the primacy of the political where political is adjunct of the state. A position worth consideration is that of Kothari, who talks of non-party political processes and sees civil society as the non-state domain of protest and challenge. Civil society may be people's action outside the state, but it has a political stance; an attempt to widen the range and arena of politics, taking it beyond the electoral and legislative politics.

In India, civil society manifests itself in organizations, be they missionary and religious, caste and communal, educational and philanthropic that are indicative of the high value attached to 'filial and fraternal solidarity'. The total number of independent groups (including NGOs and other welfare and charity organizations) on one count ranges from 50,000 to 100,000 (Vikalp 1994). A possible classification of these groups is welfare/charity, developmental, struggle-oriented social action groups and movements, legal action support, and single-issue organizations. D.N. Dhanagare has singled out the 'large number of action groups who have been trying to educate, conscientise and mobilise different marginalised sections, particularly the oppressed poor' as 'the most important development in India since the 1960s' (as quoted by Kothari 1994:6).

Until the Sixth Plan (1980–5) voluntary agencies were seen to play the traditional role in the welfare, education and medical sectors. But from the Seventh Plan (1985–90) onwards there has been a shift in that the Plan looked at NGOs 'as the eyes and ears of the beneficiaries' and government took on a partnership role with NGOs in developmental efforts.[3] Though there was formal recognition granted to NGOs and also increased funding, the importance of the *urban* sector and PCD found a place only in the Eighth Plan (1992–7), which took into account the report of the National Commission on Urbanization, 1988, and the attempt made to grant constitutional status to urban local bodies through the 65th Constitutional Amendment Bill, 1989. The concern for urban governance and PCD was writ large in the Ninth Plan (1997–2002). It talked of 'ushering in a new era of people-oriented participative planning, in which people at large and especially the poor, can participate' (Government of India 1997). The change in governmental thinking is certainly an encouraging move.

India is plagued with the crisis of governability. In the 1980s and the 1990s, the political class responded to the emerging crisis by adopting different strategies. Rajni Kothari (1989: 400) has described these as the repressive, co-optative, divisive, and diversionary tactics of the new Janus-faced structure of the state. For instance, through caste reservations (Mandalization) and religious assertions (Hindutva platform), the political class was able to defuse the emerging crisis of aspirations. To the powerful middle and upper middle classes, the safety valve opened up through liberalization. The Narasimha Rao government, in 1991, through an immediate structural adjustment programme and the New Economic Policy, indicated that India had moved from a state-led model of development to a free market model or liberalization model for economic growth.

The end of the twentieth century has brought into sharp focus the problematique of state and market, society and politics. There is a weakening of political cohesion of the Indian state reflected in coalitional politics and a fractured political process reflected in interaction between state and civil society, with the latter manifesting itself through activists, voluntary organizations, and grass roots movements. Often, one sees 'uncivil' civil society resorting to symbolic and agitational politics like hartals (strikes), *rasta roko* (road blocks), and gheraos (lock-ins) (Rudolph and Rudolph 1987: 253). What is called for is creative social commitment by generating a countervailing power in the people.

With liberalization, there is much deregulation and dismantling of government controls and downsizing of government. Selected activities are handed over to the private sector and NGOs are encouraged to work in the social development sector, especially in fields like education and health. Efforts are afoot to incorporate administrative changes like môre flat structures, numerous decision points, teamwork, and multiplicity of agencies.

All this is in keeping with international thinking. In the UN Conference on Environment and Development (UNCED) held at Rio de Janeiro in 1992, 150 nations endorsed Agenda 21(UNCED 1993: chapter 28), which emphasized the importance of participation and cooperation of local authorities. With Habitat II or the City Summit in 1996, the General Assembly of the UN officially recognized the vitality of local politics and the importance of local variations in the era of globalization. The CAPAM Conference in Canada (1994) (Bhattacharya 1997) saw the need of a strong state playing the role of a catalytic change agent concerned with macro policy-making and physical, legal, and human infrastructure building, while simultaneously strengthening civil society by 'empowering' citizens. The *World Development Report 1999* focused on the globalization and localization, and saw localization as revitalizing the local realm by raising levels of participation and involvement and providing people with a greater ability to shape their own lives. All this can result in more responsive and efficient local governments.

Civil society analysis needs special mention of the political variable that, at the minimum, implies both the political associations that play important roles in any society and the work of political compromise, restraint, and accommodation necessary for reconciling competing interests. In situations where the state is unresponsive and its democratic wherewithal does not recognize and respond to citizen demands, civil society will be characterized by assertive or even aggressive forms of activity against the state or self-protective apathy.

In discussing civil society in India, it is not enough to speak of associational activity that is essentially societal and volatile, but to relate such activity to the state: in short, to make the state the reference point. Hence, one cannot focus on civil society minus the state and vice versa. Neera Chandhoke (1995: 9) sums it best when she states: 'The state attempts to constitute the political discourse. The sites at which mediations and contestations take place, the site at which society enters into a relationship with the state, can be defined as civil society.'

Civil society provides the wherewithal for PCD. Its role can be seen to raise concerns, to hold the state accountable, to set agendas, to build social capital, strengthen democracy, establish peace and good governance, and ensure empowerment of the people in more ways than one.

NEW LOCALISM

PCD is all about development from below. It stands for 'human growth defined in terms of greater realization of human potentialities'. Government policies have to create an enabling environment within which people can effectively meet their own needs. So the focus is on the local and the civil society actors. Also, in the context of globalization, liberalization, and privatization, the nation–state is more of an enabler or facilitator rather than a provider. It has thereby enabled localities to become arenas for testing, experimenting, and working out policies. Localities have become significant sites of action, giving rise to local activism and what has been described as 'new localism'.

'New localism'[4] is all about rather fundamental political restructuring. This has two dimensions—the vertical, seen in terms of Centre–state–local relations and how they relate to each other. The other is the horizontal dimension that includes a redefinition of responsibilities between the state and organizations of civil society, between the public and private sectors at the local level. New localism gives rise to a vertical–horizontal connectivity, which continues to be in a state of flux, creating 'space' for new groups and coalitions, which are linked and not isolated from either the state or national politics. The economic rationale for new localism stems from new industrial spaces that result from globalizing and restructuring processes in which localities have a heightened awareness of their enhanced roles.[5] The political rationale for new localism is based not only on community values or even necessarily locational logic, but has an instrumental use as a political strategy to circumvent or replace outmoded structures of central bureaucracies.

Local activism is a defining feature of new localism, particularly in the context of globalization. It can give a spurt to new local development groups, structured on corporate lines, which act in partnership with or take the place of public authority. To the extent that these voluntary bodies take on tasks performed neither by the state nor the market, they function as a 'shadow state'. It is not as if the political role of local government is negated. On the contrary, local officials have a political steering role in new alternative development paths. Among other things, they have to provide directions, emphasize conditions under which politics regulates markets at the local level, maintain the local institutional infrastructure, and provide new decision frameworks for the processes of negotiation and bargaining between private interests and public authority.

Under a globalized regime, there is much happening locally. The contours of the local state keep changing with ongoing vertical and horizontal restructuring. New localism is open and deliberate. It is open to interaction with the rest of the world. It has given rise to 'new politics' that raises new issues that electoral politics cannot contain. It is about working around and transcending the prevalent institutional structures of democracy. New political opportunity structures arise, making, in a way, for a new opportunistic local state that responds pragmatically to opportunities that come its way and is not averse to gainful privatizing of local authority.

New localism encompasses proactive development strategies with emphasis on grass roots activism in the urban realm. 'Going local' means nurturing the locality and using the resources, skills, and strategies devised by the local people. It is people-centred in that it has to do with their needs, demands, and aspirations. There is emphasis on collaboration and coordination among state and non-state actors as partners in the development process. It is open and flexible, seeking ways and means to enhance people's participation. In the churning process in the local state, brought on by internal and external factors, the field is open for civil society actors through local activism to operationalize people-centred development.

PCD IN MUMBAI

Mumbai is the largest city in the Indian subcontinent. It is the 'urbs prima' in India and hailed as its commercial and financial capital. A mega city, it accounts for over 80 per cent of the financial and business dealings of Maharashtra and handles 42 per cent of India's import–export trade. It has a population of 12.6 million people as per the Census of 1991, which is approximately 1.5 per cent of the total population of India.

Migration has constituted about 23 per cent of the population growth of Mumbai during the last decade. The proportion of urban population in the state has increased from 38.7 per cent in 1991 to 42.4 per cent in 2001, as against 27 per cent at the all-India level. Half of the total urban population is concentrated in just seven cities, with Mumbai accounting for one-third of it.[6]

In Mumbai, new localism is manifest in the horizontal-vertical connectivity which is indicative of networking between NGOs, CBOs, and the like, and their linkages with the government at all levels. Initiatives for formations of new partnerships and collaborations have increased in the 1990s to support and supplement government efforts at the local level. Communities have organized themselves, particularly the downtrodden and disadvantaged, like slum and pavement dwellers, and in concert with NGOs and government have solved their problems, demonstrating PCD in action. A good illustration is the Kanjur Marg experiment relating to slum resettlement.

Mumbai houses half of its population in slums because of distorted urban development. Slum settlements keep on increasing, especially on railway property, with families living dangerously along the tracks. Although the Railways, which come under the central government, rightly claimed that the land was theirs and so would not implement the state government's policy for slums, yet they refused to shift squatters, saying that these were encroachers and moving them was the responsibility of the state government or the Brihanmumbai Municipal Corporation (BMC). It was soon realized that until and unless there was collaborative effort, the problem could not be solved.

The NGO involved was the Society for Promotion of Area Resource Centre (SPARC), which had a good track record of working for the urban poor, especially pavement dwellers. SPARC's intervention resulted in the women pavement dwellers organizing themselves and articulating their shelter needs. The Community-Based Organization (CBO) that was thus created was Mahila Milan (MM), which empowered women. MM is involved in savings and credit activity. It has demonstrated how women pavement dwellers can handle not just money matters, but look into the nitty-gritty of house building and even lobby effectively and negotiate with local and state governments.

The alliance between SPARC and MM was expanded to include the National Slum Dwellers Federation (NSDF) and its subsidiary, the Railways Slum Dwellers Federation (RSDF). The alliance members kept their individual identities and manner and style of functioning. What they shared in common was their concern for the poor and their intense desire to work through their differences and interact with government rather than confront it. Partnering was dictated by a realization that slum resettlement was just not possible without Railway finances, state government land, and local government infrastructure.

The Slum Rehabilitation Authority (SRA), a quasi-government agency, was set up in 1996. The CEO of the SRA, a dynamic and enlightened civil servant, chaired the project coordination committee that brought together representatives of the Railways, alliance, and concerned state government departments. The Railways made available Rs 13.8 million through the SRA. The alliance members, working with the BMC and SRA were able to shift 900 families in the first phase. These families were grouped into 27 cooperatives that were largely led by women who saved enough to be able to attract a housing loan from Housing & Urban Development Corporation Ltd (HUDCO) routed through SPARC to cover the cost of the initial temporary accommodation.

The Kanjur Marg experiment could succeed because of the coming together of several factors at the most opportune time. In the first place, there was the conducive policy environment supportive of slum rehabilitation and redevelopment.[7] The idea of Transfer of Development Rights (TDR) was operationalized in that extra space was sold in the open market, so that houses for slum dwellers could be cross-subsidized. The government of Maharashtra, in its Resolution of March 1997, among other things, stated that the policy objectives were 'to develop the details of the resettlement programme through active community participation by establishing links with the community-based organizations'. Apart from the involvement of civil society organizations, there was the conditionality in respect of loans of the World Bank, that community involvement must be an integral component of projects involving displacement. Above all, leaders like Jockin Arputham of the slum dwellers, Gautam Chatterjee, CEO of SRA, and D.T. Joseph from the government of Maharashtra exerted to make the gigantic project succeed.

When development is not people-centred, well-meaning schemes can fail as happened in another experiment that involves slum resettlement. The Shivshahi Punarvasan Prakalp Limited (SPPL) was set up as a company to provide free houses for 400,000 slum dwellers of Mumbai. It was the brainchild of Bal Thackeray, the Shiv Sena supremo. The state government decided to set up this company with the Maharashtra Housing and Area Development Authority (MHADA) and Mumbai Metropolitan Region Development Authority (MMRDA) as its constituents, with each contributing equally to the SPPL's capital of Rs 6 billion. Even though the number of houses was scaled down to 50,000, the scheme flopped. To begin with, the Afzulpurkar Committee in 1995 that worked out this scheme was faulty as it comprised builders and only one NGO representative. There was very poor response from private sector developers to the loan facilities offered by the SPPL. Public–private partnerships just did not take off. A number of projects initially sanctioned were taken up by developers of dubious background and many slum dwellers were taken for a ride. Many projects had to be abandoned.

There is also the case of the Jogeshwari and Mahakali caves that are a national heritage. These have been encroached upon by slum dwellers. The BMC at the local level, the Archaeological Survey of India (ASI), a central body, the Indian National Trust for Art and Cultural Heritage (INTACH), and the collector have been buck-passing and have allowed the caves to become a national shame.

A good example of an integrated approach and partnership in ameliorating the problems of migrant construction workers is Nirman, started in 1986 by the Nirmala Niketan's College of Social Work as a field project for social work students.

Construction activity is the second largest industry in India, next only to agriculture, that absorbs the largest number of the unorganized labour force. This activity could be described as temporary, seasonal, contractual, and risk-ridden, involving workers who are illiterate and unskilled. Though Nirman began with mobile crèches and other welfare activities like adult education programmes and health camps, its main thrust now is to combat the exploitative system that the construction industry perpetuates, by empowering the workers. With this end in view, Nirman initiated the Nirman Mazdoor Sanghatana (NMS) in 1990. The NMS has been registered under the Trade Unions Act.

Nirman has helped in creating awareness at various levels and among concerned parties like contractors, principal employers, medical professionals, social workers, and government and health authorities. Beginning at the micro level, it is now into networking, capacity building, and worker-related research. At the macro level, Nirman is working for policy changes, especially in matters of labour rights and labour laws.

A good example of partnership in women's empowerment is the Annapurna Mahila Mandal (AMM). The textile strike of 1974 in Mumbai led to jobless women workers forming a grass roots organization. They got down to the job they were good at, namely, cooking and providing food to migrant mill workers. Since 1985, the AMM has expanded its catering activity and has set up canteens, women's hostels, hospitals, and even a housing society. The catering scheme of the AMM is an employment generation programme. The work of the AMM bears testimony to how women can be empowered to become micro entrepreneurs. The inspiration for the government Rashtriya Mahila Kosh (RMK) that provided an alternate source of credit for poor women and the Indira Mahila Yojana (IMY) that offers schemes for women came from NGOs like the AMM.

Another example of partnering between citizens and police is seen in *mohalla* committees. These are non-political citizens' peace committees, set up throughout the city police stations to maintain communal harmony. The committees bring together members of both Hindu and Muslim communities along with police officers. Mohalla committees look into complaints related to police work, civic issues, education, sports, youth affairs, and above all promote communal harmony. It is believed that mohalla magic ensures communal peace in Mumbai and keeps it riot-free. Set up in the wake of the Babri Masjid demolition, they have been effective organs of civil society for the last ten years.

A fine illustration of PCD in the field of primary education is Pratham. It is a public charitable trust, initiated in 1994 by UNICEF, BMC, and several prominent citizens like Madhav Chavan and Farida Lambay. Its aim is to create a societal mission for achieving universal pre-primary and primary education in the city. Its goal is simple: 'Every child must go to school regularly and learn well.' Its method is to build a partnership between citizens, the corporate sector, communities, and the government.

Pratham[8] did not start with a detailed plan of action as it did not have any expertise or experience in early childhood education. So it had to network with NGOs and institutions for training. Nor did it have financial backing except for a basic seed funding of Rs 600,000 per year for three years from UNICEF.

Until Pratham took the initiative, the BMC had never supported early childhood or pre-school education. Also, it was Pratham's considered decision to improve the services of the BMC rather than develop its own independent programme. It improved on the BMC's Vasantik Varga programme and developed the Pratham *balwadi* model. The value addition to the balwadi network is the health programme for pre-school children. The cornerstone of Pratham's activity are the resource centres that are jointly developed by Pratham and the BMC. These centres plan, monitor, and evaluate academic activities in each ward while also organizing training for teachers. Pratham has a very effective bridge course programme that caters to the needs of out-of-school children with the purpose of getting them into school again. There is the Balsakhi Programme where the *balsakhi* (teacher's helper or child's friend) is linked to the school's own plan of how to improve the quality of teacher–pupil interaction in the classroom.

Today, Pratham has a presence in every slum community in Mumbai. Its programmes include approximately 3000 pre-school centres (covering 45,000 3 to 5-year-olds), 700 bridge courses (covering over 8000 out-of-school children between the ages of 6 and 12), and over 800 balsakhis working with over 40,000 children in municipal schools. There is therefore an 'education net' to enable every child to be in school. Pratham has become a large-scale community-based movement for universal primary education. With liberalization under way, the corporate sector has chipped in to help out. In 1998, computers that were phased out of ICICI were donated to Pratham to work out a project of 'leap-frogging into the twenty-first century' for municipal school children. ICICI continues its support in this regard along with others like Tata Sons and Mahindra and Mahindra. Thus, the Pratham Mumbai Education Initiative demonstrates how new localism in the field of PCD can deliver the goods.

Advanced Locality Management (ALM) is a street or area committee of citizens that is involved in civic services in partnership with the BMC. Each ALM has a nodal officer appointed by the ward officer to coordinate and redress the complaints of the ALM. To begin with, the ALM was restricted to the management of garbage. The BMC lifts the wet garbage that is used for vermi-composting and the dry part is given to rag-pickers. The ALM is now expanded to include all civic services in their localities. Every second Saturday, the ALM representative meets the ward officer, and every fourth Saturday two representatives of ALM societies from each ward meet the additional municipal commissioner along with NGOs.

There is the Action for Good Governance and Networking in India (AGNI) that works with various NGOs to build citizen awareness. Its joint action groups (JAGs) in municipal wards coordinate with NGOs like Dignity Foundation, Police–Public Mohalla Committees, and Bombay First to tackle problems eluding solution by a ward office/police station. JAGs evolve a democratic process to help an elected representative spend his or her annual discretionary fund that varies from Rs 2 million for a corporator to Rs 20 million for an MP.

The above are but a few of the civil society actors working through citizen action groups of all kinds that seek PCD at the grass roots. Theirs has not always been a success story, but the shape of things to come is clearly seen in growing local activism and citizen awareness. What is commendable is that NGOs work with strong community support. They establish horizontal ties that also bridge differences of all kinds, be they caste, class, or religion. They have high credibility given their ear to the ground. What makes for many gains is the partnership between themselves and the state.

CONCLUSION

The slogan of the day is 'Think Globally, Act Locally'. The emphasis on the local is the result of the nation-state undergoing a transformation. It has become too small to deal with global trends with the attendant risks of erosion of state's sovereignty, transnationalization of production, and standardization of consumer wants and cultures. It has become too big to cater to individual needs and, therefore, more authority and autonomy have to accrue to local institutions. In a sense, as Ash (1994: 282) states, 'there is a double movement of globalisation on the one hand and devolution, decentralisation and localisation on the other, which has been termed as "glocalisation"'.

In this emerging scenario, under a liberalized regime and in the context of participatory democracy, movements, action groups, and the like, all representative of a vibrant civil society have introduced new conceptions of power and politics. They have initiated new modes of organizations, emphasizing self-government and decentralization to effect PCD. It is new localism that is the affirmation of the local, the second democratic revolution or the 'quiet revolution in local governance'. The Mumbai experience corroborates the what, how, and why of participatory urban governance, for what Gerson Da Cunha of AGNI stated, 'We have come to the conclusion that only citizens are for citizens' is ever so true!

NOTES

1. Alexis de Tocqueville, as quoted in 'The Vision Motivating the Institute for Civil Society', Institute for Civil Society, http://www.civilsociety.org/mission.htm.
2. Anthony Black, as quoted in ibid.
3. For details with respect to voluntary agencies and the Seventh Plan, read Roy (1987).
4. For details on new localism, see Pinto (1993: ch. 2).

5. There is a view that globalization, in promoting unfettered markets, can clash with endogenous development that people-centred democracy promotes.Yet the mushrooming of NGOs itself is an indication of the growing global civil society and this too is part of the globalizing process.
6. Statistics taken from *The Economic Times*, Mumbai, 25 March 2002.
7. The 1950s and 1960s are seen as the demolition decades as the contributions of slum dwellers to the city's economy were not recognized. But the decade of the 1970s could be described as that of slum resettlement as it was a policy decision to provide the slums with civic amenities. The 1980s saw slum upgradation as the World Bank supported a Slum Upgradation Programme—a thirty-year renewable lease of land to cooperatives of slum dwellers on an 'as is, where is' basis. But the most conducive environment came in the 1990s with a focus on slum rehabilitation and redevelopment
8. This section is based on data collected from Chavan (2000), UNESCO 2000 and interviews with BMC officials and Pratham spokesmen.

REFERENCES

Ash, Amin (ed.), *Post Fordism: A Reader*, Oxford and Cambridge: Blackwell, 1994.

Bhattacharya, Mohit, 'Public Administration Today and Tomorrow', *The Indian Journal of Public Administration*, Number: Fifty Years on Indian Administration—Retrospect and Prospects, XLIII (3), pp. 323–30, 1997.

Brodie, Janie, 'New State Forms, New Political Spaces', in R. Bayer and D. Dracke (eds), *State Against Markets*, London: Routledge, 1996.

Chandhoke, N. *State and Civil Society: Explorations in Political Theory*, New Delhi: Sage Publications, 1995.

Chavan, Madhav, *Building Societal Missions for Universal Pre-school and Primary Education: The Pratham Experience*, Paris: International Institute for Educational Planning, 2000.

Dag Hammarskjold Foundation, *What Now? Another Development: A Special Issue of Development Dialogue*, Uppsala: Dag Hammarskjold Foundation, 1975.

Goetz, E.G. and Susan Clarke (eds), *The New Localism: Comparative Urban Politics in a Global Era*, London: Sage, 1993.

Government of India, *Approach Paper to the Ninth Five Year Plan (1997-2002)*, New Delhi: Nabhi Publications, 1997.

Friedmann, J., *Empowerment: The Politics of Alternative Development*, Oxford: Blackwell, 1992.

Habermas, J., *Moral Consciousness and Communicative Action*, Cambridge: Polity, 1990.

ILO, *Basic Needs Approach to Development*, Geneva: ILO, 1977.

Jon, Pierre (ed.), *Partnerships in Urban Governance*, London: Macmillan, 1998.

Korten, D.C., *Getting to the 21st Century: Voluntary Action and the Global Agenda*, West Hartford, CT: Kumarian Press, 1990.

Kothari, Rajni, *Politics and the People: In Search of Humane India* (vol. II), Delhi: Ajanta Publications, 1989.

Kothari, Smitu, 'Social Movements and the Redefinition of Democracy', *Vikalp: Alternatives*, 3 (1), 1994.

Nerfin, M. (ed.), *Another Development: Approaches and Strategies*, Uppsala: Dag Hammarskjold Foundation, 1977.

Nederveen Pieterse, J., *Development Theory: Deconstructions/Reconstructons*, New Delhi: Vistaar Publications, 2001.

Pinto, Marina R., *Metropolitan City Governance in India*, New Delhi: Sage, 2000.

Putnam, R.D., *Making Democracy Work: Civic Traditions in Modern Italy*, Princeton, NJ: Princeton University Press, 1993.

Rahman, M.A., *People's Self-development: Perspectives on Participatory Action Research*, London and Dhaka: Zed and Dhaka University Press, 1993.

Roy, Satyajit (Bunker), 'Voluntary Agencies in Development: Their Role, Policy and Programmes', *The Indian Journal of Public Administration*, Number on Voluntary Organizations and Development, 3, pp. 454–64, 1987.

Rudolph, Lloyd I. and Susanne H. Rudolph, *In Pursuit of Lakshmi*, Bombay: Orient Longman, 1987.

South Commission, *The Challenge to the South: The Report of the South Commission*, New York: Oxford University Press, 1990.

Tandon, Rajesh, 'Grassroots Democracy', *Seminar*, March, 1997, p. 39.

UNCED, *Agenda 21: Programme of Action for Sustainable Development*, New York, United Nations, Department of Information, 1993.

United Nations Research Institute for Social Development (UNRISD), *The Quest for a Unified Approach to Development*, Geneva: UNRISD, 1980.

Vikalp: Alternatives, 3 (1), 1994.

World Bank, *World Development Report*, New York: Oxford University Press, 1999.

————, *World Development Report 1999/2000. Entering the 21st Century*, New York: Oxford University Press, 2000.

10

Urban Futures of Poor Groups in Chennai and Bangalore
How these are Shaped by the Relationships between Parastatals and Local Bodies

■ SOLOMON BENJAMIN AND R. BHUVANESWARI

INTRODUCTION

Divergent ideological groups agree that economic globalization has contributed to widening inequalities: while a few are able to access infrastructure and services that are of a high quality and equivalent to First-World levels, most others are denied access to even its most rudimentary form. We suggest that an important issue of urban poverty relates to transformations in governance structures rather than technocratic factors. Emerging institutional arrangements adversely impact 'voice' and the 'manoeuvring' ability of poor groups to influence policy and implementation in their favour. Furthermore, they seem to perpetuate a situation of forced illegality.

The seriousness of the issue is accentuated when we consider that for the poor's access to jobs and economic survival is most important. As cities get globally connected, productive locations in both central city areas and the periphery become competitive terrain between those economies catering to poor (among other groups) and a globally connected economy benefiting the richer ones. In the ensuing conflicts, at stake is not only a life-giving economic process but also a political one. At stake here are not 'marginal' informal economies that with 'modernization or globalization' would vanish. There is empirical evidence to show in a variety of contexts that such economies form the dominant process (Portes 1996) and, significantly, are backed by political might (Benjamin 1996; Singerman 1997: 173). Such dualistic views informal and formal have been shown long ago to be conceptually faulty and operationally fuzzy. The persistence of use of such concepts can only be explained from an ideological viewpoint. Today, with globalization, such ideological positions appear to have been reinvented to suit a global need: improvement of the 'macro' environment to attract capital funding is essential for cities to be competitive—even if such actions replace poorer areas and deprive them of their claims. The issue here is that of increasing claims of big business on locations where access is made possible via particular types of institutional structures and policy making.

There are three important political–institutional aspects to appreciate in placing the larger argument made in this chapter. First, our earlier research at the grass roots on urban poverty in Bangalore (Benjamin and Bhuvaneswari 2001) and on local clustering economies in Delhi (Benjamin 1996) focused in part on the nature of 'voice'. This relates not necessarily to explicit protest, revealed in civil movements or empowered by public litigation. Instead, it relates to more a subtle and hidden range of institutional strategies. We termed this 'politics by stealth' or that which is set within local government or the 'porous bureaucracy' (ibid.). This allows poor groups to shape policy and implementation processes in their favour, or subvert it if required. Significantly, this was not poor groups acting alone, but most often as active and significant actors in alliance with other ones, but where they shared complex reciprocal relationships relating to land development and its regularization and local economies. Second, the effectiveness of political strategies used by poor groups relates closely to governance structures reflected in differentiated institutional circuits. Different societal groups use and shape different institutional and political circuits (Benjamin 2000; Ward 1998). The elite align with higher-level party politicians and senior bureaucratic circuits focusing on parastatal-dominated institutional domains.[1] Poor groups link to lower-level bureaucracy and local politicians via institutional forms of 'the porous bureaucracy' and strategies such as 'politics by stealth' mentioned earlier. Thus, our institutional arguments presented in this chapter are set in a highly politicized view of society where the poor form active agents of change—even if their actions are hidden. Third, much of urban conflict is centred largely on issues of land and infrastructure, and is shaped by the institutional aspects of planning. As mentioned earlier, for poor groups the motivating force is economic survival, while for the richer ones, shaping public policy to promote mega projects and their high quality infrastructure and services for efficient surplus generation in a global context.[2] Land issues thus form a key developmental issue here in both a technocratic and political sense (Benjamin 1996).[3]

The usual government approach towards poverty alleviation was that of isolated projects. While these were ineffective (severely criticized by parliamentary committees [Sethi 1992; Sivaramakrishnan 2004; UNDP and MUD&PA 2003]), they coexisted with other municipalized development programmes driven by largely local political processes. In recent times, however, there have been efforts by international development agencies to move beyond projects into holistic programmes. These are centred on 'holistic' concepts of vulnerability, 'livelihoods', a 'rights' framework, and recognition of 'social capital'— and have spurned complex and bewildering range of analytical methodology and terminology (Rakodi et al. 2002). In these frameworks, politics outside organized party systems is assumed to be an aberration, portrayed as 'vote bank'/'patron client'. Such views cut out an opportunity to trace out the political processes that poorer people use to move up in life. Our approach drawn from the realm of political economy explores the conceptual, political, and the rationality of technical agendas to question the motivation and interests that shape institutional politics.

Some of these studies specifically view the political economies of cities in the development process and as global contexts (Zukin 1991; Holston 1999; Marcuse and Kempen 2000). This chapter falls in this category to focus specifically on the political economy of institutional change. It focuses on not what is ideal, but rather on how things work on the ground and the 'rationalities' that drive this.

As Flyvbjerg (1996: 2,6) writes:

Much of modern politics, administration, and planning—and many theories about these phenomena—emphasize the ideals of modernity but do not examine modernity as it is actually experienced. . . . [T]he main question is not only the Weberian 'Who governs?' . . . but also the Nietzschean question, what 'governmental rationalities' are at work when those who govern.

It considers the urban arena as a specific realm that lends itself to a particular political analysis around land issues (impacting economic processes) and forms of institutions (municipal system among other institutions). Our conception of institutional politics moves beyond two types of binaries: That places politics within the 'implementation phase' leaving the policy realm to be driven and informed by a techno-rational ideal (Grindle 1980; Tendler 1997); That poses a binary of a state moving towards a performance of regulatory policy responding to 'market signals' set against it's 'other' of state interventions along a normative agenda to set right a clientalistic politics.' Moving beyond these binaries and dualism, we point to a more dynamic unpredictable, complicated view. This view is one that recognizes fluid events, historical accidents, and events shaped by complex local histories in addition to global trajectories. While poor groups may gain or lose clout within different institutional systems, our operating hypothesis is that institutional structures dominated by parastatals are particularly regressive environments. We have selected two cities in south India for this purpose, Bangalore and Chennai, and arrive at this hypothesis by drawing from previous work on the relationship between poverty and governance systems in Bangalore (Benjamin and Bhuvaneswari 2001). We also draw upon the growing literature on the process and impact of decentralization. A more broad-based approach is a closer look at the governance structures within which development programmes are operationalized. A key issue here has been the progress on and the impact of decentralization via the 74th Constitutional Amendment (hereafter 74th CA). Much has been written on the specifics of urban decentralization referring in particular to the 74th CA and the way this has been adopted in Tamil Nadu and Karnataka.[4] This includes a growing literature on management and governance structures in Bangalore and Chennai, including state government instituted high-powered commissions to look into the issue. A key issue is that of the relationship between parastatals (and specifically development authorities) and municipal government. This is significant since parastatals are often promoted on grounds of their technical competence with little questioning of their political positioning.

Our interest is thus on institutional aspects embedded in the nature of urban change and reflected most clearly in contests over the access and control of urban land. We look at the two cities where, like most Indian metros, parastatals, and specialized finance institutions increasingly shape urban development decisions. The choice of cities came from several factors: First, the sponsoring agencies made such a useful suggestion of Bangalore and Chennai, whose governance structures are greatly influenced by parastatal agencies. There are useful political differences. Party structures in Chennai, reflecting those in Tamil Nadu are relatively well rooted, unlike those in Bangalore whose political climate till recently was characterized by independents. Second, it seemed that local politicians in both these cities had contrasting relationships with the historical process of land development, influencing their capability for political strategy that built upon claims established by poor groups. In Bangalore, our previous research had revealed that most local politicians had very close connections and relatively uninterrupted relationships with land markets. In contrast to Chennai, it seemed that prolonged political supersession may have dislocated such links. This difference seemed to be accentuated by quite different operational styles of development authorities. The Bangalore Development Authority (BDA) selectively implemented Master Planning, while the Chennai Metro Development Authority focused mostly on regularization. Finally, both cities have been exposed to big business and global influences. This happened in different ways and had also changed institutional response. These contrasts and similarities provided a useful setting for our main hypothesis: parastatals and special agencies form key mechanisms used by increasingly authoritarian party systems to entrench dependency of the local government, and in effect poorer groups. Furthermore, such alliances relate to the congregation of big business (benefiting from such political space and access), and the party elite (benefiting from such dependence) reduce the political space of the poor and hence little resistance to anti-poor policies. We explore this hypothesis in several themes— some explored in greater detail than others due to the relatively authoritarian political climate in Chennai.

PARTY POLITICS TO POPULARIZE IDEOLOGY OR AUTHORITARIANISM?

Given that the bulk of vote banks for political parties in most Indian cities is drawn from these groups, why is it that anti-poor policies come into being and are not contested by elected representatives within the party structure? In order to comprehend this, it is useful to understand how policies are shaped within the party structure. We find that there is very little research on intra-party dynamics in the urban setting in India, leave alone specific to Bangalore or Chennai. Hence, we draw upon Subramanian's (2000) study of Dravidian parties in Tamil Nadu and informal interviews with party activists in Bangalore and Chennai. Our investigations suggest that increasingly parastatal-centred institutional settings allow a fracture in party politics where bonding happens by *authoritarian control* rather than common ideology or value. By this we refer not necessarily to an explicit dictatorial form of governance, but rather a 'democratic' structure shaped increasingly by very tight party control, often using physical and institutional might to suppress not only dissent but also forms of autonomous identities that used to till recently characterize regional and even national parties. The AIADMK, for instance, in Chennai is famous for the way it can mobilize thousands of auto-rickshaw operators at a moment's notice to immobilize the city when the party chief feels threatened. Such control is often muddied v ith the popular media driven image of vote bank clientalistic politics: 'booth capturing', carting of improvised squatters promised with food, booze, and physical violence. While these issues are certainly real, it is more important to focus on mechanisms of party control as linked to institutions shaping land and it's management. Thus, politics in Bangalore has generally been driven by complex coalitions with an important role played by independents. We are interested in a specific type of 'nourishment' that land provides to contrasting and competing political processes. At one level, and witnessed in Bangalore until the late nineties, coalition and independent political circuitry was fed by the relatively dis-aggregated and local government led 'regularization' and 'conversion' process that dominated land supply and markets. This changed in the late nineties to early 2000. Not just was the Congress (I) more tightly governed, by the party high command in Delhi, but this was paralleled by the centralization of the city's land management process to strengthen few large developers and regulate against smaller ones as being 'illegal/unlicensed'. Thus, it was not the panchayat or town councils, but rather four ministers operating directly with Delhi. Also, what was centre stage was Master Planning and politics of demolitions and the empowering of parastatal agencies like the Bangalore Development Authority (BDA). This was complimented by other forms of control: the state ruling party to change the reservation of political constituencies at the last minute to destabilize the opposition.[5]

These come at significant times, when policy discourse by major political parties in both cities has time and again alluded to Singapore as a model city for development. Significantly, this shift has happened across political parties. For example, in Chennai the Dravidian Party and currently the AIADMK policies'—which once emphasized small industrialization—support to local economies via regularization has now shifted to large development projects as a way to shape Chennai's development. For example, the city is developing a large automobile cluster and export-based industries. So is the case with the Congress party in Bangalore with its support for large mega projects, whose clearance has been obtained from the BJP at the Centre. This rules out any explicit local political opposition.[6] Thus, the issue is whether the globalizing trends of city economies polarize party influence. All this parallels the rise of a form of political authoritarianism.

To understand this situation more clearly, it is useful to use what Subramanian (2000) suggests. He distinguishes two forms of political regimes, calls *bureaucratic clientelism* and *popular clientilism* in the way benefits are distributed and policies legitimized. In *bureaucratic clientelism*, policies are often centred on large-scale development interventions, while ignoring distribution aspects. Political support comes out of benefits being (narrowly) distributed via state officials and local party bosses, often through the social elite.[7] Thus, bureaucratic regimes are characterized by the rhetoric of macro development and 'nation building' where the issue of who benefits is not as much a concern.

In contrast, *popular* clientelism builds its constituency via projects that satisfy mass and immediate needs—even if some of these may be largely symbolic. Benefits to party supporters are distributed via extensive politicized social networks of a heterogeneous mix intermediate and low-caste groups drawn from different income categories. The power of the Dravidian parties of DMK and the AIADMK in Tamil Nadu arises from their populist policies. One could perhaps understand the increasing dominance of regional parties in the urban politics in Chennai as related to the opening up of political space for a majority of excluded groups to influence the state policies. Bulk of the supporters in both the parties in urban areas are those engaged in small service, and the trade and manufacturing sector, reflecting the economic structure of the urban economy. This is true for Bangalore, where a majority of local representatives were linked to local economic activity.[8] A difference between Karnataka and Tamil Nadu politics is the nature of party candidates. In the former it is drawn from largely independent candidates (Manor 1998), whereas in the latter the cadre system is strong. Thus, the interesting thing in Tamil Nadu is the autonomy for party supporters. This commonality

of local-level political autonomy might be attributed to the relationship
between popular clientilism and a city's economic structure that shape
in turn the nature of its political claim making.[9]

A conventional explanation to the inability of poor groups to
establish political claim and influence on policies is that of 'patron–
client' forms of relationships. Within this conception, elected
representatives ignore and exploit the poor—seen as passive agents/
beneficiaries. This suggests a view of local politics being captured by
the elite and thus regressive for the poor. Such a perspective justifies
intervention external to the political ability of the poor as primary
movers themselves. This is seen to be either the national state or a
need to mobilize an independent civil society.[10] We feel that a patron–
client framework is too simplistic and demeaning to the poor. First, as
Singerman (1997) points out, such concepts are based on a utopian
notion of a politically neutral (and perhaps incapacitated), non-
clientalistic electoral contract. Our own detailed documentation of
grass roots level politics in the highly politicized neighbourhoods of
west Bangalore shows a much more complicated picture. Voters tend
to deal with the parties as a group via their caste associations, often
across religious boundaries, and via highly politicized residential
and occupational associations. Drawing from Singerman (1997),
Subramanian (2000), and our own fieldwork in Bangalore, we feel
that patron–client relationships can take different forms at the local
level, resulting in varying impacts for the poor. Rather than a dualistic
divide of interests of electorates and their representatives, our fieldwork
illustrated interest congruence between the poor, local economic elite,
and local politicians. Similarly, in contrast to a patron–client conception
of a homogenized political behaviour, there is considerable divergence
of interest between the higher-level party functionaries, and middle/
lower-level functionaries as well as the cadres. All these factors render
it difficult for parties to ignore their demands on real goods (Benjamin
and Bhuvaneswari 2001; Subramanian 2000).

What seems to have changed things is the way the elite in metro
cities have begun to chart out a political cleaver between a responsive
vote bank politics that threatens their access to resources in increasingly
contested cities. Thus, rather than patron–client conceptions it seems
more useful to analyse the complex bundle of political strings and the
larger environment that shape these. In describing a highly politicized

and 'slum'-dominated neighbourhood of west Bangalore, we have shown how political landscapes are complicated terrain characterized by complex reciprocal relationships (Benjamin and Bhuvaneswari 2001: section 4). Here, Master Planned areas, by changing the form of claims to land by poor groups, local business/trade elite, and local politicians, resulted in distinctive anti-poor environments (ibid.). Thus, it was not just the technocratic form of planning but rather the institutional setting within which it happened that seemed important to consider.

PARASTATALS AS INSTRUMENTS OF PARTY AUTHORITARIANISM?

The earlier discussion suggests a closer look at elite influence in both the political, policy-making, and implementation arena. It also suggests that in looking at the relationship between forms of politics (popular clientelism/bureaucratic clientelism) and a city's economic structure, we need to look into how the political elite in both cities come to dominate the urban political arena and institutional terrain that allow this to happen. Benjamin (2000), in commenting on the governance process in Bangalore, suggested that the rich and the poor enter into alliances with different levels of political representatives. The former ally with higher-level party politicians using non-representative parastatal structures, while the poor with local representatives and lower-level bureaucracy, usually of the municipality.[11] To understand this further, we focus on the mediating role of party hierarchies in shaping local economic fortunes. Box 10.1 discusses the corporate link in detail.

The party hierarchy mediates/filters access to decision-making relating to issues of land and regulation, and on large mega development projects, too. To understand this clearly, it is important to appreciate the transition in institutional roles from the 1970s and 1980s, to the late 1990s. Although parastatals have been a feature of urban governance since the 1970s, there was some but very limited scope for elected representatives to influence development policies at the implementation stage. An example is the regularization policies adopted by ruling parties in both the cities, largely due to internal party pressure. In such cases the concerned councillors were able to influence policies via the MLAs. In the 1990s, however, with the proliferation of parastatals for

BOX 10.1: BANGALORE'S INSTITUTIONAL TRANSFORMATIONS
TOWARDS AN 'ANTI-POLITICS MACHINE'

Since the late nineties governance in Bangalore has been characterized by
parallel systems directly influenced by this city's IT elite—the Bangalore
Agenda Task Force (BATF). (See: 'A Public Private or a Private Public: The
Promised Patnership of the Bangalore Agenda Task Force' by Asha Ghosh in
Economic and Political Weekly, vol. 40, no. 47, 19 November 2005. Web
location:http://www.epw.org.in/showArticles.php?root=2005&leaf=
11&filename=9367&filetype=html). The BATF was promoted by the city's
Municipal Commissioner—later to join the World Bank) and Chief Minister
—with aspirations to make the city a Singapore! Significantly, while reporting
to the CM, the BATF organized annual 'stock-taking' exercises where the
heads of various city management agencies including the BDA (Bangalore
Development Authority), the water supply board (slated for a privatization
programme), the city police reported on their performance and define new
targets. Such positioning also provided it's members more subtle connections.
One had representation on the state land acquisition board responsible for
mega projects. The BATF is alleged to have played a key role in hiring
French consultants to design the new Master Plan, and particularly to direct
the city elected council. In October 2001, an event widely reported in the
local language media, was the violence associated with the allocation of a
valuable plot in the Bangalore University of Agricultural Sciences to a
nationally famous bio-tech company. The company's CEO on invitation of
the then CM drafted the state's bio-tech policy. Protesting professors and
students were beaten up by the police—led none other than by the state
government's then IT secretary to 'enforce' the order. Significantly the
university's board of governors ruled against the allocation but was threatened
with removal by the state government. Six months later, these lands were
allocated to the company amidst allegations of land speculation. The otherwise
conservative English media did at one point highlight the almost incestuous
relationships between the big business and the political and administrative
elite. The news weekly *Outlook* in its' backpage edit, 'Bangalore Diary', highlighted the close family connections of the then CM, with large IT companies
and also senior bureaucrats ('Infy rules Bangalore Diary' in 17 December
2001, vol. XLI, no. 49). Officially too, the connections lay deeper: The head
of the BATF was the Managing Director of India's most known IT company,
while that company's then CEO was placed by the CM as the new
International Airport's chairperson! Such parallel systems of governance
helped the corporate sector—especially the IT and the Bio-Technology
(BT), effectively write state policy that outlined major concessions in taxes

(Box 10.1 contd)

(*Box 10.1 contd*)

expensive high grade infrastructure, and prime land on the rapidly developing outskirts of the city.

While academics and policy experts pondered over such governance changes, much of the explicit opposition came from elected representatives and especially the city council. They saw the extensive organizational influence of the BATF that from an initial advisory role, over-stepping it's limits. In particular, its members were seen to be directing specific interventions, shaping and wetting the municipal budget, prepared by the commissioner prior to its presentation to the council. (See: a) ' BATF officials accused of meddling with budget' *Deccan Herald*, Thursday, 19 April 2001: b) 'CM snubs Politicos for opposing BATF' *Deccan Herald*, 24 February 2001). To subdue opposition, the BATF seem to consolidate three areas: First, an effective control over the English media where un-written editorial policy disallowed any criticism of 'modernization' as it would threaten 'global investments' and the city's reputation abroad: Second, a concerted effort to develop a particular type of 'civil' society that could form the 'demand side' for such 'reforms'. This was in the 'Jannagraha'—a citizens' movement reflecting largely elite aspirations. Third, to host a series of measures to directly control the municipal corporation. This was via 'Proof' a 'public' forum to ensure 'Transparency and Accountability', the installation of a placement to the councils, closure of the 'Appeals' committee, institutionalizing new accounting procedures such as the Fund Based Accounting systems (F-BAS) and 'Self Assessment Tax' or SAS. One member of the BATF argued this to be also a 'sweetener' where increased budgets would be attractive this , the BATF (backed by the CM) implemented this not on the basis of political debate but rather via a 'MOU' forced on the city council by the state government threatening to delay state-local transfers. Not surprisingly, there were also pressures by the CM to appoint the wife of the then Infosys's CEO as a 'nominated' member of the municipal council (*Times of India*, 10 May 2001).

In the last months of the S.M. Krishna rule, with the weakening of that regime, councilors across party lines mounted pressure against the BATF—Jannagraha—PROOF combine—showing these to be unconstitutional and elitist. Not surprisingly, with the change of guard the new Congress (I) CM did not renew the BATF. The criticism against the BATF continued and in the November 2005 snowballed· into a major political controversy between and ex-prime minister and partner in the coalition government, the CM, and the head of Infosys. The issue focused on the special concessions on land and tax breaks, and the relative employment created by the IT. There were other controversies that came out of popular processes. Following the conflicts over water privatization in Delhi, the Jannagraha was accused by diverse

(*Box 10.1 contd*)

(*Box 10.1 contd*)

groups representing slum dwellers, Dalit interests, and other local NGOs, of promoting and facilitating privatization of water in seven smaller city councils surrounding the city. In public meetings in booth the city and also surrounding towns they accused the organization of facilitating and increase in water rates, closure of public taps and doing this with funding from the International Finance Corporation of the World Bank group and US aid routed via the Karnataka Urban Infrastructure Development Finance Corporation (KUIDFC). The KUIDFC is the parastatal designated by the state government to route foreign development aid. It set out the role for Jannagraha, what its chief described 'structured civil society participation'. The senior bureaucrat explained the rational at the inauguration of the programme's 'civil society' component, as being a way to avoid he bad press and publicity that was associated with the KUIDFC's involvement with an ADB loan in Mangalore and other coastal towns. NGOs and local groups including the Mangalore city corporation had effectively forced the KUIDFC and ADB to review developmental priorities, and in fact reduce the quantum of loan. Despite the new terminology, ground realities soon proved to be difficult going and in the months following, with extensive public protests. It is perhaps in the face of such local opposition, that while the BATF was dissolved in Karnataka, its' members have lobbied hard with other 'reform oriented' chief ministers, and specifically with the central government senior bureaucrats. They claim a role in shaping the urban agenda of the National Urban Renewal Fund (NURM)—announced in December 2005. Significantly, a key issue is that of leveraging parastatal government funds to push for institutional change that has serious constitutional implications. In the name of 'public consultations' and 'participation' as well as 'transparency and accountability' new avatars of the BATF are introduced. To provide space for 'legitimate tax paying citizens', the concept of 'area sabbas' that is built not on election but rather sabbas' while eroding municipal debate and increases the powers of the elite While returning the essentials of urban democracy to a pre-Montague Chelmsford reforms era, it also brings in what could be called as 'American style' local government—amenable to be captured by large business and cities being increasingly divided into rich enclaves and poor ghettos. Significantly, members of the BATF who have lobbied hard on this programme, use the rhetoric of 'participatory planning' to, effectively move —constitutional issues of representation outside public and political debate. Not surprisingly, the NURM funds that aim to gradually replace scheme based and other development funds and transfers are now routed in Karnataka via the KUIDFC a parastatal, and thus beyond debate by elected representatives.

(*Excerpts from Benjamin, forthcoming*)

special projects and private-public partnerships institution for financing, the inter-dependency of higher-level party politicians on local leaders was reduced. Also, land development became further centrally controlled. The commissioner of the BDA made a telling remark to one of the authors in commenting on the way their institutional philosophy related to land development had changed with the coming into office of the new chief minister:

The previous approach of regularization is over.... The emphasis is now for the authority to take over land development and enforce master planning ....The CM rings me every afternoon to check on [the] progress.

As the control of land, its development, and its management form a key political instrument, it is hardly surprising that Development Authorities are tightly controlled by the state government rather than be devolved as suggested by numerous high-powered commissions.[12] This is clearly evident in Chennai in the Chennai Metropolitan Development Authority's (CMDA) conflict with the CCMC on building regulation. Not surprisingly, as several scholars of public administration have written, these bodies are also instrumental in reducing the municipal government to a maintenance role, and local public representation and participation fractured and almost a farce.[13] In Karnataka, and Bangalore in particular, control over land development by the state party and big businesses, is reinforced not only by the conventional Development Authorities, but also by a newer genre of parastatal agencies.[14] Box 10.2 highlights this. The key issue here is that in empowering parastatals to undertake mega development, an important aspect is to undermine local authority and also access by civic society.

Changes in financial routing also reinforce the situation. An important point to note is that decision making is not only in the hand of technocrats, but rather in the highest of political authorities. The following excerpt from our interview with a senior CMDA bureaucrat in April 2002 provides insights:

Development of an inner ring road ... the east coast road in south Madras accelerated development in that area. Land along this road came under the jurisdiction of three organizations, namely, the CMDA, CMC, and the panchayats. The planners of my organization [CMDA] argued that if development is left to others they would spoil the environment. CMC argued that they should control development as the panchayat are not capable of it and the panchayat were not willing to do it.... Interested parties sought to

BOX 10.2: NON-STARTER ELRTS BLEEDS STATE WHITE

(A report of the Public Undertakings Committee of the Karnataka State Legislature, *Deccan Herald*, 30 March 2002.)

The state government established Bangalore Mass Rapid Transit Limited (BMRTL) eight years ago to tackle the problem of ever growing vehicular traffic in Bangalore City. From 1995 onwards, the government has been levying a BMRTL cess on petrol and diesel purchased in the City. Of the Rs 275 crore cess collected so far, Rs 142.84 crore has been released to BMRTL. But the company has failed to accomplish its task. BMRTL has been engaged in appointing consultancies and investing funds in financial agencies to earn interest rather than suggesting a mass rapid transit mode. Despite knowing that it would be a herculean task to mobilize Rs 4000 crore for the elevated rail transit system, which is one of the modes of transport mooted by BMRTL, officials have not bothered to convey the practical problems involved in the execution of the project to the government. The officials including the managing directors of BMRTL between 1995-6 and 1998-9 have spent Rs 17.39 lakh on foreign study tours. They were accused of wasting public money by living in luxury.

These observations about the BMRTL have been made by the Public Undertakings Committee of the State Legislature in its report for 2001-2. The report was submitted to the Legislative Assembly on 28 March. The committee, comprising 19 legislators, was headed by Congress MLA H.M. Revanna. Expressing dissatisfaction over the style of functioning of BMRTL, the committee said the government is contemplating closing the company in view of difficulties in raising an estimated Rs 4000 crore for the ELRTS project. The panel suggested that the government should take a final decision in this regard without further delay. The employees could be deployed in other government departments/offices.

The report said that in 1994, the Institute for Leasing & Finance Services (IL&FS) in its feasibility report had estimated that it would cost Rs 4000 crore to have an ELRTS for 90 km. It had suggested that in the first phase 25 km could be considered by spending Rs 1200 crore with government and private participation being in the ratio of 25:75.

The UB Group consortium, which bagged the contract, had estimated the cost at Rs 2900 crore for the first phase. The consortium expected the government to bear 93.8 per cent of the total cost. As the government is not in a position to invest such huge funds, the proposal has been shelved. The committee said that as per information given by the government and BMRTL, 300 cities spread across the world have ELRTS and only in four cities is the system running profitably. In the rest of the cities, the system is sustained by

(Box 10.2 Contd)

(*Box 10.2 Contd*)

government subsidy. The state government suffered from an illusion that the private sector might participate in the project despite knowing it would be good money down the drain. Yet, the government established the BMRTL and collected the cess from the public. At least now the government must put an end to the wasteful expenditure, the report said.

pressurize the party to resolve the issue in their favour... Eventually the then chief minister got involved and partly due to party pressure resolved it in favour of municipalities.

This is the same in Bangalore where the middle- and lower-level politicians have no say on the type of development proposed and these groups have to contend with the well-known 'benefits' that trickle down. Second, during the construction of mega projects, there is an opportunity to access inside information and play the local real estate market. Having no say in major policy issues, MLAs' work at the ward level is centred around day-to-day quick-fixing of infrastructure works in Chennai and utmost routing small investments as in Bangalore via the discretionary budget to their constituency. In this process, MLAs tend to depend on lower-level bureaucracy within parastatal institutions.[15] In parallel, there is also increased institutional control via senior bureaucrats. This implies difficulty for politicians to respond to local pressure and manoeuvre via a porous lower-level bureaucracy or via stealth politics.

Consequently, a majority of MLAs and councillors depend on senior party leaders. The structure of parastatals is such that only senior party politicians at the level of chief minister and urban development minister influence implementation of mega projects—even beyond the narrow technocratic agenda if required.

According to a senior CMDA bureaucrat:

The ELRTS line in Gandhinagar station was proposed along the side of the bank which is encroached by squatter settlements. We had to evict the squatters ... but they are from TRB's constituency [a senior politician and an ex-MP]. He negotiated with CMDA on behalf of the squatters. The dwellers were clever, they wanted the line to be shifted to the other side of the bank but my planners were adamant ... They argued that their plan was based on opening up hinterland behind the squatter settlements for development ... We would have evicted in other locations ... This was not easy ... Finally we had to shift the line and propose a bridge cutting across the settlement ... The leaders were very clever ... They told us to plan the bridge along the areas where there are shops but not residences ... They argued that in case of shops they can easily identify another location ... Finally [the] CMDA had to yield.

There are other lobbies that push for mega projects. Important are, as Box 10.2 illustrates, the significant bureaucratic lobbies at work, which today are increasingly influenced by a growing tribe of development consultants. While the latter are perhaps required due to the growing technological sophistication of the project, the issue here is one of accountability—where consultancies carried out are not in public purpose but highly profitable private enterprises.[16]

Another aspect of parastatal influence on electoral politics is the way it intervenes in land development to shape political relationships. In locations developed outside Master Planned framework, heterogeneous land uses are allowed for binding the poor and their representatives in more than one way—economic, ethnic, and neighbourhood ties. Our study in Bangalore suggests that often local representatives were involved directly in land development, most often catering to low-income groups. Their speculative returns were related to land being settled and regularized. As we have shown in detailed research elsewhere, local economy and politics were interlinked (Benjamin and Bhuvaneswari 2001). Such close ties have several political impacts. First is that they resist domination by higher-level representatives, which helps local groups to maintain their 'control' over establishing locational claims. This, in turn, due to the complex reciprocal relationship within the local community, helps to consolidate de facto tenure and thus improve land access. Second, such strong interconnections 'exclude' the imposition by central party commands of other elected representatives outside their constituency—a common feature in party politics. This intimate political arena promotes reciprocal relationships among party hierarchies, but often defined on personal rather than on party terms. Third, even higher-level political agents have to contend themselves with accommodating a variety of local leaders, who in turn need to respond to very complex community equations. All this represents a complex and highly politicized civil society (ibid.).

In contrast to the aforementioned, Master Planned areas are allocated via bureaucratic channels, setting a very different political arena in place (ibid.). First, the land development process fractures existing reciprocal links between local politicians and groups. This allows party politics to use the bureaucracy as an instrument to reinforce political control parallel to souring funds in this process. This convergence of party politics and bureaucracy leaves little scope for a dynamic local political milieu to emerge. Such processes of development promote what is traditionally defined as 'clientalistic politics' where poor groups have fragile claims.

One question that emerges is that without making more fundamental political changes (that is, making parastatals accountable to local bodies as in West Bengal, or disbanding them as in Kerala) are there administrative mechanisms to ensure greater parastatal responsiveness? Our discussion on the Joint Development Council (JDC) in Chennai explores this issue. Even though the 74th CA was enacted in both cities, this has not addressed the key issue of local control and accountability of parastatal agencies. In the Chennai case the JDC, constituted during the mayor's first tenure through a government order, is one of the measures to enhance municipality's control over parastatal activities. Chaired by the mayor, it had representation of senior bureaucrats of parastatal agencies, civic groups, and councillors. It served as a useful platform for the CMC to coordinate with a parastatal agency. However it did not make much of difference in influencing policy issues. While it is a useful first step towards municipal enhancement, such measures do not make much of a difference to strengthen local representatives. The comments of senior bureaucrats at the CMDA and the Tamil Nadu Slum Clearance Board (TNSCB) are revealing.

The JDC was a useful platform ... (The mayor) was coordinating it well... but it was represented by bureaucrats ... My boss is the minister ... my role as a chairman is only advisory ... ultimate decision is with the minister ... The mayor is on the board of CMDA ... He does raise difficult issues for us in terms of transferring planning powers to [the] municipality and regarding [the] market complex in Koyambedu. Political adjustments are there ... My minister may allow some concessions ... Equally, beyond a certain point [the mayor's] hands are tied ... for a minister is superior to a mayor and [the latter] has the compulsion to adhere to political traditions.

Further, as the JDC is constituted via a government order (rather than emerging from legislation), it is easy for ruling party at the state to close this down or dilute its effectiveness if needed. For example, the present municipal council has a DMK mayor, with an ADMK-dominated council, and the ADMK rules at the state level. Until state power passed from DMK to the present ADMK party, the mayor was said to have had significant control over the council. After that the council has ceased to function. A second interesting aspect is the politics behind the constitution of the JDC in Chennai. Senior bureaucrats and senior politicians argue that the local government was able to constitute the joint development council due to the political situation at that time and also the power of mayor within the party system. A senior bureaucrat said:

It must be recalled that historically [the] Tamil Nadu state government, in particular the then DMK chief minister, had reservations about the 74th Amendment changes. It was perceived ... as a mechanism for centre's control over state parties... though [the state] accepted [it] grudgingly ... The ex-mayor was able to bring changes ... but his power is derived largely out of the system. To put it crudely, it was a 'father-son' council. The ruling party at the state and the local level was the DMK. Second was the party dynamics within DMK, especially the struggle for succession to the present party president ... The mayor was a favoured candidate ... He was the son of the chief minister ... It gave him the proximity to other state ministers ... Furthermore there was a DMK minister at the Centre ... In addition, he was able to control councillors via the party system.

This raises a question whether in contexts like Chennai instituting instruments such as the JDC can be counterproductive for local representatives as they can allow parties to manipulate them via the mayor.[17]

[S] ran his party like a mafia leader ... However, he was able to resist party pressures when it came to policy decisions ... There was enormous pressure from his own councillors to avoid increase in property tax. But he was able to overcome it and introduce the necessary changes ... In case of conflicts between CMDA and CMC, he was never afraid or constrained from disciplining the councillors.

Our conclusion is that on some issues, like those of parastatals, there are few options, but they must be placed under direct and clear-cut control under local bodies. Second, as in the case of Karnataka, the pressures to institute them for even smaller towns must be resisted. This, however, may remain a theoretical question since the main reason for their existence is political in the contexts of globalized cities.

EROSION OF MUNICIPAL AUTONOMY

In the beginning of this paper we had suggested that municipal government provides an 'autonomous' political space for local representatives. With the advent of parastatal agencies, this space is eroded to jeopardize job-providing local economies and the political clout of local leaders. This is reflected in the growing tendency of state parties to control the council processes via special projects as will be explained later. In Chennai, the prolonged absence of council for a period of 23 years has weakened councillors' position. A majority of councillors in the present council lack experience to manoeuvre around the complex rules of the system. They rely heavily on field bureaucrats. To pressurize them, they depend on the party structure for support. This dependence on both bureaucracy and the party reinforces the fragile status of councillors. According to the councillor of ward 147 in Chennai:

In this system the councillor has virtually no power ... The municipality is telling us that here is no fund. We being close to the field level, have the capacity to ensure that citizens abide by the rules and pay the taxes. But we have no authority to collect taxes ... Councillors problems ... arise ... from lack of information and bureaucratic control ... At the zonal committee meeting, I keep telling my junior engineer that we should propose some works ... but his constant reply to us is 'Madam, we do not have any money ... it will not work' ... I depend on him for the plans and estimates to be submitted to zonal committee. So far, we have not submitted any plans for development ... I am friendly with the present ADMK chairman, and that is why I am able to get some funds for ward development.

Another important factor that weakens the councillors' position in such systems is the internal institutional dynamics that shapes the form of alliances. At the central office, the council does not have much control over senior bureaucrats who draw their support from the state and the mayor. This is linked to lack of institutional procedures, which in turn relates to the larger issue of supersession of municipality for nearly 23 years. While Bangalore has evolved procedures to bridge political fractures, for example, in the allocation of ward budgets between the central and peripheral wards, Chennai has no such systems. Budgetary allocation for a particular ward is decided at the zonal level, which is then subjected to final approval by the council. Furthermore, under the present system the mayor being elected independently has veto powers over council decisions and often tends to ally with the senior bureaucrats. Much of the key institutional decisions are resolved at the level of mayor and the commissioner. This allows for parties and at times the chief minister to control both councillors and the mayor. A comment to this effect by one of senior bureaucrats and party politicians on council process is revealing.

Irrespective of the party controlling the council, the higher-level party cadres influence development programmes. In the case of the DMK government, the mayor controlled the council and in the present government it appears to be directed by the chief minister. For example, the flyover construction under mega city programme in different parts undertaken by Stalin during his regime was aborted not immediately with the change of state government, but with the present chief minister assuming office.

Domination of the chief minister over municipal processes was also suggested in our interviews with both ruling party and opposition party councillors. The AIADMK councillor of Saidapet ward, Chennai, said:

Flyover construction is a criminal waste of municipal resources ... The mayor has wasted a lot of municipal resources ... Amma has come and stopped these programmes ... She has an excellent programmes for resolving the water problem of the city ... She is the one who introduced rainwater harvesting programme in the city.

Interestingly, the council approved the flyover implementation. However, as one opposition councillor (of ward 147) pointed out, a council resolution need not necessarily be a broad-based consensus:

The council meets once a month and always has to do quite a lot of business. In every council meeting it has become a tradition of both the parties hitting at each other, culminating in the opposition DMK party walking out during the voting ... leav[ing] the ADMK to vote ... There is a party whip that all ADMK members have to attend the council meeting and vote in support of party policies ... so a councillor and that too an opposition councillor from parties such as BJP with three members have to fight to get information or a chance to debate in the Assembly. On top of it, 33 per cent of the seats are women and that is a good fifty. Most of us are new both to the council and the party. That also helps the party structure to easily control the councillors ... During [the] DMK's rule the situation was not very different. The ADMK members used to abstain during voting, and the BJP has an alliance at the

Centre with the DMK. Irrespective of the council discussion, both parties dictate voting behaviour.

Supersession of the municipal council did not allow the emergence of a reciprocal relationship within the party structure. MLAs control constituencies directly through local leaders resulting in the councillors being dependent on the party banner and the MLAs for their votes rather than the other way round. As councillors are all new entrants, they do not have strong links with their constituents to further entrench their dependency on the party structure.

In comparison, the councillors in Bangalore enjoy some autonomy within the council. The uninterrupted functioning of the council enables them to consolidate their position within the party and also put in place institutional procedures. For example, they were able to negotiate for a system of budget allocation based on the development status of the wards (interview with Rame Gowda, ex-councillor, standing committee chairman, Bangalore City Corporation [BCC]). Councillors, irrespective of party affiliation, have access to a significant sum for infrastructure investments in their ward. Access to this budget is important in consolidating their electoral base at the ward level, and in turn for autonomy within the party structure discussed in the later section. Furthermore, the established relationship between bureaucracy and many of the councillors, and knowledge acquired over the years, render it difficult for the latter to dominate them. In contrast to Chennai with its strong commissioner (and mayor alliance), the BCC has had a string of commissioners, changed as a result of strong local political pressures. Its mayor, although selected by the party system, has tenure of only a year.

In Bangalore, although procedures are in place and councillors' positions are relatively empowered, the council is rendered ineffectual through larger parastatal structures mentioned earlier. For example, specialized cells were created within the municipality for the implementation of mega city programmes in Bangalore and infrastructure projects in Chennai. These projects were monitored directly by their designate parastatals and, in cases, directly by the private corporate sector. The role of the council was limited to secondary-level accounting procedures. Interestingly, such centralized control is reinforced by the guidelines of the projects to ensure 'accountability'. The council had no say in the design of such projects. Further, intervening in project implementation is equally difficult as it was controlled by senior bureaucrats, often with the support of high-ranking ministers. Another more serious development is the monitoring of the corporation by external bodies such as Bangalore Agenda Task Force (BATF). This force, dominated by corporate members supported by the chief minister, fixes targets for state agencies, including the BCC.

The impact of such centralizing control is severe on the poor as they find it difficult to contest such decision-making. In Bangalore, for instance, especially targeted are commercial structures, apart from blocking efforts at regularization. In the case of Chennai, the ELRTS resulted in large-scale evictions of squatter settlements. A quote by a party activist in Mylapore is useful:

For the ELRTS project, around 5000 families have been shifted from Mylapore and its neighboring ward ... They have been sent to three different locations ... Even now Langford Garden is going to be shifted ... They say the Mylapore bus terminus is going to shift there ... MLA cannot do anything.. for Langford Garden people. He has talked to the concerned organization and bought some time... [but] eventually they'll be shifted ... But we help the poor ... make sure their names are on the list of evictees so that they at least get a house in the new area.

Another situation in the Chennai case is the trend to 'clean up' the city—again affecting a large number of the poor on the economic front. Along with this institutionalization that creates an illusion of 'a planned city', there is a redefinition of legality. Initially, the interventions of courts were sought by the poor to protect occupancy rights and in effect maintain a diversity of tenure that fitted well with the general regularization policies. With the promotion of mega projects, the institutional emphasis is on homogenizing tenure and claims. The courts are drawn upon by public authorities to enforce middle- and upper-income groups' claims to contested locations as a way to create an urban setting conducive to them. A quote from an interview with BJP district secretary on the situation of hawkers is revealing: 'Hawkers around the temple tank ... are also going to be shifted ... Nothing can be done [by us] ... There is a court order that the government has to implement'.

In Bangalore it is significant that the BDA used strategies of initiating demolitions on a weekend so as to avoid the aggrieved party to obtain a stay. Another was to initiate the process during the day when mostly women and children would be present. When the public suggested that the BDA should clearly identify plots especially under 're-conveyance' prior to demolition, the BDA responded that this responsibility was that of the public. This suggests that both the political arena and also legal space are stacked against them.

STRUCTURES OF FINANCE REFLECT FORMS OF CONTROL

Have infrastructure financing patterns since the 1990s further disadvantaged municipalities? Our evidence on this issue is very preliminary given the absolute lack of information. This is not only due to its complex technical nature or recentness, but also mainly due to non-transparent institutional structures and lack of involvement of elected representatives on this issue. However, even on the strength of existing evidence, there seems an important case to merit more detailed and specific research. Large-scale interventions are promoted based on two assumptions. One is that large investments are required to make the cities competitive in the global arena. Second is that large cities need mega infrastructure projects to deal with their problems. In many ways, the central government's Mega City Scheme is centred around the core of these ideas and justifies the focus on scale by specifically disqualifying local projects that are ordinarily handled by municipal bodies (NIUA 2000). This goes against the spirit of the 74th CA, formulated in the same time period of 1992, and there is also little empirical research available to support such technical rationale. Furthermore, its actual operation suggests that the stress is on 'municipal reform' rather than the creation of infrastructure as purported in the original idea—an issue we shall see that may impose greater political control.

This section illustrates the political nature of financial instruments and as mechanism for control and perhaps even 'capture' of municipal arena by higher-level state agencies and the private players. It relates to recent literature that has emerged about the situation in other Indian cities like Ahmedabad, which too have embarked on the process of 'going to the market' (Kundu 2002; Mahadevia 2002). Research on that case suggests a need for caution and much more careful analysis on several grounds:

1. The path of going to the market (made initially possible on account
of revenue enhancement due to mainly octroi) 'bloats' the municipal
budget leading to investment in 'supply-side' infrastructure in terms
of road widening, urban renewal, and flyover construction through
the borrowings (ibid.). This includes 'escrowing' some of the
remunerative octroi posts to redeem the bond (ibid.). Significantly,
the Ahmedabad Municipal Corporation (AMC) also has to adhere
to certain additional conditionalities, like maintaining an average
credit ratio, pledging municipal assets with certain asset coverage,
create a sinking fund, and also, changes in macro policies to 'protect
the interests of the investors' (ibid.).

2. The extensive urban renewal threatens large number of the poorest
with displacement. Significantly, it is not the slums on private lands
that are under threat but those on public land 'reserved' for 'city
development projects' (ibid.). In the case of the proposed river
front beautification programme, at risk are 8000 households many
of whom are living for the last two generations (ibid.).

3. The state government by threatening to withdraw the octroi tax in
effect threatens the financial underpinnings of the municipal
government after it has invested in supply-side infrastructure
investments and needs to pay back the market borrowings. Similarly,
to pay back HUDCO funds, 'octroi *nakas*' are escrowed (ibid.)—
leading to arguably political control by the central government.
Hence, one could argue that centralized political control by the
state and central governments is reinforced.

4. The NIUA report in a study on the mega city projects suggests
that investments made on 'remunerative' projects with these funds
have not given expected financial returns and led to many local
bodies to ask for a reduction in the interest rates on these—thus
raising the issue of the efficacy of such supply-side infrastructure
investments—as promoted by several development agencies and
private sector consultants. Also, detailed budget documents show
that while project-based funding of infrastructure has links to
institutional borrowings, none of the projects had any specific sources
of revenues (ibid.). This adds in effect to the increased revenue
expenditure on general administration—substantial increase brought
about by the Fifth Pay Commission (ibid.).

5. To pay back such borrowed funds, a worst case scenario would be
a sharp rise in taxes, user charges, and perhaps, the selling of

municipal government properties (ibid.). While the latter would eventually dry up as a source of revenue, the former would lead to political problems.

6. One of the first areas to be 'cut' in this situation is usually the social sector—health and education, and items that directly benefit the poorer groups (ibid.). Significantly, the AMC may choose to tax the slum areas at a nominal level (ibid.). To further worsen the situation, actions to ban and evict hawkers from important public places to keep up a global image hurt those families which have been pushed to this occupation as a coping strategy in the face of declining economic prospects. As Mahadevia writes: 'With the gradual withdrawal of subsidized public facilities, a significant section of the city's population will be denied access to basic facilities. This will increase their overall vulnerability' (2002: 119).

7. Significantly, while the start of the process of 'going to the market' was made easier by initial soft loans from the World Bank, these were replaced by newer financial institutions like HUDCO, HDFC, and the US Housing Guarantee funds (via USAID) besides capital bonds—following market rates of interests (ibid.). Thus, the spectre of a debt trap looms ahead for the AMC. As Kundu writes: 'It is very frightening to imagine the kind of financial crises the AMC will be plunged in, if the project, launched through the bond money, fails financially and the state refuses to bail it out, which it can do legally' (2002: 163).

The experience of the AMC is significant since, as we shall note later, there are strong pressures by the central government, by some state bodies under advice by international development agencies, and consultant 'experts' for local bodies to tap the market.[18] Not surprisingly, the AMC in a memorandum to the Gujarat government has suggested that the state government should take over the development of big infrastructure projects while the AMC could handle the maintenance of these (ibid.: 160). The model of development, as Mahadevia notes, is one that is exclusive and serves the elite. Here, it is significant that a recent issue in Karnataka's legislature has been the state's increasing debt, a point noted by the central government's auditor-general, as this has reached threatening levels due to extensive infrastructure 'supply-side' investments made. Similarly, in the coastal cities of Mangalore and Udupi, home to Karnataka's vocal population and birthplace of the banking industry, local groups and the municipal government have protested against the terms at which the infrastructure loans have been taken by the Karnataka government from the Asian Development Bank. This protest has spread to eight of the ten towns along the coastal region. The point here is not that infrastructure is not needed but this issue is the process and rationale by which this happens. With the disempowering of local bodies, their control by bureaucrats with allegiance to state and national governments, with the co-optation of local elected representatives by an authoritarian party politics, local bodies become pawns in a larger political play that threatens their autonomy and ability to operate strategically. The victims are the poorest—as vividly demonstrated in our detailed studies of Bangalore's efforts at urban renewal in its central market areas (Benjamin and Bhuvaneswari 2001: section 3). Assumptions that a caring civil society via NGOs could alleviate this suffering revealed on the contrary their self-seeking actions to use the situation to reinforce their control over local groups to establish their relationship with funding agencies (ibid.).

Earlier, in most cities, municipalities controlled infrastructure financing and development. They drew both on general municipal funds and also on developmental charges imposed for land development as new land was privately settled. Some municipalities, like Kanchipuram in Tamil Nadu, directly drew on domestic funds like the Life Insurance Corporation (LIC) to fund development. Not only are interest rates lower by a substantial amount—between 8 and 10 points (NIUA 2000), but there was still local control over the investment of funds. Subsequently, when city improvement trusts were created within local governments (as in Bangalore and Chennai), there was still a close working relationship and direct political control. This situation also allowed for community-based partnerships wherein local associations seeking infrastructure improvements would collaborate on joint funding and at times including a contribution from the councillors' allocations. All this was also possible since service provision was an integral function of municipalities as in Chennai or as a separate undertaking under the control of municipality as in the case of Delhi. In effect, this institutional relationship allowed them to coordinate city development and respond to electoral demands.

In the 1970s and 1980s, the responsibility for infrastructure development was shifted to parastatal agencies. Parastatals, drawing finances from the state (as in Bangalore) or from external aid agencies (as in Chennai), opened up avenues for the latter to control city development. With this shift municipalities lost out on both economic and political fronts: on the economic front, municipalities lost out on ways to tap urbanization gains via development charges; and politically on their strategic local control over development as pointed out by Kanchipuram council chairman:

Kanchi is famous for its nine temples ... bringing in substantial revenue. However, the municipality does not benefit from it. The temples are under the archaeology department. The tourist tax goes to the central government. Although the city generates substantial revenue through tourism, the municipality do not benefit from it. In addition, land development beyond G+1 is regulated by the state government... that also cuts out a main source of revenue, which the municipality could have earned. All these are removed, and then we are asked to go to the market for loans. What is the logic? Instead we prefer to tap the different ... revenue streams rather than take loan and burden the municipality.

Box 10.3 traces the patterns of infrastructure financing and development in Chennai. Chennai drew on external aid for infrastructure finance, which was routed through the CMDA. As can be inferred from this box, aid agencies and central government have a greater influence on policies.

FINANCING AND IMPLICATIONS FOR POLICY

Infrastructure development in Chennai was financed via three major urban development projects since 1975. The Madras Urban Development Programme (MUDP) 1, MUDP 2, and subsequently the Tamil Nadu Urban Development Programme (TNUDP 1) were implemented with World Bank assistance. Funds were routed via the CMDA, which was responsible for project planning and monitoring. With TNUDP 1, a special project management cell was created within CMDA and a separate Madras Urban Municipal Fund for use of project funds.

With the completion of the project in 1996, the World Bank initiated a shift in policy to promote public–private partnership. It led to the creation of intermediary institutions such as the Tamil Nadu Urban Finance Infrastructure Services Limited (TUFISIL). In parallel, the state government instituted a parastatal agency, the Tamil Nadu Urban

---

BOX 10.3: EXCERPT FROM THE L.C. JAIN REPORT COMMISSION ON THE 74TH CA IN TAMIL NADU

The nature of the interaction between the CCMC and the CMDA is defined in the following manner in the L.C. Jain Commission report:

Delegation of Powers: The Corporation of Chennai has been delegated with powers by CMDA to issue Planning Permission for ordinary buildings, i.e., buildings with four dwelling units, each unit not exceeding 300 sq.m or commercial area not exceeding 300 sq.m or building comprising not more than two storeys. The proposed second floor for residential purpose where ground floor and first floor are in existence for more than three years also come under the category of the ordinary building. The Corporation is also entrusted with powers by CMDA to issue Planning Permission for Institutional Buildings not exceeding the height of 15 m. The Corporation of Chennai could also sanction the subdivisions and layouts not exceeding the area of two hectares under the powers delegated by the CMDA. *The Planning Permission Applications for Special Buildings and Multi-storeyed buildings are directly sanctioned by CMDA and forwarded to the Corporation for issue of Building Permits by the Commissioner, Corporation of Chennai. The commissioner has delegated these powers to the chief engineer (general), Corporation of Chennai. The Building Applications for Special Buildings and Multi-storeyed Buildings are scrutinized and if they comply with building rules framed under the CCMC they are placed by the city engineer to the chief engineer (general) for sanction.* Wherever there is any conflict between Development Control Rules and Building Rules, the Development Control Rules shall prevail as per T&CP Act. As far as the factory buildings are concerned, the Planning Permission and building permits are issued by the commissioner, Corporation of Chennai as provided under Sec. 288 of CCMC Act. The city engineer of the Corporation of Chennai sanctions the Planning Permission Applications and Building Applications for ordinary buildings.

Interaction with CMDA: The chief engineer (general) of Corporation of Chennai is a member of the multi-storeyed building panel and attends the panel meetings at CMDA. The city engineer is the member of the Technical Committee recommending the reclassification applications and attends the meetings of the Technical Committee at the CMDA.

Finance Infrastructure Corporation (TUFICO). Besides these two, there are other financial intermediaries for specific sectoral projects, such as the Tamil Nadu Power Finance Corporation (TPFC).

Both TUFISIL and TUFICO draw part of their finance from private markets, are attracted to invest given the low risk, high levels of non-performing assets, and the economic slow down. The rest is from international capital and state funds. The World Bank has provided TUFISIL with a grant capital, while TUFICO has access to central and state governments' grants.

TUFISIL is registered as a private trust, and is headed by an ex-bureaucrat. Besides the government of Tamil Nadu (GoTN), the other main partners are the ICICI, HDFC, and IL&FS (Infrastructure Lease & Financing Services). The former own 49 percent of the share and the rest by other three partners. The Tamil Nadu government is represented in the trust board by the chief secretary of the state and the secretaries of CMDA, Finance, Housing and Urban Development, and Department of Municipal Administration (DMA). Its main objectives are:

1. Strengthening the managerial, financial, and technical capacity of urban local bodies through an institutional development programme.
2. Mobilizing resources for basic urban infrastructure investments (water supply, sewage, and sanitation; solid waste management; drains; road transport; street lighting, etc.) from the capital market.
3. Securing sustainable funding sources for the urban infrastructure investments through Tamil Nadu Urban Development Fund (TNUDF) and municipal bond issuance beyond the bank's line of credit operations.

TUFISIL lends directly to municipalities, in most cases with guarantees from the state government. In order to ensure regular repayment, the municipality's accounts are escrowed. Escrowing, meaning intercepts allowing TUFISIL to have first access to funds that reach the municipal accounts to cover their risks and is instituted through an agreement with the bank. Although loans are sanctioned only after the council meeting, the reality is that substantive decisions are not open to a council debate, where the entire consequences of such loan are debated and minuted. One of the councillors pointed out that often such controversial decisions are slipped in as part of larger grouping of issues, with the result that not many councillors are aware of the implications. Given the widespread civic implications, there is no procedure that allows for broader public debate.

Our initial investigation in Chennai and to some extent in Bangalore, raises the following issues.

LOCAL ACCOUNTABILITY

In the 1990s, in addition to higher-level state institutions, private actors emerged as key players in urban areas. Municipalities as in the case of Tamil Nadu are increasingly pushed to source funding from capital markets. Institutional forms via which the funds are routed may take the forms of: (a) project-specific parastatal (PSP); or (b) public–private partnership (PPP) agencies. In both the cases, several issues are involved. First is that of local accountability (and political control). Parastatals, as we described earlier, have no electoral mandate and are controlled by bureaucrats, as advised by external consultants with little systemic accountability to the elected body.

In the case of the Mega City Scheme, too, it is significant that the constituent clearing committees responsible for the operational features have mainly bureaucrats with little real or strategic role for the elected body (NIUA:13–14). The case is almost of bureaucracy and technocracy heavy parastatals or disempowered local bodies proposing projects, which presuppose a particular large project-centric development agenda, being reviewed by even higher level and powerful bureaucratic bodies. It is significant that a key issue has been the repayment of mega city funds since these are pitched at much higher rates (at 15 to 17 per cent from ICICI and IDFC (Infrastructural Development Finance Company), plus 2 per cent as cover for state guarantee) than those available from HUDCO or LIC (at 12 per cent, to even 8 per cent). Where the financial performance of the projects undertaken under this scheme has been rated as excellent (as in Bangalore), it is significant that these same projects have either seriously threatened the fiscal health of the local body, contributed to the increasing state deficit, and/or been regressive to the poorest of citizens who use the city as an economic setting. This last point relates to the key issue of how local bodies or parastatals on their behalf view ways to raise funds to pay such expensive finance—leading to the issue of reform. The NIUA documents (NIU.: 30) provide a key illustration of this process. It is here that we see many of the institutional contradictions emerging. The issue here is not only one of increasing user charges, to 'use land as a resource', but rather the creation of new parastatals (as

TABLE 10.1: IMPACT ON POOR GROUPS AND THEIR LIVELIHOODS
AS A RESULT OF A MEGA PROJECT IN BANGALORE

Actors	Before the implementation of mega projects	After the implementation of mega projects
Retail traders	• More business transactions due to clustering of wholesale and retail business in one place. • Access to different clientele group—especially the floating population in the market. • Low rents.	• Not even 10% of previous sales transaction is taking place. • No security from anti-social groups and no parking. • Sharp rise in rent and also lump sum amount required for advance. • Clientele limited to regular customers mostly the bulk buyers. The majority clientele of small buyers are cut off. • Wholesale shops increased from 108 to 300.
Hawkers	• Income (daily)= Rs 150–200 after food and bribe expenses. • Fewer hawkers in the ward. • Low cost of trading due to less police harassment and clustering of businesses under a single roof. • More business opportunities partly due to clustering.	• Income = Rs 50–80 daily (after bribes). • Increased competition with hawkers pushed out from other locations. • Increased competition with retailers and consequent conflicts. • Less business (previously all the markets were situated at one place) due to splitting up of markets. • Increase in the cost of trading due to erratic police raids and BCC raids. Hike in bribes.
Coolies Shop coolies Head loaders Market coolies	• Organized and negotiated for income with shop-keepers. • Fluctuating income dependent on floating population. • Income stability for those connected to particular shops. • Those not connected depended on floating population—unstable incomes.	• No significant change. • Increase in income due to dispersal of markets since the hawkers now depend on them. • Initially a decrease in income and opportunities for shop coolies. However, most moved to become head coolies where they can charge more but face unstable incomes.

Source: Benjamin and Bhuvaneswari (2001:138).

the Karnataka Urban Infrastructure Development Financing Corporation [KUIDFC] in Karnataka) and in the case of Tamil Nadu—enacting new legislation that dilutes the proactive provisions of the Tamil Nadu Urban Local Bodies Act, 1998, to empower the CMDA. Thus, the form of institutional restructuring is at the core of the issue—and with this, as we discuss later, come new forms of centralized political control.

In the case of PPPs, control established over municipalities seems more sophisticated. Such institutional forms, as in TUFISIL described later, are complex. Although registered as a private agency, it is dominated by state-level bureaucrats and aid agencies. If this includes a state administrative representative, presumably to ensure a public mandate, there seems little reason as to why there should be no political representative. TUFISIL, for example, is structured both as a trust and as a private business undertaking. At one level, we were given to understand that such institutional structures reduce corporate/income tax burdens. We are concerned with the larger accountability issue—of taking refuge in the private domain but being able to access public funds and influence public policies on the utilization of such funds. The point is not that the role of private financing institutions is not important, but that control should remain with local elected representatives to ensure that such funds are utilized in ways that are responsive to local needs. It is significant to mention the experience of Alandur municipality within the Chennai metropolitan area, wherein the council decided to reduce the loan burden by sourcing community contribution. In this, context, the chairman involved both TUFISIL and TUFICO, with a lead role. In this, the chairman of the council played a key role in building the bridges between the community and the different institutions.

WEAKENING MUNICIPAL CONTROL

Does the present structure with little local accountability allow for greater control and 'capture' by private groups? An assumption guiding both PSP and PPP is that municipalities lack technical capacity to design projects and to monitor them. A key issue here is that of control. For instance, even if some part of the project requires a high degree of technical sophistication, the specialized group appointed could report to the municipality. Prima facie, it seems that project

BOX 10.4: URBAN RENEWAL: OF LOST INCOMES, INCREASED
BRIBES, AND COURTROOM 'PROXIES'

The pavement hawkers claim that before the flyover construction and the
market complex, for an investment of Rs 100 per day, they earned between
Rs 150–Rs 200. After the urban renewal, this has now reduced to between
Rs 60–80 per day. Also, they are no longer sure of the possibility of doing
business on a regular basis. Police harassment has increased and so is the
bribe amount paid to the lower level corporation inspectors. At the time of
the study, our team witnessed one such incident of police raid. A few
minutes before our arrival at the scene, a policeman thrashed one of the
woman hawkers and collected Rs 25 in the morning. We also saw in front
of us, a poor person buying vegetables from a hawker adjacent to the
woman hawker being beaten up and being spat upon. Later in the afternoon,
when we passed that location, we found that the Sub-Inspector came once
again, objected to the trade, seized the goods, and thrashed the hawkers.
Our team members met the woman who was beaten up earlier that morning
three hours later. She was still waiting with her basket, hoping to do
business in the afternoon. She hoped that a new policeman that would
come in the afternoon would allow her to do trading. We found that this
was now the norm, where hawkers like her were raided in the morning,
and waited for the change in shift in the afternoon to undertake trading.
Thus, half the day was spent with no business and if anyone tried to buy
any of their wares, they risked being beaten (like the person we witnessed).
However, there are days when hawkers have to wait till late evening for
starting their business. They claim that prior to the flyover construction
and the new market complex, they were earning between Rs 150 and 200
and at times, between Rs 200 and 250. This has now reduced to Rs 60 to
Rs 80 per day. Also, the instability in business is a serious issue. According
to one of the hawker leaders:

In the past, for an investment of Rs 50, I was able to earn a profit of Rs 60 after all
the expenses. The bribe to the authorities used to be Rs 2 and 0.50p respectively
for the police and the BCC officials. Now the bribes paid are Rs 5 per vendor for
one shift a day. Each vendor has to pay for three shifts. This is in addition to the
weekly bribes to the Sub Inspector. The police increased the daily commission
(Camul) from Rs 5 to Rs 10 arguing that the shopkeepers are paying rent to the
Corporation which the footpath vendors do not pay. Also, sales are no longer
guaranteed. There are days when I return back home with no income. Now if I
invest Rs 1000, I earn only Rs 150 after two days.

For instance, Kamraj is a fruit hawker on the pavement outside the market
and living here for the past 25 years. From the year 1990 onwards, he

(*Box 10.4 contd*)

(*Box 10.4 contd*)

started his own business. In the old market, if he invested Rs 500 he would get Rs 100 to 200 as a net profit after meeting all the expenses (such as food and bribing the officials). Bribes in those times were lower for the police and BCC officials—Re 1 to Rs 2. At present, this has worsened. On the day when interviewing him, 15 March 2000, he invested Rs 500 and by 11.30 a.m. earned Rs 50. Out of this he paid Rs 10 to the police and BCC officials. Later in the day there was a police raid and business got disrupted. While it is also true that there were fewer sellers then and more buyers in the old market, he feels that he led a comfortable life before the new market was constructed. He also feels that other pavement hawkers too have been affected and are no longer sure of a regular income.

(Excerpted from Benjamin and Bhuwaneswari 2001:138.)

design is hence taken out of municipal control, allowing for private consultants and higher levels of government to dominate. We refer to an experience of Kanchipuram municipality.

Kanchipuram has had a history of borrowing from the Life Insurance Corporation. In the case of TNUDP, the design was done by Tamil Nadu Water Supply Board (TWSSB) and money was directly transferred from GoTN to TWSSB from our devolution funds . . . This was directly adjusted for loan repayment during the last financial year. The municipality had no control over design or implementation. Once TWSSB left the scene, we were not able to draw water via those pipelines on account of design fault. However, we are saddled with the loan. We are paying for something, which we do not benefit [from] (Commissioner, Tamil Nadu government).

Furthermore, loan conditionality may impose forms of 'reforms' that may not emerge out of a public process. For instance, in the context of our preceding discussions, seemingly technical issues (accounting procedures and relationships, computerization) could have serious political implications in the way they alienate local elected representatives from decision-making. The issue is not one of relevance or urgency of such reforms, but the way decisions are influenced. If these are thrust on municipalities from above, they could seriously weaken local voice of both politicians and through them the general public. Important here is the link of some of the key private financiers (for example, IDFC) with aid agencies such as the World Bank/USAID and through the latter to other private investor bodies like the US realtors' association seeking higher and secure returns. Since these involve some form of central government clearances, an issue here is opening up the financial system to much higher levels of political control.

One example is the manipulation of local councils via devolution funds. These are an important source for loan repayment and for raising matching municipal contribution. This in effect allows for the ruling parties at the state to delay project implementation in municipalities led by opposition parties, as it happened in Alandur municipality. A senior officer of TUFISIL said:

The water supply and drainage project was promoted by the chairman ... along with the then commissioner. The former belongs to DMK, and had filed public interest litigation contesting the election result of the present chief minister. The commissioner who worked then on the project has been changed and the present commissioner—an AIADMK representative—does not have a cordial relationship with the chairman. On account of this political situation, the project has been delayed ... Although the state government does not have the capacity to stop the devolution fund, enough damage can be done by delaying the project.

The question of manipulation of institutional structures by party politics, though not unusual, relates to the undermining of municipal autonomy via such institutional structures. Institutional mechanisms such as TUFISIL and TUFICO are justified as 'necessary as they impart financial discipline on the municipalities'. However, the influence of state-level bureaucrats on the board of TUFISIL for example, together with the control of ruling parties over devolution funds raises questions for a municipality's autonomy.

ECONOMIC IMPACTS ON MUNICIPALITY

Third, is the implication for municipalities' finance in terms of costs and risks? Loans are offered at rates above the market rate, raising the issue if local bodies can directly access the market without institutional mediation. A chartered accountant in looking at the documents we collected raised an issue on the cost of the loan. While loans are offered on the market for rates varying between 10 and 12 per cent, and on the international market at about 2 per cent, it seems strange that loans to municipalities are offered at rates above 12 per cent and up to 16 per cent. According to the commissioner of Kanchi municipality:

Between the different financing institutions there is considerable difference in the lending rates ... There are interest advantages between the two organizations. Whereas TUFISIL loans are given at 16 per cent, TUFICO's lending rate is around 12 per cent. But the mechanism of loan repayment is the same ... escrowing the municipal account or adjusting the state devolution fund against these loans.

When this was raised with a private financing institution, they pointed to the lack of creditworthiness of many municipalities. However, creditworthiness appears to be not a clear-cut issue as it is made out to be. As the same CA who looked at the report commented, 'Many private companies with high losses of above 96 crores [960 million] are rated under AA+ the highest credit rating, such accreditation need not reflect the actual financial health of a particular institution.'

This seems important since informants suggest that there is substantial amount of finance available with private infrastructure companies. With liberalization the market is opened up for large market players such as the ICICI, IDFC, HDFC, and IL&FS to tap domestic and international capital (often routed in parallel to development aid). Significantly, the Mega City Scheme promoted by the central government is key to opening up the institutional system to these financial intermediaries rather than strengthening the operational systems of institutions like the LIC and HUDCO, which local bodies could directly approach. The experience of Kanchipuram municipality, in Tamil Nadu is revealing, as the chairman comments:

We were not keen to take up loans from finance institutions. TUFICO's earlier proposal ran up to Rs 1.5 crore [15 million] which has been slashed by the council to 25 lakh [2.5 million] to those items which are perceived to be absolutely essential.

Experience of TUFISIL during the creation of the pool financing mechanism corroborates the possibility of municipalities being pushed to take loans that are not necessarily favourable. A senior official of the government of Tamil Nadu says:

In the creation of pool financing, TUFISIL obtained 50 per cent guarantee from [an aid agency] ...There was pressure from the concerned funding agency to take a financing institution as another guarantor. However, the cost of guarantee was quite high ... it could be avoided only because the government of Tamil Nadu came forward to be the second guarantor. Most infrastructure financing companies such as IDFC are loaded with funds but not many takers.

Consequently, cash-starved municipalities are pressurized to take loans irrespective of their future health. As the state stands as a guarantee for most of these loans, the finance institutions are assured of getting back their finances.

Linked to this is the issue of risks. While the costs of loans, especially via PPPs, are high, risks are borne alone by the municipality. This is more serious when municipalities already face a fund crunch in terms of inadequate central/state transfers and political pressures from under-serviced settlements. Financing institutions protect their loans through mechanisms such as escrowing municipal accounts and a state government guarantee. In most cases, loan repayments are anyway adjusted against state government transfers to local government. According to a TUFISIL official, in case of a state guarantee: 'There is always a guarantee to get back the loan from devolution funds'.

Although in the case of Chennai municipality, the officials were not willing to comment on repayment arrangements for TUFISIL and TUFICO loans, the use of devolution funds for loan repayment was confirmed from other municipalities.

Mechanisms of escrowing and the adjustment of these loans against transfers imply that municipalities could lose their control over their own funds. Discussions with councillors in Chennai indicate that often many are not aware of the loan repayments through escrowing of municipal accounts. Knowledge of financing of major infrastructure projects seems to be limited to the higher-level bureaucrats and few elected representatives. While a common counter-argument is that the councillors are not interested in city-wide issues, and tend to think and act in a partisan way, it still remains that knowledge about such projects is taken out of the public domain. Also, there are few instances as in the case of Alandur mentioned earlier where the council could take a lead role in deciding on the nature of investments.

CONCLUSION

Our description of the political milieu shaped by institutional relationships and in particular by that of municipal body and parastatal agencies raises several questions of responding to social change: where poor groups feel empowered, are able to secure stable livelihoods, legitimately claim public investments especially in basic infrastructure, and are able to secure claims to locations that help them move out of poverty. One set of questions is constitutional in nature. To what extent can the 74th CA expect to empower local representatives and governments? Are centrally-driven constitutional amendments capable of creating an environment for progressive change? More generally, is it realistic to expect legislators, administrators, and constitution writers to frame watertight rational frameworks and institutional structures to counter regressive politics? Or is it that one's actions need to be necessarily embedded in this politics to internally strive for change? This relates thematically to the argument by Flyvbjerg:

Modernity relies on rationality as the main means for making democracy work. Constitution writing and institutional reform are the main means of actions, in theory as well as in practice, in the modernist strategy of developing democracy by relying on rationality against power ... While power produces rationality and rationality produces power ... power has a clear tendency to dominate rationality in the dynamic and overlapping relationship between the two ... But if the interrelations between rationality and power are even remotely close to the asymmetrical relationship ... then rationality is such a weak form of power that democracy built on rationality will be weak, too (1996: 234).

Insights from Bangalore and Chennai show that legal backing alone is not sufficient for municipal empowerment. Pressure for legislative change has to emerge from the grass roots, shaped necessarily by conflict, and that this happens over a longer term.

In many ways, this relates closely to the issue raised by Justice Krishna Iyer in his public lectures on 'judicial activism' and specifically in an essay on methods and approaches to select the chief justice (Iyer 2002). These are in the context of the serious regressive impact on the poor by rulings from higher-level courts, including the Supreme Court, and cases of corruption among the judiciary.[19] The issue is not the anti-poor judgements pronounced but the 'rationale' and procedure used to develop that rationality used. It is hardly surprising that at the centre of this controversial judicial activism is in fact the normative planning process and that too promoted by Development Authorities in the most undemocratic fashion and centred around one of the most authoritarian legislations, namely, the Land Acquisition Act. If so, then legislation and the actual operation of the law must focus on the way it shapes political space around municipal government and be reflected in day-to-day operational procedures. The focus must be, in a sense, 'law in process' shaped by a dynamic of civic action and political change.

The second set of questions relates to the limitations and real scope of techno-managerial approaches. We have addressed this issue adequately in the main text (the approach of the Mega City Scheme and the ELRTS in Bangalore). Our intention here is to underline the point that it is not only the practice and technical arrangements but rather the location and institutional structures from which these are practised. In this context, reform and development aid being channelized via autocratic development authorities are likely to be counterproductive. This is just as simplistic as assuming that promoting civic participation and consultations via select NGOs is likely to represent 'public voice' and act as a forum for it. In both cases, the arena again must be municipal—of control if not of operational location. This is most likely to help techno-managerial approaches to be shaped by the locality of the issue. Note that we do not argue against technocracy. Cities are increasingly complex systems, but this does not mean that technocracy raises itself above the civic-political domain.

The third set of questions relates to forms of economic development. Here, there is an urgent need for policy makers to recognize the complexity and value of local economic systems rather than be enamoured by the big, beautiful, and simple. Perhaps technocratic policy makers in a fractured society will always do so, and the question may be the setting, which forces a more local below-your-nose attitude. The political construct of choosing the high ground—away from local claims and promotion of expensive and regressive mega projects that come with this—can only be addressed via political pressure and accountability.

In essence, we return to Ferguson's anti-politics machine and in specific its institutional and political underpinnings. Such a machine could be seen to be constituted by the conventional process of planning, what is presently mainstream judicial activism, popular notions of civic society organized neatly via NGOs, and promotion of corporate economies—all forming an anti-politics machinery set to subdue an activist and locally responsive political arena centred around municipal government. We also return to the need to understand power relationships as they operate in real life for poor groups as active agents. Commissions set up to review progress on the 74th CA can focus even more closely on the operational relationships and terrain of parastatals and specifically on land issues. Activism needs to be moved not only by advocacy driven from a moral high ground, but rather from a more sensitive understanding of micro-level strategies and the importance of stealth. In parallel, it should be more sensitive of the local political process.

There are other broader questions to be addressed:

1. Does the emerging forms of economic globalization, spur a self-reinforcing political and institutional process forming the mechanics of the anti-political machinery?
2. Is the persistence of parastatals related to the way cities address two forces: one, an increasingly globalized and influential elite; and another, a trend towards high centralization if not authoritarian party politics?
3. Are these related to the way Indian metros fracture along enclaves for the rich and ghettos for the poor?
4. Is contemporary urban poverty closely related to reduced voice and weakened claims of the poorest as brought about by fractured institutional access?

If so, it is important to:

1. Understand underlying institutional dynamics of urban space being shaped into differentiated but competing economic terrains;
2. Move beyond binary/dualistic frameworks of Formal–Informal, Policy–Implementation, Civil–Political;
3. Stress the economic and political centrality of land issues as an essential feature of urban contestations, rather that view it in its narrow techno-managerial aspects;
4. Focus more closely at the political terrain of municipal/panchayat bodies as significant arenas through which poor groups establish claims. As part of this to locate political processes as influenced by centralized party systems, and those connected to local constituencies. To consider the politics of the 'day to day' in addition to 'election time';
5. Recognize the politics of the 'high ground' of policy making now set within the globally connected parastatal apparatus and the way these are influenced by lobbies of the elite including 'civil society'.

NOTES

* An initial form of this paper was presented at a Workshop on Local Governance organized by the Centre for Study of Law and Governance, Jawaharlal Nehru University, New Delhi, in collaboration with UNDP and UNCHS at New Delhi, 11–12 April 2002. Comments by a fellow panellist and also from other participants are duly acknowledged. The paper is based on fieldwork in Chennai and Bangalore where several people helped the team. Any mistakes/omissions remain the responsibility of the authors. Comments are welcome and can be e-mailed to: solomonbenjamin@hotmail.com or bhuvanaramanin@ yahoo.co.in.

1. As we shall explain below, by parastatals we refer to special-purpose agencies instituted for specialist technical functions—and under the political control of higher levels of government. In particular, we focus on Development Authorities responsible for city planning, land issues, and the provision of basic infrastructure. We also discuss other service provider agencies like those responsible for water and sanitation.

2. Public interventions for the latter are critically important: to access land in productive locations and in large parcels needed for mega urban design projects; to keep CBD areas beggar- and squatter-free; to fund the high-cost off-site quality infrastructure; and to access cheap institutional finance and secure public guarantees against its default. All this is made possible by institutional settings dominated by parastatals, and explicit support of higher-level political and administrative actors (ibid.: Benjamin, forthcoming).

3. Clustering economies tend to evolve in 'flexible' types of land settings (Benjamin, forthcoming). Flexible settings refer to the functional and economic aspects of land, constituted by 'pro-poor' aspects positively affecting institutional access, economic social mobility, and political empowerment of poorer groups. Flexible land settings have three characteristics:

   (a) A loose regulatory environment specifically oriented towards mixed land use to allow for enterprises to locate in close physical proximity, important when most poor households start enterprises using social and ethnic connections.

   (b) A diversity of tenure claims and forms. This diversity of enterprises is made possible via a variety of rental and ownership markets, and forms of tenure. Diversity of tenure is perhaps the single most important factor that facilitates poor groups' access to land in urban locations.

   (c) Possibility for incremental development within a wide range of infrastructure settings. Entrepreneurs and poor groups usually start small and expand in relation to demand. What starts off as a back-room operation often expands to take over the entire ground floor, while the residence shifts into new quarters on higher floors.

   These characteristics also relate to how neighbourhood residents, especially the poor, can access finance tapping into real estate surpluses directly connected to land issues, community savings mechanisms, and also trade-based finance circuits (Benjamin 1996: Ch. 5). Research in Bangalore clearly indicates the connections of various types of poor groups to such financial circuits, it is important in terms of access to cash flow (Benjamin and Bhuvaneswari 1999: 81). Even the poorest groups operated as active agents and interconnected with complicated financial circuits, each characterized by particular types of instruments, rates of returns, and fitting in to a particular ethnic and cultural cycle of a trade/manufacturing/fabricating activity and its participant groups.

4. See, for instance, Pinto 2000; Benjamin and Kumar 1999; Benjamin 2000; L.C. Jain Commission 1993; Mohanty 1986; Subramanian 2000a, 2000b; Chandrashekar et al. (1997); Jayaraman (undated). Some of these are more academic works, while others focus on specific policy issues, including commissions set up by the state government.

5. The ex-deputy mayor in Mangalore (Janata Dal's lone candidate) mentioned that in the recent local elections, for the first time the local political circles were surprised by the systemized poll rigging while the bureaucratic system being coerced to 'look the other way'. Significantly, the ruling party imposed on the local political landscape relative newcomers with little political experience but with greater dependence to 'party interests' rather than more established candidates of the local unit. In Delhi, too, perhaps the model for centralized 'authoritarian' party politics, local elections are fought by relatively unknowns or politicians with non-local constituencies imposed by the party structures. This form of politics also allows itself for particular forms of organized criminal politics. Rajni Kothari mentions how the communal violence in 1984 was actively organized and facilitated by the then ruling party to murder almost 2000 Sikhs over three days, and more recently, the carnage in Gujarat where such systemized violence continued for over two months.

6. This issue came up within civic groups and local politicians in Mangalore protesting against the detrimental impact of Asian Development Bank (ADB)-funded large infrastructure projects. Despite the regressive impact to local political constituencies, the ruling Congress (I) municipal councillors were constrained by their party directives on these projects, and the opposition BJP councillors bound by the party HQ's in Delhi, which had supported these projects. The ex-deputy mayor mentioned to one of the authors how one of the factors that led to her ouster via illegal means may have been her opposition to this project and instituting a municipal resolution that argued that the Mangalore Municipal Corporation should go for funds loaned by local banks at 2 per cent rather than ADB funds being loaned at 12 per cent, not counting any penalty charges.

7. Subramanian (1999) analyses the reasons for Congress' decline in Tamil Nadu. During Congress regime, under the chief ministership of Kamraj, the state witnessed rapid economic growth. Policies were centred on heavy industries. The popularity and rapid growth of DMK in part were linked to questioning of the narrow distribution benefits to elites.

8. For example, in the case of Chennai municipality, according to party activists and the MLA of Zone 11, of the 155 councillors more than 65 per cent were associated with trading sector, and the remaining were professional politicians but with links to local service industry. Similarly, De wit (1995) found that a majority of employment was linked to textiles, small manufacturing, and trade. Moreover, as per our information, a majority of councillors derive their political clout from these economies and land development that service them.

9. Subramaniam (2000) points to the wide divergence of policy interest and activities at the top and at the lower levels in the case of Tamil Nadu. Partly due to this, the policies of parastatals influenced heavily by the state political parties and the World Bank of the 1970s and 1980s were focused until recently on regularization. Similarly in Bangalore, during the Janata Dal regime, in the late 1980s and early 1990s, the period of a spectacular real estate boom, policies were related to land regularization, re-conveyance, and a strong emphasis on small-scale infrastructure development.

10. This viewpoint is found across ideological divides. Putnam's (1993) work, attractive to the conservative and the large NGO community, has been influential to promote a 'de-politicized' benevolent society. Harriss (2001), in a well-founded critique, however, also views local politics as being one of the capture by the local elite. Tendler, in looking at this issue in Brazil, justifies the interventions of the higher-level state institutions and bureaucrats to overcome capture by local elite. These positions complement the social movements' literature, centred around Castell's work on the need to mobilize the poor outside the influence of political parties.

11. See, for example, the alliances between Krishna and the corporate sector. The BATF, which we discuss in the later half of the chapter, is headed by Nilekani, the president of Infosys. This task force constituted with the support of chief minister aims to develop Bangalore as a 'Singapore'.

12. If one were to take a cynical view of the issue, it is hardly surprising that the TOR of commissions to 'decentralize development' remains so broad-based to include various functions of municipal state governance rather than specifically focus on the core issue of land. This merely serves to confuse the issue and provide a way out by the commissioning authority to select and choose the easier options and not address the core issues.

13. M.N. Buch, himself a senior administrator and one-time vice-chairman of the Delhi Development Authority, has written extensively on fractured public representation and influence on the Master Planning process. See Buch 1985. Also see Mohanty 1987; Pinto 2000: ch. 8.

14. For instance, while the expressway authority (Bangalore Metropolitan Infrastructure Corridor Development Authority) has no political represent-ation, it includes a representative of the private corporation (its private partner) on its governing board. A similar situation is with the international airport development authority. This organization's chairman (a post which

is normally given to an elected official) is the CEO of an Indian IT giant. Another instance is of the Infrastructure Development Company of Karnataka (IDeCK) set up by the government of Karnataka and the Infrastructure Development Finance Company (IDFC) (an autonomous institutional finance corporation).

15. Based on interviews with MLAs in south Chennai constituency.
16. This is paralleled in the area of governance reform, stressing simplistic accounting practices with minimal understanding of the political circumstances, but highly profitable for the accountancy professionals which takes to these avenues of employment in the development business.
17. There are some issues specific to Chennai that may be of interest. A third issue is the control wielded by state government on municipality even after the 74th Constitutional Amendment. The current conflict between the state and local government in Chennai illustrates this. With AIADMK's accession to power, and in particular since the present chief minister assuming office, the mayor's functioning has been affected. The conflict between the state and the local government centres on holding of two posts by an elected member. The present mayor also holds an MLA seat. The Bill prohibiting elected representatives to hold two offices was introduced in the legislative assembly on 22 April 2002. The opposition party DMK met it with stiff resistance. Within the council, this has affected the relationship between the mayor and the deputy mayor, the latter belonging to the AIADMK party. Senior politicians and media reports suggest that this is a move to increase ruling party's control over the council. In the present system the mayor has more powers and can veto the council and the commissioner. The meetings of joint development council were abandoned. According to an opposition councillor, the council has come under the control of the AIADMK party, with the mayor keeping away from the council business and other DMK councillors having not much space to manoeuvre the system:

For the last one month meetings [have been] chaired by the deputy mayor... who is new to this office. Often there is considerable confusion in these meetings....Being elected by the citizens, he is not 'directly accountable' to the council. It is hence difficult for the ruling party to control the council via party machinery. If S is moved, the deputy mayor, an ADMK candidate with not much experience can be manipulated. (A councillor in Chennai).

The ongoing political conflict in Chennai illustrates the limitations of the 74th CA in empowering local representatives. Although senior bureaucrats and politicians point to the procedural lacunae:

Either the mayor should be given more powers to conduct business or the system of mayor's election need to be changed. In the present system, it is hardly possible for the council to conduct any business.... Parties will continue to influence.... Probably it is better for a mayor to be selected/elected by the majority party as in other states. (An MLA)

18. Debolina Kundu notes how despite the technical support the AMC received from USAID and the rigorous examination of the project proposal by the CRISIL, awarding the former the highest rating, 'lack of project management support and AMC's routine approval process' could come in the way and delay the implementation of the proposals. It is all the more surprising because this happened after SEBI scrutinized the bond prospectus and got it revised before the approval process (2002: 165).

19. We refer to the series of pronouncements made in high courts in metro cities, which effectively criminalize vast groups of poor from accessing land and sources of employment in small and tiny trade and manufacturing activities.

REFERENCES

Amis, P., 2001. 'Rethinking UK Aid in Urban India: Reflections on an Impact Assessment Study of Slum Improvement Projects' *Environment and Urbanization* 13 (1), 2001.

Aunde, Sanjiv, 'The "Rational" World of Parastatals: Reflections on the ELRTS' mimeo, 2002.

Benjamin, S., 'Neighbourhood as Factory: The Influence of Land Development and Civic Politics on an Industrial Cluster in Delhi, India', unpublished Ph.D. dissertation, Massachusetts Institute of Technology, Department of Urban Studies, 1996.

————, 'Governance, Economic Settings, and Poverty in Bangalore', *Environment and Urbanization*, 12 (1), 2000.

————, 'Pro-Poor Cities in Global Settings: The Interplay of Land, Economic Setting, and the Politics of Governance', *Geo Forum*, forthcoming.

Benjamin, Solomon and R. Bhuvaneswari, 'Democracy, Inclusive Governance and Poverty in Bangalore', Working Paper 26, International Development Department, Birmingham: University of Birmingham, 2001.

Buch, M.N., 'Information Needs for Urban Planning and Development: The User's Perspective', *Nagarlok*, 17 (4), 1985, pp. 46–52.

Chakravarty, S., 'The Big Foul-up: Violent Protests Against a Bid to Shift Polluting Units Leave the Government Groping for an Alternative', *India Today*, 17 December 2000.

Chandrashekar, B.K. *et al.*, *The Committee on Urban Management of Bangalore City*, Bangalore: Government of Karnataka, 1997.

DELPHI, 'Study of the Silk Reeling Cluster at Ramanagaram, Karnataka', for the Swiss Development Cooperation (SDC), Bangalore, 1998.

————, 'Study of the Silk Weaving Cluster at Kanchipuram, Tamil Nadu', for the Swiss Development Cooperation (SDC), Bangalore, 2000.

Ferguson, James, 'The Anti-politics Machine: "Development"', in *Depoliticization and Bureaucratic Power in Lesotho*, Minneapolis and London: University of Minnesota Press, 1996.

Flyvbjerg, Bent, *Rationality and Power: Democracy in Practice* Chicago: University of Chicago Press, 1996.

Grindle, Merilee S. (ed.), *Politics and Policy Implementation in the Third World* Princeton, NJ: Princeton University Press, 1980.

Harriss, John, *Depoliticizing Development: The World Bank and Social Capital*, New Delhi: Leftword Books, 2001.

Holston, James (ed.), *Cities and Citizenship*, Durham: Duke University Press, 1999.

Iyer, V.R. Krishna, 'The Indian Judicature', *Frontline*, 19(11), 2002.

Jain, L.C., *Report on the Entrustment of Powers to Urban Local Bodies*, Chennai: State Planning Commission, Government of Tamil Nadu, 1997.

Jayaraman, S., 'Role and Functions of Urban Local Bodies under 74th Constitution Amendment Act and State Finance Commission', available at http://www.tn.nic.in/TN74thAmendment.pdf, undated.

Kundu, Amitabh and Darshini Mahadevia (eds), *Poverty and Vulnerability in a Globalizing Metropolis: Ahmedabad*, New Delhi: Manak Publications. See in particular Chapter 3, 'Interventions in development: A Shift Towards a Model of Exclusion', by Darshini Mahadevia, and Chapter 4, 'Provision of Infrastructure and Basic Amenities: Analysing Institutional Vulnerability', by Debolina Kundu.

Kundu, Debolina, 'Provision of Infrastructure and Basic Amenities: Analysing Institutional Vulnerability', in Amitabh Kundu and Darshini Mahadevia (eds), *Poverty and Vulnerability in a Globalizing Metropolis*, Ahmedabad: Manak Publications, 2002.

Mahadevia, Darshini, 'Interventions in Development: A Shift towards a Model of Exclusion', in Amitabh Kundu and Darshini Mahadevia (eds), *Poverty and Vulnerability in a Globalizing Metropolis*, Ahmedabad: Manak Publications, 2002.

Manor, James and Richard Crook, *Democracy and Decentralization in South Asia and West Africa: Participation, Accountability and Performance*, Cambridge: Cambridge University Press, 1998.

Marcuse, Peter and Ronald Kempen, *Globalizing Cities: A New Spatial Order?*, Oxford: Blackwell, 2000.

Mitra, S., 'Planned Urbanisation through Public Participation: Case of the New Town, Kolkata', *Economic and Political Weekly*, 37(11), 2002, pp.1048–54.

Mohanty, L.P.N., 'State–Municipal Relationships: An Analysis of Collaboration and Control in India', *Nagarlok*, 16 (4), 1986, pp:16–29.

Navlakha, Gautam, 'Urban Pollution: Driving Workers to Desperation', *Economic and Political Weekly*, 35 (51), 16 December, 2000

National Institute of Urban Affairs (NIUA), 'Impact Assessment of Mega City Scheme', Research Study 87, New Delhi: National Institute of Urban Affairs, 2000.

Pinto, M., *Metropolitan City Governance in India*, New Delhi: Sage Publications, 2000a.

——, 'Impact Assessment of Mega-City Scheme', Research Paper No. 87, New Delhi: National Institute of Urban Affairs, 2000b.

Portes, Alejandro, 'The Informal Economy', in Susan Pozo (ed.), *Exploring the Underground Economy*, Michigan: Kalamazoo, 1996.

Putnam, R., *Making Democracy Work: Civic Traditions in Modern Italy*, Princeton, N.J.: Princeton University Press, 1993.

Rakodil, Carole, T. Lloyd Jones, *Urban Livelihoods: A People Centred Approach to Reducing Poverty*, London: Earthscan Publications, 2002.

Satterthwaite, D., 'Reducing Urban Poverty: Constraints on the Effectiveness of Aid Agencies and Development Banks and Some Suggestions for Change', *Environment and Urbanization*, 13(1), April 2001. See Table 2 (p.154).

Sethi, J.D., 'Review of Urban Poverty Schemes' in *Economic Times*, 15 July 1992.

Sharma, K., *Rediscovering Dharavi: Stories from Asia's Largest Slum*, New Delhi: Penguin Books, India, 2000.

Singerman, Diane, *Avenues of Participation: Family, Politics, and Networks in Urban Quarters of Cairo*, Cairo: American University in Cairo Press, 1997.

Sivaramakrishnan, K.C., 'Municipal and Metropolitan Governance: Are they Relevant to the Urban Poor?' Paper presented at the Forum on Urban Infrastructure and Public Service Delivery for the Urban Poor, Regional Asia National Institute of Urban Affairs, New Delhi, June 2004.

Stackhouse, John, *Out of Poverty and into Something More Comfortable*, New Delhi: Penguin Books, 2000.

Subramanian, K.P., 'Impact of the Tamil Nadu Urban Local Bodies Act 1998 and Building Rules 2000 on Development Control System', *Nagarlok*, October–December, 2000a, pp. 77–85.

———, 'Role of Local Bodies in Planning and Development', 1999, *http://www.tn.nic.in/TN74thAmendment.pdf.*

———, 'Sustainable Chennai Project (SChP): A Case of Misunderstood Concept', *Nagarlok*, 2000b, pp. 47–55.

Subramanian, Narendra, *Ethnicity and Populist Mobilization: Political Parties, Citizens and Democracy in South India*, New York: Oxford University Press, 2000.

Swami, P., 'A Raw Deal and Desperation: Another Saga of the Deepening Hardships that Textile Mill Workers Face in Mumbai', *Frontline*, 18 (8), 2001.

Tendler, Judith, *Good Governments in the Tropics*, Baltimore: Johns Hopkins University Press, 1997.

Thomas, Fredric, *Calcutta: The Human Face of Poverty*, New Delhi: Penguin Books, 1999.

UNDP and MUD&PA, *National Strategy for Urban Poor: Urban Livelihoods*, Project document of the Ministry of Urban Development and Poverty Alleviation, and the UNDP programme, 2003, pp. 6–8.

Ward, P., 'The Successful Management and Administration of World Cities: Mission Impossible?' in Paul Knox, Taylor Peter (eds), *World Cities in a World System*, Cambridge: Cambridge University Press, 1998, ch. 17, pp. 298–314.

Zukin, Sharon, *Landscapes of Power: From Detroit to Disney World*, Berkeley: University of California Press, 1991.

11

Developing a Quantitative Framework for Determining Devolution of Funds from the State Government to Local Bodies*

■ AJIT KARNIK, ABHAY PETHE, AND DILIP KARMARKAR

INTRODUCTION

That the Indian economy is undergoing a process of transition for some time now is incontrovertible. Whilst the winds of change started blowing since the mid-1980s, the process has gained impetus only of late. Indeed, this process has been hastened and intensified in the last decade or so, especially after the onset of liberalization and globalization in early 1990s. There have been several ramifications encompassing different sectors as well as the way we have been administering and organizing our economic affairs. The ongoing changes have implied modifications in rules and regulations, and indeed have affected the institutional architecture concerned with organizational environment of the micro and macro policy management. This has meant both setting up of new institutions as well as refashioning existing ones. One of the ramifications of assimilating the impulses of change has been that the central government has had to initiate the process of improving its housekeeping in terms of fiscal discipline. More specifically, it has had to contain its fiscal deficit. This, given the lethargy of tax and non-tax revenues, has meant severe control on its expenditure. In a word, Indian leaders and policy makers and, consequently, the general public have had to take a lesson in the art of letting go of institutions (zero-based thinking) and learning to 'pay for your lunch'. These lessons and the accompanying pressures and adjustments have had to percolate down quickly to the second and third tiers of government.

The central government has introduced the 73rd and 74th constitutional amendments leading to transfer of additional functions to the local body governments (LBs henceforth). This granting of constitutional sanction and recognition to local bodies is administratively, politically, as well as economically welcome. For it will lead to 'power to the people' as also put the burden of accountability via performance checks on the LBs. This can also result in self-government in the true sense of the term (as Lord Rippon had envisaged), without fear of arbitrary and ad hoc encroachment by higher levels of governments. The amendments—in their various provisions—also allow the LBs to go beyond the traditional duties of looking after conservancy, water supply, roads, and such other basic amenities, and set up 'plans for development with social justice'. However, there are some problems.

If the well-intentioned and well-drafted constitutional provisions are to result in genuine change at the ground level, then the functions listed in the schedules cannot be discretionary but must be mandatory. The states need to be pressurized to take urgent steps to bring about the necessary legislative changes to remedy this unhappy situation. We wish to stress further that devolution of functions, if they are to be both realistic and meaningful, must be matched by economic power and authority. This alone will give LBs the power to control as well as perform, and hence they can be legitimately asked to shoulder the responsibilities coupled with accountability. It is in this context that we commend the constitutional amendments, for making it mandatory on the part of the state governments, to constitute state-level finance commissions (FCs) with a mandate to recommend principles and methodology as regards the devolution of funds to the LBs.

BACKGROUND

This chapter is based on the results of a much larger study carried for the UNDP/UNCHS. The objective of the study was to help evolve criteria for allocation of funds as per the State Finance Commission recommendations from the state to urban local bodies (ULBs) to strengthen decentralization efforts by ULBs. The study consisted of three segments. The first segment dealt with the following:

1. Implementation of recommendations of the Tenth Finance Commission (GoI 1995) in Maharashtra.
2. Criteria developed by the First State Finance Commission (GoM 1997a) for devolution of funds and their application.

3. Instances and examples of criteria used by other states for such devolution.
4. Implications of the Eleventh Finance Commission (GoI 2000) recommendations for Maharashtra.

The main focus of the first segment is to provide the background ' against which the functioning of ULBs in Maharashtra takes place. In the second segment we shift our focus to the actual functioning of ULBs in the state. The major components of the coverage of the second output was:

1. Evaluation of the general revenue and expenditure pattern of ULBs in Maharashtra and the level of services provided in cities.
2. Assessment of data gaps in the aforementioned areas.
3. Detailed revenue–expenditure information and service delivery standards for a representative sample of cities, namely, Pimpri-Chinchwad, Thane, and Navi Mumbai.
4. Comparison of the data and levels of income–expenditure and services, with various norms proposed from time to time.

The third segment, on which this paper is based, is concerned with evolving a formula-based devolution procedure to ULBs. The specific elements of this chapter consist of weighted devolution criteria, including a mathematical model, for transfer of resources from state to ULBs—striking a balance between equity and efficiency considerations.

CONCEPTUAL FRAMEWORK

SOME PRELIMINARIES

There are several approaches or methods in existence for formulating an approach towards devolution of funds to local bodies. Some of these have, at least, partially a theoretical basis, while some others are purely ad hoc (informed by political and such other exigencies). There are some premises or propositions that we presume in working out our conceptual framework.

To begin with, realistic and pragmatic attitude demands that we should assess and delimit the relevant objectives that are to be addressed. Not every 'good' objective needs to be incorporated in the objective function of every governing body (such as an LB). This point bears some elaboration. Burdening any given institution with several objectives leads to several problems. The multiple objective criterion decision–problem is often saddled with internal conflicts. This is generic to the class of such decision–problems as a whole. There is always the issue of prioritization of multiple objectives and the related problem of assignment of relative weighting pattern. There is a more important issue involved. The situation outlined above leads to almost an impossible situation with respect to accountability and evaluation of the concerned institutional performance. The game of passing the buck and general obfuscation is easily played. Also, given the total quantum of funds available for disbursal, it would be quite wrong to expect too much. At least as of now, one can expect that provision of local services with predominantly public goods character needs to be met through disciplined operations of LBs. For other things such as 'social justice', which involves redistributive effort on a large scale, perhaps a higher level initiative is the answer. Burdening an LB with too many responsibilities makes evaluation of its functioning difficult.

Devolution schemes involve assignment of revenues of higher-level government to lower-level government on the basis of some formulae. Though the origin of such revenues may be reflected in such formulae, we believe that it is not necessary and that the formulae should inter alia be based on some exogenous factors such as population and some other measures of need.

There is an ongoing debate on 'dangers of decentralization for macroeconomic governance'. While there are protagonists of both views, the consensus seems to be veering round to the view that, provided there is a stable and committed macroeconomic environment, and careful attention is paid to the design of institutions, application of decentralization principles does offer a significant potential for improvement of macroeconomic governance and efficiency. There is, of course, the theoretical consensus that for some of the functions, empowerment of local governments leads to more realistic and efficient choice of projects and implementation mechanisms. At any rate, Indian policy makers have unequivocally thrown their weight behind this strategy. It cannot be overemphasized that for this design to be translated into action it needs the backing of substantial resources. Thus, the quantum of resources to be devolved to the LBs has to be significantly hiked from the low historical values if the whole exercise is to be meaningful.

Decentralization also entails that there should be no dictates from the top about what needs to be done. The presumption must be that awareness of local conditions, political awakening at the grass roots, and accountability enforced by regular, free, and fair elections will surely help local bodies take appropriate decisions. Globally set purposive devolution should be done away with in such a situation. Neither should funds to be devolved be tied to tax sources emanating from relevant area. This is essential, especially in the context of data problems and the possible variability in the devolution package over time. Of the allocative, distributive, and stabilization functions of public finance, LBs should be confined to take care only of the first, and the other two should be monitored at a higher level of governance.

OUR APPROACH

Our approach, specifically and importantly, will comprise five cardinal principles or 'panchtatva', abbreviated as PEACE. PEACE stands for: (a) political feasibility; (b) equity; (c) adequacy; (d) computational transparency; and (e) efficiency. Let us now elaborate briefly on each of these, leaving the details of specific variables to be incorporated and the weighting patterns (with justification) to be employed for discussion at a later stage.

Political Feasibility

Administrative and technical agents (like bureaucrats or economists) often come up with brilliant plans or schemes. However, the best laid plans risk coming to naught unless they are laced with a healthy dose of realism. This, in the main, means that the implications of implementing or operationalizing the plans have to be politically palatable (and perceived to be so!). Pragmatism, therefore, demands that due weight be given to political considerations. In concrete terms this implies the following:

1. The devolution structure recommended should not vary in distance from the existing devolution pattern by too much since such radicalism will be quite unacceptable to political agents. This translates into symbols as:

$$\delta(dp^r, dp^e) \leq \varepsilon \qquad \qquad \dots (11.1)$$

where,

    d is the metric,

    dp^r is the recommended pattern of devolution,

    dp^e is the existing pattern of devolution, and

    e is the politically acceptable level of tolerance.

2. The corollary is that, *as a norm*, none of the LBs must get fewer funds (in absolute terms) in comparison to the existing scenario as a result of our recommendations. The newer (innovative and/or stricter) criteria should in effect apply to the sharing of the feast in an incremental sense.

3. Transition in regimes should be informed by gradualism rather than radicalism. Nature and politics obviously move continuously rather than in catastrophes. This means that if, a is the weight or proportion dedicated to newer criterion, then:

$$\alpha = o \ |0.5| \qquad \qquad \dots 11.2$$

that is, a should be of order 0.5.

Equity

Equity is a crucially important *need-based* component. An authority that assumes a paternal role vis-à-vis its citizens can ill afford to neglect this aspect. Distributional considerations are paramount. Non-homothetic growth may be a natural phenomenon in some cases, but has weighty objections lined against it in the context of political economy. To repeat, if the power has to go to the people and their aspirations are to find articulation through the functioning of LBs, they have to be empowered and fortified with adequate funds (resources) to carry out at least the minimal normal functions. This reflects what is 'needed' by the relevant LB. There is normally a tendency to overestimate one's own needs (both because one really believes it and also as bargaining strategy). In deciding the actual devolution there has to be some sense of the *absorptive* capacity of the LB. Sudden increase in funds will lead to inefficiencies in terms of consumption as well as production use.

    There are several parameters that select themselves automatically. These can be categorized into two types: one, the global indicators;

and two, the local indicators at the level of LBs. Global here is being used in the sense of district level. These are assumed to be shared (to some extent at least) by the LBs in that district. At any rate, very little information (consistent and reliable) is available at a level of disaggregation lower than the district. While the rural sector does not figure in our study, it needs to be noted that urban and rural sectors display strikingly different qualities in terms of quality and quantum of data available. This perforce leads to different treatment of the two sectors in terms of intensity and detail.

The need for equity is not just based on moral-ethico-political precepts. Post Keynes and given the interdependant nature of a maturing economy, it is dictated by sturdy economic sense. Unless a basic level of development and dynamism is achieved in the rural sector, the urban sector will find it successively more difficult to grow and develop (suffocated as it will be by effective demand). The huge market potential for both consumption and producer goods (which is so very essential for a vibrant economy) will remain a distant chimera.

Adequacy

Scarcity is omnipresent; indeed it is the raison d'être for economics and economists. The resource gap between what is available and what is 'needed' will be with us in the foreseeable future. One way out of the difficulty is to increase the central pool of funds to be disbursed to a substantial extent. Given the context of the withdrawal of the state from many traditional spheres, one cannot realistically expect too much by this route. The LBs must learn to stand for, and help, themselves. This solution has its own limits and is beset with problems; however, there is no readily available alternative. Efforts for closing this gap by LBs must be lauded and rewarded by clubbing it with the efficiency criteria.

There are many issues—data problems apart—that are involved here. For instance, there is the question of the extent to which sub-national governments may be allowed to set their own taxes. It is feared that excessive latitude in this regard can create unacceptable level of complexity and administrative burdens, as well as spatial inequities and distortions in allocation of resources. Within limits, these problems need to be tolerated in the interest of gaining the benefits of decentralized government. There is the other issue of changing regulatory practices in order to allow a greater access to the credit markets for LBs. This is especially important in the context of the large capital requirements for infrastructure development. Which of these is the better option is a moot question answerable only in terms of actual empirical evidence. Indeed, rather than a clear option, this involves a selection of a proper mix of these and similar such possibilities. The need to try out innovative experiments, however, is beyond doubt. One of the important lessons that can be learnt from evidence elsewhere is that it is better if commercial principles are followed and the LBs have to compete for capital with other borrowing agencies in the interest of efficient utilization of resources.

Computational Transparency

Checking and replicating the devolution pattern as given by our formulation should be transparent and simple. Adhocracy in setting the devolution pattern has the great defect that it makes even discussion and criticism difficult. Also, there is a loss of credibility and all kinds of suspicions about motivation begin to surface, which is counter-productive. The word 'simple', used in the context of devolution pattern, is being used as an antonym of complex. Of course, given the multitude of factors that need to be considered, the whole algorithm is bound to become somewhat complicated. However, a detailed road map can be set out, which can be followed by users of the algorithm without continuous guidance by its creators. Computational transparency also lends itself to constructive discussion in that it is possible to undertake the exercise of scenario building and simulation, and present it to the ultimate policy maker. Also, the logical structure can be traversed backwards and forwards, thus making it useful.

Efficiency

This is really a cornerstone of our conceptual framework. In the present context of the Indian economy, whence we are in the process of making changes in the way we conduct our macro-management affairs, there can be no doubt about the importance of having *incentive-compatible systems* in place. As economists, we would push very hard for this component to be the most important (weight-wise) in the scheme of things. However, political feasibility as well as adequacy requirements restrain us from going too far. Incentive compatible system implies that every effort reflected in performance gets a reward and every slide on the efficiency front is penalized. Also, there is a static and a dynamic component to this criterion. For example, if an LB is well off in its current performance terms, this will entitle it for a reward. Further, if its performance involves a switch in regime (that is, from being relatively better an LB becomes absolutely better off; illustratively, this will happen when its small deficit changes into surplus), once again a bonus may be given to the LB. Alternatively, a unit may be badly off, but if it shows improvement (a return of the prodigal to the fold!) it would be entitled to a bonus.

Given that the total funds that are being disbursed under this criterion are not very large, the signalling aspect of this criterion needs to be underlined. There is a further point to be made here. Logically, efficiency as a criterion can conflict with some of the other components in our conceptual frame. This is a standard problem of a multi-objective decision function that we referred to earlier. Thus, it is conceptually necessary to set up the decision function in an add-on fashion rather than in a single simple formula. Of course, ultimately the whole exercise can be consolidated and hence a single formulation is implied, even by this approach.

Before turning to the mathematical formulation, we would like to comment on two issues that we believe to be of crucial importance. The first is about the rural–urban break-up as far as resources go and the second is with regard to data problems.

It is important to note that urbanization is more than a demographic phenomenon. It is a societal transformation along the rural–urban continuum. At the beginning of the twenty-first century, cities and towns form the frontline in development campaign. Within a generation, the majority of world's population will live in urban areas and the number of urban residents in developing countries will double to around 2 billion. *The urban transition offers significant opportunities for countries to improve the quality of life for all its citizens through sustained economic growth leading to broad social welfare gains.*

In the context of political and fiscal decentralization along with the general environment of globalization, the shifting of trade and production towards cities with market advantage needs to be noted. The industrial and commercial activities located in urban areas account for half to four-fifths of GDP in most developing countries. The development of urban areas is closely linked to rural economy through exchange of goods, services, capital and social movement, and employment opportunities. Against the backdrop of these comments, let us look at the Indian situation vis-à-vis the resource flows from the FCs. This examination is important even though, as we have stated earlier, the rural sector is not relevant to our study. The reason is that there is a close nexus between the rural and the urban sector and to some extent the problems of urban sprawl and urban decay that we see in Indian cities is due to the neglect of rural areas. Thus, in some ways, to alleviate urban problems it may be required to uplift the rural areas and offer considerable support to rural local bodies (RLBs). Strengthening RLBs will create better living conditions in rural areas and blunt the incentives to migrate to urban areas.

The FCs at the centre have suggested it to be 80:20 division in favour of rural segment, and many at the state level have been following suit. Indeed, in Maharashtra the actuals show the division pegged at 88:12, which is completely unacceptable to us. Now, at the national level urbanization is of the order of 27 per cent. Thus, given the economies of scale involved in servicing the people who are rather more densely packed in urban settings, 80:20 may not appear terribly skewed. However, given that Maharashtra is one of the most urbanized of states, with 42 per cent urban population, devolving only 12 per cent defies reasoning. (Further, even within ULBs, municipal corporations [MCs] get a huge proportion so that the councils get a pittance.) Whilst it may perchance be true, that the ULBs are in a better position to raise revenues on their own, it needs to be remembered that whether it is education or health or water supply or sanitation, the ULBs are called upon to do much more than the RLBs. The consequences of non-provision in urban areas are likely to be more severe and immediate.

In all arguments that one comes across in this regard, there is a clear bias in favour of rural section, captured in the phrase: 'India lives in its villages'. Everything to do with cities is frowned upon almost as an evil! (Just as the West is caricatured to be bad, so, within India, cities are caricatured as hotbeds of crime and immorality.) It should be borne in mind that 90 per cent of revenues and 60 per cent of our GDP is contributed by the cities; yet at the municipal level they receive as revenue only 0.6 per cent of the GDP. Even the plan outlay for urban development over plans has come down from 8 to 2.6 per cent of the total plan outlay. We think it to be incontrovertible that whereas from a historical perspective there is an undoubted primacy to rural (chronological as well as logical sense) vis-à-vis urban segments, it is restricted to only the initial causation. When one comes to discussing the perpetrating causes of growth and development, there is a role reversal. The future is decidedly urban. The earlier we recognize it explicitly the better it will be for all of us. The point here is that we would like the devolution to be 60:40. But it is not feasible since it would be too drastic a departure from historical path and also the scale economies referred to earlier come into play. Further, as a rule RLBs are poor and they cannot be starved of committed expenditure (in terms of salaries, etc.), for then we would not allow them to become healthy enough to look after themselves. We have also to take cognizance of the argument that at least in part, the urban malaise is due to rural underdevelopment and hence, helping the rural segment in fact helps the urban segment.

We will now turn to the data situation. Theoretical arguments are one thing, but for them to be relevant they need to be operationalized in empirical terms. That is possible only if there is a strong database available. The data on LB-specific parameters such as area, population serviced, backwardness, and production levels is simply not available. The data for these characteristics is available only at the district level. The distributional characteristics at the LB level have perforce to be given a go-by. One is forced here to make a heroic assumption that the district-level characteristics are uniformly distributed across LBs. This is far from satisfactory, especially if one wants to introduce efficiency criteria based on service delivery as well as financial performance.

In this day and age of information technology, and for a forward-looking and IT-savvy state like Maharashtra, it may not be too much to expect a better data system. We thus very strongly recommend that there should be a cell set up on a permanent basis that would be involved in data collection and monitoring the quality of the same. Indeed, such a cell would also be helpful in collecting and computing the component of our scheme that needs to be computed in an iterative fashion over time, being dependant on the data that would become available in the future.

EMPIRICAL EXERCISES

The approach discussed here focuses on districts of the state of Maharashtra. We will be estimating the devolution that will take place to each district. Before that we need to identify the criteria, such as population and area, according to which devolution will take place. Once this has been determined, we need to have in place the characteristics of the districts that will determine the weighting pattern according to which the share of each district will be computed.

Availability of Resources to be Devolved

It is imperative that we know the size of the cake that is to be divided among districts and local bodies before we recommend the actual devolution. As per the pattern observed over the years 1995–6 to 1999–2000, the following points may be made:

1. The total revenue receipt of the state government was Rs 956 billion, of which
2. ULBs received total grants of Rs 27 billion, and
3. RLBs received total grants of Rs 193 billion.
4. The sum of the grants received by the ULBs and RLBs, which was Rs 221 billion, was 23.11 per cent of the total revenue receipts of the state.
5. Of the total of Rs 221 billion received by the LBs, the share of ULBs was 12.27 per cent and the share of RLBs was 87.72 per cent.
6. The rate of growth of revenue income for the state has been observed to be 10.15 per cent p.a. over a five-year period. It is expected that this rate of growth will continue in the future as well.

However, if one carefully looks at the year-to-year changes, there is significant variation. Table 11.1 shows the variations over the years.

Given such wide variations and the difficulty in predicting the actual quantum that would be available from the state government over the next five years, we felt that it would be best to set out our methodology and the consequent distribution of funds to RLBs and ULBs assuming a notional amount to be distributed during 2001–2. The notional amount that we have assumed is Rs 10 billion. The

TABLE 11.1: YEAR-WISE DEVOLUTION OF FUNDS TO
LOCAL BODIES

Year	Devolution (Rs billion)	Change (%)
1995–6	31.54	–
1996–7	37.77	19.7
1997–8	42.50	12.5
1998–9	47.66	12.1
1999–2000	61.53	29.1

actual amount to be devolved to LBs could be seen as some multiple
of Rs 10 billion and can easily be worked out using the algorithm
that will be developed in the study.

It may be noted that the notional amount that we have employed
is the assumed devolution to the local bodies. We do not attempt to
estimate the level of total revenue income of the state government.
Further, we do not attempt to estimate the share of local bodies in
the total revenue income of the state government. We believe that
predicting or estimating the total revenue income is fraught with
uncertainty, which is best avoided in the building up of the model
that we develop here. As far as the share that would be available to
local bodies is concerned, we believe it will be a negotiated value
and no view can be taken regarding this at this moment.

We divide the total devolution going to ULBs into two
components: need-based devolution and efficiency-based devolution.
The former will be allocated 60 per cent of the notional amount of
Rs 10 billion and the latter 40 per cent. A diagram of the entire
devolution scheme is given at the end of the chapter.

APPROACH TO NEED-BASED DISBURSEMENT

A variety of criteria have been used by the various central finance
commissions for disbursement of funds to states. Many of these have
changed in importance over the years. For example, the weight on
population has been going down over the years. However, as far as the
Central Finance Commission recommendations are concerned, no
distinction needs to be drawn between the geographical boundaries
of the state and the jurisdictional authority of the state government.
The jurisdictional authority of the state government exactly matches

the boundaries of the state. This convenient state of affairs breaks down when one is concerned with disbursements below the level of state governments.

The largest geographical entity inside a state is the district. Most of the detailed information, such as, distance from highest income, and index of backwardness, is available only for the districts. As far as ULBs are concerned, apart from financial data, information is available on their population and area. This is a much better state of affairs than for RLBs: there is not even an accurate estimate of the number of villages in Maharashtra!

As far as financial data is concerned, criteria such as tax effort and fiscal discipline have no relevance at the level of the district; these are relevant only at the level of local governments.

Given the difficulty involved in reconciling the characteristics at the district level and those at the local government level, we have adopted a three-stage strategy for the devolution of need-based funds:

- *Stage 1:* We use some specially selected criteria in combination with estimated shares for each district to arrive at the disbursement to each district. (There are 34 districts in the state of Maharashtra.)
- *Stage 2:* Having obtained the disbursement for each district we then seek to employ certain other criteria to determine the disbursement among class of urban local governments, whether MC, MC-A, MC-B, or MC-C.[1]
- *Stage 3:* Finally, we develop a method for distribution of funds to each ULB with a class of ULB or urban local government.

As far as the efficiency-based allocations are concerned, we have been able to devise a methodology that directly targets ULBs.

CRITERIA USED FOR NEED-BASED DISBURSEMENT IN THIS STUDY

The criteria that are used in this study will now be discussed:[2]

1. *Population:* Population of the urban segment alone is considered here.
2. *Area:* Area of urban segments of the districts is considered.
3. *Distance from district with highest per capita income:* The rationale for this is fairly clear. By this criterion, the district with the highest income will get the least disbursement (possibly equal to zero). We

preferred to use this criterion as compared to measuring distance from the per capita state domestic product (SDP) of Maharashtra. While the final set of shares of districts emerging from the alternative would be very similar, we felt that measuring distance from highest per capita income would be a superior alternative. Measuring distance from per capita SDP would have resulted in a mixture of positive values (where the per capita income of a district is smaller than the per capita SDP) and negative values (where the per capita income of a district is greater than the per capita SDP). This mixture of positive and negative complicates computation of shares of districts. The alternative employed here, while conveying a very similar picture, eases computation considerably.

4. *Inverse income:* This criterion instead of using per capita income uses the reciprocal of per capita income as a characteristic. Compared to the distance criterion, the inverse income criterion allocates shares, which are relatively higher not only for the poorest states, but also the richest states at the cost of middle-income states. The exact procedure used is discussed below.

5. *Backlog as a backwardness indicator:* The earliest information on backlog of development (with respect to roads, education, electrification, etc.) comes from the government of Maharashtra (GoM 1984). The report had computed the expenditure that would be involved in clearing the backlog in different sectors, such as roads, irrigation, village electrification, education (general and technical), health services, water supply, land development, and veterinary. These expenditures were reported for each of the 26 districts that were in existence at that time. While we did feel that the picture that was presented by the report of the Fact-Finding Committee might not have changed much over the last decade and a half, it was nonetheless better to obtain more recent information on backlog. We have obtained this from the GoM (1997a). The main advantage of using the later report (ibid.), apart from using more current information, is the fact that information was available on districts that came into existence after the first report of the Fact-Finding Committee (GoM 1984).

The total quantum of expenditure that would be required to eliminate the backlog as estimated in 1994 has increased substantially as compared to the expenditure estimated by GoM

(1984). While it reports a total of Rs 31 billion (excluding Mumbai), the GoM (1997a) estimates a figure of Rs 151 billion, an increase by 4.75 times. We have made use of the backlog indicators given in the GoM (ibid.) as a separate criterion to capture the backwardness of a district.

6. *Income from (mining + secondary sector + tertiary sector) as a proportion of total income of the district (distance approach):* Here we assume that all income created in the mining, secondary sector, and tertiary sector originates in urban areas and distance from the highest (mining + secondary sector + tertiary sector) income district in a manner similar to that employed in criterion number (3).

The criteria, along with the weights used in this study are given in Table 11.2. In deciding weighting pattern, past practice as well as informed judgment is crucial. Some of the considerations that were important in the determination of weights are:

1. Too high a weight on distance discriminates rather strongly against the high-income districts as compared to low-income ones. While efforts must be made to reduce the gap between districts, better performance must not be penalized by too high a weight on this characteristic.

2. The weight given to backlog is in keeping with the recommendation of GoM (1984). Besides, it was felt that this characteristic

TABLE 11.2: WEIGHTS FOR CRITERIA FOR DISBURSEMENT

Criteria	Weights
Distance from highest per capita income district (DIST)	0.150
Backlog in terms of backwardness indicator (BACK)	0.150
Urban Population (UP)	0.150
Urban Area (UA)	0.200
Income from (mining + secondary sector + tertiary sector) as a proportion of total income of the district (distance approach) (MST-DIST)	0.150
Inverse (mining + secondary sector + tertiary sector) income (INVMST)	0.100
Number of municipal corporations (MCS–weight)	0.015
Number of 'A' class councils (A–weight)	0.015
Number of 'B' class councils (B–weight)	0.035
Number of 'C' class councils (C–weight)	0.035

would be correlated with distance and too high a weight would discriminate against better of districts rather excessively.

3. The central finance commissions have been progressively reducing the weight attached to population. While the weight given to this characteristic by the Tenth Finance Commission was 0.20, this was reduced to 0.10 by the Eleventh Finance Commission. While we agree that too high a weight gives populous jurisdictions excessive allocation, we felt that the weight given by the Eighth and Ninth Finance commissions would be appropriate for an exercise that is being conducted for the first time in the state.

4. For provision of local public goods, it is *area of coverage* that is probably more important than the *number of beneficiaries*. Local public goods are more susceptible to congestion than pure public goods, and hence area of a jurisdiction combined with its population would be adequate to estimate the need for funds of a local body within a district.

DETERMINING SHARES OF DISTRICTS FOR NEED-BASED DISBURSEMENT

Having identified the criteria to be used for disbursement and assumed certain weights for these criteria, the next step is to estimate the shares of districts under each of these criteria.[3] We will now discuss the way in which we estimated the shares of districts. It will be noted that there are certain criteria that are global, in the sense that these are applicable to the district as a whole, both its rural and urban segments. On the other hand, there are other criteria that are specific to the urban segment alone. We will first discuss the derivation of district shares based on global criteria and then look at shares derived from segment-specific criteria.

One important decision had to be taken while determining the shares of districts and this pertained to the inclusion or exclusion of Mumbai from the exercise. Given the dominant presence of Mumbai in all spheres of the state, including it distorts the picture completely. Hence, we have excluded Mumbai from all computations in our exercises. We devise a separate method to compute the share of Mumbai.

Global Criteria

1. *Distance from highest per capita income district* (DIST): Distance is defined as the gap the between the highest per capita income of a

geographical area (say, district) and the per capita income of other areas. Thus, defining:

$$\text{Distance} = Y_n - Y_i \qquad \qquad 11.3$$

where,

Y_n is the highest per capita income among all districts, and Y_i is per capita income of another district.

The share of a district is given by:

$$S_i = N_i(Y_n - Y_i) / \sum_{i=1}^{I} N_i(Y_n - Y_i) \qquad \qquad 11.4$$

where,

N_i is population of the *i*th district.

The construction of the formula is such that the poorer the district, larger its share in revenue sharing arrangement. This will also imply that highest-income district would get zero share. Note that we have excluded Mumbai from these computations.

2. *Backlog* (BACK): Given the total amount of expenditure for eliminating the backlog of all districts in the state (excluding Mumbai), we obtain the share for each district as ratio of the backlog expenditure for a district to the total backlog expenditure. Naturally, districts with a higher ratio will command a greater share of disbursement according to this criterion.

Urban Criteria

1. *Urban population* (UP): Share of the urban segment of the district under this criterion is computed as:

$$Q_i = N_i / \sum_{i=1}^{I} N_i \qquad \qquad 11.5$$

where,

N_i is the urban population of the *i*th district.

2. *Urban area* (UA): Share of the urban segment of the district under this criterion is computed as:

$$AS_i = A_i / \sum_{i=1}^{I} A_i \qquad \qquad 11.6$$

where,

A_i is the urban area of the *i*th district.

3. *Income from (mining + secondary sector + tertiary sector) as a proportion of total income of the district (distance approach)* (MST-DIST): As stated earlier, the rationale for this criterion is the hypothesis that the overwhelming proportion of income in mining, secondary, and

tertiary sectors is generated in urban areas. The higher this proportion is for a district, the better off it is and should qualify for a lower share by the needs-based approach. The method for generating weights is exactly as given for 'Distance from highest per capita income district' under global criteria above. The only difference is that under the usual distance criterion, we use distance from highest per capita income to generate shares, here we use distance from highest ratio of income from (mining + secondary sector + tertiary sector) to total income.

4. *Inverse (mining + secondary sector + tertiary sector) income* (INVMST): This is computed as follows:

$$\text{Share of a district, } B_i = (N_i / Y_i) / \left[\sum_{i=1}^{I} (N_i / Y_i) \right] \qquad 11.7$$

where,

N$_i$ is the urban population of ith district, and

Y$_i$ is income from (mining + secondary + tertiary) sectors of the ith district.

5. *Weights for ULBs*: Separate weights have been assigned depending on the number of various levels of ULBs present in a district. The shares for the district are then computed in terms of the ratio of number of ULBs of a particular level (say, number of MCs in Thane) in the district to the total number of ULBs in that level in all of Maharashtra (say, total number of MCs in the state of Maharashtra).

EFFICIENCY-BASED DISBURSEMENT TO ULBs

The total amount that has been set aside for efficiency-based disbursement is 40 per cent, that is, Rs 4 billion, will be available for this purpose out of the notional amount of Rs 10 billion.[4]

We view efficiency in two broad ways:

1. Performance
   (a) Levels (DR)
   (b) Changes (DDR)
   (c) Recovery of arrears in property taxes (PTAX)
2. Efficiency
   (a) Administration (ADMIN)
   (b) Public goods (PG)

The separation between performance and efficiency allows a division of the funds reserved for efficiency-based disbursement: we set aside 12.5 per cent of these funds for performance and 87.5 per cent for efficiency.

Performance: Levels (DR)

This is understood in the sense of overall fiscal balance. We have adapted the measures that have been proposed by the Reserve Bank of India for evaluating the fiscal performance of Indian states. The measure of performance levels that we have used may be called 'Own deficit' of a ULB. This is defined as:

$$DR = \frac{(\text{Total Expenditure} - \text{Own Income})}{\text{Total Expenditure}} \qquad 11.8$$

Own income of a ULB consists of octroi, property tax, water charges, conservancy and sanitation, street lights, licence fees and entertainment, and building rents.

Obviously one can compare only similar ULBs. Hence, we compute for each ULB but compare it only with a similar ULB. The performance of a ULB in the municipal corporation category cannot be compared with the performance of a ULB in the councils A category.

This measure gives an indication of the dependence of ULB on resources (such as grants) from a higher level of government. As defined, DR may be positive (indicating an own deficit) or it may be negative (indicating surplus). Creating a set of weights for indicators that are both positive and negative creates major problems of comparability. We have overcome this problem by adopting a rule that only ULBs with a surplus, that is, a negative DR, will receive a bonus and that the total amount allocated for DR will be shared between ULBs (in a particular category) in proportion to the level of their surplus.

It needs to be noted that allocation according to DR will use values of this ratio for the latest year for which data is available. Hence, it is not possible to set out allocations to ULBs according to this criterion for a number of years in the future. *DR will have to be computed afresh every year and then allocations determined.*

The amount set aside for DR is 5 per cent of the Rs 4 billion available for efficiency-based disbursement, that is, Rs 200 million. This amount has to be distributed between various classes of ULBs in some proportion. Using the broad division between municipal corporations and municipal councils, we believe that the share of the former should be 25 per cent of the total. This represents a lowering of the historical shares that have been allocated to municipal corporations in Maharashtra. Among the councils, MC–C are deemed to be weakest in financial terms and the share of this class must be highest, followed by MC–B, and then by MC–A. Thus the division of funds is MCs: 25 per cent; MC–A: 20 per cent; MC–B: 25 per cent; and MC–C: 30 per cent.

Performance: Changes (DDR)

The indicators generated out of performance (DR) may be termed static indicators, that is, indicators for a particular year. We also need to reward ULBs that show improvement over time. For this we look at the changes in the ratio DR that has been defined above. Given the way in which DR is defined, an improvement over time would be reflected by a decline in the value of the ratio. Hence, if DDR is negative for a ULB, it indicates an improvement in performance. Only ULBs with negative DDR will qualify and the amount set aside for this indicator will be divided among ULBs in the same manner as DR.

As in the case of DR, it is apparent that allocations according to DDR will need to use changes in the values of DR for the latest year for which data is available. It is clearly not possible to set out allocations to ULBs according to this criterion for a number of years in the future. DDR *will have to be computed afresh every year and then allocations determined.*

The amount set aside for DDR is half that reserved for DR: 2.5 per cent of Rs 4 billion, that is, Rs 100 million, has been set aside for DDR. This amount is distributed among the various classes of ULBs in the proportions set out above.

Performance: Recovery in Property Taxes (PTAX)

While some aspect of recovery of taxes is reflected in DR, it was felt that we should also specifically focus on recovery of a specific tax. Property taxes which are already important and are likely to be even more important for the fiscal health of a ULB. All ULBs face severe problems in the recovery of property taxes, leading to current year's arrears and accumulated arrears for previous years. The measure of performance discussed here compares recovery of current and accumulated arrears in property tax in a year with total current demand and arrears in property taxes.

$$PTAX = \frac{(Current\ Demand\ and\ Arrears\ in\ Property\ Tax\ Collected)}{(Total\ Current\ Demand\ and\ Arrears\ in\ Property\ Taxes)} \quad 11.9$$

The need to use the latest data on property tax recovery is paramount, which means it requires a continuous data collection process.

The amount set aside for PTAX is 5 per cent of the Rs 4 billion available for efficiency-based disbursement, that is, Rs 200 million. Once again this is distributed among various classes of ULBs in the set proportions.

Efficiency: Administration (ADMIN)

Apart from overall performance, a local body must be efficient in providing services, that is, public goods, to the citizens. The ability to provide such services will be severely compromised if expenditure on administration captures a large part of the resources available to a local body. Consequently, we need to devise an indicator that will penalize a ULB for spending excessively on ADMIN to the detriment of public goods provision. The indicator that we use is given by:

$$ADMIN = \frac{Expenditure\ on\ Administration,\ Salaries,\ Pensions,\ etc.}{Total\ Expenditure} \quad 11.10$$

The higher is this ratio for a ULB, the lower will be its share in allocations under this head.

Given that a total of Rs 4 billion is available for disbursement under the efficiency-related criteria of which Rs 500 million are reserved for performance, the amount available for efficiency is Rs 3.5 billion. Of this amount we reserve 25 per cent for ADMIN, that is, Rs 875 million. As before, this amount is distributed among classes of ULBs in the proportions determined earlier.

Efficiency: Public Goods (PG)

We believe that the main objective of decentralization should be to provide local public goods to citizens in a way that reflects their preference structure. Under public goods we include education, libraries, free reading halls, sanitation, solid waste management, drain, mechanical and electrical facilities, fire brigade, water supply, epidemics

and public health, and roads and street lighting. The indicator used is
given by:

$$PG = \frac{\text{Expenditure on Public Goods}}{\text{Total Expenditure}} \qquad\qquad 11.11$$

A possible objection to the use of this ratio is that part of the
expenditure on public goods may be for salaries of the bureaucracy
in charge of public goods provision. This includes salaries of engineers
in charge of, say, sanitation as well as salaries of clerical staff. It could
be argued that while expenditure on salaries of engineers is important
for service delivery, that on clerical staff is not. While we agree with
the sentiments underlying this view, the current availability of data
precludes us from operationalizing such an approach. It must, however,
be mentioned here that such data collection is not possible even for
higher levels of government; hence, to expect it at the level of local
bodies, while laudable, is far too ambitious.

It has also been pointed out, not only in the context of public
goods provision, but more generally, that a broad division between
revenue (current) expenditure and capital expenditure will also be
indicative of the efficiency of a ULB. While we agree that this is
indeed true, and the dominance of revenue expenditure over capital
expenditure is a problem that afflicts all levels of government, at the
moment such division of expenditure is not available at the level of
local bodies.

It was pointed out earlier that mere spending on public goods
need not result in superior service delivery. It should be clear that we
are using expenditure on public goods as a proxy in the absence of
data on actual service delivery. However, we would like to make a
strong recommendation for collection of data on actual provision of
public goods by each corporation and council. This actual provision
must be compared to the minimum norms that are available from a
variety of sources, such as Mumbai Metropolitan Regional
Development Authority (MMRDA) and Zakaria Commission.

Given that a total of Rs 4 billion is available for disbursement
under the efficiency-related criteria, of which Rs 500 million are
reserved for performance, the amount available for efficiency is Rs
3.5 billion. Of this amount 25 per cent was reserved for ADMIN,
which left 75 per cent for PG—Rs 2.6 billion. As before, this amount
is distributed among classes of ULBs in the proportions determined
earlier.

SENSITIVITY ANALYSIS

In this subsection we suggest examining the influence of a change in the weighting pattern of the various criteria that determine need-based allocations to districts and subsequently to ULBs. This exercise is important especially if one bears in mind that the weights set for the criteria are not sacrosanct and may be changed according to the judgement of the user of the methodology developed here. We have set up some alternative weighting patterns and so as to enable comparison with the devolution arrived from the initial weighting pattern. Table 11.3 gives the weighting pattern under four different scenarios. We have also included the original weighting pattern used earlier for ready reference.

We do not report the details of the changes in allocations as a result of the changes in the weighting pattern. These details right down to the last municipal council are available in Karnik *et al.* (2002).

TABLE 11.3: WEIGHTING PATTERN UNDER VARIOUS SCENARIOS

Criteria	Original scenario	Scenario 1	Scenario 2	Scenario 3	Scenario 4
DIST	0.150	*0.050*	0.150	0.150	0.150
BACK	0.150	*0.250*	0.150	0.150	0.150
UP	0.150	0.150	*0.100*	0.150	0.150
UA	0.200	0.200	*0.250*	0.200	0.200
MST-DIST	0.150	0.150	0.150	*0.250*	*0.000*
INMST	0.100	0.100	0.100	*0.000*	*0.250*
MCs	0.015	0.015	0.015	0.015	0.015
Council A	0.015	0.015	0.015	0.015	0.015
Council B	0.035	0.035	0.035	0.035	0.035
Council C	0.035	0.035	0.035	0.035	0.035

Note: Highlighted numbers show the changes in a particular scenario relative to the original scenario.

DATA GAPS

An exercise such as the one carried out in the UNDP/UNCHS study and discussed conceptually in the previous section is highly data intensive. The more accurate and detailed the data, the better targeted are the disbursements likely to be. Such data will facilitate well-targeted disbursement on grounds of efficiency as well as equity. While we have been able to obtain data of fairly good quality, which has made for a rich analysis, looking to the future of decentralization and disbursement of funds to strengthen ULBs, we are .in a position to point out certain data gaps.

The ideal situation for targeting disbursements is the availability of detailed data at the level of the local body. This will include, apart from information on the financial performance of the local body, other 'real' data, such as, total income generated, population, area, poverty ratios, level of backwardness, and quality of infrastructure (separately for water supply, sanitation, street lighting, etc.). However, as we have found out during the course of our exercises, much of such 'real' data are available only at the level of the districts, while at the level of local bodies only financial data is available in detail. Even as far as some local bodies were concerned, there were data gaps with respect to availability of financial data. This was more likely to be the case at the level of C class councils.

The next step in the decentralization process is one where we go beyond the level of the ULB, that is, beyond the MCs, councils A, B, and C. This would imply going to the level of wards within each ULB. While the concept of decentralization could logically extend to the ultimate unit in the jurisdiction, that is, the citizen, practically we need to set some limits. These practical limits will have to be set by constitutional provisions relating to the decentralized unit. At the moment, such provisions have been put in place up to ULBs only. Further, there are no provisions at the level of state acts, which extend decentralization below the level of ULBs.

In spite of this, it remains a fact that functions of the ULB get decentralized to the ward level. Hence, we can say that actual service delivery takes place at the ward level and consequently, the functioning of the wards should be a matter of concern to us. However, it needs to' be borne in mind that wards or ward committees do not have functional autonomy and, more importantly, do not have financial autonomy. Wards have to functions as per the dictates of the chief officer and standing committee of the ULB.

Despite this, since actual service delivery takes place at the level of the wards and hence citizens' welfare is crucially determined at this level, it would be important to assess the functioning of the wards. Naturally, for such a task to be undertaken, far more detailed data would have to be available. This, however, is likely to be a formidable task: in Mumbai MC alone there are 23 wards and at the moment we do not even know how many wards there will be in other MCs and councils. To undertake the task of data collection at the ward level will be gigantic, however desirable the objective may be. We have not been able to collect any information beyond the level of the ULB. That said, we do strongly recommend that a pilot study for data collection at the ward level be instituted.

Bearing in mind the data gaps that we have discussed, we would like to recommend a centralized, autonomous agency for collection, analysis, and updating of a variety of data.

CONCLUDING REMARKS

The purpose of this chapter is to present a methodology for a systematic and transparent formula-based disbursement of funds to ULBs. The methodology presented has had to innovate on the basic approaches of Central Finance Commissions' disbursement procedures. However, there is one major difference that has been pointed out: while the jurisdictional authority of the state government exactly matches the boundaries of the state, this convenient state of affairs breaks down when one is concerned with disbursements below that level. Hence, we have devised a three-step procedure that operationalizes the proposed procedure. The procedure, however, makes significant demands on the data gathering mechanism. This is especially true if the extension of the procedure has to take into account actual service delivery by ULBs. Hence, it is our strong recommendation that not only the state of Maharashtra (which is the focus of this study) but other states should institute a permanent data collection machinery that will provide continuous inputs for the operationalization of the proposed procedure.

It has been pointed out that the methodology developed in this paper depends critically on the quality of data that is available.[4] There can be no disagreement on this issue. The better the quality of data, the better will be the results of the exercise. In fact, efforts to strengthen the database of local bodies should be one of the major recommendations, not just from this chapter, but from all efforts at deepening fiscal decentralization. The point about excessive number of criteria in the needs-based devolution scheme (see Note 4) is well taken. However, given the diversity of Indian states and the diversity of local bodies within the states, we felt that offering as much flexibility, in form of a plethora of characteristics, to the users of the methodology was desirable. In specific instances, users can emphasize or de-emphasize certain characteristics by increasing or reducing (even setting equal to zero) the weights on the criteria. Our objective in this paper was to demonstrate the full capability of the method and leave it to the user to tailor the method according to local requirements.

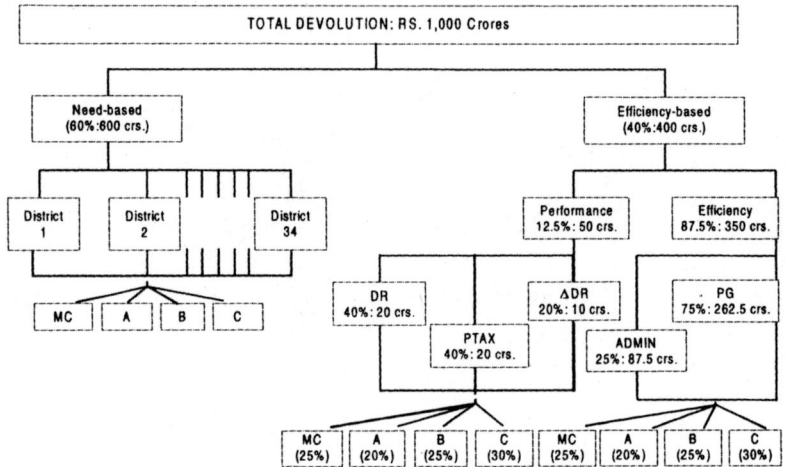

FIGURE 11.1: DEVOLUTION SCHEME

NOTES

* We would like to thank the participants at the JNU/UNDP/UN-HABITAT Workshop on Local Governance, Jawaharlal Nehru University, 11–12 April 2002 for excellent comments on the paper. The usual disclaimer applies.
1. Professor Ravi Srivastava pointed out at the JNU/UNDP/UN-HABITAT workshop that the presence of so many characteristics in a devolution scheme could lead them to work at cross purposes. We believe that with an appropriate weighting scheme—including a weight of zero for some of the criteria—this problem can be overcome. The reason for using so many criteria is to offer as much flexibility to the user of the methodology as possible.
2. Karnik *et al.* (2002) give the detailed mathematical formulation of this procedure.

3. Karnik *et al.* (2002) give the detailed mathematical formulation of this procedure.
4. This point was made at the JNU/UNDP/UN-HABITAT workshop by numerous participants, especially, Professor Amitabh Kundu.

REFERENCES

Government of India (GoI), *Report of the Tenth Finance Commission*, New Delhi: Government of India, 1995.

———, *Report of the Eleventh Finance Commission*, New Delhi: Government of India, 2000.

Government of Maharashtra (GoM), *Report of the Fact-Finding Committee (FFC) on Regional Imbalance* (V.M. Dandekar, Chairman), Mumbai: Planning Department, Government of Maharashtra, 1984.

———, *Report of the Indicators and Backlog Committee* (Volume I: Relative Levels of Development, Backlog, and Removal of Regional Imbalances), Mumbai: Government of Maharashtra, 1997a.

——— (1997a) *Report of the First Maharashtra State Finance Commission*, Government of Maharashtra, Mumbai.

Karnik A., A. Pethe, and D. Karmarkar, 'Evolving Criteria for Allocation of Funds as per the State Finance Commission Recommendations from the State to Urban Local Bodies to Strengthen Decentralization Efforts by Urban Local Bodies', Draft report of the research study, New Delhi: UNDP/UNCHS, 2002.

12

Urban Local Bodies and District Administration
An Empirical Examination of Some Issues Relating to Urban Water Supply in Karnataka

■ K.P. KRISHNAN

INTRODUCTION

Writings in political theory going back to James Stuart Mill make out an educational and empowerment role for 'local government'. Public finance literature traditionally treats urban water supply as a local or municipal public good, calling for its provision by the local or municipal government. The 74th Amendment to the Indian Constitution in effect adopts this view and urban water supply figures as an item in the Twelfth Schedule. Municipal legislations of Karnataka, which predate the Constitutional Amendment, also treat urban water supply as an obligatory function of the elected urban local bodies. In practice, however, like many other Indian states, the government of Karnataka has established a statutory body for planning, preparing, and executing schemes for providing supply of drinking water and drainage facilities. Operation and management of these assets, however, continue to be with urban local bodies.

This chapter questions the conventional wisdom of treating all of urban water supply (UWS) as a local public good. It does this empirically by taking Belgaum district of Karnataka as an example. The main argument of the paper is that UWS has components that are 'local'—the retail distribution within the urban area—but it has components—intake, treatment, bulk distribution, etc.—that are 'regional' and not 'local' in the sense in which it is defined in economics. Their provision, therefore, has to be by a 'regional' entity. This region could be a historically evolved administrative unit like a district and the entity the district officer. Theoretically it could also be more than one district, but this paper confines itself to district as a unit and looks at the argument on economies of scale more carefully to make the point about the advantages of aggregation.

The chapter has three sections. The first is a brief overview of the theory. The second section describes in brief the urban scenario in Karnataka, including urban governance legislation and structure, and the institutional framework for the provision of UWS. The third section applies theoretical arguments of the first section to Belgaum district and argues the case for a district-level urban development agency to exploit economies of scale and synergies in elements of UWS that are regional. This argument derives additional strength when one looks at the various other urban development programmes that offer similar economies of scale and scope.

THE THEORY OF LOCAL GOVERNMENT

Local government is a broad term referring to levels of administration and governance beyond the state or provincial governmental structures. This is what is often called the third tier of the government, and includes both urban and the rural structures.

THE POLITICAL SCIENCE PERSPECTIVE OF LOCAL GOVERNMENT: AN OVERVIEW

Local government, according to a well-known political theorist, 'has seldom been treated with elegance and precision' (Mackenzie 1961). He goes on further to lament, 'If you scan the textbooks of political thought you will find no accounts, or very shoddy accounts, of theories about local government.' Though this was said over forty years ago, the position is perhaps not very different today. Notwithstanding this, however, in practice, even during the British regime, there were conscious attempts by the then reformers to evolve local government according to certain principles that were influenced by the general tenor of contemporaneous English political thought.

Lord Ripon's famous Resolution of 1882, often considered a watershed in the constitution, powers, and functions of municipal bodies, bore the stamp of English utilitarianism. John Stuart Mill, for example, basically valued local government as the public education of the citizens. The Ripon Resolution on local self-government was in consonance with this utilitarian philosophy. An oft-quoted passage of this resolution is:

In advocating the extension of local self-government, and the adoption of this principle in the management of many branches of local affairs, the Governor-General-in-Council does not suppose that the work will be in the first instance better done than if it remained in the sole hands of the Government District Officers. It is not, primarily, with a view to improvement in administration that this measure is put forward and supported. It is chiefly desirable as an instrument of political and popular education.

The resolution envisaged the small beginnings of independent political life through the introduction of local government and the supersession of the more autocratic system—the district administration.

Later constitutional reforms did not lose sight of the role of local government in the total framework of government. The Decentralization Commission of 1909 recommended almost a total elimination of official control and conferment of freedom on the municipal bodies to raise local taxes and to have complete control over their budgets. The next impetus came in 1918 from the Montague-Chelmsford Report, which insisted on the educative principle, advocated extended franchise, and pleaded for complete popular control in local bodies. According to the Ripon Resolution, the 'autocratic system' of district administration should gradually give way to local government and the district officer was to watch the performance of local bodies at best from without. However, after this period, in response to rising Indian political demands, Indian constitutional reforms in subsequent years were directed more and more toward the provincial and central governments. The local government was gradually receding in the background. Though the Simon Commission recommended going back to the Ripon Resolution, effectively urban local government reforms, in a political sense, did not figure in the agenda of the nation till the time the 73rd and 74th amendments to the Constitution were taken up.

THE ECONOMIC PERSPECTIVE OF LOCAL GOVERNMENT:
LOCAL PUBLIC GOODS

To fully appreciate the economic arguments for 'local government', it is necessary to set out briefly the economic arguments for government itself. Inter alia, this rests on the role of the government as a provider of 'public goods'.

What economists call 'pure public goods', have two main distinguishing features:

1. Their consumption is characterized by 'non-rivalry': Consumption by one agent does not affect its availability to be consumed by any other.

2. Their consumption displays 'non-excludability' of potential consumers: There is normally no feasible way of preventing some from consuming the services of this good.

The result of these characteristics of public goods is that the market mechanism will fail to achieve a 'Pareto optimal' allocation of resources. The basic reason for market failure in the provision of public goods is because the benefits that these goods give rise to are not limited to the particular consumer who purchases them (as is the case for private goods), but becomes available to others as well. In other words, benefits derived by any one's consumption of a social good are 'externalized' in that they become available to others. In the case of private goods, the benefits of consumption are 'internalized'. Market mechanism is based on exchange. Exchange occurs only when there is an exclusive title to the property that is to be exchanged. Therefore, application of the exclusion principle tends to be an efficient solution in such a situation. In the case of 'public goods', it would be inefficient to exclude any one from partaking of the benefits when the participation would not reduce the consumption by any one else. So even if feasible, exclusion would be undesirable. As a result of this non-excludability, consumers will not voluntarily offer payments to the suppliers of public goods and there is no revelation by consumers of how much of the service they want and how much they value that service leading to 'free riding'. This is referred to as the problem of 'preference or demand revelation' in respect of public goods. Articulation of the demand for public goods to enable the provision of it in the necessary measure, therefore, becomes an important economic role for government.

Once this demand articulation is done, the general principle for optimal allocation of public goods is the same as the one for goods in general, namely, that economic efficiency is achieved by providing the mix of output that best reflects the preferences of the individuals who make up society. This allocation theory as applied to the public sector leads to the conclusion that public services should be provided and their costs shared in line with the preferences of the residents (Musgrave and Musgrave 1976). Moreover, given the fact that a political process is needed to secure preference revelation, it follows that particular services should be voted on and paid for by the residents of the region who are the beneficiaries of the service. Therefore, services that are nationwide in their incidence should be provided for nationally, and local units should provide for services with local benefits, and still others such as highways should be provided for on a regional basis. Given the spatial character of social goods, there is thus an a priori case for multiple jurisdictions. Each jurisdiction should provide services the benefits of which accrue within its boundaries, and it should use only such sources of finance as will internalize the costs. This is the basic economic argument for provision of certain categories of public goods by local governments.

In an application of the basic principles of welfare economics to the provision of public goods and services by state and local governments, Tiebout (1956) showed that competition among communities will result in their supplying the goods and services individuals want, and the production of those goods in an efficient manner. Tiebout was originally concerned with the problem of preference revelation, that is, how will individuals reveal their preferences of public goods? Voting pattern is not a good answer, as voters cannot express in detail their views about particular categories of expenditures. Referenda cannot be a frequently employed tool on account of organizational and expenditure constraints. His argument was that individuals could 'vote with their feet'. Their choice of communities revealed their preferences toward locally produced public goods in the same way as their choices of products reveal their preferences for private goods. Therefore, a sort of a market-type solution will emerge according to him for the provision of public goods.

THE BASIC ECONOMIC THEORY OF 'DECENTRALIZATION'

There are other additional reasons that Oates (1972) marshals in favour of the provision of local public goods by local governments. These are:

1. Decentralization also leads to greater experimentation and innovation. A variety of approaches in the long run promises greater technical progress in the modes of provision.

2. Competitive pressures from an enlarged number of producers will lead to adoption of the best technique.
3. In a decentralized mode expenditure decisions are tied more closely to real resource costs.

In the US, for example, any programme to provide a new service or an improved service is as per legal requirement always accompanied by the increase in property tax rates necessary to fund it or the increase in 'user charges' necessary for its provision. Hence, this leads to more explicit recognition of costs. Oates in fact went on to show in his famous 'decentralization theorem' that where cost savings from centralized decision-making are absent, it is always preferable to provide the public good on a decentralized basis. The optimal degree of decentralization will vary substantially among different societies and the determinants are best established empirically. The theoretically ideal solution is 'perfect correspondence'. In the case of perfect public goods, the optimal form of federal government to provide the set of 'n' public goods would be the one in which there exists a level of government for each subset of the population over which the consumption of a public good is defined. This would be sufficient to internalize the benefits from the provision of each. In other words perfect correspondence would mean jurisdictions for determination of the level of provision of each public good by including precisely the set of individuals who consume the good. Optimality is achieved in a Pareto sense by 'benefit pricing', that is, by equating price with marginal cost.

In summary, therefore, for a public good, the consumption of which is defined over geographical subsets of the total population and for which the costs of providing each level of output of the good in each jurisdiction are the same for the central government or the respective local governments, it will always be more efficient or at least as efficient for local governments to provide the Pareto-efficient levels of output for their respective jurisdictions than for the central government to provide any specified and uniform level of output across all jurisdictions. The basic rationale is if each local government, or local body as they are called in India, reaches Pareto optimality then welfare maximization takes place. However, it is useful to keep in mind that this approach does not take into account economies of scale, which can reduce unit cost. An important conclusion that emerges from these propositions is that for a given population size, the welfare gain from the decentralized provision of a particular local public good becomes greater as the diversity in individual demands within the country as a whole increases and as each geographical grouping of consumers becomes more homogeneous in terms of their demands for the good. The determination of the optimal sized jurisdiction involves a trade-off between the increased cost savings from the joint consumption in larger groups versus the greater benefits from more responsive levels of consumption in smaller groups.

This public-finance-theory-led conclusion, however, needs to be qualified. More recent literature on the subject draws attention to the issue of the capacity of local governments to handle matters involving technical and financial complexity. For example, the World Bank (2000) candidly states, 'Even a well meaning political team cannot overcome incompetent [local] administration.' Improving local services requires an effective local administration. Lack of capacity at the local level and the need for massive increase in skilled staff are the arguments most frequently (and often factually correct) invoked against decentralization. While these capacity constraints are surmountable, they deserve serious attention and the regional governments (state governments in the case of India) need to provide technical support to local governments as part of the process of decentralization.

URBAN WATER SUPPLY

Urban water supply is traditionally regarded as local public good, the provision of which should ideally be entrusted to local governments or local bodies. For instance, the World Bank (1994) says, 'Two features of water make its supply a "local" service that can be administered in a decentralized way. These are:

- water is expensive to transport over long distances &
- it is cheap to store.'

Therefore, the article goes on to say that there is a good case to vest the responsibility to provide water in the jurisdictional local body.

Municipal legislations in most states in India have adopted this principle and urban water supply is normally listed as an 'obligatory function' of the local body. The 74th Amendment to the Constitution of India is, in the opinion of the author, a tacit recognition of the idea that urban water supply is a local public good. Entry 5 of the Twelfth Schedule of the Constitution (read with Article 243 W) says that water supply for domestic, industrial, and commercial purposes should be a function entrusted to a municipality.

Decentralization in Practice: A Summary

What is, however, interesting is that the motivation for decentralization—as it is observed in practice—appears only tangentially related to administrative or economic reform. Political analysts have in fact suggested that decentralization stems from a more fundamental cause: the need of national political leaders to accommodate or deflect increasingly strident demands for power sharing by groups that have traditionally been excluded from it. Prud'homme (1993), for example, has characterized decentralization as 'political strategy by ruling elites to retain most of their power by relinquishing some of it'. Other scholars have analysed the reasons for decentralization in specific regions of the world. Hall (1993), referring to Africa, has attributed this to the conspicuous failure of the centralized state and characterized decentralization as an attempt by bankrupt central governments to create a new target for political dissatisfaction (again without relinquishing real power). Other scholars have looked at the former Eastern bloc countries, Latin America, etc., and come to similar conclusions. Whatever the underlying cause, what appears to be clear is that the decentralization now occurring or that which has occurred recently is not a carefully designed sequence of reforms aimed at improving public sector performance. It more often takes the form of a reluctant and disorderly series of concessions by central governments attempting to maintain political stability. The result is that decentralization has brought about a change in the structure of urban service delivery; it has not necessarily brought improvement.

In the opinion of this author, this is more or less true of the Indian situation, too. An attempt will be made in this paper to examine the above observations with reference to urban water supply. Though in a political and legislative sense, UWS functions have been entrusted to local bodies (that is, a change of structure), there is no improvement in the delivery of service. The reasons for this are many and complex. This chapter will focus on economic arguments and advance the view that in part it is because some components of UWS are more appropriately handled at the level of a district and by a district-level agency rather than by local bodies. Belgaum district of Karnataka is taken as an example to empirically illustrate this argument.

KARNATAKA

Karnataka, with nearly 34 per cent of the state population living in urban areas, has a higher degree of urbanization than the Indian average of 27.78 per cent.

URBAN GOVERNANCE IN KARNATAKA: THE LEGISLATIVE FRAMEWORK

Karnataka has 216 urban local bodies (ULBs) categorized into four types based on certain criteria prescribed in the relevant legislations. The legislative provisions on the subject are to be found in two acts, namely, the Karnataka Municipal Corporation Act of 1976 (hereafter the KMC Act) and the Karnataka Municipalities Act of 1964 (hereafter the KM Act). The paper will use the term ULBs when referring to all these categories of bodies. ULBs carry out many obligatory functions prescribed in the laws. As noted already, we will focus on one of these functions, namely, water supply. Table 12.1 provides data on ULBs in Karnataka.

URBAN WATER SUPPLY IN KARNATAKA

Capacity Creation

As per Section 87(j) of the KM Act, 'Obtaining supply of or an additional supply of water proper and sufficient for preventing danger to the health of the inhabitants from the insufficiency or unwholesomeness of the existing supply when such supply or additional supply can be obtained at a reasonable cost' is an obligatory function of the ULB. There are further provisions in the Act dealing with inspection of the water supply works, drainage, etc.

Besides this, the other important provisions on the subject are to be found in the Karnataka Urban Water Supply and Drainage Board Act 1973 (hereafter the KUWSDB Act). The net result of these legislative provisions can be summarized as follows:

1. The legislative provisions contained in the KM Act enjoin the ULBs to ensure provision of water supply to the residents of their area, but the Act is silent on the method or how this provision is

TABLE 12.1: CLASSIFICATION OF URBAN AREAS IN KARNATAKA
AS PER STATE MUNICIPAL LEGISLATION

Category	Criterion for classification	Number	Relevant legislation	Urban population (%)	Urban area (%)
Municipal corporation (MC)	Population size of 300,000 and above	6	Karnataka Municipal Corporation Act 1976	21.00	15.41
City municipal council (CMC)	Population size of 50,000–299,999	40	Karnataka Municipalities Act 1964	19.21	11.70
Town municipal council (TMC)	Population size of 20,000–49,999	82	Karnataka Municipalities Act 1964	33.28	61.86
Town panchayat (TP)	Population size of 10,000–19,999	88	Karnataka Municipalities Act 1964	26.51	11.03
Total		216		100.00	100.00

Source: GoK (1995).

to be ensured, presumably leaving this to the discretion of the ULB.

2. The KUWSDB Act prescribes the method for this provision by conferring monopoly powers on the Board for planning preparation and execution of schemes. This Act explicitly prohibits local authorities from preparing and executing any scheme the cost of which is more than Rs 50,000.

Operation and Management

As per the acts, both the ULBs and the Board have been given powers as regards O&M of the schemes, and the state government the discretion to decide as to whom this should be entrusted. Prior to 1996 there was no explicitly articulated general policy of the government of Karnataka (GOK) on O&M relating to UWS. At the time of sanction of individual schemes, specific arrangements used to be specified for O&M, but these were of an ad hoc nature. Till

1996 in practice it was the Board that carried out O&M functions. This was, however, not the result of any statutory or contractual obligation, but an informal arrangement.

Government Order No UDD 204 UMS 95 dated 15 November 1996 (hereafter the 96 GO) contains the extant policy of the GOK as regards O&M of UWS schemes. As per this GO, the state government directed the municipalities to take over O&M wherever the Board had completed the schemes.

Hence the total picture, as of now, is clear in terms of the following bifurcation:

1. investigation, preparation, and execution of schemes for creation of capacity and augmentation thereof is the responsibility of the Board; and
2. once created, their O&M, collection of water charges, etc., is the responsibility of the ULBs.

Though the formal policy continues to be as stated in the 96 GO, in view of the continuing complaints about non-availability of water and poor quality of service in most urban areas, there are periodical demands for a review of this policy. The latest pronouncement in this regard is a statement by the chief minister of Karnataka in his 2001–2 budget speech. The CM said, 'I am proposing that while ownership of water supply schemes remain with municipalities, maintenance will be handed over to the KUWSDB, which will impose and collect water rates.' This pronouncement has not led to any revised government order or guidelines yet and the 96 GO prescriptions on O&M continue.

Current Service Levels of Water Supply Provision

Bodies like the WHO and the Central Public Health and Environmental Engineering Organization (CPHEEO) have prescribed per capita water supply norms based on the category of urban settlement. However, effectiveness of service provision is more than merely meeting the recommended litres per capita daily (LPCD) levels. Any measure of water supply service effectiveness has to be multidimensional and at a minimum should include many other elements like:

• duration and pressure of the supply;
• equitable coverage; and
• quality of water supply.

Neither the Board nor the ULBs have data on these indicators, rendering it difficult to get even a minimal idea of service effectiveness. What, however, comes out clearly in discussions with ULB officials, legislators, and citizens is that actual household-level water availability is woefully inadequate. There is anecdotal and other evidence to show that the availability of water figures that are used in the official literature are way off the mark in terms of physical availability at the individual household level. In the estimation of this author, on an average the actual availability at the level of the household is likely to be of the order of 30 to 40 per cent of the stated bulk capacity of the water supply in most urban areas of the state.

Problems and Diagnosis

Inadequate provision of water is, therefore, a major problem in most ULBs in the state. In the absence of any data on the other indicators, it is difficult to state with confidence anything about the overall effectiveness of UWS in the state. However, given the frequently reported complaints in the media and in the legislature about quality of water, infrequent provision of water, lack of adequate pressure, etc., the picture is likely to be worse when one looks at the other indicators of water and overall service effectiveness. To achieve complete coverage, the prescribed LPCD levels, and the acceptable levels of quality, the urban water supply systems in the state need

- more investment for capacity creation and distribution improvements; and
- perhaps, more importantly, better management of existing systems.

Given the focus of this chapter, we will skip the investment inadequacy part and examine the management and institutional aspects in more detail.

MANAGEMENT AND EFFICIENCY ISSUES

The question that we look at in the context of poor service levels is: How effective has the utilization of the capacity created with past investments been?

As regards the utilization of created capacity and other efficiency indicators, reliable data is not available. The position in respect of

TABLE 12.2: INDICATORS OF EFFICIENCY OF UTILIZATION OF
WATER SUPPLY CAPACITY BY SELECTED
CORPORATIONS

Criteria	Belgaum	Hubli–Dharwar	Mangalore	Mysore
Total capacity (MLD)	41	111	93	132
Current production (MLD)	39	90	85	127
Percentage served through house connections	35.00	48.00	56.00	61.00
Percentage served through illegal connections	20.00	18.00	30.00	20.00
Total NRW (%)	51.00	60.00	48.00	51.00
Cost of water delivered (Rs/cum)	6.2	8.9	4.3	4.9
Average tariff charged (Rs/cum)	5.4	3.7	5.4	3.2
Collection efficiency	86.00	64.00	86.00	70.00
Annual operating surplus or deficit (Rs million)	–24	–83	1	–60

Source: Presentation to GoK in February 1999 by Anglian Water International
Private Ltd.

some indicators for some municipal corporations is as given in
Table 12.2.

Board officials are of the opinion that these figures are generally
correct and, if anything, on the conservative side. Similar data for
other ULBs is not available either with the Board or the ULBs. The
expectation, however, is that it is likely to be similar or worse.

In conclusion, it can be said that with the Board primarily
responsible for building assets and ULBs responsible for running the
system, there is diffused accountability. ULBs are not involved in any
meaningful way in the creation of the assets and, therefore, complain
that many defects in the running of the system go back to the
construction phase. Board officials on the other hand insist that the
service levels are bad because ULBs:

1. do not carry out preventive maintenance and are not technically
   capable of carrying out or supervising breakdown mainten-ance;
   and
2. do not have trained staff for O&M, procurement of quality
   material, maintenance of stores, inventory.

The result of all these is:

1. an enormous amount of asset creation;
2. often this is not necessarily assets or capacity of the right type;
3. very low O&M expenditure and very poor O&M practices; and
4. lack of a genuine sense of ownership of the water supply system by the operator (namely the ULB).

leading to:

1. unacceptably high levels of non-revenue water (NRW);
2. commercially and economically unviable water operations; and
3. poor levels of service to the consumers.

BELGAUM DISTRICT: A CASE STUDY

In addition to the reasons for poor outcomes in the urban water supply sector outlined in the previous section, the reason that we want to put forward in this chapter is the inappropriate level of entrustment of some components of the water supply function. Some components of UWS are more akin to 'regional' rather than 'local' public good in the view of this author and hence should be executed by 'regional' authorities and not by local bodies. This section of the chapter will attempt to show empirically with the help of data relating to Belgaum district of Karnataka this 'regional' aspect of some of these elements. Thereafter it is shown that the appropriate 'region' for the entrustment of this function is the 'district' and the appropriate agency to execute it the 'district administration'.

THE DISTRICT OFFICER AND ULBs

The point about the dominance of the political motivation (as opposed to economic or organizational motivations) in whatever urban de-centralization has taken place thus far in India and elsewhere was referred to in the first section of this chapter. This motivation is apparent when one takes a look at the powers vested in the district officer in municipal affairs. Appendix to this chapter enumerates the powers of the deputy commissioners of districts under the KM Act.[1] Even a cursory examination of the appendix will show that the primary focus of the legislation is supervision and control of ULBs. Either in this legislation or in other subordinate legislations there is no reference to the economic and inter-ULB coordination role of the district officer or the district administration. The basic thrust of the legislation framework is political governance and administrative accountability. Economic principles underlying the concept of local public goods as well as issues like economies of scale in municipal service provision do not find a mention in the legislations; nor is there evidence of municipal sector policies being informed by these considerations. The position is the same when it comes to urban water supply. Deputy commissioners of districts do not figure in decision-making mechanisms on UWS either in terms of legislative provisions or by administrative guidelines. Only in times of drought and acute shortage of water supply, as the authority administering calamity relief, do deputy commissioners come into the picture. In the normal course, they and hence the district administration are completely divorced from this sector.

URBAN PROFILE OF BELGAUM DISTRICT

Belgaum with 24.06 per cent of its population living in urban areas is the fourteenth most urbanized district in the state. Given that Karnataka has 27 districts, it is the median district in terms of degree of urbanization. It is a big district with a large number of urban areas making it a good district for an analysis of this kind. Table 12.3 summarizes the urban and municipal profile of Belgaum district.

The poor resource base and the low skill employee base of ULBs are obvious when one looks at the figures in Table 12.3.

MUNICIPAL AND URBAN WATER SUPPLY IN BELGAUM DISTRICT

The institutional framework for UWS in Belgaum district is the same as in the rest of the state. The Board is in charge of capacity creation and ULBs are in charge of day-to-day operations and maintenance. All problems relating to UWS that were listed in the context of the state apply equally to this district. The basic data relating to the bulk water supply service in urban areas of Belgaum is described in Table 12.4. Attention is drawn to some interesting features of the urban drinking water supply scenario of Belgaum district:

1. Out of 16 urban areas, not even one is dependent on groundwater as a source for the water supply scheme.
2. One ULB has a combined surface source and groundwater-based scheme.

TABLE 12.3: URBAN AND MUNICIPAL PROFILE OF BELGAUM DISTRICT (1997–8)

S. No	Name of ULB	Category	Population	Revenue (Rs 1000)	Expenditure (Rs 1000)	No. of employees	Group D employees
1	Athani	TMC	39200	10785	9937	88	76
2	Chikkodi	TMC	32820	7185	6221	73	59
3	Nippani	CMC	28000	23139	21591	169	118
4	Sadalga	TP	20207	902	991	11	5
5	Konnur	TP	14937	2316	2464	27	22
6	Moodalgi	TMC	29894	2216	2502	27	20
7	Hukkeri	TP	19906	4951	5837	26	21
8	Sankeshwar	TMC	32511	6102	6471	54	42
9	Khanapur	TP	16501	5927	6147	33	23
10	Gokak	CMC	52808	13930	14206	95	75
11	Soundati-Yellamma	TMC	33136	10480	9265	72	54
12	Kudachi	TP	19852	1775	1812	17	12
13	Raibag	TP	16000	1281	1504	16	11
14	Ramdurg	TMC	31822	4313	4073	67	50
15	Bailahongal	TMC	43215	9672	8448	74	60
16	Belgaum	MC	500000	234493	233801	2110	1477

Source: GoK (2001).

3. The average urban area is at a distance of nearly 9 km from its water source. If Belgaum City Corporation (BCC) is included, this average is more than 12 km.
4. In all urban areas, the source of the water supply is outside the geographical boundaries of the ULB.
5. The average urban local body has a water supply pumping capacity of approximately 5 MLD.
6. Two of the 16 urban areas do not have water treatment plants (WTP). The average capacity of the WTP where it exists is nearly 6 million litres daily (MLD) if one excludes the BCC and 10 MLD including the BCC.
7. Equally interesting is the range of these parameters. There are ULBs at a distance of only half a kilometre from their source of water and ULBs at a distance of 45 km from their source. Likewise, there are ULBs with pumping capacity of less than 1 MLD and ULBs with over 50 MLD. Similar is the situation in the capacity of the WTPs.

TABLE 12.4: URBAN WATER SUPPLY IN BELGAUM (BULK)

S. No.	Name of ULB	Category	Population as per 2001 Census	Water supply source	Distance of ULB from source (in kms)	Pumping capacity (in MLD)	WTP capacity (in MLD)	Design PCD
1	Athani	TMC	40915	SS	12.00	2.72	4.54	60.00
2	Chikkodi	TMC	32820	SS	20.00	5.44	5.44	70.00
3	Nippani	CMC	58061	SS	9.00	8.00	9.08	70.00
4	Sadalga	TP	20207	SS	1.50	4.54	4.54	95.00
5	Konnur	TP	17978	SS	0.30	4.54	4.54	90.00
6	Moodalgi	TMC	29894	SS	7.00	4.54	4.54	130.00
7	Hukkeri	TP	19906	SS	20.00	15.89	19.07	50.00
8	Sankeshwar	TMC	32511	SS	25.00	common scheme	common scheme	90.00
9	Khanapur	TP	16563	SS	1.50	2.27	2.27	90.00
10	Gokak	CMC	67166	SS	0.50	4.54	4.54	90.00
11	Soundati–Yellamma	TMC	38212	SS	3.00			NA
12	Kudachi	TP	19852	GW+SS	2.50	0.70	No WTP	35.00
13	Raibag	TP	15924	SS	3.50	0.75	No WTP	60.00
14	Ramdurg	TMC	36639	SS	5.00	1.36	Only sand filter	50.00
15	Bailahongal	TMC	43215	SS	7.00	5.83	5.83	90.00
16	Belgaum	MC	506235	SS	45.00	54.48	54.48	108.00
	Total		930809					

Source: Data collected by the author.

Notes: SS = surface source; GW = groundwater.

Table 12.5 captures the details of the retail and distribution aspects of urban water supply in Belgaum district.

TABLE 12.5: URBAN WATER SUPPLY IN BELGAUM DISTRICT
(RETAIL AND DISTRIBUTION)

Name of ULB	Category	No of properties in assessment record	No of water supply connections	Water supply coverage ratio (%)	No. of public taps	Length of water distribution (in Km)
Athani	TMC	6905	3853	55.80	84	15.00
Chikkodi	TMC	7870	2639	33.53	95	14.25
Nippani	CMC	8933	6182	69.20	1481	26.00
Sadalga	TP	4500	876	19.47	45	3.20
Konnur	TP	3182	1100	34.57	34	6.00
Moodalgi	TMC	4271	531	12.43	26	10.00
Hukkeri	TP	4500	559	12.42	10	3.00
Sankeshwar	TMC	6500	2616	40.25	24	18.00
Khanapur	TP	3915	1240	31.67	32	6.00
Gokak	CMC	9404	5878	62.51	250	18.00
Soundati- Yellamma	TMC	7304	2426	33.21	70	28.00
Kudachi	TP	1850	744	40.22	12	4.00
Raibag	TP	3400	901	26.50	16	5.00
Ramdurg	TMC	5559	2000	35.98	33	10.00
Bailahongal	TMC	8842	4016	45.42	238	38.00
Belgaum	MC	46019	29301	63.67	601	600.00

Source: Data collected by the author.

IS URBAN WATER SUPPLY IN BELGAUM DISTRICT A 'LOCAL PUBLIC GOOD'?

In the first section of the chapter we dealt with the concept of local public goods. It was brought out clearly there that absence of scale economies in the provision of a service is a major argument in favour of local provision of the service. We first examine whether there are scale economies in urban water supply. We do this from two viewpoints.

The first relates to the O&M norms of water supply schemes. The Government of India (GoI 1999) has prescribed minimum O&M staffing pattern for surface-source-based water supply systems. Table

TABLE 12.6: O&M STAFFING NORMS FOR SURFACE SOURCE–
BASED WATER SUPPLY SCHEMES

Capacity (MLD)	EE	AEE	AE	Jr Manager	Operators	Helpers/ fitters	Electrician	Watch-man
0–5	0	0	1	0	7	7 + 1 for every 8 km of raw water raising main + 1 for every 8 km of clean water raising main	2	6
5–25	0	0	1	0	7	11+ 1 for every 8 km of raw water raising main + 1 for every 8 km of clean water raising main	2	6
25–50	0	1	0	1	7	10 + 1 for every 8 km of raw water raising main + 1 for every 8 km of clean water raising main	3	6
50–75	0	1	1	1	7	17 +1 for every 8 km of raw water raising main + 1 for every 8 km of clean water raising main	3	6
75–150	1	1	0	4	20	10 + 20 fitters and 2 helpers for every 6 km of pipeline	3	6

Source: GoI (1999).
Note: EE: Executive Engineer
       AEE: Assistant Executive Engineer
       AE: Assistant Engineer.

12.6 summarizes these norms. A quick look at this table reveals that if there were to be common O&M staff for a cluster of ULBs, there are considerable savings in staff strength and hence salary expenditure that can be achieved while providing better quality urban water supply service. Given the overall financial weaknesses of the ULBs, any such savings would be of considerable importance to ULBs.

The second aspect relates to what is known as regional or combined water supply schemes. As noted already, most UWS schemes are now surface-source-based schemes at some distance away from the consuming urban area centres. There is, therefore, a long bulk water transmission pipeline in each of these schemes. These pipelines run through many rural and urban settlements en route. Many of these settlements do not have their own water supply schemes. Therefore, there has been strong demand to provide water from these pipelines to intervening villages. Non-provision has led to considerable tensions, law and order situations, and damage to pipelines. Hence, the GoK in 1996 issued an order on en route village schemes to share the capital costs of constructing these schemes. Since the intervening villages also rely on the same surface source, a slightly higher capacity transmission main was considerably less expensive than a parallel transmission line only for the village/s. Similarly, the cost of the pumping facility at the source and the water treatment plant get shared over a larger number of people and the per capita cost comes down considerably.

There is considerable literature in the US context, which shows that there are clear network economies at work in water supply and for most ranges of capacities that we are interested in, economies of scale are positive and more than the dis-economies of large organizations. For instance, Kim and Clark (1988) looked at data from 60 water utilities in the US for the 1970s and came to the conclusion that there are significant economies of scale in water treatment, but not in distribution. The study also found that utilities on the whole also experience economies of scope if residential and non-residential water services are treated as separate products/services.

Presumably motivated by this sort of an argument, the GoK order on en route villages encourages regional water supply schemes. However, the implementation record of the 17 regional water supply schemes taken up so far is dismal. Cost sharing has not taken place the way it was expected. Worse still is the fate of the schemes after creation. For example, in Belgaum district there is a fairly new regional water supply scheme for Hukkeri–Sankeshwar and 16 en route villages. This scheme draws raw water from a source at Hidkal Dam across the river Ghataprabha. It covers a total population of 150,000 people. In addition, there is a small industrial demand component in the scheme. This scheme is designed for a total capacity of 20 MLD. The scheme was commissioned in 1998 at a cost of Rs

125 million. In the initial few months after completion, for the operation of the pump set and water treatment plant, the town municipal council at Sankeshwar deputed some operating staff. Thereafter, since the other bodies involved allegedly did not share the recurring costs, the scheme is in complete disuse and is slowly becoming non-functional, and will need some capital expenditure to repair. Since the scheme caters to a large number of local bodies, both urban and rural, no single body has come forward to claim it or operate it. The Board has estimated that the O&M of the scheme will cost approximately Rs 3 million per annum. The story is the same in cases of other completed regional water supply schemes.

The simple point here is that bulk water supply provision for drinking water to urban and rural settlements is not a local public good but a regional one. However, the institutions created by law and practice are all 'local' and there is no regional institution that can address such issues. The distribution of water within the settlement, whether rural or urban, is, however, a local public good that is best managed by the ULB or the village panchayat concerned. Table 12.7 summarizes the critical features of Belgaum district urban water supply, which brings out these points clearly. The local public good, namely, retail distribution of water to households through individual connections is under-provided as reflected in the low percentage of properties with water connections. Similar is the position when one looks at the retail distribution pipeline length as a percentage of road length in each ULB. The ULBs have a comparative advantage in the provision of this local public good. Therefore, what may be required is an unbundling of UWS into its constituents. The facility for water intake at source, bulk transmission of raw water, treatment of water, bulk transmission of pure water, etc., appear prima facie to be more 'regional' in their spatial characteristics and hence in accordance with principles of multi-unit finance provided by 'regional' bodies. On the other hand, distribution within the local area is clearly a local service and is best provided by the local body.

NON-URBAN WATER SUPPLY ASPECTS OF AGGREGATION AND
THE CASE FOR DISTRICT URBAN DEVELOPMENT AGENCY

The preceding discussion has brought out the fact that there are clear, definable, and separable components of urban water supply

TABLE 12.7: URBAN WATER SUPPLY FEATURES OF BELGAUM DISTRICT

Percentage of urban population	22.12
Total no. of ULBs & their	
classification　　Municipal corporations	1
City municipal councils	2
Town municipal councils	7
Town panchayats	6
Percentage of urban population dependent exclusively on ground-water as source of drinking water	0
Percentage of urban population dependent on a mix of groundwater & surface source	2.13
Percentage of urban population dependent on surface source for drinking water	97.87
Percentage of properties in urban areas of the district without municipal water supply connection	38.55
Average length of internal water distribution pipelines in the district (km)	50.28 including BCC 13.63 excluding BCC
Average distance from source to ULB (km)	10.175 including BCC 7.85 excluding BCC
Average ULB water pumping capacity (MLD)	8.26 including BCC 4.70 excluding BCC
Average ULB water treatment capacity (MLD)	10.02 including BCC 5.98 excluding BCC

that are 'regional' in character in terms of economies of scale and their characteristics. Public finance literature suggests that the provision of these components is best done by regional entities and not by local authorities. The question is which are the appropriate 'regional' authorities for the discharge of this function? The obvious answer seems to be, the 'district authority'.

The revenue district is a historical and a geographically compact entity. The district officer is an established and recognized office and his role in municipal affairs is as old as ULBs themselves. However, given the technical nature of the assistance that needs to be provided to ULBs in the context of water supply and the need for coordination across ULBs and collective decision-making, what may be more appropriate is a 'district urban development agency' (DUDA) with adequate technical and other functional capacity like finance and audit. It is not proposed to go into details of the constitution of the DUDA in this chapter except to say that it should comprise all the elected and executive heads of ULBs. In this sense, it can become like an urban zilla panchayat and become the urban arm of the District Planning Committees, which are mandated by the 73rd and 74th constitutional amendments.

There are a number of other urban and municipal functions besides UWS that offer economies of scale and scope, which can be fully exploited by an agency like a DUDA. Some of them are illustrated here. This list, however, is not intended to be exhaustive.

1. *Swarna Jayanti Shahari Rozgar Yojana* (SJSRY): The SJSRY seeks to provide gainful employment to the urban unemployed or under-employed poor through encouraging setting up of self-employment ventures or production of wage employment. The programme lays strong emphasis of creation of community structures for the delivery of benefits. The scheme itself recommends the constitution of a DUDA to work under the overall guidance of the district officer. One of the major functions proposed for the DUDA is to promote and facilitate convergence with various functional departments at the district/city/town level.
2. *Integrated Development of Small and Medium Towns* (IDMST): This centrally sponsored scheme is to improve infrastructure facilities and promote dispersed urbanization. The scheme provides for many components and central assistance in the form of grants, ranging from Rs 4.8 million to 27 million. Project preparation, engineering design, scrutiny of payments, and actual design and execution all offer scope for aggregation and economies, which can be done by the DUDA.
3. *Solid Waste Management:* The Municipal Solid Waste (Management and Handling) Rules, 2000, have been notified under the Environment Protection Act of 1986. These apply to all municipal authorities in the country. Under Section 5, the deputy commissioner of the district has the overall responsibility for the enforcement of the provisions over the territorial limits of his jurisdiction. The rules prescribe how municipal solid waste has to be managed

and handled right from collection, segregation, storage, transportation, processing, and disposal. Detailed guidelines have been issued on various aspects of landfill sites, including site selection, facilities at sites, specification of landfilling, pollution prevention, water quality monitoring, ambient air quality monitoring, plantation at landfill sites, closure of landfill sites, and post-care. Likewise, Schedule IV of the rules prescribes the standards for waste processing and disposal facilities including composting standards. Given the capacity of an average urban local body in terms of the finances as well as human resources, it is but necessary that the deputy commissioner at the district level plays a significant role in ensuring adherence to these rules in ULBs. Besides this, and more important from our point of view, almost every activity mentioned above calls for a minimum economic size of operation and the DUDA becomes the logical agency to exploit these economies.

4. *National River Conservation Plan* (NRCP): The NRCP provides funding to ULBs essentially to prevent river pollution. Various components like sewage treatment plants are permitted under this scheme. Given the size argument, there is scope to build treatment plants that are common to two or more ULBs. This again is something the DUDA can facilitate.

CONCLUSION

The basic argument for the role of the district administration in municipal affairs that is sought to be made by this chapter rests on the non-local nature of some components of urban water supply and the aggregation advantages of the provision of this and some other services at the district level. All these arguments are summarized in Table 12.8. What is done here is to take known attributes of local public goods and show that urban water supply has elements that are clear departures from these.

These departures from necessary attributes of local public goods clearly point to the need for a regional agency to discharge these functions and there is considerable advantage in vesting these functions in a district urban development agency.

TABLE 12.8: COMPARATIVE ANALYSIS OF ATTRIBUTES

Attribute	Local public good	Urban water supply in Belgaum	Remarks
Nature of service	Variations in preferences of consumers (demand side) and possibility of variations in production to meet this demand.	Barely minimal requirement provided with no scope for any product or service variation	UWS does not meet with the required attribute of local public good in this regard.
Spatial dimension	Restricted both in terms of the availability of the service and the ability to control its geographical dimensions.	Source of water supply in every urban area of Belgaum district is outside its respective geographical boundary. It is not possible nor economical to spatially restrict the pipeline to only the end point urban area while ignoring the intervening villages.	UWS or at least some components of UWS do not meet with the required attribute of local public good in this regard.
Scale economies	Usually not present in a significant sense.	Clearly present in many components of the service like • source management • water treatment • bulk transmission pipeline • O&M, including in manpower required for O&M.	UWS or at least some components of UWS do not meet with the required attribute of local public good in this regard.

NOTES

1. Deputy commissioner is the formal designation of the district officer in Karnataka.

REFERENCES

Government of India (GoI), *The Manual on Water Supply and Treatment*, New Delhi: Central Public Health and Environmental Engineering Organization, Ministry of Urban Development, 1999.

Government of Karnataka (GoK), *Municipal Statistics 1995,* Bangalore: Directorate of Economics and Statistics, 1995.

———, *Municipal Statistics 1997–98,* Bangalore: Directorate of Economics and Statistics, 2001.

Hall, J., 'Consolidating Democracy', in D. Held (ed.), *Prospects for Democracy,* Palo Alto: Stanford University Press, 1993.

Kim, H. Youn and Robert M. Clark, 'Economies of Scale and Scope in Water Supply', *Regional Science and Urban Economics,* 18, 1988, pp. 479–502.

Mackenzie, W.J.M., *Theories of Local Government,* Greater London Papers No. 2, London School of Economics and Political Science, 1961.

Musgrave, Richard and Peggy Musgrave, *Public Finance in Theory and Practice* (Second edition) Kogakusha: McGraw-Hill, 1976.

Oates, Wallace E., *Fiscal Federalism,* New York: Harcourt Brace Jovanovich, 1972.

Prud'homme, R., 'On the Dangers of Decentralization', mimeo, 1993.

Tiebout, Charles, 'A Pure Theory of Local Expenditures', *Journal of Political Economy,* 64(October), 1956, pp. 416–24.

World Bank, *Infrastructure for Development* (World Development Report 1994), Washington, DC: World Bank, 1994.

———, *Entering the Twenty-first Century* (World Development Report 2000), Washington, D.C: World Bank, 2000.

APPENDIX: FUNCTIONS AND POWERS OF THE DEPUTY
COMMISSIONERS OF DISTRICTS IN MUNICIPAL AFFAIRS AS PER
THE KARNATAKA MUNICIPALITIES ACT, 1964

Subject matter and Section of the KM Act	Limits
Powers to transfer any officer or servant of a municipal council to a service of any other municipal council or of any other local authority or of any government department. (Sec. 320)	
Filling up of vacant posts (Rule 3 of KM [Recruitment of Officers & Servants] Rules, 1971) (a) Group 'D' (b) Group 'C' Appointment, promotion, preparation of seniority list, etc. of group 'D' & group 'C' posts (Rule 4 of KM [Recruitment of Officers & Servants] Rules, 1971)	With prior permission of government
Power of inspection and supervision (Sec. 304)	
Confirmation of auction sales in CMCs and TMCs (Rule 39 of KM [Guidance of Officers, etc.] Rules, 1966). Read with Sec. 72 of KM Act	For values not exceeding Rs 1 million
Receiving copies of every resolution passed at any meeting of municipal council and to nominate any other officer to receive from the president (Sec. 43[d]).	
Application of municipal fund (Proviso [b] to Sec. 83)	
Discretionary functions of municipal councils—organizing public receptions, etc —previous sanction of (Sec. 91 [o])	
Prohibition of expenditure not budgeted for (Sec. 286 [d] [i])	
To certify the amount due under Sec. 296 (1) (Sec. 297)	
To remove councillors in respect of TMCs (Sec. 41[1])	
Removal of president/vice-president from office for misconduct in the discharge of his duties, etc. in respect of TMCs (Sec. 42 [10])	
To issue direction to president and vice-president to hand over charge (Sec. 46 [2])	
Sanction to deposit surplus funds in government treasury (Sec. 85[1])	
To direct any municipal council for analysis and inspection of water supply through pipes (Sec. 90)	

(*Appendix contd*)

(*Appendix contd*)

Subject matter and Section of the KM Act	Limits

To cancel or to diminish any earlier arrangement made by yearly contribution to any municipal council for any educational or charitable institution or any promise purporting to bind itself or its successors, etc. (Sec. 92)

To accord sanction to levy fee on persons attending *jathra, urs*, etc. (Sec. 137 [1])

To require municipal council to impose any tax for raising additional funds (Proviso to Sec. 141).

To demolish any building erected contrary to the provisions of sub-Sec. (1) & (2) (Sec. 189)

Regulation or prohibition of certain kinds of cultivation (Sec. 237)

To close certain areas from using for disposal of the dead (Sec. 255 [1])

To prohibit certain areas from being used for industrial purposes specified in Part I or Part II of Schedule XIII (Sec. 256 [2])

To prevent extravagance in employment of establishment. (Sec. 311 [1])

Powers to direct persons in custody of municipal fund to pay government dues (Sec. 314).

13

Mainstreaming Gender in District Plans in Madhya Pradesh*

■ ANWAR JAFRI AND VIKAS SINGH

This chapter attempts to understand and assess the role of women, and the expression of women's concerns in the planning process at the village and district levels of governance in Madhya Pradesh (MP). It is based on the initial findings of a research project supported by the UNDP and UN-Habitat, titled 'Gender Mainstreaming in District Plans', in three districts of Madhya Pradesh. The purpose of the chapter is to put some of the ideas and hypotheses emerging from the first phase of the research study for discussion and debate so that feedback and suggestions can be incorporated into the study design, thereby making it more relevant.

In this study certain aspects of Indian democracy are looked at from close quarters. As we all realize, 'Indian democracy is apt to look very different from different perspectives.'[1] Here, we share experiences and perceptions of planning processes and other micro-dynamics at the panchayat and district levels in the context of an evolving panchayat policy in MP. Perception of these dynamics can provide us rather contradictory outcomes. When we look at panchayats historically and from the perspective of national and international politics, then the ongoing changes in panchayats on the national scene and especially in Madhya Pradesh to strengthen and deepen democracy seem very remarkable. However, when we look at the grass roots situation from the point of view of the poor, the women and the Dalits, with their immediate and pressing needs, then many of our claims start looking hollow. The points of view of the poor need to be understood and addressed if panchayats are to retain meaning for these sections of people.

OBJECTIVES OF THE STUDY

As evident from the title, in this study we aim at assessing the degree of women's participation and the incorporation of women's issues in what is called the 'district plan'. The district plan in MP is an annual document supposed to be prepared by the district planning committees (DPC) for each district by consolidating the village plans prepared by individual gram panchayats through discussions in the gram sabhas.

It is important to note that consolidation of the village-level plans is central to the concept, and therein lies the raison d' être for the DPC, which was born of Article 243ZD of the Constitution of India. The article provides for the establishment of the DPC 'to consolidate the plans prepared by the Panchayats and the Municipalities in the district and to prepare a draft development plan for the district as a whole'. The composition of DPCs, however, varies from one state to the other, and so do the functions that they have been entrusted, as well as the intensity and nature of planning exercises that they undertake. In Madhya Pradesh, a minister of the state government is nominated by the state government as chairperson of the DPC and, beginning 1999, in what is described as an attempt at administrative decentral-ization, the DPC was allocated additional administrative responsibilities that earlier rested at the state capital. The body was also rechristened as '*zilla sarkar*' or district government. Howe.er, while the DPC has been entrusted with major responsibilities, its role in planning—its constitutional existence— seems to have suffered. But for an exercise in progress, for the year 2002–3, which we will dwell upon later in this text, nowhere in the state have district plans been prepared (Khanna *et al.* 2001).

The Madhya Pradesh Panchayati Raj Act[2] provides for the preparation of plans at all levels of the panchayati raj institution. At the village level, the gram vikas samiti is responsible for preparing a plan for 'overall development' of the village and submitting it, for approval to the gram sabha (Section 7-F). The responsibility of preparing an annual plan for 'economic development and social justice' of the panchayat area and submitting them to the *janpad* panchayat for integration into the janpad plan has been entrusted to each gram panchayat (Section 49-A). In the case of the janpad panchayat, Section 50 (1-A) makes it mandatory for it to prepare an annual plan with respect to schemes relating to economic development and social justice. It is also supposed to consolidate the plans prepared by the gram panchayats in its area with its own plan and submit the consolidated janpad plan to the zilla panchayat. Similar provisions also exist for consolidation of plans of the janpad panchayat into the plan at the zilla panchayat. The janpad and the zilla panchayats also have the responsibility of guiding the janpad and the gram panchayats, respectively in the formulation of plans.

The DPC, in turn is supposed to consolidate the plans prepared by the panchayats and municipalities in the district. The emphasis in these acts on formation and consolidation of plans on the basis of what may be called 'territorial' units of governance is worth noting. It bears a marked contrast with the traditional sectoral mode of planning and implementation manifested in the line departments. Thus, in the extent of success in the shift from the 'line' mode of planning and implementation to these 'units of territorial governance', and in achieving the integration required for the purpose could well lie the key to understanding the extent of empowerment of self-governance institutions.

The primary objective of the research project was to understand the 'gender aspect' in the process of preparation of the district plan, as well as the plans formulated at lower levels, namely, the janpad and the gram panchayat, on which the former is 'supposed' to be based. The total sample for this study is to be three districts of Madhya Pradesh and five villages to be selected from each of these districts.[3]

However, from preliminary discussions with government officials and PRI representatives, and initial visits to a few villages, it was clear that any comprehensive planning process based on consolidation of village plans was just not taking place. Going to one village after another, trying to understand and observe the 'birth of a baby that never gets born' did not make sense although we did indulge in this for a while. We realized that we should instead accept a broader meaning of the words 'plan' and 'planning'. While there are no formal planning exercises taking place in the villages, some form of 'plans' are made and implemented. Making proposals and plans to get funds from different sources and then 'action plans' for utilizing them— whether in a written or oral form, in a formal or an informal setting— all this is obviously taking place. We, thus, included an informal meaning of planning being followed, along with the formal plan or plan-like exercises, such as the annual budgeting and action plan preparation, wherever these existed.

The slightly reformulated objectives around which this research was designed were broadly as follows.

At the Village Level

- Understand the different kinds of planning exercises taking place at the village and panchayat level and the role played by women, particularly women panchs, in these exercises.
- Understand the relative weightage that women's concerns and interests carry in these plan exercises, and whether and how these find a place in the final plans.
- Assess the impact of selected schemes focused on women's development. Observe the role that women, particularly women representatives and other village level 'women leaders',[4] play in enhancing this impact.
- Understand the difference that panchayati raj, and the positive discrimination for women in it, has made to the expression of women's concerns.

At the Janpad Level

- Understand the nature of consolidation/forwarding/sanction exercises carried out at the janpad panchayats with respect to village- and panchayat-level plans.
- Understand the role played by women janpad panchayat members in activities/decisions related to the village level plans, particularly components related to women's concerns or priorities.

At the District Level

- Understand the planning process at the district level and its linkage to village-level concerns and priorities, expressed through annual plans or otherwise.
- Analyse the allocation of resources in district plans for gender-related issues and interventions.
- Analyse any specific tools that may have been used for gender mainstreaming in district plans.

METHODOLOGY OF THE STUDY

Selection of Districts in Madhya Pradesh

Three districts have been selected for this study, but as of date data has been collected in only one: Dewas. The three districts selected are Gwalior—a developed area; Mandla—a backward area; and Dewas—

an area that can be considered somewhere in between the other two
on the basis of basic development indicators. Table 13.1 justifies this
selection on the basis of literacy, irrigation, forest cover, and the SC/
ST population.

TABLE: 13.1 CHARACTERISTICS OF DISTRICTS STUDIED

	Literacy	Irrigation	Forest cover	ST population	SC population
Gwalior	57.7	44.2	23.6	2.9	20.4
Dewas	44.1	18.5	26.03	15.0	18.2
Mandla	37.3	3.5	40.4	60.3	5.2

Note: All figures are percentages and taken from the MP HDR.

Geographically, the locations are distributed over MP: Gwalior is
situated in the north, Dewas in the west, and Mandla in the east of the
state. Gwalior has a high urban base and Mandla low. The same order
seems to be followed by these three districts when it comes to diversity
of political activity as well as the number of voluntary and non-
governmental organizations known to be active.

SELECTION OF VILLAGES

Five villages were to be selected in each district for the study of
panchayat functioning, the planning process, and the role of women
members. The following broad criteria were fixed to make a
representative selection of the villages:

1. One large village, which is on the roadside, and has a mixed population of different castes; having a primary and middle school;
   population over 2000.
2. One medium–sized village; mixed population of different castes.
3. One village with a majority of tribal population/poor and backward;
   away from the road; not too small in size; with a middle school.
4. One village with a majority of SC/poor and backward.
5. Finally, one village whose panchayat generates a larger revenue,
   through industry or quarrying or some other commercial activity,
   to provide example of a panchayat with larger untied funds that
   could be used for planning.[5]

As reflected from the characteristics of the villages selected, we are trying to capture a diversity of conditions, but not too keen to forget very interior areas or very small villages. The reason for this is that in any case we do not expect much in the way of planning in smaller and remote places. Our hunch seems to have been borne out in the first district that we covered. However, it is interesting to see whether much of planning and gender inclusion exists even in reasonably well-to-do, mixed villages of the first two types defined earlier. With the same logic, we decided to select tribal and SC villages with middle schools so that they are not too small.

When it came to actually making the selection of the villages, we found that in case of panchayats with more than a single village, the selection of any single village cannot fulfil our data needs. We needed to cover each village in the panchayat to get a full picture of the local dynamics, as well as the representative views of the women panchs and other groups. Thus, in the first district we ended up selecting five panchayats, which meant covering altogether 12 villages instead of the expected five.[6] The actual gram panchayats were selected through discussions with local resource persons so as to ensure a 'representative selection' from the viewpoint of the characteristics discussed earlier.

Semi-structured personal interviews, written reports, and documents were the major source of information at the district and janpad level. At the district level, the respondents included district administration officials, including the collector, the district planning officer, the zilla panchayat officials, zilla panchayat members, and officials from the panchayat and the Integrated Child Development Scheme (ICDS) department. At the janpad level, the respondents included present and former janpad panchayat members and officials in the janpad panchayat office. A significant number of the respondents were women. The documents studied included the district plan document, and orders and circulars related to planning in addition to annual reports.

Structured interviews (on questionnaire formats)[7] and focused group discussions were the major tools used at the village level. The key respondents included panchs, sarpanchs, up-sarpanchs, former panchs, panchayat secretaries, treasurers, anganwadi workers, women leaders, and members of gram sabha. The majority of the respondents interviewed belonged to marginalized sections, particularly women. Focused group discussions were held with diverse groups, with emphasis on marginalized sections. The action plan and the annual budget were taken from the panchayat secretary, as were the minutes of gram sabha proceedings.[8]

Before discussing the field situation and the perceptions gained about the objectives of this study, it would be useful to have a brief look at panchayat legislation in Madhya Pradesh since the 73rd Constitutional Amendment. This will provide the background setting in which the action of our study takes place.

PANCHAYATI RAJ LEGISLATION: PRESENT SCENARIO

Panchayati raj politics and policies have evolved at a brisk pace in Madhya Pradesh since the original Act was introduced in 1994.[9] It would facilitate our understanding of the present panchayati raj dynamics if we gain an understanding of the main features and spirit of the amendments made to the original Act.[10] To clarify the context of these changes, we briefly outline the relevant features of the 73rd Constitutional Amendment and then take up the Madhya Pradesh Act and some of its amendments. Needless to say, the status of the state-level legislation sets the environment for the dynamics of panchayats at each of the three levels.

THE 73RD CONSTITUTIONAL AMENDMENT

A national framework for establishing panchayati raj in the states was laid down through the 73rd Constitutional Amendment of Parliament. The important features of this framework were:

1. a three-tier system of panchayati raj;
2. a gram sabha in each village wherein all members would have a say in the formulation and monitoring of panchayat plans and development schemes;
3. direct elections to fill all seats at all three tiers;
4. reservation of seats at all levels of panchayats for women, Dalits, and tribal groups[11];
5. regular review of panchayat finances and recommendations through the state finance commissions; and
6. regular elections for panchayats.

Over and above the basic framework of the 73rd Constitutional Amendment, the states have added other features to their panchayat legislation, which has provided the special flavour to panchayati raj in each state. We look at the recent evolution of the Panchayati Raj Act in MP.

EVOLUTION OF THE PANCHAYATI RAJ ACT IN MADHYA PRADESH

A number of amendments have been made to the Panchayati Raj Act in MP since its initial passage in 1994, so much so, that now the name of the Act itself has been modified to the Panchayati Raj and Gram Swaraj Act. In fact, some observers have interpreted the high number of amendments to the Act as an indication of inadequate debate and preparation while introducing the initial Bill itself (Buch 2000b).

Amendments to the state Act include, on the one hand, what could be considered tactical changes to take care of specific issues and problems not foreseen at the outset of the Act itself. On the other hand, there have been a couple of major amendments to the Act providing a new dimension to decentralization and panchayat functioning. In whatever way we look at the large number of amendments, some of them have reflected alert and deft handling of sensitive panchayat issues by the state government, while others seem to reflect the increasing pressures of state politics on panchayati raj. Some of these amendments have a direct and important bearing on issues of decentralization as well as the role of women and Dalits in panchayat dynamics. We give here brief descriptions of some of the amendments.

LINKS BETWEEN THE THREE TIERS OF PANCHAYAT

An organic link has been created between the gram panchayats and janpads, and between the janpads and zilla panchayats. Through an amendment in the state Act in 1997, one-fifth of the sarpanchs are now members of the janpad panchayats by rotation each year, and all the janpad presidents are members of zilla panchayats. They cannot, however, be members of any standing committee of the janpad/zilla panchayat, whereas the MPs and MLAs have been specifically included in the standing committees.

CASUAL VACANCIES IN THE PANCHAYATS

The original Act had the provision for the gram panchayat's up-sarpanch/vice-president to carry out the duties of the sarpanch/president in case of a vacancy caused by a no-confidence motion being passed against the sarpanch, or due to some other cause such as death. This provision was found to motivate a large number of no-confidence motions, instigated by the up-sarpanch/vice-president, especially against Dalit sarpanchs, and even more so when they happened to be women.

The sixth amendment to the state Act in 1997 made it mandatory for an acting sarpanch to be elected from the same reserved category as the original sarpanch. This means that if a Dalit woman is removed from the office of sarpanch through a no-confidence motion, the new sarpanch to officiate till elections are held must be a Dalit woman from amongst the panchs.[12]

PROVISION FOR RECALL

The eighth amendment to the state constitution in 1999 has introduced a provision of 'recall' of the sarpanch or a panch of a village panchayat. This process can be initiated if at least one-third members of the gram sabha/ward for a sarpanch/panch give notice and at least half of the tenure, that is, two-and-a-half years after the elections, is over. In the case of sarpanch, this is in addition to the provision of no-confidence motion, which can be tabled by the members of the gram panchayat but only one year after the election and at least six months before the expiry of the tenure. So now a sarpanch can be removed by the elected members of the gram panchayat as well as by the members of the gram sabha, though he/she is directly elected by the latter (Buch 2000b; Mathew 2002).

GRAM SABHA MEETINGS

In the initial Act of 1994, the gram sabha in Madhya Pradesh meant all voting members of the panchayat. In case the panchayat consisted of more than one village, all the members of the panchayat were supposed to collect together at one place for the gram sabha meetings. The concept has now been amended. Gram sabha now means the gram sabha of each village, which now needs to meet independently and take decisions regarding the village schemes, selection of beneficiaries, and other issues.[13]

PANCHAYATI RAJ AND GRAM SWARAJ ACT

The Panchayati Raj and Gram Swaraj Act was introduced in January 2000 and was primarily aimed at increasing the power of the gram sabha. The gram sabha is the village council, which was originally meant to debate and monitor the programmes of development prepared by the village panchayat. However, by the introduction of an amendment in the earlier Act, a number of powers of the gram panchayat have been taken away and the gram sabha made directly responsible for planning and taking decisions through its committees.

In effect, the main content of the new Act has been to introduce a number of committees (to be precise, eight) with the membership to be decided at an open forum of the gram sabhas.[14] These committees have taken over the role played earlier by the elected members of the panchayat. The new Act was introduced in 2001. At the ground level there still seems to be a marked confusion and lack of clarity about the respective roles of the panchayat and the gram swaraj committees set up. In many instances the panchayats still continue with their earlier functions. So it would be too early to judge the quality of functioning of the gram swaraj provisions. But some interesting things about the background of this Act and its aftermath can be noted.

What were the main reasons for introducing the new Act called 'The Madhya Pradesh Panchayati Raj Avam Gram Swaraj Adhiniyam, 2001, which placed emphasis on the term 'Gram Swaraj'? Popular belief says that the state government was concerned about two major factors:

1. the increasing influence of the panchayat members, especially the sarpanch, in the affairs of the panchayats;[15] and
2. the continued failure of gram sabhas to meet regularly and to be an effective body in providing the necessary checks and balances to the elected panchayats.

So, it was with the objective to give more powers directly to the gram sabha, through its committees, and to encourage greater participation by gram sabha members in the panchayat affairs that the amended Act was brought in.

We shall report later our observations on the present status of the gram swaraj committees in the villages. However, there is an added complication to this whole affair. It seems the state government was carried away in a wave of enthusiasm and decided to increase the required quorum at gram sabha meetings from 10 to 20 per cent.

QUORUM FOR GRAM SABHA

In the earlier Act, a quorum of 10 per cent was required for holding the gram sabha in a village. However, in the amended Act in MP, it is specified that one-fifth of the population of any village (20 per cent) will constitute the quorum.[16] The amended Act further specifies that while ensuring the quorum, one-third of the members should be women, and SC/ST members should be represented in proportion to their population in the village.

PLANNING AT THE DISTRICT LEVEL

It was for the year 2002–3 that annual district plans were prepared for the first time in Madhya Pradesh.[17] In earlier years, there has been no attempt for even horizontal consolidation of departmental plans at the district level, leave alone vertical consolidation of village level plans to form a district plan. The only planning exercise taking place at the state level was those instances where individual departments are expected to provide annual departmental plans to the state planning board on the basis of the ceiling fixed for the department. The ceiling is in turn based on negotiations between the department and the state planning board on the basis of total plan funds available with the board, the funds allotted to the department in the previous year, and the department's record in terms of utilization of the allotted funds. (Khanna *et al.* 2001). The plan funds accruing to different departments are transferred to them individually at the state level in different instalments. The department at the state level then provides individual districts with their shares, which are largely based on the previous year's figures. Here, it should however be noted that in accordance with the provisions of the 73rd Constitutional Amendment, a number of schemes meant for rural areas have been transferred to the zilla panchayats from different departments and, therefore, funds for these schemes, which earlier used to flow to the departments, now flow to the zilla panchayat through the panchayat and rural development department. Thus, while sectoral departments have lost their importance after having been deprived of many important schemes, the zilla panchayat itself has been fitted into the traditional departmental mode.

It is important to say here that while individual departments are expected to provide their annual plans to the state planning board, the nature of this planning exercise too can hardly be described as comprehensive. The annual planning exercise is largely based on the achievable numbers under different schemes, which in turn are distributed over districts. The role of the district-level departmental officials is at best consultative in nature (ibid.). Moreover, for all centrally sponsored schemes, clear guidelines exist from the central government for division of available funds among the districts. Therefore, the department at the state level too has little discretion. For instance, in the case of the Indira Awas Yojana, an important housing scheme targeting the poor below-poverty-line (BPL) clear guidelines from the central government are in place for distribution of funds under the scheme, according to which the total funds have to be divided in proportion to the combined SC and ST population of the district. To that allotment, the state government is expected to add its 25 per cent share.

The departments in the districts, thus, only get 'informed' of the 'targets' available to them for the year. The strict predefined distribution criteria in not only spatial, but also functional, and partly explains the lack of comprehensive planning exercises at the district as well as higher levels. The strict criteria in turn seems to be an effort at ensuring just and proper utilization of limited plan funds, leaving little scope for 'untied funds' at different levels. What is, however, worth noticing is the implicit linkage between 'proper utilization' and 'centralization'. Among other explanations, this betrays a lack of trust by higher institutions on their subordinate institutions, an institutionalized practice that may well be the major stumbling block on the path towards decentralization.

While the space available to the district for planning may not be ideal, the district does have access to limited amount of 'untied' funds for which planning is possible. Important among these are the local area development funds available with the MP and the MLA, and the resources generated within the district. In addition, it is also possible for the zilla panchayat to plan for that part of the component of funds under various schemes that have been left to its discretion. Similarly, it is possible for the janpad to plan for the untied funds available to them. However, neither the Khategaon janpad panchayat nor the Dewas zilla panchayat prepare any periodic plans.

PROVISIONS FOR DISTRICT PLANS, 2002–3

An exercise for district planning was initiated in the state beginning 2002–3. For the preparation of this plan, a team of three—the district collector, the district planning officer, and a resource person selected from a college in the district—was trained. In this exercise, 30 per cent of the state's resources are earmarked as untied funds for the districts, to be distributed over districts as their figure for plan ceiling (GoMP 2001). These schemes for the districts are, however, to be divided into state and district sectors. The former is to include large and medium projects, and the projects that are inter-district in nature; while district sector schemes include small projects and projects that do not go across district boundaries. In this exercise, each department at the district level is to prepare plans based on the following considerations:

1. last year's level of expenditure of the department in the budget;
2. 20 per cent increase or decrease over the last year's budget; and
3. overall budgetary ceiling for the district.

The process of preparation of the district plan is to be coordinated by an executive committee, chaired by the collector, with the project officers and district-level officers of development department, re-presentatives of lead bank, rural banks, cooperative banks, National Bank for Agricultural and Rural Development (NABARD), represent-ative of Madhya Pradesh electricity board, and the resource person as members. The district planning officer is the member-secretary of the committee.

The executive committee is to constitute working groups for various sectors that are to prepare the recommendations to be used as guidelines for preparing plans by different departments. The departments are to present their annual/five-year plans to the district planning office, where the corresponding sub-committee of the DPC is to discuss the plans. The executive committee is to consolidate the district plans prepared by departments in predefined sectors, based on the sub-committees of the DPC. The draft plan is required to be first approved by the district planning committee and then finalized by the plan board, after consultations with districts/department representatives. The departments at the state level are to then include the departmental proposals from the districts in their proposal, to be approved by the finance department without any modifications.

DISTRICT PLAN, DEWAS

In accordance with the above-outlined provisions, the district of Dewas, one of the districts being studied, has prepared a district plan. The total plan amount of Rs 222.9 million is divided among twenty departments. Departments with a plan of more than Rs 10 million are rural development (39.6 million), public works (27.8 million), school education (38.7 million), public health and engineering (14.5 million), SC/ST and OBC welfare (26 million), planning (21 million), and women and child development (15.7 million).

According to the members of the coordination committee, the plan was prepared by individual departments and compiled by the district planning officer. The district collector is said to have personally supervised the whole process, doing much of the work himself because of the lack of experience and expertise in some of the departments. The plan was, however, formulated at the district level itself without formal processes for the involvement of block- and village-level institutions. When asked, the coordination committee members ascribe this to the problems of time and experience among the department officials. Here it will be worth recalling the planning department's circular, described in the earlier section, and the conspicuous absence of any provision for preparation of plans below the district levels from it. The chairperson of the coordination committee (the district collector) was of the opinion that unless sizeable 'free' funds are available, bottom-to-top planning, as it is called, is not possible. He thus explained the case of his district. Of the total amount of Rs 220 million (of the 300 million earmarked for the district, the state kept the rest for state sector schemes), more than 160 million was committed, while another Rs 15 million had to be committed to water harvesting works because of specific directions by the state government. An additional Rs 10 million had to be earmarked for construction of road in a certain part of the district, which is facing unrest. In addition, there are the unavoidable requirements of medicines for hospitals and the like. Therefore, the district was hardly left with any funds to plan for.

Another aspect worth noting is that in this exercise the panchayats are simply construed as another department and there is no provision for their inclusion in the planning process other than their membership in the district planning exercise. This district planning exercise therefore, has little in common with the planning exercise provided for, by the Panchayati Raj and Gram Swaraj Act. On another note, for the last two years the zilla panchayat members have been simply dividing the untied funds available with zilla panchayat among themselves, as shares of their constituencies (though it not necessary that they spend those funds in their constituencies alone).

THE VILLAGE: ANNUAL PLANS AND
BUDGETING EXERCISES

In this section we discuss our initial observations of gram panchayat dynamics and the present role that women play in it. This helps us to understand the process that goes under the term 'planning'. We should keep in mind, however, that it is a time of flux, with many new provisions in the legal framework concerning responsibilities for planning, under the Gram Swaraj Act. Most 'planning' activities at the village level, however, still seem to follow from the older system.[18]

The text is based on first impressions from the field, a reading of the questionnaires, and the data collected in the form of field notes and notes on focused group discussions. A more exhaustive analysis of the survey data, which is yet to be collected from two more districts, will be carried out. The conclusions drawn here are, therefore, to that extent, tentative.

Five panchayats, namely, Ajnas, Padyadeh, Neemavar, Lakdani, and Patrani, consisting altogether of 12 villages, were identified for the fieldwork. Table 13.2 provides a brief on each of these panchayats.

Except one panchayat, Patrani, annual budgets have been submitted by each of these panchayats, followed by action plans. The exercise of annual budgeting is a task that panchayat office bearers have to undertake every year. The standard exercise is that every year in about January they receive a letter from the government asking that annual budgets be prepared and submitted to the janpad by a certain date.

TABLE 13.2: CASTE BACKGROUND OF PANCHAYAT MEMBERS IN FIVE SELECTED PANCHAYATS

Panchayat	Villages	Person in-control*	Sarpanch	Up-sarpanch	No of panchs**								
					Total	SC		ST		OBC		General	
						men	women	men	women	men	women	men	women
Ajnas	1	Sarpanch's husband	ST female	OBC male	19	2	1	3	1	2	2	5	3
Padyadeh	4	Sarpanch	General male	ST male	13	2	1	2	2	2	1	2	1
Lakdani	3	Sarpanch's husband	OBC female	ST male	13	1	1	4	3	-	-	3	1
Patrani	1	Sarpanch and his godfathers	SC male	OBC male	12	3	2	4	1	1	1	-	-
Neemavar	1	Sarpanch	ST female	OBC male	19	1	1	2	1	3	2	6	3

Notes: * By person in control, we mean the de facto person in charge of the panchayat, as per common perception. Of the three women sarpanches in the panchayats of our study, in two cases the husbands were in charge.

** Includes the up-sarpanch

This, however, may not be a serious exercise for the demand made by the panchayat and the nature of proposals sent does not affect the quantum of fund inflow. This is decided by the higher authorities under other considerations. The budgeting exercise is, therefore, a simple one, the amount accruing under each head in the previous year being generally increased by an average of 10 per cent. In addition, often activities/amounts are proposed under the MP/MLA funds, Indira Awas Yojana (IAY), the Matratva Sahyata Yojana (National Maternity Benefit Scheme), and others, which never seem to materialize through this channel.[19] The assured funds are those under the Jawahar Gram Samridhi Yojna (JGSY)—the redesigned Jawahar Rozgar Yojana (JRY), in which all funds, except for a small amount demarcated for the state for trainings, flow directly to the panchayats—and the funds from the State Finance Commission, called the 'moolbhoot' or basic panchayat funds. However, even in the case of these funds, the budgeting exercise does not make a difference to the amount that is to come, which is generally determined by supply factors. What may, however, be important, even if marginally, are the activities proposed in the budget. And this is where the extent and nature of public participation in the budgeting exercise is of interest to us.

We found that it is the secretary who prepares the panchayat budget in consultation with the sarpanch (or her husband) and a few other panchs. The nature of the exercise may vary from a discussion in the panchayat meeting to a rather closed exercise between the sarpanch (or her husband), the secretary, and those panchs who may be part of the inner coterie. It is important to note here that the majority of respondents, panchs, and general villagers alike said that budget preparation is the responsibility of the sarpanch and the secretary. Some included the up-sarpanch among the decision makers.

On the other hand, the sarpanchs, along with a small number of panchs from their supporters, claimed that the exercise is carried out in the gram sabha. Only the case of Padyadeh panchayat was different. Here, the sarpanch, a dominant male from the Bishnoi caste[20] who is politically active at the district level, claimed that the budget exercise is done in the gram panchayat and does not concern the gram sabha. In the case of another panchayat, Ajnas, where the sarpanch's husband, though controlling the situation on behalf of his wife, is popularly perceived to be sincere, a significant number of respondents[21] said that the budget, though prepared by the sarpanch and the secretary, is read out in the gram sabha.[22]

In addition to the annual budget, in 2002 the panchayats had also been asked to submit an annual action plan.[23] To this end, guidelines for an action plan, from the panchayats and rural development department were circulated to each gram panchayat. It is important to note that these guidelines do not contain any format and simply compile the guidelines of each scheme, and the gram sabha's and panchayat's role therein. While this may be construed as leaving spaces for the panchayat's discretion, the lack of a proper format also perhaps means that these action plans, prepared in triplicate on register sheets, may not support actual implementation or monitoring. In the five panchayats that we studied, except for Patrani, where the plan was yet to be submitted, action plans had been submitted by all the panchayats before mid-March. The action plan document is relatively more detailed than the budget document, though the formulation is similar. The details include the activities/work planned under each budget head and the location of each work. The budget heads, in addition to the stock heads of JGSY and moolbhoot funds, also include proposals under the IAY, Eleventh Finance Commission, Matratva Sahayata Yojana, MP/MLA funds, etc. It is the works, and their location, proposed under the JGSY and the moolbhoot funds that seem to have some specific relevance under planning.[24] It is only to this extent that the planning process and the level of participation of different segments, and for our study, participation of women from different socio-economic strata, assumes importance.[25] However, this process is more or less the same as that for the annual budgeting exercise.

It is clear from the preceding discussion that as per the existing impression in the villages, the main actors in the planning process are the secretary and the sarpanch (or the de facto sarpanch, as the case may be). They may be acting in close consort with a small number of supporters from amongst the panchs. The scene of action where decisions regarding the budget and action plan are taken could be either the panchayat meeting or informal meetings of a subgroup of loyalists. The decisions seem to be shared with the gram sabha as a formality, and also to take its formal concurrence.

In the next section we specifically consider the role of women in panchayats and their participation in decision-making processes.

WOMEN'S INVOLVEMENT IN ANNUAL PLANNING AND BUDGETING EXERCISES

How regularly and effectively do women members attend panchayat meetings? And when they do, what is the nature of their participation?

From our observations in the selected panchayats, we found that while only a limited number of women regularly attended panchayat meetings, the rest on an average were present in three to four meetings in a year.[26] However, in one panchayat, that is Neemavar, women's attendance was significantly higher than in the other panchayats. In fact, according to some respondents, women outnumber men in the panchayat meetings there.[27] There are also some women panchs, who may have attended only one or two meetings in their total period of membership.

Of those women who do attend, few are vocal in their concerns and opinions, while the large majority either sit silent or may utter a few muted sentences. What are the factors that determine their participation or lack of it in panchayat meetings?

There are a number of factors that determine whether a woman panch attends panchayat meetings and the regularity of her attendance. In the 12 villages that the study team visited, we found three women representatives who were enthusiastic about attending panchayat meetings of their own accord and even taking the initiative in ensuring that meetings are held. Two of these women are panchs in Ajnas panchayat while the third is the sarpanch of Neemavar village.[28] While the Neemavar sarpanch is of tribal background and a single woman, of the two active women panchs in Ajnas, one is from the ST category while the other is from the SC category. It could be worth noting here that two of these women work as *dais* (midwives). All three women are active and mobile, and have a reputation of being very vocal and dynamic among their peers.[29] Panchayat meetings in both these places are held quite regularly. In addition, the sarpanchs of Ajnas and Lakdani, who happen to be women, attend the meetings whenever they are held, though it is their husbands who hold sway during those meetings. The wives remain more or less mute 'signing bodies'. These two husbands also decide all matters related to the panchayat, including the dates of the meeting.

Almost all the rest of the women panchs interviewed during the study betrayed a relatively lackadaisical approach towards panchayat meetings. This impression was also supported by the perceptions of their peers in the village. However, the regularity of their attendance varied. On an average, only about 50 per cent of women are said to attend any given panchayat meeting in four of the five panchayats. As mentioned earlier, in the case of Neemavar, almost all women are said to attend. When specifically questioned, they ascribed a variety of reasons for their low participation in panchayat meetings. Some of these are individual or locality-specific reasons, while most others are commonly shared. The most common reasons expressed were:

1. Women find themselves ignored and dismissed by the sarpanch and the panchs, particularly the male panchs. This is a very common assertion in all panchayats, except, of course, Neemavar. They say that whenever they attend meetings, they are reduced to mute spectators and when they do speak they are all but dismissed as 'ignorant uneducated womenfolk'. They describe the little participation that they are able to manage in the panchayat as not worth the trouble of going to the meeting. This could be the main reason that explains the difference between Neemavar panchayat where the woman sarpanch dominates, and the other panchayats where the men dominate. Again, the case of Ajnas panchayat is different, where women panchs have a significant voice, even though the sarpanch is dominated by her husband. However, in Neemavar one woman panch respondent, an SC agricultural labourer, said that the sarpanch does not listen to her and dismisses her as uncouth. However, in spite of this complaint, she continues to regularly attend panchayat meetings.

2. Women members reported that they were not 'properly informed' about meetings. This meant that either they were not informed at all or they were given very short notice. Also, they were not informed about the agenda of the meeting. Often, the panchayat peon comes to them for signatures after the meeting was already over. The lack of proper information is explained by different factors in different situations. One reason seems to be that the sarpanch avoids properly informing certain people who he/she believes are pitched against him/her. This becomes evident from the case of one of the panchayats, namely, that of Patrani, where the sarpanch's detractors dominate the panchayat. The sarpanch, therefore, avoids calling the gram panchayat meeting, and as this chapter describes

later, explains it away through the gram swaraj provisions, which have all but made gram panchayat meetings redundant. In the case of Neemavar panchayat, the up-sarpanch professes to be in control of 12 of the 19 panchs. In other cases, the sarpanch may command clout over the panchayat and finds it unnecessary to invite women whose opinions he may have scant regard for. For instance, in the case of the panchayat Padyadeh, the sarpanch, a male from the dominant group and with enough clout, considers women panchs to be irrelevant. In some other cases it is possible that the panchayat's messenger just did not bother informing women who are not regular in attending.

3. The women themselves may be deterred from attending the meetings due to factors such as losing a day's wages, social and domestic pressures, or individual hesitation. That attending panchayat meetings means losing wages is a common complaint of working-class women. The continuing drought in the region and the resulting lack of surplus have further aggravated the situation. Some women panchs also figured among people who have permanently or temporarily migrated for wage labour opportunities. In addition, some women panchs, generally from well-off upper-caste families, expressed reservations about sharing a common and open platform with men, and perceived panchayats as male arenas. This trait was commonly seen in households that are represented by a male panch in addition to the female panch. In such cases it is the son, husband, or brother-in-law who takes the initiative. In one panchayat, Patrani, many of the women panch respondents said that they do not go to the panchayat meetings because of the conflicts among the men in the panchayat. It should be noted that there is severe groupism in this panchayat and the sarpanch is supposed to be a proxy of one group of the dominant Meena community. This is resented by the Scheduled Caste panchs and also panchs representing the interests of other Brahmin and Meena groups.

4. The distance of the panchayat headquarters from a village and the lack of female company to go to the meeting may also act as hindrances.[30] This factor was commonly witnessed in panchayats that consisted of more than one village. For instance, in Padyadeh the panchayat headquarters is about 2 km from the village of Khirnikheda. With no private modes of transport, it is difficult

for the women of Khirnikheda to attend the meetings. The option of walking to the meeting is only exercised if a woman can get company and has enough spare time. The situation is worse in Ratanpur village of Lakdani panchayat, which is about 7 km from the panchayat headquarters. One of the women panch respondents interviewed in this village had resigned from the gram sabha because of the logistical problem of attending meetings. Her husband had to take her to the gram sabha every time on his bicycle and that took a lot of time and energy.

From these accounts it is clear that on an average only a small number of women attend gram panchayat meetings, the exception being a panchayat dominated by a woman. An even smaller number of women participate with enthusiasm and initiative in the meetings. The low participation in gram panchayat meetings means that women lose out on a platform on which their concerns could have been given a place. In addition, when meetings or infomal get-togethers are held at the sarpanch's house then the women are deprived of all chances to participate.[31] However, most respondents feel that irrespective of their presence, it is the sarpanch or his/her proxy and the 'inner group', which generally includes the secretary and a few other panchs, who decide. This may also remain true for deciding work locations and selection of beneficiaries under different schemes, processes of more consequence than the relatively inconsequential one of preparing action plans and budgets. However, in most of these cases, the gram sabha can have substantial leverage. Let us now dwell on this space provided by the gram sabha.

THE GRAM SABHA AND ITS COMMITTEES

Another opportunity for the women to influence the components of the plan is in the gram sabha.[32] As we have mentioned earlier in this chapter, through an amendment in January 2001, the state Panchayati Raj Act was amended, so much so that it was renamed. The amended Act provides for separate monthly gram sabhas to be held in each of the constituent villages of the gram panchayat. And each gram sabha is to have eight standing committees, of which the eighth, namely, the gram vikas samiti, is to be constituted of the presidents of the other seven samitis. There are fair provisions for reservation for different groups in each of the seven committees, including the provision for annual rotational presidency among SC, ST, OBC, and other categories. Under this rather bold attempt at direct democracy, the responsibility for making all the major decisions has been entrusted solely to the gram sabha, while operational decisions are to be made by the vikas samiti or its president, the sarpanch. In the following section, we shall try to analyse the space that these institutions provide for and the difference that they have made to our research concern, 'the reflection of women's concerns in plans and planning processes'.

We begin by stating that after more than a year of the Act's enforcement, valid gram sabhas, with due quorums—the cornerstone of this attempt at direct democracy—are exceptional cases. Sometime in the latter part of 2002, gram sabhas were held for the express purpose of setting up the gram swaraj committees after strict orders from the state. As reported to us, deficit quorums in the gram sabha meeting were often completed by complementary methods of door-to-door signatures and/or proxy signatures. Thus, the committees were set up but have yet to start functioning in any sense.

On an average, there have been four to five attempts at holding gram sabha meetings in the single village panchayats since the new Act with enhanced quorum needs and requirement of monthly meetings of the gram sabha. However, because of the strict criteria of quorum (20 per cent of the voters have to be present and one-third of them need to be women), all of them were reported failed.[33] While some of them were suspended after deciding on new dates, in other cases the signatures of those present were taken and the rest filled through door-to-door and proxy signatures.

Where the proceedings of the gram sabha are concerned, the noteworthy part is that the sarpanch puts the agenda of the meeting in the public domain. The panchayat's agenda primarily includes decisions on works to be implemented under different schemes and the selection of beneficiaries, primarily under the IAY, in addition to the ratification of the budget, plans, etc. This may or may not be followed by a 'public debate'. Certain other issues of concern to the people or the village may also be discussed. The nature of the debate varies on the basis of the constitution of the gram sabha on that particular day, the relative clout of the sarpanch and his detractors, and the issue under consideration. It is necessary to outline a few important points here. The number of women in the panchayat meetings is generally, as expected, only a fraction of that of men. A turnout of 15 to 20 per cent women of the total turnout is generally considered good. However, according to popular village perception, among women, the turnout of SC/ST women is better than that of those from the backward and general castes. This, in spite of the fact that being economically poor, the direct economic opportunity cost should evidently be higher for them. There is also the widespread 'complaint' of male respondents, particularly from the general and the OBC castes, that these women (SC/ST) come to the gram sabha only with individual or household demands and problems, and not to contribute to the task of 'village development and expression of women's larger needs' in the public forum. However, of more than fifty women respondents interviewed during this study, hardly any (except the sarpanchs and couple of panchs) had attended a gram sabha meeting. This goes to show the relatively low significance of the present gram sabha forum.

An important conclusion emanating from the survey is that a large majority of the respondents ascribed their absence from gram sabha meetings to not being appropriately informed of the meetings. The standard procedure is of informing through drumbeaters (*dondi*) who announce date, time, and venue of the gram sabha and the issues to be discussed—a procedure that most sarpanchs say was followed. While it is possible that some of the people may be beyond the range of the drumbeater's shouts, others say that the drummer does not mention the issues.

As for the gram sabha committees, while they have been formed in all the villages, they are active in none.[34] While in most cases they were formed in gram sabhas, called after the express orders of the state asking for the samitis to be constituted, in at least one, Patrani, the samitis were formed by the sarpanch. In this particular panchayat, the sarpanch himself asserted that he formed the samitis on his own. Even in other cases, the sarpanch is said to have played the dominant role in the formation of the committees. In certain cases, lest there be administrative problems, sarpanchs have taken care to ensure that panchs got included in the gram vikas samiti. This arrangement ensures that gram vikas samitis are substituting for panchayats to support local political alignments.[35]

REFLECTION OF WOMEN'S CONCERNS

A few of the research questions were designed to assess the issues of concern to women; the extent to which they were able to voice them in public fora; and the way these concerns was received and the outcomes. Preliminary analysis of the answers received brings out some points of interest.

Though they vary from one village to the other and the respondent's socio-economic background, the basic needs of drinking water, sanitation, health, education, housing, and wage opportunities dominate the expressed concerns of women. Of these, the needs of drinking water, health facilities, and education are most widely shared among respondents from different locations and socio-economic backgrounds. Installation of hand pumps, establishment of hospitals, and improvement in their services, and establishment of schools and their upgradation are among the most vocally voiced demands in almost all the villages. In at least one panchayat, Padyadeh, the need for drinking water and latrines predominated women's concerns. In another panchayat, Patrani, wage labour, health, school, and water were the dominant concerns. One set of explanations for the difference between the two panchayats is that the former panchayat, Padyadeh, is located in the vicinity of the block headquarters, Khategaon, where schools and health are not a major problem. Moreover, even from the service angle, the Auxiliary Nurse Midwife (ANM) and other health workers have few problems going to that panchayat as it is close by. Supply of wage labour is not a problem, first because of the relatively prosperous agriculture in this Narmada valley village, and second, because the proximity to Khategaon provides opportunities for labour. Their main concerns, therefore, remain drinking water and sanitation, facilities that do not result from the obvious advantages that Padyadeh otherwise seems to have.

The concerns of the women of other villages are similar and perhaps fall in the range expressed by the two cases illustrated. In certain cases, for instance, in the case of the Muslim women of Ajnas panchayat, the need for construction of a pathway and drainage system in their colony was voiced. They complained of negative discrimination in the allocation of funds to their colony. Women of other panchayats expressed similar needs as well particularly, those belonging to the deprived sections. Here, it is also important to note that while general and OBC women belonging to prosperous or middle-class houses gave a higher prioritiy to school and hospital in their and generally women's concerns, women belonging to the deprived segments expressed concern about drinking water, wages, anganwadis, and sanitation in their colony, in addition to school and health.

The concerns expressed by women respondents in the survey differ slightly from the concerns that they expressed in different village forums. A pointed question was asked about the issues that they had raised in the gram panchayat and the gram sabha. The demand for hand pumps and pathways in their colony dominated the response to this question. To an extent, this is explained by the fact that the large part of the funds available with the panchayat is traditionally used towards such needs. Therefore, the women panchs negotiate for getting these facilities for their hamlet or colony. In addition, the generation of wage labour schemes by the panchayat was another major demand in Patrani. Moreover, there are two other demands that women respondents have not emphasized in the interviews but have been voiced in gram sabhas. These are the demand for Indira Aawas Yojana houses and to be registered in the BPL. Another concern that the women raise with the panchayat is of proper supply of midday meal at schools. Again, pertinent demands the panchayats are accountable for.

It is, thus, clear that women only raise those issues in the panchayat and the gram sabha that they know these bodies are capable of providing. They do not raise those related to hospitals and schools in which the panchayats have limited authority. In these situations there are cases of women approaching even the collector and the MP/MLA. It is evident from a comparison between the concerns expressed by the women to the interviewers and in the panchayat forum that many of these are reflected in the design of the government schemes that the panchayat implements. The problem, however, lies in the quantum of resources available with the panchayat and the extent to which a fair share is used for the concerns of the deprived segments, including women. Considering that deprivation continues at unabated scales, it important that the state not only earmarks a larger share of the resources for rural development but also assures its proper utilization by ensuring a controlling role for the deprived segments. This raises a host of issues related to examining the policy matters in the context of gram swaraj, as well as capacity building of gram sabha members

who are expected to wield more power. How and to what extent
that is possible under the present conditions and differing priorities
and politics of various sections are issues we must face.

We end by recalling Bardhan (1999), in that 'the pace and patterns
of development are not all pretty and wholesome'. And then using
his quote of Adam Michnik, a veteran of the Polish struggle for
democracy:

Democracy is neither black nor red. Democracy is gray.... It chooses banality
over excellence, shrewdness over nobility, empty promise over true competence.... It is eternal imperfection, a mixture of sinfulness, saintliness and
monkey business. This is why the seekers of a moral state and of a perfectly
just society do not like democracy. Yet only democracy—having the capacity to question itself—also has the capacity to correct its own mistakes.[36]

NOTES

* This chapter is based on the initial findings of a research project supported by
  the UNDP and UN-Habitat, titled 'Gender Mainstreaming in District Plans'
  in three districts of Madhya Pradesh. We wish to express our gratitude to
  UNDP and UN-Habitat for this support.
    The field study and its organization received unstinted support from a
  number of colleagues in and outside Eklavya. We thank them all, and
  especially A.N.Tripathi and Amitabh Dongre, Rajesh Bhadoriya, and Thomas
  Toscano, as well as Kirti, Sandhya Gurjar, Savita Verma, and Anju Trivedi.
1. See Dreze (2002) for a more detailed discussion on relating different
   viewpoints.
2. This Act is now termed the Madhya Pradesh Panchayati Raj and Gram
   Swaraj Act after the latest amendment.
3. For details of selection of districts and villages, see the section on 'Methodology
   of the Study'.
4. It is not unusual to find 'natural community leaders' amongst women at grass
   roots levels. Interestingly, we have observed this phenomenon mainly amongst
   tribals and Dalits, and more rarely amongst higher castes. In the latter case,
   the role of husband or family becomes crucial, whereas for the Dalits or
   tribals, the basic abilities of the woman may be sufficient for her being
   accepted as a community leader. Also see Jafri (2001).
5. Although panchayats have acquired the powers to raise their own revenue, it
   is still rare for them to do so to any substantial degree. We could identify
   only two panchayats in Khategaon block, out of a total of 73 panchayats, that
   had their own revenue sources, mainly from sand and stone quarrying.
   Panchayat members are still hesitant to levy house and other taxes on fellow
   citizens in the village as this is considered politically unsound, and also
   because of a lack of personnel in the panchayats for collection purposes.

6. See Table 13.2 for details of the panchayats and villages selected in Dewas district.

7. Refer to the appendix for the questionnaire format which is available with the authors.

8. It may be pertinent to mention here that in certain cases the secretary either refused to share the documents or claimed temporary inaccessibility of documents.

9. For a review of Panchayat Raj in Madhya Pradesh, see Buch (2000b).

10. Some of these are examples to understand how legislation could be used effectively to support decentralization and pro-poor dynamics. Other examples show the need for greater care and foresight before plunging into legislation. The raising of the required quorums for gram sabha meetings to 20 per cent seems to us certainly one such case of misplaced enthusiasm. Still other aspects of legislation such as gram swaraj must remain interesting but debatable issues as to whether their time had come.

11. For a lucid discussion on the reservation of women in panchayats, see Buch (2000a).

12. This is said to have effectively nipped in the bud the ambitions of many an adventuring up-sarpanch/vice-president. However, although on a lesser scale, no-confidence motions against sarpanchs still continue, with probably the majority being against Dalit women.

13. A joint gram sabha meeting for a panchayat with more than one village was not seen to be working. It was difficult for members, especially women, to go to other villages for meetings. Even in the case of a single-village panchayat with a population of over 1000, gram sabha meetings may become too crowded if held properly. This problem however, does not arise in most cases since the quorum of 20 per cent is rarely if ever met in practice.

14. The committees to be set up by the gram panchayat are as follows: gram vikas samiti, agriculture, health, education, infrastructure, natural resources, social justice, and village security. The committees are to be set up at an open meeting of the gram sabha, and each committee except the first, that is, the gram vikas samiti, elects its own president. The gram vikas samiti consists of the seven presidents of the other seven committees, and the sarpanch and up-sarpanch of the panchayat. Each committee makes a plan of work and recommendations for its own sector and the gram vikas samiti puts together these plans in the form of a village development plan. This plan has to be presented to the gram sabha.

15. It is a fact that under panchayati raj, the post of the sarpanch had gained considerably in importance and weight (read 'funds commanded'). Since the sarpanch provided various certifications to people which are necessary for applying for loans, schemes, or projects, he was not to be taken lightly or questioned at a gram sabha meeting. Thus, the people did see a sarpanch as a 'growing centre of power'. The introduction of the Gram Swaraj Act was

thus often greeted initially in villages by ordinary people as well as panchayat members as the 'ouster of the sarpanch'.

16. It is not clear why the government decided to increase the quorum from 10 to 20 per cent of the population when the requirements of the 73rd Constitutional Amendment did not demand such an increase. The framers of the new Act probably felt that with the inclusion of such a substantial number of gram sabha members in the gram swaraj committees, their interest and involvement in affairs of the gram sabha would see a marked increase. At least in the last one year since the quorum has been increased, holding a 'proper gram sabha meeting' with the requisite quorum has become even more difficult and seems to be a rare event.

17. An exercise in district budgeting is said to have been attempted once, a few years ago. However, we are yet to get further details on the nature of this experiment and why it was not continued.

18. At the field-level, planning is still largely considered to be the role of panchayats, mainly those of the secretary and the sarpanch. Some adminis-trators and field activists suggest that gram swaraj samitis may become more lively and 'real' with the allocation of more funds to these village level bodies. This hypothesis remains to be tested.

19. MP/MLA funds are non-tied funds and, therefore, can be utilized in a variety of ways. However, they never seem to materialize through the direct channel. Funds for schemes such as Indira Aawas Yojna are also based on BPL lists and decided at the state level. MP/MLA funds are reported to be channelled through specific contacts and relationships of sarpanchs. Unless such contacts exist, sarpanchs do not even consider it worthwhile to directly approach their area MP or MLA for sanction of these funds.

20. The caste has thereafter been categorized as an OBC. However, because the sarpanch got elected on a general seat and was from the general caste at the time of election, in this paper, we consider him as representing the general castes.

21. It is perhaps necessary to differentiate between the respondents who answered the question and claimed to know, and others who either did not answer the question or claimed ignorance. While ignorance itself tells us a few things, it is necessary that their number should not be used to dilute the responses of those who knew and were disposed on one side or the other.

22. Though the gram sabha may not be valid technically because the quorum requirement of 20 per cent is not met.

23. There are conflicting views on whether action plans were submitted in earlier years, too. We are yet to get a final word on this.

24. It is not clear to us why the government insists on having proposals prepared for schemes such as the Indira Aawas Yojana, as well as for the MP/MLA funds. In the case of the latter, there are no 'known systems' in place for linking disimbursement of these funds to any 'need-based planning'.

25. We have always heard abundant tales of long lists of 'demands' sent by gram panchayats, which are never even acknowledged by the janpad panchayat.

26. Panchayats are expected to hold a meeting at least once every month.

27. Neemavar is a notable case, with a highly vocal and confident Dalit woman sarpanch, who is also a practising midwife.

28. This figure may seem somewhat more respectable if we compare it to the number of active or enthusiastic male panchayat members. Although the average attendance by male members is certainly higher, it does not mean a much higher quality of participation by most of them. This aspect needs to be observed in greater detail.

29. It is important to underline that Dalit and tribal women members of panchayats as well as of the gram sabha may be enjoying some overall advantages over rural women from upper and OBC groups. The Dalit and tribal women have a better chance of being selected as members of panchayat or as sarpanch for their personal characterstics. Upper-caste members seem to be selected for the position or influence that their husbands enjoy, and such women are often not very active on selection. See also Jafri (2001) for some case studies.

30. The factor of distance may lose its significance when gram sabha meetings and gram swaraj committees start meeting regularly for each village separately.

31. This, as we have said earlier, is an option generally practised when the sarpanch avoids his detractors in the panchayat. In this case, the sarpanch may use the option of getting the woman panch's signature at her home, even in exchange for a small cash payment, as per some accounts.

32. The other institutions formed under the Gram Swaraj Act are yet to function actively. Considering the state's emphasis on these institutions, they could emerge as more central to the planning process in days to come. See section on 'Panchayati Raj Legislation: Present Scenario'.

33. A study from West Bengal reports an average of 16 per cent attendence at gram sabha meetings against a requirement of 10 per cent (Ghatak 2002). In the light of Madhya Pradesh's present record, we should consider the option of reverting to a 10 per cent quorum requirement at gram sabha meetings.

34. These are the committees formed after the amended Panchayati Raj and Gram Swaraj Act. See notes 14 and 15 on evolution of panchayati raj.

35. The stand-off seems to be between a gram sabha body and the panchayat itself.

36. Reported in the *New Yorker*, 9 December 1996.

REFERENCES

Bardhan, Pranab, 'Democracy and Development: A Complex Relationship', in I. Shapiro and C. Hacker-Cordon (eds), *Democracy's Value*, Cambridge: Canbridge University Press, 1999.

354 LOCAL GOVERNANCE IN INDIA

Buch, Nirmala, 'Panchayats and Women' in George Mathew (ed.), *Status of Panchayati Raj in the States and Union Territories of India 2000*, New Delhi: Institute of Social Sciences, 2000a, pp 34–41.

———, 'Madhya Pradesh' in George Mathew (ed.), *Status of Panchayati Raj in the States and Union Terri-tories of India 2000*, New Delhi: Institute of Soci`l Sciences, 2000b, pp. 165–83.

———, 'Gram Swaraj: (Dis)empowering the Marginalized', *Hindustan Times* Bhopal II Anniversary Issue, 25 February 2000c.

Dreze, Jean, 'On Research and Action', *Economic and Political Weekly*, 2–8 March 2002, pp. 817–19.

Ghatak, Maitreesh and Maitreya Ghatak, 'Recent Reforms in the Panchayat System in West Bengal', *Economic and Political Weekly*, 5 January 2002.

Government of Madhya Pradesh, *The Madhya Pradesh Panchayati Raj Adhiniyam, 1993*, 1995.

———, Madhya Pradesh Act no. 19 of 1995, *The Madhya Pradesh Zila Yojana Samiti Adhiniyam*, 1995.

———, Madhya Pradesh Act no. 2 of 1999, *The Madhya Pradesh Zila Yojana Samiti (Sansodhan) Adhiniyam*, 1999.

———, Human Development Report, Madhya Pradesh 1995.

———, *The Madhya Pradesh Panchayati Raj Avam Gram Swaraj Adhiniyam, 2001*, 2001.

———, various circulars, 2001–2.

———, District Plan, Dewas, 2002.

———, District Plan, Mandla, 2002.

———, District Plan, Gwalior, 2002.

Khanna, Amod, Y., Singh, Amitabh Singh, Leena Singh, and Chitra Khanna, 'District Institutional Framework Analysis: With Particular Reference to Madhya Pradesh', 2001.

Jafri, Anwar, 'Promises and Problems of Panchayati Raj: Experiences from Madhya Pradesh', in Imrana Qadeer, Kasturi Sen, K.R. Nayar (eds), *Public Health and the Poverty of Reforms*, New Delhi: Sage Publications, 2001, pp. 379–97.

Mathew, George, 'Panchayati Raj and its Enemies', *Panchayati Raj Update* (Hindi), 7(1), January 2002, pp. 6–7.

Murthy, Rajani K. (ed.), *Building Women's Capacities: Interventions in Gender Transformation*, New Delhi: Sage Publications, 2001, pp. 17–42.

Panchayati Raj Adhiniyam 1993.

14

Accountability in Local Governance
Infrastructure Development in the Industrial Townships of Faridabad and Gurgaon

■ AMITA SINGH

Like most industrial townships of India, Faridabad and Gurgaon are also gasping for adequate infrastructural needs. What makes their study a special one is their proximity to the capital city and the enormous gap between the promises and practices on one hand and between formulated policies and their implementation on the other. It is interesting to find out the role that infrastructure plays in the expansion of industries and also in foreign direct investment. The outward flight of foreign capital from these two industrial towns in the last few years may have much to do with the global economic recession, but when the small-scale industries' associations and their employees were interviewed they seem to be utterly agonized with the failure of government in providing them with basic requirements such as electricity, telecommunications, and transportation. They were in distress even for water due to the massive fall in the groundwater level and sewage disposal facilities, but this is not the focus of this study.

This study highlights the changes that local governance hsa undergone due to rapid infrastructural developmet as a prelude to attracting global investment in these cities. At least one Indian industry, the information and communication technology is booming and if the annual revenue projections are to be believed, it has the poential of crossing $ 77 billion by 2008 whcih excludes the $ 10 billion transactions of e-commerce, (NASSCOM-McKinsey Study Report 2002). Gurgaon and to some extent Faridabad provide a very attractive domain for the spread of BPO companies besides the top twenty IT transnational companies which have already started their operations here. One important research question emerges in this new relationship between state institutions, technological system, and the whole process of defining human history which created villages, land systems and community controls over what has suddenly been thrown open to business. This study also discovered that the fast growth fo infrastructure projects in the city which was required to sustain global technology had an inverse effect upon the processes and administrative institutions of democratic state which brings it close to the observations on democracy made by Hirsh (1965) and Posner (1961). This has been so because even though there has been a strong motivation to create governance structures for the facilitation of service delivery yet these new structures mostly based upon the models of public–private parnerships could not promote equitable development (Fukuyama and Wagner 2001: 191). Thus controls shifted from state apparatus to technological and business regimes which were governed by efficiency doctrine which in the purely agricultural locales of these two cities encouraged group dominance as an accepted system for the survival of traditional communities inhabiting these cities. These models of two cities have shown the ability of local governance being stymied by the creation of new agencies which worked in total disregard to transparency, accountability, and regulatory dynamism needed to inculcate a sustainable infrastructual growth. Citizen's choice, welfare, and public distribution became a matter of public choice which reduced the ability of local governance to voice the marginalized.

In the early 1970s, when Delhi planned to dislocate industries of its north-west region to the neighbouring state of Haryana, a glimmer of hope prevailed amongst the entrepreneur community for a more respectable business environment. The relatively clean environment and the promised optimism for further expansion encouraged the potentially ambitious small-scale sector to virtually rush and catch the train to Haryana. Globalization and liberalization sent these hopes further skyrocketing, leading to massive empires of collaborations, of the indigenous to the transnational. Faridabad and Bahadurgarh were the earliest of the chosen industrial estates, while Gurgaon became the hub of industrial activity only in the last decade of 1990s. The catalytic effect of the Haryana State Industrial Development Corporation (HSIDC) made Haryana the so-called 'new paradigm state in modern India'. In the last three decades

Haryana can claim to have transformed, and its people are a more enterprising community than what they were a decade ago.

Ironically, the ground problems started surfacing by 1999 and threatened this newly achieved status of a forward-looking industrial state. Entrepreneurs seem to be disheartened and disillusioned. A large number of industries started freezing further expansions into the state. Infrastructural constraints such as roads, electricity, sewerage, and water constitute their major grievances. The industrial boom appeared to be coming to a close, inspiring researchers to explore this dramatic shift and prodigious backfiring in economic activity within this short span of time. The progressive thrust of industrialization, growing number of state-of-the-art corporate offices, shopping arcades, and telecom-munication linkages did not appear attractive enough to sustain business opportunities in Haryana. The tall claims for providing world-class infrastructure, adequate power supply, water availability, easy accessibility, and sewerage were not enough to prevent the outgoing industries.

In this study the two towns of Gurgaon and Faridabad are taken as sample towns to survey the impact of infrastructural constraints on industrial activity. Faridabad started losing economic activity which in the mid-1990s began to be passed over to Gurgaon to the detriment of entrepreneurs and also the neglect of equity issues in development. The study looks into the impact of infrastructure growth on this trend of unbalanced and downsliding business in these towns. The study treats infrastructure as a grass root government activity that is essen·ial for people and business to thrive in a synergetic manner. The fact that these services are so essential for people implies that they be provided with a well-governed and transparent local government system so that a healthy trend of industrialization could set in motion a sustainable mode of development. Considering the enormity of the nature of infrastructural parameters and the limited focus of this chapter, the three basic parameters of industrial infrastructure such as electricity, transport, and telecommunications are treated exclusively, whereas other parameters such as waste disposal, water availability, and social infrastructure (schools, housing, hospitals, clubs, and hotels) have been studied only in relation to the others. The study is based on the hypothesis that the centralized government services have not been able to ensure increased business and FDI because of their inability to see local governance as the core implementer of their policies. The prevailing mess at the local governance level is directly responsible for the infrastructural management. On the contrary, the experience from the states of Gujarat and Karnataka has shown that a well-governed local office has been able to attract business even with minimal infrastructure. Privatization has released enormous energy for growth, but the litmus test is that of the ability of local governance to channellize industrial development. The innumerable links between the local-government-provided services and the entrepreneur have to become transparent and well oiled for a sustainable economic activity in these prime industrial townships.

THE PROBLEM

Infrastructure development and promotion largely depend upon the way it is visualized, prioritized, and pursued by local administration. Only an honest, transparent, and corruption-free local administration can inspire infrastructure growth; otherwise any amount of investment in this sector may just fatten local officials. These infrastructure constraints also impregnate policy with enormous socio-economic problems, which over a period of time threaten the survival and existence of industrial development. Retrofitting is always more expensive and it leads to a political imbroglio in which economic activity is the major casualty.

'Infrastructure' is an enabling act of government through capital investment. Faridabad and later Gurgaon became examples of transformed villages and their rural fringes are a challenge for local urban governance. It is by and large the result of two forces working in opposite direction, one is local empowerment through the strengthening of panchayati raj institutions and second is strengthening official control over land acquisition policies to expand road, electricity, and network of industrial estates. As urbanization and industrialization progress, the pressure of infrastructure expansion compromises procedural norms at the 'game players' level, which in the ultimate prescribes 'rent' for each service thereby increases their transaction cost and discourages industries from locating in that area. The local agencies spend more time looking for big grants from the central government and donor agencies rather than providing high-quality services to prospective businesses. In the rush to share the loot, local officials fail to demonstrate an amicable and transparent management ability. This is also encouraged by the increasing dominance of political power in these prime cities. Ades and Glaeser (1997) have studied three prime factors that enable these cities to become dominant in economic ativities. They are the trade barriers, poor internal transport, and the concentration of political power. Gurgaon and Faridabad have three additional factors in common to make them dominant: the proximity to Delhi, powerfully organized agricultural groups, and a weak coalition of parties in power at the Centre, which in an effort to woo the state government prefer to abstain from considerations of political and administrative ethics. Thus, a free hand is given to the administrator at the local area dealing with land issues.

As these two towns were urbanizing, the local government service provisions came to a controversial stalemate. Many small-scale manu-facturing units felt that it was cheaper for them to manage at least their water supply and waste disposal without government intervention since their units were located on the rural fringes of the towns. Since low rural densities allow natural systems to provide water and dispose wastes in a more unrestrained manner, local governance gets confined to minimal regulatory role. But increasing urbanization and density of population do create the need for increased power supply, transport availability, and telecommunication links besides the need for related social infrastructure. This also increases the local government per capita expenditure not only because of extensive service provisions, but also due to higher unit cost of services, which were quite cheap in earlier days of industrial activity. Increasing infrastructure investment and its relation to the city sizes have raised queries about the social efficiency, equitability, and accountability of services available. It has been studied (Wheaton and Shishido 1981: 17–30) that federal and decentralized systems where the local administration has the power to formulate policy and levy taxes, basic services are better managed. After the 73rd and the 74th Constitutional Amendment acts, panchayats and municipal committees are pursuing decentralized decision-making on infrastructure spending and policy by specifying taxes and the regulatory mechanism for local business.

Hence, with the expansion of economic growth activities, local administration is faced with some major challenge which become indispensable to their process of political empowerment, this is increasing their efficiency by decentralizing and sharing regulatory burdening activities with users.

Haryana government has been attracting investment decisions through perfect advertising of the infrastructure facilities and official support to entrepreneurs. The inflow of industries, which began in the decade of the 1970s, has also brought large population with it. Faridabad, which is the ninth most industrial town in the country, better known as the industrial hub of Haryana, whereas Gurgaon, which has grown in the last decade only, has achieved the status of the third biggest software exporting township in India after Bangalore and Hyderabad. The city size has increased explosively. In the 1991 Census (Census of India 1991) Faridabad had a population of 1,477,240 and Gurgaon 1,146,90 although the total area of Faridabad was around 600 sq.km less than Gurgaon. In the decade following (Census of India 2000) Faridabad added a population of 700,000 out of which 400,000 was concentrated in the city's central zone alone. In the same decade, Gurgaon's population increased by 500,000 and unlike Faridabad, the total concentration of this population was in the town. The result of this explosive expansion has led to a big gap between services, customer citizen demand, and consumer grieances. Table 14.1 shows the comparative increase in the number of factories and the number of people employed in them in Gurgaon, which promises to provide relatively better infrastructure than

TABLE 14.1: EMPLOYMENT IN THE ORGANIZED SECTOR

Year	Organized sector	1000 or more factory workers	500 or more factory workers	100 or more factory workers
Faridabad 1995	—	8 factories; 16,038 workers	21 factories; 13,942 workers	—
2000	1,18,120	6 factories; 9818 workers	7 factories; 3926 workers	85 factories; 15,337workers
Gurgaon 1995	—	—	3 factories; 1762 workers	30 factories; 6895 workers
2000	59,306	1 factory; 1087 workers	4 factories; 2361 workers	42 factories; 8298 workers

Faridabad: The Table also shows the declining trend of industries in Faridabad.

At present around 118,120 employees in Faridabad and around 59,306 employees in Gurgaon commute on a regular basis to their place of work through roads. This has led to an increased demand for means of transport, roads, and other civic amenities. Table 14.2 shows that the increase in population of these towns has not apparently matched the increase in the length of metalled roads and means of public transport. On the contrary, the fleet strength of Faridabad and Gurgaon transport has substantially decreased and private transportation system, with opaque and arbitrary regulations, has become a flourishing trade. This has not only made public transport system less responsible and expensive, but has also implanted transport mafias working in tandem with local administration to discipline commuters who question their arbitrariness. The fact that outsourcing of transport services has not been accompanied by an equally compelling drive for structural and procedural reform of the transport licensing authority and toll tax units at the borders, much is left to the discretion of local operators. The transport mafia are largely taking over casteist colours in the process of encountering stiff competition for contracts. The Yadavas and the Gujjars, the two main communities in Gurgaon have consolidated their familial and kinship groupings to influence local administration to get trucks,

TABLE 14.2: TRANSPORT SCENARIO

Years	Length of metalled roads (km)	Length of metalled roads (% of total)	Length of metalled roads (km per 100,000 population)	Vehicles on road	Fleet strength	Total Kilo- metreage (km/ 100,000)	Accidents
Faridabad							
1995	1192	56.63	81	180,960	222	251.60	1126
2000	1206	57.29	82	145,628	213	233.56	1317
Gurgaon							
1995	1691	61.27	147	39,456	236	260.58	840
2000	1696	61.45	148	83,743	212	213.34	912

tempos, and buses while sowetines they also get each other's vehicles impounded at the border checkposts. Since local administration has developed diverse interests in building a nexus of local operators in business, it fails out on some core duties of the transport system management (TSM), leading to major bottlenecks during peak hours in the two towns and their adjoining highways. Thus, improved road infrastructure and a complementary modal split[1] unless accompanied with decentral-ization of local regulatory authority for sustainable improvement may continue to prevent and obstruct growth of demands for accountability of local bodies.

Another area of entrenched corruption is the electricity department. Table 14.3 shows that between the years 1995 and 2000, the number of LT (low transmission) and 11 KW lines have not been laid in accordance with the proportional growth of the number of industrial and commercial electricity connections over the town. As a result, the local functionaries, such as, linesmen billing departments, office of SDO and Executive Engineer become the breeding ground of corruption. This has encouraged electricity thefts and also politicization of regulatory bureaucracy at the bottom of departments, such as, linemen, billing clerks, and meter readers. During this study, one was intrigued by several incidents of connivance of the local administration with local politicians on serious issues like power thefts, transferring location of tube wells, meter change, new meter installations, billing, load increase, and cable extensions. Many such decisions were made at the level of the local linemen, involving at most the SDO. Sometimes the executive engineer or the superintendent engineer expressed their disgust with people who

TABLE 14.3: POWER SCENARIO

Year	LT lines	11 KW lines	Transformers	Industrial connections	Commercial connections
Faridabad					
1995	7071	2992	5732	14,640	32,229
2000	7332	3271	6634	13,832	27,555
Gurgaon					
1995	8298	3086	4819	7646	19,416
2000	8442	3203	5780	9360	23,510

failed to report such malpractices to higher authorities. However, they tried to downplay the difficult exercise of getting jobs done within the existing colonial pattern of the office structures and procedures.

LAND: THE VORTEX OF LOCAL GOVERNANCE

During the last decade, which saw the launching of New Industrial Policy, these two towns have been the main providers of land for industries and firms, both national and transnational. Their proximity to Delhi and easy availability of land from villages has brought some of the big manufacturing industries to them. Faridabad has Escorts, Eicher, Whirlpool, Goodyear, Lakhani, and Bhartia Cuttler Hammer. Gurgaon has largely attracted service industries and most of the MNCs headquartered in Delhi, like Coca-Cola, PepsiCo, Motorola, GE Capital Services, Hughes Software Systems, Nestle India, and Gillete India. What has been of particular concern is that these companies and factories have been coming in faster than the administrative changes required to manage them with an equivalent speed and transparency. The old colonial regime of tehsildar, junior engineers, and SDOs along with their band of linemen and foremen continues to drive the consumer to distress. This rapid growth of industrial townships had been quick to develop an impermeable layer of grass roots fixers, which is ready to crack the hierarchy for a fee fixed according to the type of services required. What is astounding is the immense cooperation of different departmental functionaries at the local level to sustain this fixer zone of corruption, which in this short span of few years became a most sought-after alternative mode of employment for local villagers who had given their land to government for industrialization. According to a survey conducted in four offices of local administration (Police, District Town and Country Planning, Gurgaon Telephones (pre-BSNL), and Dakshin Haryana Bijli Vitaran Nigam) through informal yet structured inerviews with their heads and questionnaires circulated to people (around 150 residents of DLF, Palam Vihar and South City in New Gurgaon) revealed that most transactions were conducted through fixers as intermediaries to administration. This, not only made each transaction expensive but also emboldened bureaucracy to be corrupt.

Residents experienced:

1. Registration of land had 2 per cent of the registered amount as the tehsildar's fee.
2. Electricity connection and associated services (meter installation, fixing load, changing defective meters, and getting bills corrected) had different rates ranging from Rs 1000 from the domestic consumer to an amount that ran into thousands from an industry.
3. Telephone connection—Rs 1500 for the dealing clerk and Rs 500 to the local lineman, Rs 200 or more after installation depending upon the desperation of the consumer.
4. Private developers called 'colonizers' ruled through their private security and made regular monthly payments to local police stations for better coordination in dealing with law and order problems. At least one major developer which the local administration refers to as a parallel state government during the regime of Chief Minister Om Prakash Chautala was found to be making regular payment to local police. Some local residents complained of victimization by the mafia maintained through retired army personnel as they failed to register their complaints at the local police station. A rush for an SHO posting in the colonizer area is revealed by the fact that the average tenure of an SHO in Sector 29 police station which constituted the hub of builders activity was three months only.
5. Till April 2002, dealing with telephone complaints was on payment by the complainant. The long-serving junior engineer posted at the telephone exchange in DLF Phase II (who was later transferred in March–April 2002) had no hesitation in revealing that the linemen were not paid by the government. The reason given was that the government has downsized the number of linemen but the services to be attended by them have only increased due to a spurt of population density and so at the local level as a junior engineer he has to hire people and also allow them to fend for themselves. So a stream of such ad hoc non-government local service providers survived on whatever they could bargain for with the customer.
6. The procedure of Change of Land Use (CLU) certificates which were obtained from the Town and Country Planner, was rooted into most arbitrary regime of money power, 'the den of

corruption'. This impacted upon changes in PRI Act (1992) and Land Acquisition Act of 1894, giving a very wide amplitude to 'public interest' as a pretext for acquiring land from villages.

Thus, grass root administration presented a picture of a nightmarish maze of detours and deviations, which affected local administration in four different ways:

1. It made the settling and sustaining exercise too disheartening for a promising new entrepreneur in a new surrounding.
2. This also led to the industry-focused infrastructure development which led to the neglect of services to residential areas.
3. Rise of service providing mafias in twin cities and construction companies, used them to settle their scores with defiant residents and business units in their areas by withdrawing their infrastructural facilities arbitrarily at will.
4. Shrinking of deliberative bodies in local administration as functioning of local administration became too erratic. While it was too swift to act on some complaints, it was totally inert on others. Small-scale industries became subservient to the demands of local operators.

Even with the promise of class infrastructure, economic activity was challenged by this regime of corruption laid out at the bottom to squeeze new residents out of the new city. As investment grew, so did the share of the local service providers.

LAND DEVELOPMENT AND ALLOTMENT

Most institutional changes made tried to answer the questions brought out from land mal-administration. The problem of land development is at the root of this infrastructural array in most developing countries. In India, this is one dominant factor that continues to blur all efforts towards cleaner layout programmes for infrastructural expansion. Being an overpopulated country with high population density, the service delivery mechanism of the government is fraught with insurmountable land management problems. This is also the area of severe infestations of land mafias and their nexus with the long line of political and administrative decision makers. Haryana's rise to an industrial state has been due to the fact that the industrial land is available to potential entrepreneurs. However, development of industrial estates has not been as speedy as the growth of industries and households. A large number of aspiring entrepreneurs are left without any alternative but to explore an informal or even an illegal settlement on inadequately serviced land. This is in part related to inadequate resource allocation for infrastructure and poor inter-agency coordination, but once it is allowed, the situation inflates into a Frankenstein administrative dilemma. Land management involves a number of interrelated procedures. To ensure that developed land is available to entrepreneurs both private and public and that the available land is put to its most productive use in both economic and social terms, a series of measures are required. First comes the most essential ingredient, *the legal framework,* which ensures that land can be easily bought and sold. Second are the *procedures and regulations* to ensure the development of land at an affordable cost. The third measure is that of *land taxation* to promote equity and efficiency in land use. Fourth is a *transparent and corruption-free local administration.*

The *problem of acquiring land* for infrastructure and industrial development is the first major administrative jungle that every prospective entrepreneur has to cross. Smaller villages in Haryana have been transformed into industrial townships and large industrial cities with TNCs' corporate offices operating within them. Although the state government claims to have developed 82 industrial estates through its developmental agencies and several more are being developed, industrial activity is still much faster than the growth of these industrial townships. The District Town and Country Planner (DTCP) claims that the controlled areas that fall at the rural–urban fringes are real centres of planning for further industrialization. In Gurgaon alone, it comprises something of a third of the total land in the district out of which only 9.5 per cent of the areas are urban, thereby leaving more than 90 per cent area of the state free from any of the controls of acts enforced by the government. There is a lot of infrastructural mismanagement considering the fact that the municipal committee and the panchayats are not obliged to function within this area and the Town and Country Planner (TCP) cannot undertake work without an officially declared plan for that area. They may more reasonably be termed as the 'areas of dilute governance'. Land purchased within the controlled areas need a CLU certificate from the DTCP, which land purchased outside the controlled areas does not require. This has set in motion a dangerous trend going around the whole of Faridabad and Gurgaon. Since the industrial townships have not been able to develop plots, these industries have started buying plots directly from the farmers and managing to obtain (CLU) certificates from the of Town and Country Planning Department (TCPD). This is not only threatening the rich and fertile land of the Haryana farmers and creating a new industrial slum that could discharge hazardous effluents untreated over ground, poisoning the already depleting groundwater but also increasing the transaction cost of common services to citizens exorbitantly. Increased power thefts, grabbing land, and preventing competition have become the order of the day in controlled areas of industrial townships. The TCPD enjoys its freedom to keep the dagger hanging over new entrepreneurs settled in the controlled areas and in the absence of any clear-cut demarcation of industrial and agricultural lands, the problem is only exacerbated. This problem is also aggravated in some areas by divergences prevailing between modern legal concepts and popular perceptions of land rights rooted in religious and traditional beliefs. A large number of bank-supported projects suffer from delays in land acquisition and land tenure problems. The suprintendent engineer (SE) of Gurgaon admitted that the major bottleneck for expanding power infrastructure in the district is the acquiring of land for setting up any infrastructure unit. A 66 KW sub-station is pending construction in Sector 29 and another in Sector 42 for the inability to acquire land from the Haryana Urban Development Authority (HUDA). The speculative Gurgaon SE lamented that this is an un-necessary delay since there already exists a previous agreement with HUDA to supply land for infrastructure purposes without delay to concerned departments.

The second problem is that of the *land registration system*, which is still undertaken within the old colonial structure in which the tehsildar retains an all-encompassing regulatory empire. His regime expands from the identification and transferring of landownership to the assessment and collection of the property taxes, which is right now the most attractive domain of ruling politicians. In certain districts adjoining Delhi, like Gurgaon, and Faridabad, which had seen the rapid spurt of industrial activity in the last decade, entrepreneurs have become the milch cattle of local service administration (like that of electricity, waterworks, and telephones), which have almost started drawing parallel salaries from industries. The tehsildar works through a band of document writers and clerks who check file documents. It was found that the tehsildar generally remains absent from office in the first half of the day and returns to his office at almost the closing time for the court. This was the situation of Gurgaon Tehsil between March 2002 to November 2002 during which the survey was conducted. On several occasions it was also observed that the district collector who may be higher in hierarchy was ironically working on the directives of the tehsildar since he was more directly associated with the Chief Minister. The enormous amount of money which passed through this channel made a mockery of the demands for clean administration in a globalizing state. It was frightening to see the nexus between corruption and infrastructure growth.

The World Bank has been undertaking projects related to site and services upgradation since 1973. These have focused on secure land tenure to project beneficiaries and institutional strengthening of land-related agencies. While the legal procedural system has been structured in countries such as Cameroon and Tunisia, land regularization and land registration has also been undertaken in Brazil and Thailand, and the property taxation mechanism has been sufficiently improved upon in Indonesia, yet Haryana, the model industrial state, has its land management roots deeply entrenched in the Land Acquisition Act of 1894 with a highly vulnerable public interest doctrine to serve different meanings. As a result, the award for land acquisition was on rates fixed by the district commissioner (DC). So the sole competent authority under revenue law to assess such rates continued to be the DC (claims under Section 9 of the Land Acquisition Act, 1894). This made Faridabad and Gurgaon the most sought-after and enticing administrative posting for all positions related to land management such as the tehsildar, subdivisional magistrate (SDM), and DC. In the last decade, at least the two chief ministers, Bansi Lal and Bhajan Lal, in Haryana survived upon their own men in these positions and the trend continued more vigorously in Om Prakash Chautala's tenure also. The document writers at the tehsildar's office who happen to be the middlemen to most customer dealings revealed that these positions by virtue of the enormous money inflow have become an important ingredient for the political survival of chief ministers in this state. To get a posting on these two positions in Gurgaon and Faridabad one either has to be the chief minister's kin or be able to pay a big amount. Land was the prime source of revenue for Haryana and thus attracted special political attention.

In 1995, on 9 February, the government constituted a committee comprising the following officers as a process to decentralize power hereby concentrated in the DC. Changes referred to:

- divisional commissioner as chairman;
- deputy commissioner as member secretary;
- representative of the concerned member department; and
- district revenue officer as the concerned member.

This also restricted the DC's discretion to determine the market price of land not on the basis of the five-year sale average but only on the basis of a year's sale average. Section 5A of this New Land Acquisition Act, 1995, also enabled the landowner to refer to the court under Section 18 of the Act.

However, this new Act could not change ground rules for four reasons:

1. The reference to the court could only be made through request to the DC. This allowed the DC to manoeuvre the acquisition and sale of land from farmers and panchayats. It also brought corruption of higher offices down to the lowest functionary in land administration. Middlemen in service administration thrived in Gurgaon and Faridabad.
2. The hearing of objections was done through a joint inspection committee comprising of DC and few other government officials. The absence of NGOs and panchayat members from this committee made it as centralized as the earlier structures.
3. The changes in legal system had been so fast and so unrelated to the grass roots network of lower functionaries in administration that most farmers did not know and did not believe that any change has actually arrived. Most of the village lekhpals continued to be strongly disruptive of legal changes undertaken in the post-73rd and post-74th Amendment era to raise participation and voice of Dalits and women. The mindset of both the bureaucrat and the village hierarchy remained the same.

4. These changes were more cosmetic in nature since they lacked the political will for implementations. The historic and societal casteist and land-based structures in Faridabad and Gurgaon were so strong that mere procedural decentralization was too soft a device to prevent them from working in connivance.

INFRASTRUCTURAL DEVELOPMENT THROUGH THE HSIDC

The Haryana State Industrial Development Corporation (HSIDC) has been one of the most potent agencies for infrastructure development in the state. The infrastructure policy of the state government had designated it as the sole developing agency for the whole industrial infrastructure in Haryana. It was established in 1967 as a public limited company owned by the government of Haryana. Ironically, it could develop an infrastructure planning cell to facilitate the industrial infrastructure division in planning, sourcing, and distribution system for water supply, surface drainage, and sewerage system for all industrial estates only in as late as 1997. The Industrial Policy, 1999, has categorized these industrial estates on the basis of the level of infrastructure and it is on this basis that they are   priced. These are classified as:

1. *High-intensity infrastructure industrial estates:* These estates shall have constructed sheds, industrial plots, internal roads and parking facility, sewerage and storm water disposal systems, internal electrification, telecom facilities, solid waste disposal system, recreation centres, parks, banks, post office, and medical facilities.
2. *Medium-intensity infrastructure industrial estates:* These estates shall have only industrial plots, internal roads, water supply, open drainage system, and power supply at the external source.
3. *Low-intensity infrastructure industrial estates:* These estates shall have the provision of only approach road and power supply at the external source. The price of land will be low and units will be permitted to develop their own internal services. These estates will be built to encourage large-scale units.

As an effort to provide a financial infrastructure, Haryana Financial Corporation (HFC) and the HSIDC have been operating to meet the requirements of medium- and small-scale industries. However, few members of the Gurgaon and Faridabad Small-Scale Industries Association revealed in the questionnaire circulated that most of the small-scale units were not able to manage funds and loans from these institutions. Besides this constraint, the government had introduced many new taxes in the name of infrastructure development, like the fire tax, professional tax, licence fee, and the backbreaking hike in the electricity charges. The Industrial Policy, 1999, aspired towards a reorientation of their role to focus on venture capital, small and medium enterprise (SME) renewal, and investor escort services (see India Infrastructure Report 2001). It is claimed that these changes are likely to bring a major transformation of services at the level of people.

DECENTRALIZING TRENDS IN INFRASTRUCTURE-LED GROWTH

The globalizing era of 1990s saw the launch of New Economic Policy and a trend towards relaxing controls on private investors towards a major industrial revolution. This matched with the global revival of the concern for managing infrastructure potential (see Estasche and Sinha 1994: Estasche 1995). The need for competition and a harmonized integration with global economy changed the domestic environment even in these two towns also. It was admitted in the Industrial Policy statement of 1992 that 'a reorientation of the development vision was needed in recognition of the new paradigms that put the industrial policy initiatives in the context of an overarching economic development policy'. While the 1992 policy statement focused on providing incentives for attracting investments in the industrial sector the Industrial Policy of 1997 adopted *infrastructure-led growth*.

This new policy initiative was directed to revitalize industrial growth and lay the foundation of a vibrant economy. An investor-friendly climate through better infrastructure layout become the new concern of the state government. The new approach proposes to achieve a coordinated development of all sectors of economy that comprehensively address economic value addition (EVA). The institutional mechanisms for the variety of measures needed for land development would be revamped so that fast-track clearances and

investor-friendly climate is created. Simplification of rules and an
effective monitoring and grievance redressal mechanism is expected
to accelerate the modernization of the erstwhile colonial administrative
processes. The service sector was recognized as the driver of future
economic growth. Taxation reforms as a measure of fiscal prudence
in prioritizing public investment were undertaken in the context of
expanding and strengthening the existing infrastructure through its
own resources and for encouraging private sector participation in
infrastructure development. The realization that infrastructure is at
the core of industrial activity is evident by the fact that the state
government has plans to set up an Economic Development Board
under the chairmanship of the Chief Minister to act as the supreme
body for overseeing infrastructure initiatives.

The revamping of the institutional mechanism focused upon three
areas:

1. An *empowered committee* would be constituted under the
   chairmanship of the chief secretary to suggest policy initiatives,
   monitor implementation of policy, and coordinate with various
   departments of the government to achieve the objectives set forth
   in the policy. This committee has not yet started functioning in
   Gurgaon and Faridabad.
2. *The Industrial Assistance Group* (IAG) to be suitably strengthened
   and restructured to act as the nodal institution for providing
   assistance to investors, escort services for venture location,
   information on investment policies, procedures, and clearances.
   The presence of this group was not in the knowledge of any
   district functionary.
3. The government would constitute a *standing committee* wherein
   representatives of industrial associations will be associated to study
   existing laws and procedures relating to setting up of new industries,
   and to suggest modifications and alterations that eliminate delays
   and expedite clearances. This group will also recommend
   amendments to and deletion of various laws and enactments that
   have outlived their utility.

However promising this may appear, the ground rules are still
formulated in the offices of the tehsildar, SDO, and DC. As Sebastian
Morris observes (2001:2) that the slow infrastructural growth has
been due to the fact that the working of government in policy, rule

and law making roles was maimed by inadequate skills, knowledge, and activism and most by the systemic ills such as lack of competency, power of vested interests, graft and corruption. This is mainly so because 'We hope to highlight interesting and thus far underplayed aspects of law, policy, administration, structure of organizations and institutional arrangements. The overarching design of political institutions can constrain regulatory organizations' (Morris 2001:3).

In Haryana, the state government adopted a system of deemed clearance/approval for implementing projects. Under this system the certificate of deemed clearance shall be issued by a single-window service (SWS) for projects having fixed capital investment (FCI) up to Rs 300 million. For projects having FCI of Rs 300 million and more, such certificates shall be issued by the Industrial Assistance Group (IAG). It is observed that certain requirements like the time schedules fixed for giving sanctions and approvals and the visit of inspectors to industrial units should be kept to a bare minimum statutory requirements, but this has encouraged self-regulation in industrial associations. The procedures governing NOCs and consents from Haryana State Pollution Control Board (HSPCB) also need to be streamlined. The IT industries in large and medium categories set up within approved industrial estates and having sewer connections have been rewarded by allowing them exemption from seeking consent from the HSPCB. These efforts are strengthened by the setting up of the District-Level Industries Grievance Redressal Committee headed by the deputy commissioner and the State-level Monitoring and Grievance Redressal Committee headed by commissioner of industries, which remove obstructions in industrial activity, including those of infrastructure. The state government is also in the process of setting up an Infrastructure Development Fund (IDF) to act as a catalyst for mobilizing and channellizing private resources into infrastructure development of the state. The Economic Development Board (EDB) is expected to act as the apex empowered body responsible for overall development, planning, policy formulation, and a 'single window' for approvals and award of concessions for IDF applications to state infrastructure projects. The IDF will be constituted out of the resources to be raised by the government and will have the option for institutional and private sector participation. The fund shall be professionally managed with advisory assistance from an independent professional body. Individual viable infrastructure projects will be considered as referred to it by EDB on user charge basis for funding through special purpose vehicles (SPVs). The state government has also set up an Infrastructure Development Board to coordinate private and public sectors engaged in the infrastructural development. At present, the Foreign Direct Investment (FDI) Board with its office in Delhi is also involved in the infrastructure development issues. An Integrated Infrastructure Development Centre is being set up in Sirsa to look into the infrastructure problems of expanding industries.

The government has also supplemented these efforts by taking a big leap in this new industrial policy directed towards modern management techniques through the use of information technology. Transaction automation and information data banks are being introduced in administrative agencies and this has left bureaucracy at the local level sulking at least for the time being. The changes that have actually acted as whistle-blowers to decentralization can be discussed under the following areas of infrastructure services.

TOWN AND COUNTRY PLANNING (TCP) OFFICE

The division of powers between the HSIDC and HUDA for developing land for industrial and commercial purposes has boosted development since the powers of the DC and the tehsildar are substantially curtailed. These agencies have a corporate structure, they have weaker hierarchies and greater professionalism. Their boards also have at least three non-official members. The District Town Planner (DTP) under all possibility would work with the zonal administrators. Out of the total five zonal officers in the whole state, these twin industrial towns get two, but they also have to coordinate their work with the 11 estate officers posted in four different land acquisition divisions of the state. Being the local official, the DTP continues to enjoy more power than its counterparts in local infrastructure-related decisions. However, the survey of the office revealed that the mindset of grass roots functionaries was still rooted in the colonial bureaucratic norms and surprisingly the office had very few numbers of those aware of the decentralization drives being undertaken within their offices. A more integrated collaboration with the grassroots panchayat administration, local NGOs, and the industries' organization was required for the planning of infrastructure projects which was still amiss. Also, the number of officials in planning committees of the TCPD far exceeds the non-officials. The government has in the recent past introduced extra development charges (EDC) for the prospective industry in the region with the objective of utilizing this money for infrastructure needs and improvements. It is difficult to relate these extra charges over industries with the improvement of infrastructure in the corruption-infested lower hierarchies of the related offices. The terms and conditions that decide the EDC keep the industrialist gasping for breath in his effort to seek minor approvals and finally the guillotine drops over the developmental plan.

POWER DEPARTMENT

Power sector reforms undertaken after the Haryana Electricity Reforms Act 1997 have focused upon decentralized governance at the grass roots and privatizing power generation or contracting out power related services (see Glen 1992). The intractable and the entrenched corruption in this department and the tendency towards deviations from rules led the government to restructure and bifurcate the Haryana State Electricity Board. Now Dakshin Haryana Bijli Vitaran Nigam (DHBVN) looks after the distribution aspect and the Haryana Vidyut Prasaran Nigam (HVPN) deals with the supply side only. Another corporation called the Haryana Power Generation Corporation (GENCO) is responsible for operation, maintenance, and expansion of the existing Panipat and Faridabad Thermal Power Stations and the Western Yamuna Canal Hydroelectric Project. Inspired by these reforms the superintendent engineer of Gurgaon district took some severe measures to root out corruption from his office at the lower levels of SDOs and linemen. First, he shifted the dilapidated and pathetically run office from Sector 18 to a more open and modern construction in the midst of Sector 31. The concerned officials who had little incentive to visit the old office because it was without a proper toilet, drinking water, and the basic canteen facilities become more regular in attendance. As they became more visible, the role of middlemen and touts on its own got substantially reduced. The table of every dealing clerk, from record-keeper, those dealing with change of meter and defective bills, and linemen is visible to every visitor. Secrecy in dealings is also muted in comparison to the past as the SDO, who is the only grass roots official for the people–government interface is now made to sit in the office for a larger part of the day. On top of it, the executive engineer also occupies a room in the same office. Earlier his office was placed far away from this office for lack of space and the lower clerks had no fear that he would ever come to their dingy set-up. Entrepreneurs now heave a sigh of relief as most jobs for which they had to pay large sums of money to the invisible chain of local operators are now going straight into business with the SDO. The Small-Scale Industry Association members say that this has only replaced the invisible with the visible, and the operations are at least assured. Efforts are also being made to prevent power thefts and sudden tripping of transformers. The SE's office has been connected with digital panel meters or indicator clocks to show the cycle per second frequency of the current. Once the frequency falls below 50, it is immediately ordered to shut down electricity supply. Earlier the lower offices had to seek permission to shut off supply and in the process led to major trippings. The introduction of the computerized information system at the dispatch centres has brought visibility into the decisions of electricity regulations.

A major decentralization effort has been achieved after the Haryana Electricity Regulation Act 1997. Both in Faridabad and Gurgaon the power to sanction load has now been decentralized. This was earlier being done at Hissar, which meant a lot of distress to consumers. Thus, it led to increased corruption because out of desperation, the industrialists were ready to pay any amount to the local operator who could do the running around for them.

A Citizens' Charter has also been formulated. It is expected to clarify electricity rates, the role of the regulatory commission for electricity complaints, procedures for Bijli Adalats and agendas for Bijli Sabhas, tariff guidelines, and the rights of consumers. Industries have already started benefiting from the changes towards decentralization. Now there are no continuous cuts in electricity for the industries and they are allowed to operate even during the peak hours of 6 to 9 p.m. Earlier this was the grey-regime of the junior engineer and the SDO who could impose heavy penalties on industries found operating during peak hours. They have also lost some power with the installation of electronic meters. The local bureaucracy was found to be so frustrated and helpless in dealing with these private operators because they are, as one JE puts it, 'not only politically backed but have also been wiping out their income sources'. Power remains one of the 'most critical infrastructure' (Das *et al.* 2000). especially in areas taken over by colonizers in Gurgaon and Faridabad.

TELECOMMUNICATION

Telecommunication has been recognized as the core of infrastructure policy. Reforms in other areas could begin only through the expansion of telecommunication. The spectacular growth of the telecom industry is directly related to the globalizing and liberalizing trends in the economy and, therefore, Gurgaon became the beneficiary of the reform process undertaken by the government in the recent past. In comparison to Gurgaon, Faridabad lags behind in speed and innovation. The corporatization of the Mahanagar Telephone Nigam Limited (MTNL) and Videsh Sanchar Nigam Limited (VSNL) in 1986, and the development of the switching technology products by the Centre for Development of Telematics (C-DOT) paved the way for the Telecom Policy, 1994 (TP-94), and Telecom Policy, 1999 (TP-99). This increased competition and also improved basic services to consumers. Faridabad and Gurgaon are already within the local Delhi mobile telecom-munication system. However, these changes in technology in tele-communication policy also required a complementary system of legal and consumer rights framework to increase the system's accountability towards the people. The major change towards transparent functioning of this regime of new companies was the creation of the Telecom Regulatory Authority of India (TRAI) Act, 1997. Its main tasks were tariff fixing through a cost-based tariff policy and of dispute settlement. In doing so it even gave judgements that were against the government.

New entrepreneurs recollected that a few years ago, the task of settling in these twin cities of Haryana was a nightmare. Like vultures, these floor-level workers made life miserable for the newcomers. From billing to fault repair of telephones, the administrative system was laden with inertia and greed. When the Department of Telecom-munication (DOT) was changed to Bharat Sanchar Nigam Limited (BSNL) in 2000, the expectations were belied because the new system continued to function with old guards. However, the general manager, Telephones, Gurgaon posted in 2001–2, refers to it as a landmark in the history of telecom since it set in motion the decentralizing process in local governance.

The *first* step towards decentralization is achieved through the introduction of data circuits. This enables even the lowest-level worker to receive information about the functioning of the system. This leads the fragmented and loosely grouped field offices towards better coordination and integration. The data circuits were found to be so successful that their number almost doubled from 175 in 2001 to 399 in May 2002.

The *second* step towards decentralization is the introduction of the optical fibre cable connectivity network for all industries. The change as claimed by the GM of BSNL Gurgaon, provides the telephone connection almost 'on demand', or within 24 hours. This weakened the entire community of local operators surviving on the red-tapism of decision-making.

The *third* development was aimed at changing the procedural norms to bring accountability, transparency, and speed to the local offices. Earlier the data officer would pass the demand to the SDO for evaluating feasibility and here the demand note would be subjected to three to six months of long wait. Now the demand note is handled directly by the commercial officer who prepares the advice note within 24 hours and issues connections to industries.

The *fourth* development has been the creation of the 'data user forums' and the 'earmarking of officers for the account holders for industries'. Thus, each local officer of the SDO level is made responsible for a small group of industries so that problems could be taken care of on a more personalized plane.

The fifth development was the setting up of a call centre in June 2003. This call centre functioned as an online provider of information to all customers as well as prospective customers.

At the ground level these changes had a revolutionary impact upon customer services. But it also exposed the widening gap between the higher and grass root lower bureaucracy. While the upper bureaucracy as found bubbling with new initiatives in technology and competition, intra-oraganizational lower bureaucracy looked at it as if it was a conspiracy of the bosses in the big offices against the lower workers in the field. Thus, during the course of the survey, not a single lineman or JE believed that the changes could ever bring customer satisfaction because 'technology is ultimately what they create at the ground level'. Moreover till 2003, Touchtel of Bharati Infotel was the only competitor for BSNL.

The GM of BSNL Gurgaon, Sri Kant Sharma, and his team associates are blaming the 'mindset' of customers as well as the local bureaucracy that continues to plague their customer dealings. When industries and local businesses get desperate, they think of only the wrong way out and in the process make a monster of a mild devil. On his personal initiative, he had organized the 'Jan Sunvayees' and 'Telephone Adalats' in different areas every month. This has motivated the workers, SDOs, and JE to make efforts towards efficient services to consumers. This was done to prevent existing BSNL customers from switching over to private company providers. The SDO for the DLF Corporate Park said that this has been highlighted as an issue concerning the reputation of local offices which then onwards get personally involved in not allowing even a single connection pass out to the new private providers.

The last factor is about the difficult coordination among HUDA, Municipal Committee, Panchayats, and the Town Planners Office concerning the cable layout and other associated services. This actually takes a very long time, extending to a year or more. Larger decentralization has mde departments more accountable, but at the same time increased problems of coordination amongst them. Information technology has come to Gurgaon in a big way, transforming the attitudes, procedures, and functioning of the local bureaucracy reeling under the empire of inertia and corruption. This promises to coordinate faster with associated offices as attitudes change.

TRANSPORT

The roads in Gurgaon and Faridabad have been trying to survive the onslaught of increased business and density of population. Due to lack of adequate fleet, the transport department is contracting out to private companies. The two towns have also witnessed as never before the enormous rise in the per capita trip rate or an average number of trips made per person per day. This has been so not only due to the cheaper and more standard shopping and educational options available in Delhi, but also due to the increase in the disposable incomes of people living here. The trip lengths are also growing due to the physical growth of these towns. The *modal split* in favour of personalized motor vehicles is growing, together with an increased number of supply trucks from Rajasthan supplying marble, and chartered taxi and bus services for bringing employees to work. Gurgaon and Faridabad have a large and ever-growing fleet of privately run Tata Sumo, Qualis, and Tata Indica taxis. In 1999, after protests from the residents welfare associations of several HUDA sectors, these services were stopped by the DC, but on the personal intervention of the chief minister in 2001 they were allowed to serve even on roads with narrow carriageway width. The transport department could not be bothered with an issue the chief minister himself had given the green signal to. Moreover, there existed a grey area in the way these private transporters are being promoted. The highly subsidized financing for the Tata Sumo and then the Qualis has unleashed a stream of less trained and insolent drivers on narrow roads to Delhi. The police at the checkpost failed to show any registered cases against rash taxi drivers. Most booked cases were against heavy motor vehicles such as trucks or goods carriers.

In both towns transport offices were located in ill managed and unhealthy locations near the city bus stations. The staff lacked training, imagination, and creativiy. Their failure to perceive problems was due to the lack of studies on modal split or the requirement of a multi-modal transport system. Since private companies and individual entrepreneurs were entering business in a big way, contracting out is becoming an administrative norm. The congestion on roads has also a major bottleneck, and government officials have failed to strengthen Citizens' Charter on the rights and duties of citizens. Transparency of administration is required in the following areas:

1. Setting up of information booths for bus service users. The interior administration of both towns remains difficult, but it is intractable in Gurgaon. For those who have to pass through these town junctions towards projects coming up on the other side of the town, it is a nightmarish drive.
2. Planning of roads in which median cuts, intersections, and flyovers are designed to serve the needs and convenience of the developer rathan than people's safety and convenience.
3. Relationship between traffic police and transport departments. Every month several buses belonging to the recalcitrant parties are impounded at the border.

4. Management of petrol pumps. The DC is not bothered about the sprouting of a number of petrol pumps selling adulterated petrol. The community, caste bonds are so strong that the local administration also works in tandem with their brethren.

Transport officials, are already in the process of winding up to contract out to private operators but unlike the other departments where contracting out has improved services there are three major fears here:
1. Services are likely to become more expensive. This would take t.em out of the reach of poor commuter and also students.
2. The town of Gurgaon is notorious for the Yadava–Gujjar tussle. This has only increased in recent times. In seeking bus contracts with the TNCs operating in these areas, politics rules over reason and politicization becomes the norm of conducting business.
3. With transport department endowed with a regulatory role, increased competition with private operators may have to be sustained an a health system of transparent regulations.

CONCLUSIONS

An enormous amount of discontent had been surfacing amongst the entrepreneurs who were shown the golden trail to Haryana in the mid-1990s. Faridabad, Ballabgarh, Bahadurgarh, and Gurgaon, which were the trailblazers in earlier times, gradually started showing a depressing and retrogressive growth by 1999. The main reason being that the small-scale industries, which had earlier rushed to Haryana, felt deceived and cheated. With the government's complete focus upon Gurgaon, other major townships had been left to fend for themselves. The concern for infrastructure management has been completely lacking in other strategically important townships.

Faridabad's industrial estate became a virtual slum. The basic drainage and sewage lines are in an appalling state of neglect. The adjoining modern industrial estate of Bahadurgarh started showing a downward trend. Similar is the case for several other industrial estates, including Gurgaon, where most of the manufacturing units started freezing further expansion. The main grudge was the gap between high infrastructure expenses and low quality of services. The government has been collecting a fairly large amount of money from industries as EDC for providing infrastructure facilities, but despite the exhorbitant increase in EDC in 2003 and an estimated revenue collection of more than Rs 6 billion, the situation remained appalling at the ground level. In the last 20 years, HSIDC and HUDA have been able to develop only 3000 small plots as against the required number of around 15,000. In most of these industrial towns even the government has failed to contain the threatening drop in the groundwater level, which has made the subsoil water brackish. In Gurgaon, the water table dropped to a threatening 300 ft at many points which may soon create desert-like conditions in the region. This, added to the lack of sewerage or alternate drainage system in these areas, could turn it into a health hazard. The Sonepat–Gurgaon water supply channel has been insufficient and the government has shown complete ignorance of new trends such as water regenerating and water-harvesting in this desertifying industrial state. All this is equally true for both Faridabad and Gurgaon. The findings may be summarized into following points:

1. The government has focused too much on technology to the utter neglect of the changes required for transforming the grass roots bureaucracy, which are the real service providers to the people. The regime of the linemen, SDO, and junior engineers thrives and consumers who take action against them suffer persecution in various ways. This is overtly true for the large number of senior citizens, women and people who are not part of any NGO or RWA.
2. While the higher offices boast transformed regulatory systems, the service providers at the lower levels are neither affected nor interested in these new changes. Electricity goes off for days altogether with the same age-old problem of burnt transformers, fallen poles, and power thefts. Telephones still function through open boxes with a jumbled bunch of wires hanging out. One windy day and all the telephones could go off.
3. The focus of grass roots administration has been industries and residents who are politically powerful. This has raised serious issues of equity in infrastructure policies. For the local administration there are levels of priorities listed clearly for providing services on the basis of their saleability.
4. The new technological revolutions associated with TNCs have come in faster than the evolutionary pace of development on

the social front. This is a great reason for the turbulence on land.

5. Decentralization measures have cleaned up many channels for customer services, but local bureaucracy does not implement them. This decentralization process has helped the new breed of middle-class educated citizens who have the capacity to file legal complaints and reach consumer courts.

6. A new network of associations like residents' welfare associations, data user groups, industrial associations, and the Society for the Urban Regeneration of Gurgaon (SURGE) are major forces for the regeneration of the bureaucratic functioning but opaque system of governance reduces their role.

The decentralization efforts in the government do not ensure better services to the people unless they are complemented with necessary legal changes in consumer laws, that will also treat a citizen as a consumer, impose financial penalties on the departments that delay in providing services, aim at an open tribunal to deal with infrastructural problems, and implement the Citizens' Charter lying dormant in many departments. The favourite method of achieving accountability of local administration, which has been the transfer of officials, is the most insignificant and sometimes dangerous option. It does not end corruption, but ensures its endless flow. Such officials should be dealt with in open forums of industries and residents' welfare organizations. Unless the government takes infrastructure seriously, economic development will never be able to perform optimally and may also continue to stagnate. The prime challenge for sustainable governance in Gurgaon and Faridabad, as in the rest of the country today, is to sustain a higher growth within a transparent constitutional and legal framework capable of speedy delivery to investors and pro-poor services.

NOTES

1. Modal split is the proportion of trips undertaken by different modes of travel such as walk trips, vehicular trips, and intermediate public transport trips, such as rickshaws. A complementary modal split would mean a multi-modal transport system.

2. Private investment in infrastructure: The World Bank, OFCF (Japan), DFID(UK), CIDA(Canada), and USAID were expected to invest in the state. After 1998

when the initial $60 million investment for the whole of Haryana including Faridabad and Gurgaon by the USA came through for power sector reforms, there has been little progress here to feel proud about.

REFERENCES

Ades, A.F. and E.L. Glaeser, 'Trade and Circuses: Explaining Urban Giants', *Quarterly Journal of Economics*, 110(1), 1997, pp. 195–227.

Census of India (1991), Changes in the Extent of Availability of Infrastructure Facilities in Small Towns during 1971-81, Delhi: Controller of Publications, 1997.

————. *Population Indicators*, net site. Government of India, 2000.

Das, Anjana, Jyoti Parikh, Kirit S. Parikh, 'Power, the Critical Infrastructure', in Kirit S. Parekh (ed.), *India Development Report* 1999-2000, New Delhi: Oxford University Press, 2000.

Estache, Antonio (ed.), *Decentralizing Infrastructure: Advantages and Limitations,* Washington DC. World Bank, 1995.

Estasche, Antonio and Sarabjit Sinha (eds), *Does Decentralization Increase Public Spending on Public Infrastructure?* Washington, DC: World Bank, 1994.

Fukuyama, Francis, Caroline Wagner, 'Governance Challenges of Technological Revolutions', in John de la Mothe (ed.), *Science, Technology and Governance,* London, New York: Continuum, 2001.

Glen, Jack D., *Private Sector Electricity in Developing Countries: Supply and Demand,* Washington DC: World Bank, 1992.

Hirsch, S., 'The US Electronics Industry in International Trade', *National Institutional Economic Review*, 34, 1965.

Morris, Sebastian, 'Overview', in Sebastian Morris (ed.), India Infrastructure Report, *3 I Network, Infrastructure Development Finance Company, Indian Institute of Management Ahmedabad and Indian Institute of Technology Kanpur,* New Delhi: Oxford University Press, 2001

NASSCOM Mc Kinsey Study Report, 'Strategies and Implications for Indian IT Companies', http://www.nasscom.org.

Posner, M., *International Trade and Technological Change*, Oxford Economics Paper (13), 1961.

Wheaton, William C. and Hisanobu Shishido, 'Urban Concentration, Agglomeration Economics and the Level of Economic Development', *Economic Development and Cultural Change*, no. 30 (October), 1981, pp. 17–30.

15

Transparency, Accountability, and Governance
Local Government in Kerala and Karnataka[1]

■ V. Vijayalakshmi[2]

Transparency and accountability are vital factors in the effective performance of local government including both political representatives
and the bureaucracy. Conceptually there is little disagreement on the
political and administrative dimensions of accountability, and their
relation to the institutions of local government. Transparency and
accountability are expected to reduce rent-seeking in development
activities. There is, however, a wide gap between normative principles
and the actual manifestation of accountability. Political and bureaucratic
processes, hierarchical social environment, low citizens' participation,
and lack of deliberation have undermined accountability in governance.

The decentralization reforms in India, effected through the 73rd
Constitutional Amendment (1992) provided a common framework
for the panchayati raj institutions to be devised by the state governments. Issues pertaining to transparency and accountability have been
left to the discretion of the respective state governments. Measures to
ensure the accountability of public officials, therefore, varied across
different states. Kerala for instance has instituted participatory planning
and budgeting, which may be considered as contributing towards
accountability. On the other hand, Karnataka, which had the earlier
advantage of having established decentralization reforms in the 1980s,
even before the Constitutional Amendment, had not taken specific
measures to enhance accountability, other than the minimal requirements through the gram sabhas. This chapter examines the factors that
determine accountability in the institutions of local government in
Kerala and Karnataka.

Conceptually, there is little disagreement on the political dimensions
of accountability in local government. The representatives have clearly
defined functions and duties to perform. They have a tenure of five
years to represent the interests of their constituencies and to be

instrumental in the planning of developmental activities. Under these circumstances, a non-performing representative is as culpable of not carrying out the duties and functions of a representative as another who may be actively engaged in rent-seeking activities. Transparency and accountability are expected to reduce less desirable activities such as rent-seeking. There is, however, a wide gap between normative principles and the actual manifestation of accountability. Clearly, there is every reason to assume that representatives are not inherently predisposed towards being answerable for their actions during their tenure. Thus, including the principle of accountability within the functions of representatives is to ensure that they act in a manner that is above reproach. However, while accountability could be seen as an essential component of the role of a representative, this function cannot be taken for granted. Specific institutions have to be created to ensure the accountability of representatives. As there are conditions that hinder accountability, or variations that are clearly evident from place to place due to social and political situations, it is necessary to take account of local existential realities. Institutions that facilitate accountability include the scrutiny of political parties (in opposition), citizens' forums, the media, regular elections, as well as specific institutions created to enhance accountability such as ombudsman, audits of various kinds, and the gram sabhas. The judiciary is also a system that is expected to ensure that individuals function with probity and within the limits of the law. In this sense, it affects the functioning of representatives (or is intended to) and answerable for their actions.

While accountability is expected from the representatives as well as the bureaucracy, in this paper we are particularly concerned with political accountability, that is, accountability of the representatives. Accountability implies that the representatives are to communicate to the electorate the activities that they have carried out in their capacity as representatives, and also that they are answerable for these actions. This accounting involves not only electoral accountability, where the citizens can vote out their representatives or the party they belong to, but also legal, institutional and procedural features to enforce accountability (Shiviah 1994). The chapter examines the measures of accountability and their effectiveness in local government in two states, namely, Kerala and Karnataka. The analysis is based on data collected in two districts in Karnataka (Mandya and Udupi) and Kollam district in Kerala. Both these states, to varying degrees, have instituted legal, regulatory, and participatory measures through which the accountability of the representatives in local government can be enhanced. The effectiveness of these measures is discussed, as well as the political and social processes that hinder or reduce the effectiveness of the institutions of accountability. Finally, the implications these have for the quality of representation, the legitimate role of the bureaucracy, and rent-seeking are also discussed.

POLITICAL DETERMINANTS OF ACCOUNTABILITY

Accountability entails the process of carrying out the representatives' assigned mandate, and the willingness to face the consequences of their official actions, which would be published through acts of periodic reporting (see Inbanathan 2001; Helgason 1997; Polidano and Hulme 1997). The process through which accountability gets established is, however, an empirical question, which is reflected in various forms (on different forms of accountability, see Blair 2000). The notion of accountability has two interrelated dimensions—direction and essence. The former implies that there is an agent who exercises control through sanctions and the latter refers to the method through which the relationship is established. In a democracy, representatives are accountable to the citizens and one of the means of accountability is elections, where the electorate can exercise its power and decide whether to retain the representatives in office or replace them with others (on electoral accountability see Ferejohn 1999; Prewitt 1970). Where electoral accountability is more or less the only means by which the electorate can directly influence the course of democratic represent-ation, the responsiveness to the voters is higher if the political party ensures accountability, or the representatives have the intention of contesting and winning the next elections through voters' approval of their record in office. The electorate normally has little opportunity to indicate its views about governance between elections.

Electoral accountability in the context of local government in these two states has severe limitations mainly because the reservation of seats often prevents the re-election of candidates to a second term (see Inbanathan 1999, 2000; Vijayalakshmi and Chandrashekar 2002).[3] Also, electoral accountability alone does not take into consideration the reaction of the constituents to specific issues. Under the circum-stances, to what extent would there be any accountability if the possibility of re-election is low? While carrying out certain actions may be considered objectionable (if they were corrupt acts, for example, in which case legal provisions can come into force), there is virtually no provision for the voter to take action against a representative who is not doing anything at all that is, who is completely non-functional. In a state such as Madhya Pradesh, the right to recall has been brought into existence, though how it functions in practice is not clear. There is, however, the recognition (in Madhya Pradesh) that the voter need not wait for five years to replace an elected official who is not an effective representative.

Notwithstanding the principles related to accountability, it is not likely that representatives would accept their failures or any contention that they have abused their official position and public resources. If one of the yardsticks of their performance is the fulfilment of the expectations of the electorate, ascertaining the effectiveness of the representatives is problematic since there is no indication that communication between the electorate and the representatives is sufficiently well-established. While the expectations and demands of the citizens who voted the representatives to power are not binding (Manin *et al.* 1999), accountability cannot be seen entirely in isolation from representation of peoples' interests. Accountability and respons-iveness have overlapping areas of 'obligation' to the electorate (Shiviah 1994), which may not always have a bearing on effectiveness. It is important, therefore, that the representatives explain their actions (questions of how and why) and do not assume that pointing out the output alone is sufficient 'accountability'.

There is also the question of whether the assertions of the represent-atives can be fully accepted or supported by physical evidence. How should the effectiveness of the representatives be assessed? The actual accountability to the citizens depends primarily on the output that is visible, and the availability of adequate information. However, since output alone is not indicative of the effective utilization of public funds, the citizens should have more information. Transparency in governance facilitates citizens' comprehension of the functioning of representatives.

In local government where the re-election of individual represent-atives is limited, political parties, both those in power and opposition, have a more enduring presence in the polity. It is, therefore, in the interest of the political parties that representatives who are party candidates play a more effective role in governance and representation. While the ruling political party would like to hide its wrongdoings, the opposition would want to emphasize them to gain political advantage. In both Kerala and Karnataka there was more than one political party at the local level, and their influence in local government largely depended on the number of seats each occupied in the panchayats. The composition of the party has a significant influence in local government, that is, intervention would be high if there is less difference in numerical strength between the ruling and the opposition parties.

The impact of de facto politics (non-representatives taking over the functions of representatives, who now remain only as nominal representatives), and elite dominance of the political space, reduce representatives' accountability. In institutions of local government, often individuals not elected to panchayats are involved in carrying out or influencing panchayat activities, for political gains, and/or commissions. Elected representatives get caught between the social and political imperatives, of the elite and party-centred politics.

A crucial factor in the process of accountability is citizens' involvement in governance. The implication here is the 'demand factor' that the citizens are aware of what is legitimately due to them from the elected representatives and the officials. It entails not only communicating their preferences to the representatives but also being informed about the management of public funds and the outcomes of panchayat decisions on development works. The important distinction here is between fulfilling the interests of the constituents, which is an important facet of representation, and of being 'responsive' (see Philips 1995; Pitkin 1967),[4] and answerable to them. In being responsive, the development programmes have to be more oriented to citizens' needs, and avenues such as gram sabhas need to be effective for the constituents to articulate their preferences and indicate their views on issues concerning local governance.

There is, however, a political dimension to responsiveness, *ex ante* accountability as referred by Moncrieffe (2001: 27).[5] Responsiveness is not to be seen in abstraction but is related to representation. Being responsive involves representing the interests of the constituents, and acting towards improving the welfare of the citizens. Since interests are not identical, it is not an easy task to decide which section of interests should be represented. In a minimalist perspective of democracy, the representatives can use their own discretion and decide what is best for the country or constituency (in Przeworski *et al.* 1999; Manin 1997; Schumpeter 1942; Burke 1774).[6] While such a perspective is not acceptable in participatory democracy, representatives can be accountable even without being responsive and vice versa.

Considering the avowed participatory nature of local governance, accountability and responsiveness are seen here as related, obverse sides of the same coin as it were. Understanding the factors that contribute to or constrain such a process is important to our understanding of accountability itself.

ACCOUNTABILITY: KERALA AND KARNATAKA

Measures of accountability in Kerala and Karnataka can be broadly classified as legal (legal framework where the direction of accountability is clearly specified) and regulatory (accounts audit, performance audit, ombudsman, vigilance and technical committees); and participatory measures (gram sabhas, beneficiary committee, development seminars). Of these measures, convening gram sabhas is mandatory under the 73rd Constitutional Amendment, and to be followed by all the states. Measures to promote transparency such as right to information, publishing information on the finances of the panchayats, and display of information at the work site of the project being implemented are intended to enhance accountability.

Gram sabhas and accounts audits are found in both Kerala and Karnataka. The two states have incorporated elements of citizens' audit, in the gram sabhas in Kerala and *jamabandhi* in Karnataka. Kerala's interest in transparency and accountability can be traced to the vision document on decentralization of power in the state (Sen Committee's recommendations). Measures to enhance transparency and accountability were instituted within the functioning of the panchayati raj institutions. The people's campaign on decentralization, which worked closely with Kerala Shastra Sahithya Parishad (KSSP), a state-wide movement on popularizing science, oriented the people to various provisions of the Panchayati Raj Act. Although Karnataka had brought in several innovative measures through the 1983 Panchayati Raj Act, the efforts to enable transparent, accountable, and participatory governance were not sustained over a period of time. When the 1983 Act was framed, the concept of accountability was not discerned in the present manner. Hence, gram sabhas were considered adequate for accountability in the panchayats. While comparing Kerala and Karnataka, it may be pointed out that Karnataka's efforts have made greater changes in the political sphere and less in the administrative and fiscal areas. Kerala has made substantial efforts towards fiscal decentralization in addition to political decentralization.[7]

Kerala

Kerala has incorporated several participatory measures. The Kerala Panchayati Raj Act has provisions for the participation of citizens in planning and made it a requirement that the reasons in support of a decision should be evident, with sufficient information made available to the public. This was furthered by the Sen Committee's recommend-ations, following which amendments were made in the year 2000 to the Kerala Panchayati Raj Act. One of the recommendations was to increase the participation of the people in the decision-making process and minimize the role of the bureaucracy in the implementation of development programmes. Creation of new structures of accountability and transparency, such as scrutiny through a beneficiary committee were intended to facilitate a greater role of citizens in governance and enhance the answerability of the representatives. The institution of ombudsman made it possible for citizens to file petitions on any irregularities in the planning and implementation of the development programmes. The relatively high awareness among the people of the various measures of accountability can be attributed to the efforts of the Left Democratic Front (LDF) government, which carried out an intensive campaign to disseminate information on the new panchayati raj system.

Performance audits are intended to be independent of government control and have their own standards.[8] Despite this, the audit was conducted by state government officials, thereby reducing the scope for independent functioning. The performance audit is meant to be a corrective mechanism, and the panchayat officials were of the view that it was more of a facilitating exercise. In its actual working, the report that is produced is not a public document, although elected representatives have access to it. Despite the emphasis on transparency, information on official performance continues to be a closed area.

The institution of ombudsman, when first introduced by Kerala, comprised seven members, including a high court judge, two district judges, two secretaries to government (all retired officials), and two eminent public citizens nominated in consultation with the leader of the opposition party.[9] The ombudsman takes action on the complaints made by the citizens, and this essentially works as a redressal mechanism. It is also empowered to order corrective measures. One of the problems with the institution of ombudsman was that it was overloaded with complaints on the beneficiary selection, and technical aspects of projects undertaken by the panchayats. In the year 2001, out of the 3244 complaints received by the ombudsmen, only 799 (34 per cent) were settled. The redressal time was too long to have any positive impact on the issue at hand. Even complaints about misappropriation of funds and corruption charges were looked into after protracted delays, long after the project was completed and the bills cleared. The composition of the institution of ombudsman was reduced from seven to one by the United Democratic Front (UDF) government (after it was elected in the year 2001), further reducing its effectiveness. Where petitions were filed with the ombudsman and technical committee, alleging misappropriation of funds and poor quality of work, they were not pursued by the petitioners. When the delay in examining petitions resulted in the work being completed, the petitioners did not consider it worthwhile to pursue the matter. Besides this, appellate tribunals constituted at the district level are to receive appeals from the citizens against decisions made by the local government. The tribunal is meant to act as a redressal cell on complaints related to the issue of licence and permits.

The other important measure was the formation of beneficiary committees to implement public works. According to the Act, after the plan document is approved, gram sabhas/ward committees should be convened to discuss the project to be implemented. A committee of seven to 15 person and a chairperson is to be constituted by the gram sabhas. The beneficiary committee enters into an agreement with the gram panchayat, and is paid the expenses of the project in instalments with a periodic review by the expert committee. Implementation through beneficiary committees is intended to minimize the role of contractors and middlemen in carrying out public works, and enable speedy completion of the work that is undertaken.

While the idea is well conceived, the extent to which it succeeds in containing corruption largely depends on the nature of the formation of these committees and their effectiveness. In the eight gram panchayats that we studied, the beneficiary committees existed only on paper for the purpose of official records. The individuals listed as members did not take any interest in the actual implementation of the public works.

The formation of beneficiary committees was not uniformly based on formal rules and procedures. Some were formed without any consultation in the gram sabhas/ward committees (as we observed in two gram panchayats). Beneficiary committees that existed only for official records were found in five out of the eight gram panchayats studied, and the citizens were aware of it. The citizens also considered it a formality in carrying out the development work and were not concerned with the composition of the committee. Although the main aim of the beneficiary committees was to minimize the role of the contractor, it was found that the public works, in most cases, were awarded to contractors. The representatives were of the opinion that it was not possible for the beneficiary committee members to take time off to fulfil the administrative procedures, and get clearance from the technical committee. The beneficiary committee in some panchayats has become a cover for the engineer, contractor, official and elected members nexus in the implementation of the development work.

While there existed problems in the participatory implementation of development activities, there are no measures taken to strengthen the beneficiary committees. On the other hand, the UDF government, which is in power in the state, reduced the limit for the development work to be implemented through contractors to Rs 25,000 which during the Peoples' Campaign did not have any such limit. Community participation is minimized with the new regulation, which has specifications for even the development work which costs Rs 25,000. The community can only be involved if 70 per cent of this is mud work.

For greater transparency in decision-making in governance, several measures were institutionalized. All the plan documents, papers related to prioritization of beneficiaries, bills and vouchers of public expenditure are open to public scrutiny and/or reference. While it is also mandatory that the statement of expenses and other important details of public works be displayed at the site in Malayalam (the local language), it was not successful as a source of information. Often it was only displayed for a day to fulfil the requirement, and was later removed. We did not encounter cases where members of the public objected to lapses in transparency.

One of the measures taken to reduce corruption in development work is by vesting gram sabhas (also considered as a mechanism of 'social audit') with multiple responsibilities of providing forums for accountability, monitoring the performance of the beneficiary committees, deciding the norms and criteria for beneficiary selection, and identifying the needs of the local people.[10] The gram sabhas were not effective as a forum of accountability or in exposing and reducing corruption.

While there is scope for direct participation of the citizens through gram sabhas convened four times in a year, the question is whether the people made use of this forum to demand more effective governance. In all the panchayats, attendance in the gram sabhas was below the required quorum (which is 10 per cent of the adult population). There was, however, a higher proportion of women who attended the gram sabhas. One of the reasons for this was that women who were members of self-help and micro-credit groups promoted by the panchayat were asked to attend the gram sabhas by the panchayat representatives, to fulfil the requirement of quorum, but they still did not meet the 10 per cent figure.

For greater accountability and transparency in beneficiary selection, the panchayats in Kerala developed a format of giving points to the various applicants based on certain criteria. A local committee comprising the president, the ward member, and selected members of the public scrutinized the applications. The beneficiary list with the scores obtained by each applicant was to be read out in the gram sabhas. The final list of beneficiaries should be displayed in the gram panchayat for a minimum of 15 days. If the criteria of awarding points were not adhered to, the applicants for the beneficiary scheme can register their protest in the gram panchayat office. Opinion on the scoring scheme being followed was mixed. Despite the elaborate procedure of giving scores, it was not uncommon for applicants to submit fictitious medical reports, to score more points. Also, there were instances where the list presented in the gram sabhas was later altered in the gram panchayat. There were a number of complaints about the beneficiary selection, indicating greater public awareness of the various schemes, and protests against the politics of patronage.

The panchayats have also set aside 1 per cent (mandatory) of the total allocation of funds for disseminating information on income and expenditure. This includes publicizing the proposed plan of action by distributing copies of it to all members of the village one week before the gram sabhas. Similarly, the statement of expenditure of the gram panchayat is to be printed and made available to the constituents who are interested in such information. While the statement of expenses was available in all panchayats, the agenda for action was not circulated a week in advance of the gram sabha meeting.

KARNATAKA

One of the problems in the case of Karnataka is that accountability and transparency did not get adequate emphasis in the Karnataka Panchayati Raj Acts, or the subsequent amendments. The gram sabhas, which were constituted in the 1983 Act and even before the 73rd Constitutional Amendment, were intended to be a forum where accountability could be manifested. When the 1983 Act was formulated, the concept of gram sabhas was well ahead of what then existed. It was expected to function quite effectively in transparency, account-ability, and, most importantly, participation. Subsequent years have shown that gram sabhas have not served this purpose.

The two important measures of accountability adopted by Karnataka are gram sabhas, and jamabandhi (in existence since 2001). Gram sabhas were envisaged as deliberative forums where the constituents meet and indicate their preferences and needs on development activities. They were also to assess the performance of the representatives and the activities of the panchayats. They are the only formal channel for people to communicate with elected members and officials. Earlier it was mandatory that the gram sabha meetings be convened at least twice a year, but this has been increased to four times a year in every village, and jamabandhi to be conducted once in a year.

As in Kerala, the gram sabhas in Karnataka too were associated with government programmes and were attended mostly by those who were prospective beneficiaries in the programmes. People's participation in planning of the development programmes of the panchayats was low. While there were exceptions in some parts of Karnataka (for example, Dakshina Kannada, Udupi), in most other places, the gram sabhas were a mere formality where those who attended were either reduced to being spectators or were consumers of the beneficiary programmes. Although it is required that the gram sabha meeting be convened in every village, the venue was usually the panchayat headquarters. Grama sabhas, thus, failed to be a deliberative forum and a channel of communication between the representatives and the constituents, and far from being an effective means of accountability. Except for the members of the gram panchayat who attended the gram sabha meetings in their village, the representatives of the upper tiers did not attend the gram sabha meetings.

Jamabandhis were introduced in the year 2001 and are an assessment of the functioning of the gram panchayat by the electorate. While they are meant to enhance the accessibility of citizens to information, the objective was not achieved in the panchayats we studied, as the citizens were not aware of the programme. Conducted once a year, and for just one day between 15 August and 15 September, the method of public audit of the gram panchayat financial records has several limitations. The jamabandhi is conducted by the officials at the taluk level, and the executive officer has the responsibility for preparing the report of the public audit. Citizens were informed about the contents of the public audit report as there is no provision for public discussion, for example in gram sabhas (see Sivanna and Babu 2002).

In Karnataka, it was mostly the informal channels of communication between the representatives and constituents that were in operation, and no measures have been institutionalized for transparency in the utilization of public funds. The Karnataka Right to Information Act, 2000 enacted by the state leaves much to be desired in its effectiveness. While the citizens may in principle have the right to information, various provisions in the Act restrict the process of acquisition of information. For example, the citizens are expected to specify the purpose for which the information from the government is sought.[11] The time taken to provide it is often too long. The form in which the data is given is not complete and difficult to comprehend because of inconsistency in presentation.

FACTORS AFFECTING TRANSPARENCY
AND ACCOUNTABILITY

We examined factors that affected the level of accountability in panchayats. While comparing Kerala and Karnataka, it is important to note that they have different levels of financial devolution. While this in itself is not a decisive criterion for greater or lesser accountability, it influenced the perception of representatives and citizens on the activities of the panchayats. The explanatory factors in accountability are presented in Table 15.1. Accountability level was the dependent variable (the accountability score was arrived at using indicators on measures of accountability and their effectiveness). The independent variables that were used include civil society participation (both citizens and representatives), participation in the political party, transparency measures, participation of the citizens in gram sabhas, gender, de facto politics, political orientation of the citizens, different tiers of the local government, and the composition of ruling and opposition parties. Dummy 1 was given to Kerala where 40 per cent of the funds are devolved to panchayats and the measures of accountability are institutionalized. The $R2$ was 0.947, indicating a high correlation (see Table 15.1).

The institutional measures acted as a catalyst in accountability. There was a significant relationship between the institutional measures and representatives' accountability in governance. In Kerala, the various measures of accountability, and the wide promotion during peoples' planning campaign about them have created an environment where citizens are aware of these issues.

In both the states, the measures to enhance accountability have been introduced at the level of gram panchayats, without adequate focus on the upper tiers. In Karnataka, there are no participatory measures involving the representatives of the district and taluk panchayats, and our studies have shown that the representatives of the upper tiers hardly attended the gram sabha meetings. Although not a common pattern in Karnataka, public forums comprising the representatives and the citizens were formed in Udupi and Dakshina Kannada districts at the taluk and district levels, to deliberate on issues related to development and governance. *Janasamparka sabhas* were convened by MLAs about once a year, and attended by local people, panchayat representatives, and officials, to discuss local problems.

Political orientation among the citizens contributed to the demand for accountability. In both the states, there was a high correlation between the interest shown by the constituents (in matters related to political parties, campaigning, attending political meetings, demonstrations, interaction with the representatives and officials, and filing petitions or writing letters of protest), and their perception of accountability. Political activity generates more interaction in the public domain acting as a channel of accountability. Engagement in political activity was low among citizens in Karnataka (the exception being coastal Karnataka), as compared to Kerala. A related factor in the greater political activity in Kerala, which we have also seen in coastal Karnataka, was the active media, and publicity of the activities of the panchayats in newspapers at the local level.

The political activity of the citizens not only fulfilled a part of the requirement of accountability through interaction with elected representatives, but also enhanced citizens' information about the funds available to the panchayats. In Karnataka, the low levels of political activity and the absence of transparency measures limited people's awareness of the panchayat activities and the funds they received. The correlation between information level about the activities of the panchayat (including the funds received) and accountability was 0.739 in Kerala, which is significant at 0.01 level; and −0.678 in Karnataka, significant at 0.01 level.

There was no significant relationship between civil society participation and accountability in governance (see Table 15.1). Although civil society participation scores of the representatives and the constituents in Kerala were much higher compared with those in Karnataka, it did not contribute to the level of accountability. When participation in political parties was considered independently of other kinds of associational activity, it was significantly related to accountability.

While associational activity did not significantly influence accountability (see Table 15.1), our analysis indicates that it enhanced the inform-ation level of the people. In Kerala and Karnataka, the correlation between associational activity and citizens' information level was 0.691 and −0.572 respectively which was significant at 0.01 level. The dif-ference in the information level of the citizens of Karnataka and Kerala can be largely explained by the variation in civil society participation.

TABLE 15.1: MULTIPLE REGRESSION ANALYSIS
OF ACCOUNTABILITY

	Un-standardized coefficients B	t
(Constant)	0.238	0.231
Transparency measures	0.934	33.484 ★
Representatives' participation in civil society	3.27E-03	0.135
Participation in gram sabhas	-9.01E-02	-1.417
Information level of the citizens	5.25E-02	2.286 ★★
Citizens participation in civil society associations	4.66E-02	1.148
Political orientation of the citizens	8.75E-02	2.139 ★★
Taluk/block panchayat	-0.679	-2.636 ★
Zilla/district panchayat	-1.142	-3.856 ★
De facto politics	-1.713	-3.856 ★
Composition of the ruling and opposition parties	1.139	2.664 ★★★
State-Karnataka	-0.815	-3.445 ★

R2 0.947
Dependent variable: Accountability level
Number of observations: 380

Note: ★ Significant at 1 %
    ★★ Significant at 5 %
    ★★★ Significant at 10 %.

The numerical strength of the opposition party or parties at all levels affected accountability in the panchayats. Panchayats where a majority of the members belonged to a single party and those where the margin of strength between the parties in the panchayat was less were examined. In the latter case where no single party had adequate numbers, there was more pressure on the representatives not only from other representatives but also from constituents of a different party background. In both the states, in those panchayats where the numbers of the opposition and the ruling party were close, there was greater accountability, compared with the panchayats where a single party was dominant. The findings point out that the practice of accountability and transparency was better in panchayats where the parties were of almost equal strength. In Karnataka, this was more evident in the case of district and taluk panchayats than at the village panchayats (where elite dominance was greater than the political party influence). Those panchayats where the two major parties Janata Dal (Secular) (United) alliance and Congress (I) had an almost equal number of seats, the one in opposition kept a closer watch on the functioning of the panchayat and the observance of procedures. In Karnataka, although there were consultations at panchayat meetings on how the funds are to be spent, the implementation of programmes was not transparent.

Corruption was widely prevalent in panchayats, which is another indicator of low level of accountability. In Karnataka, the representatives did not consider it wrong to accept commissions or *percentages* (as it was also referred to). There was also an opinion among the elected representatives that commissions paid were not bribes.[12] The expenses incurred during elections were given as one of the reasons for accepting commissions. There was a variation in the election expenses across the three tiers, and the representatives stated that they had to spend their personal funds on election expenses. In addition, the representatives elected to executive positions had to spend money to get the support of the panchayat members. The higher the election expenses, the greater was the tendency to accept bribes and commissions, and to maintain secrecy. The election expenses of the representatives were higher in Mandya district than in either Udupi (in Karnataka) or Kollam (in Kerala). Also, representatives considered elective positions as an opportunity to make money to further their political interests and a source of income. While kickbacks were paid in the implement-ation of panchayat works in Kollam district in Kerala and Udupi district in Karnataka, the members at least did not justify it.

While accountability is entailed in elective positions, the social and political processes constrain its manifestation. The following sections discuss clientelism and politics of patronage, which affect the way representatives perceive accountability.

CLIENTELISM AND ACCOUNTABILITY

Accountability among the representatives was weak, although it was not at the same level in Kerala and Karnataka. While patronage relations contributed towards limiting accountability in local institutions in both the states, in Karnataka (for detailed discussion, see Inbanathan 2001) it was further aggravated by lack of transparency and low levels of information. The representatives did not consider accountability a crucial aspect of representation. In Karnataka, the perception of accountability was such that they considered themselves accountable to their families (particularly among women) and patrons, while constituents rarely figured in their reckoning. For most women there were constraints in their interaction with the constituents and officials since male family members and patrons were involved in the actual functioning of the panchayats, rather than the women representatives. The justification was that their family spent money during elections and played a supportive role, and similarly the patrons and/or party gave them the opportunity to enter the panchayats and hence, they should be accountable to them. In Kerala, however, the representatives were considered accountable to the constituents, although the manifestation of accountability varied. Among the Left party representatives, accountability was to the party and its supporters while the representatives belonging to UDF (particularly the Congress [I]) did not demonstrate any overt accountability to the party. In neither case was there noticeable accountability to the people, notwithstanding the claims of representatives.

In both the states, the representatives (including both men and women) were drawn into the practice of commissions in panchayats earlier in their career as panchayat representatives than into other responsibilities, or development of their skills. Part of the reason for this was the entrenched corruption network comprising officials and contractors. While the institutional structure is clear about the accountability of elected representatives to the people, and of the officials to the representatives, reality does not always correspond to this principle. The inexperience of the representatives, their lack of awareness of the rules and procedures, and the paucity of information on development activities contributed to a dependence on the officials. This largely reduced the accountability of officials to the elected representatives. Although it cannot be justified, the officials were of the view that their accountability to the elected representatives was low because of the poor administrative capability of the latter. Such a view cannot be generalized as the representatives in the taluk and district panchayats in Karnataka had relatively high levels of administrative and political skills, which had a bearing on the representatives' accountability in the utilization of public funds.

Representatives at all levels of local government either received commissions themselves or indicated others who received commissions. There was a difference in the magnitude of corruption between the gram panchayats in Kerala and those of Karnataka. It was not anything to do with the level of accountability but more related to the funds devolved to the lower tier of panchayats in these two states. In gram panchayats in Karnataka, only a few members were recipients of commissions as the possibility of commissions being offered itself was limited. Representatives in executive positions (president) admitted to receiving commissions, while the ordinary members did not receive monetary benefits. In the upper tiers of panchayats in Karnataka, the incidence of accepting commissions was high. The elected members gave an account of the money they received, or more often about what other representatives received for awarding contracts, and as commissions from panchayat programmes. Out of 67 taluk panchayat representatives 32 admitted that they received commissions. In the zilla panchayat, 27 representatives (out of 47) admitted to having received money while carrying out their duties in elective positions. In Kerala, the representatives were not willing to admit having received commissions, although they indicated that commissions were part of the implementation of panchayats' programmes.

In Karnataka, the 'commission culture' was so pervasive in the panchayats that the representatives did not even regard it as corruption. Representatives in all the tiers of the panchayats justified accepting money. Accepting commissions was not considered as inappropriate since they spent money from their private funds during elections. For 32 per cent of the representatives, the money they spent in securing positions in the panchayats was for the pay-offs involved. Lack of transparency in how the money was spent still continues, even in the panchayats of Kerala, as the emphasis in accountability is on the outcome, rather than on questions of how and why such expenses were incurred.

ELITES

There was a close relationship between elite dominance and account-ability in the panchayats of Karnataka. The political network showed a central core of elites perceived as influential in the political and local community affairs. There were distinct segments of power with members of elites (which included panchayat members as well as those who were not panchayat representatives) at the centre, followed immediately by the bureaucracy, and at the periphery there were representatives other than those in the inner circle. The elites were from locally dominant caste groups who occupied leadership roles (such as community elders), belonged to prominent political families of the area, and had access to and control over various structural resources. They had a political base and occupied important party positions, were members of civil society associations, and had contacts with prominent politicians, MLAs and MPs. By virtue of their social, economic, and political positions, these individuals wielded considerable power. The elites at each level of panchayats had more than one of these characteristics.

While elite dominance of panchayats was common in all the tiers, there was a difference in the perception of who among the elites influenced the functioning of the panchayats at different levels. At the gram panchayat, the elites were individuals who were community elders and were often from the land-owning group. Some of them (30 per cent) were also prominent party functionaries. The social, political, and economic power enabled the elites to influence the functioning of panchayats whether or not they were representatives. They played a significant role in selection of candidates, mobilizing support for them during elections, and in keeping the election competition under their control.[13]

In some cases, when members of the elites were not eligible to contest because of the reservation of seats, they ensured that their supporters, or women from their own families were elected. The vote in such cases was for one of the elites who could swing the votes in favour of the candidate. The elites supported several candidates in the gram panchayats, as their political reputation in local politics depended on the number of representatives who were elected through their support. In gram panchayats where a significant percentage of the representatives was elected unopposed, the local elites played a prominent role in choosing the representatives. The consensus arrived at was between the local elites, who selected the candidates, and was not the popular choice of the local people. Although in principle, people had the right to contest, it was not feasible to oppose the powerful elites. In taluk and zilla panchayats, women's selection as candidates was related to the identity of their patron and the political and economic standing of their families. Power was concentrated with the elites and not automatically derived from the elective positions.

There is a close link between elites and the patronage system. Despite reservation of seats for various sections of the population, the control over panchayats and local politics by the elites continued and the patronage system has taken new forms. The elites who were in politics influenced the panchayats through the members they were instrumental in getting elected. Although, in principle, the individual who occupies the elective position is answerable, the representatives often found themselves in situations where they were not party to the decisions taken. Hence, they were not the decision-making authorities, and the actual decision makers were not elected representatives, and therefore not accountable.

LEFT DEMOCRATIC FRONT (LDF)— PARTY CENTRALIZATION IN KERALA

One of the paradoxes of decentralization in Kerala is the party centralism in the functioning of the panchayats where the LDF was in a majority. This was in contrast to the greater autonomy in the functioning of the Congress (I) and other United Democratic Front (UDF) allies. While the LDF government played a vital role in furthering decentralization in the state, the strong influence of the Front in the functioning of the panchayats continues (even though the state has now a UDF government). The LDF made important decisions of the panchayats. The gram panchayat representatives often did not have the choice to decide within the panchayat forums on issues such as beneficiary selection, awarding contracts, and other development work. Although it is not uncommon for political parties to take decisions regarding the candidates for executive positions, and suggest names for the committees (standing committee, sectoral committees, and the chairpersons of these committees), the role of the Left parties was far more than a facilitating one. The CPI(M) and CPI have well-spread party organizational networks extending to the village. The Left parties held weekly meetings to monitor the functioning of the panchayats. All the representatives of the LDF were expected to attend these meetings and report on the happenings in the panchayats.

One of our observations was the selection of inexperienced women representatives to committees such as public works and finance, when there were other representatives with more experience in public office. Since it was decided in the party forum, there was less overt opposition to these nominations. The party functionaries, however, considered it easy to control the functioning of the panchayats by having weak candidates in strategic positions. This is similar to the elite domination of panchayats that we found in Karnataka.

The stronghold of the Left parties in the functioning of panchayats in which their parties were in a majority has mixed consequences for transparency and accountability in governance. Accountability of the representatives was more towards the party.[14] While it can be argued that the party is an important factor in public accountability, there were some less desirable consequences. Since the support margins were close in Kerala, the political parties used the panchayats to keep their vote banks intact and this took the form of patronage politics. While patronage was also a factor in the Congress (I) party, the LDF was more centralized in decision-making. Although the representatives were emphatic that they did not bring party politics into local governance, the bias towards their party supporters was evident in their functioning as representatives.[15] While political parties can play a facilitating role in ensuring that institutions of accountability are effective, it can also become a hindrance if they have an overbearing presence in the functioning of the panchayats. There was a strong perception among the constituents, not supporters of the Left party, that the Left parties were more biased towards their own supporters. Such a perception of the party being biased was more prevalent in the Left-dominated panchayats than among the Left supporters in the UDF panchayats. Although the representatives belonging to the Left parties did not like the control of the party, there was no open dissent and they usually accepted the party dictum quite voluntarily.

CONCLUSION

Lack of transparency and accountability is among the many interrelated problems in the panchayats of Karnataka and Kerala. While measures enhancing accountability are valuable, it is not simple to determine the efficiency of the panchayats from these parameters alone. The practices leading to effective governance, as we have seen in the case of Kerala, have the potential to bring citizens into direct interaction with the local government. Also the process of decision-making in government is more open to public scrutiny. However, accountability or lack of it in governance is not an isolated problem, but endogenous to the social and political process. An understanding of the social and political structures that sustain rent seeking in local governance may be useful for strengthening accountability practices.

There are multiple challenges to accountability in local government. Despite political decentralization, there is limited administrative decentralization often leading to an overwhelming presence of the bureaucracy in local governance. The role of bureaucracy and elected members is an integrated one involving planning and implementation. The bureaucracy plays an advisory role in planning, and has a major role in the implementation of development works. The representatives have a crucial role in planning, but only a supervisory role in implementation. In practice, the lack of experience of the representatives and limited channels of information has led to an excessive dependence of the representatives on the officials. This dependence also leads to a nexus between officials and representatives in rent-seeking.

Prior to the reservation of seats, the elites dominated elective positions, and voting was only one of the ways to legitimize their ruling position. When wider representation is enabled through the reservation of seats in positions of governance, there are two entities with differences in power and resource bases affecting the political process. A substantial number of individuals belonging to disadvantaged groups are elected to positions of decision-making in governance, but do not have power; and elites who are powerful because of their social and economic position, even if they were not elected representatives influenced governance. The commitment to effectiveness and responsiveness is often undermined when the same individual does not hold authority and power. In local governance, electoral values attached to responsiveness and patronage (either to individuals or the party) are far greater than the value attached to accountability.

Accountability was undermined when elites not elected to local institutions played an important or sometimes even decisive role in the functioning of the panchayats. Accountability and responsiveness thus get associated with different entities, that is, the representatives and elites or the representatives and the party. The elites and party influence the representatives into being responsive to their (that is, elites/party) expectations of what the constituents wanted, that would give them political advantage. Accountability is diluted when there are conflicting factions restraining the functioning of the representatives. Populist politics and claims for credit for getting work done frequently clashed and became constraints to accountability. Thus, the need to have a central position for the ordinary members of the constituency lost out to the greater prominence given to other individuals and social entities. This is where the institutions of local governance showed a decided weakness. Far from being responsive and accountable to the voters, these attributes were either completely absent or were corrupted to an extent that their real significance in local governance was very weak.

NOTES

1. This paper written in 2002 was based on two studies— 'Democratic Decentralization in Karnataka', and 'Decentralized Governance, Representation and People's Participation in Kerala', both financially supported by Ford Foundation.

   The paper was presented at a workshop on Local Governance organized by the Centre for Study of Law and Governance (CSLG), Jawaharlal Nehru University, New Delhi, in the year 2002. Some of these issues were also discussed at the George Washington University, Washington DC. I am grateful for the comments of participants at both these places. I am also grateful to Anand Inbanathan for suggestions and comments on earlier drafts.

2. V. Vijayalakshmi, Consultant Sociologist based in Bangalore, India.

3. The reservation of seats brings into the election process candidates who are contesting panchayat posts for the first time, and who are not likely to contest again as in the next election their constituency may be reserved for a group to which they do not belong.

4. The dimension of representation is the expectation from the representatives and 'responsiveness' of those in government.

5. Moncrieffe refers to responsiveness as 'ex post accountability'.

6. Burke asserted that representatives should use their discretion and judgement, rather than always doing what their electorate told them to do (Edmund Burke, 1774 'Speech to the Electorate of Bristol'). Schumpeter went even further and suggested that the electorate may not have the capacity to make rational judgments in governance, and hence, other than voting in their representatives, they (the people) had nothing else to do.

7. Transfer of power in these three areas—political, administration, and financial —is considered essential for effective decentralization (see Manor 1999).

The limitations of Karnataka's decentralization efforts are rooted in this asymmetrical devolution.

 8. It was envisaged that its functioning should be similar to that of the Comptroller and Auditor General of India.

 9. The government of Karnataka also plans to introduce the institution of ombudsman.

10. In Kerala and Karnataka, 'social audit' in panchayats is used to refer to people taking stock of the activities of the panchayats in gram sabhas.

11. For a comment on the Right to Information in Karnataka, see Nikhel Dey and Vinod Vyasulu, 2002, 'Setting the Rules for Engagement—Right to Information in Karnataka'.

12. In local parlance it is also referred to as *mamul* which is the amount given for getting work done, although in principle nothing should be accepted for carrying out that work (see Vijayalakshmi 2003).

13. Elites controlled the selection of the candidates and also ensured that not too many candidates entered the electoral competition. They often paid money to some candidates to make them withdraw their candidature.

14. It needs to be pointed out that in Kerala, the LDF and UDF, each have had stable electoral support of a little over 45 per cent of the vote share, with minor swings in electoral fortunes in successive elections. This has often led to the practice of sectarian politics to retain the support base.

15. For example, some Congress members stated that the call for tenders to carry out public works was published in the regional newspaper *Deshabimani* published by the LDF, which was read only by Leftist parties' supporters, and not in *Mathrubhumi* and *Manorama*, which were read by people belonging to all political parties.

REFERENCES

Blair, Harry, 'Participation and Accountability at the Periphery: Democratic Local Government in Six Countries', *World Development*, 28(1), 2000, pp. 21–39.

Burke, Edmund, 'Speech to the election of Bristol', in R.J.S. Hoffman and P. Levack (eds), *Burke's Politics, Selected Writings and Speeches*, New York: A.A. Knopf, 1949 (1974), 114–17.

Dey, Nikhel and Vinod Vyasulu, 'Setting the Rules for Engagement—Right to Information in Karnataka', unpublished paper, Bangalore: Centre for Budget and Policy Studies, 2002.

Ferejohn, John, 'Accountability and Authority: Towards a Theory of Political Accountability', in Adam Przeworski, Susan C. Stokes, and Bernard Manin, (eds), *Democracy, Accountability and Representation*, Cambridge: Cambridge University Press, 1999, 131–53.

Government of Kerala, Committee on Decentralization of Powers (Chairperson: S. B. Sen), Second Interim Report, 1996.

Inbanathan, Anand, 'Decentralization and Affirmative Action: The Case of Panchayats in Karnataka', *Journal of Social and Economic Development*, 2(2), 1999, 269–86.

———, 'Power, Patronage and Accountability in the Panchayats of Karnataka', Working Paper No. 68, Bangalore: Institute for Social and Economic Change, 2000.

———, 'Representation and Accountability in Local Government: The Panchayats of Karnataka', Working Paper 96, Bangalore: Institute for Social and Economic Change, 2001a.

———, 'Patronage and Representation in Karnataka's Panchayats', Unpublished paper presented at Workshop on Decentralization, Bangalore: Institute for Social and Economic Change, 2001b.

Manin, B., *The Principles of Representative Government*, Cambridge: Cambridge University Press, 1997.

Manin, B., Adam Przeworski, and Susan C. Stokes, 'Elections and Represent-ation', in Adam Przeworski, Susan C. Stokes, and Bernard Manin (eds), *Democracy, Accountability and Representation*, Cambridge: Cambridge University Press, 1999, 131–53.

Manor, James, *The Political Economy of Decentralization*, Washington DC: World Bank, 1999.

Moncrieffe, Joy M., 'Accountability: Idea, Ideals, Constraints', *Democratization*, vol.8 (3), 2001, 26–50.

Pitkin, Hanna, *The Concept of Representation*, Berkeley: University of California Press, 1967.

Phillips, Anne, *The Politics of Presence: The Political Representation of Gender, Ethnicity and Race*, Oxford: Clarendon Press, 1995.

Polidano, Charles and David Hulme, 1997. 'No Magic Wands: Accountability and Governance in Developing Countries; *Regional Development Dialogue*, 18(2), 1997, 1–16.

Prewitt, Kenneth, 'Political Ambitions, Volunteerism, and Electoral Accountability', *American Political Science Review*, LXIV (1), 1970, 5–17.

Przeworski, Adam, Susan C. Stokes, and Bernard Manin (eds), *Democracy, Accountability and Representation*, Cambridge: Cambridge University Press, 1999.

Schumpeter, J.A., *Capitalism, Socialism and Democracy*, Harper: New York Press, 1942.

Shiviah, M., 'A Perspective on System and Measures to Enhance Accountability in Panchayati Raj (Consistent with its Status as a Vehicle of Genuine Local Self-Government)', in Amitava Mukherjee (ed.), *Decentralization: Panchayats in the Nineties*, Delhi: Vikas Publishing House, 1994.

Sigurdur Helgason, 'Towards Performance Based Accountability: Issues for Discussion', Public Management Service, OECD, 1997.

Sivanna, N. and Devendra Babu, *Panchayati Jamabandhi in Karnataka: An Evaluation Study*, Bangalore: Institute for Social and Economic Change, 2002.

Vijayalakshmi, V. and B.K. Chandrashekar, 'Authority, Powerlessness and Dependence: Women and Political Participation', Working Paper No. 106, Bangalore. Institute for Social and Economic Change, 2002.

Vijayalakshmi V., 'Rent-seeking and Gender in Local Governance', Paper presented at the Symposium on Reconstructing Corruption, University of East Anglia, Norwich, England, 30 April to 2 May 2003.

The Salience of Poverty, Participation, Transparency, and Security in Good Urban Governance

■ RAMA NATH JHA

In recent years the Government of India's most concerted and widely shared urban initiative was its launch of the National Good Urban Governance Campaign in September 2001. The launch that witnessed participation of more than 1,500 urban representatives, as cross-sectional as possible, resulted in a set of Recommendations for National Action Plan for Good Urban Governance' (MoUD&PA, GoI 2001). Six issues that got identified as fundamental to good urban governance and found universal acceptance in the launch were the issues of urban decentralization, municipal finance, urban environment, integration of the poor and marginalized, transparency and civic engagement, and municipal management and capacity building.

Of the six cited issues, urban decentralization has drawn a great deal of attention. The devolution of administrative and financial powers from the state to the civic bodies and further down to ward committees has been widely considered as axiomatic to the promotion of good urban governance. Urban finance, the accompanying concepts of innovative resource mobilization, and private sector participation have not been far behind in terms of the importance attached to them as matters central to good delivery of civic services and quality of urban life. So has urban environment been a favourite in seminars and workshops, and urban sustainability and the need to prevent the degradation of urban ecosystems have been subjects of enormous concern.

In comparison, issues of urban poverty, civic participation, transparency of tools of urban governance, and an emerging fundamental issue of security of citizens in body, property, and livelihood have not drawn as much care and notice. This article is an attempt to dwell on the centrality of these issues in good urban governance. In the Indian context, their salience is enhanced. For while decentralization is essential to local empowerment, mere devolution of powers does not necessarily translate into good civic governance. This is amply demonstrated by many cities where devolution is large and yet governance is poor. While resources are critical, mere richness of the urban coffers does not lead to good delivery of services and an improved quality of life. What better proof of this than the instance of Surat. This is decidedly one of the country's richest cities and yet was visited by the plague, which rode in on its piles of filth. The same city went on to emerge from its trauma as one of the cleanest cities in the country. While we fight the battle for urban environment in Delhi in the areas of air pollution, solid waste management, and water and sewerage, the critical social issue of urban poverty and growing slums continues to adversely impact the city's social sustainability. And while in parts of our country we reach heights of industrialization and abilities for creation of wealth and business opportunities, the uphill struggle of cities to ensure security of life and property and livelihood are eroding their competitive edge. These facts are further proof of the mutually interdependent and reinforcing nature of the principles of good urban governance. They cannot stand in isolation and ensure good municipal governance unless all ingredients are in place to play their respective supportive roles.

The importance of participation and transparency has assumed added significance in the light of a visible change in popular perception about how governance should be re-engineered. There is now growing belief that all administrative action should be people-centred rather than rule-centred, outward-looking rather than inward-looking, inclusive rather than exclusive. There is insistence that governments should examine themselves primarily from the viewpoint of outputs and delivery of governance, rather than merely from the viewpoint of processes. This chapter attempts to deal with each of these issues in some depth.

First, a disquisition on the salience of urban poverty to good municipal governance.

It would not be very original to state that urbanization in the developing world has been too quick for comfort. It is now widely accepted that this intensity and rapidity of urban growth has largely been on account of the urbanization of poverty, of the rural poor fleeing rural deprivation, and congregating in cities in tiny hovels and in dingy, dark lanes to discover tools of survival. The results of such growth have been troublesome for cities, and their sustainability has been rendered increasingly suspect. This is because more and more of their inhabitants live in rising filth, disease, illiteracy, fire, and crime, all contributors to urban non-sustainability. And these are consequences not because the poor have brought in disaster, but because the cities have either ignored the rising phenomenon of poverty or have failed to foresee, comprehend, and proactively integrate this phenomenon into the planned settlement. While cities have relished the services and the value additions that poor men and women bring into the city as industrial workers, sweepers, cleaners, domestic assistants, and hawkers of myriad wares, there has been little concern about where they would live in order to provide these sought-after services. The concomitant of the neglect of poverty as a key ingredient in urban planning has substantially been the collapse of urban sustainability. With the passage of time and the rise of urban poverty, it increasingly dawns on city governments that the single most important factor that will destroy cities will be their inability to deal with the poor. Let a few facts walk us to this truth.

One of the chief consequences of the urbanization of poverty has been the proliferation of urban slums. As cities have expanded, their slum populations have risen even faster, leading to greater percentages of city populations in larger cities living in informal settlements and in squalid misery. The reasons for such proliferation are starkly clear. Urban planning has thought broadly of residential needs, but has not sufficiently examined the customized requirements of different groups of people, in particular the poor. It has zoned lands as residential, but left its use to be determined largely by market forces. Since the poor are priced out of all decent land zoned for housing, they find shelter on lands that are zoned open, ecologically unfit and hazardous for residence, or reserved for other activities. Their settlements are built without valid permission, without infrastructure, and without any modicum of planning. Attempts to apply the law by either eviction en masse or relocation without stakeholder consultation have generally failed, largely because decisions have been taken entirely from the point of view of the state, in disregard of the needs of the poor. Moreover, the indomitable human will to survive has almost always excelled the administrative zeal to regulate. But the impact of such settlements has been sad both for the city as well as the poor. The informal city has unplanned the formal town, and thrown many of its services into disarray. Laws, rules, and regulations on which cities stand have been compromised. The poor on the other hand have lived in constant fear of eviction, in miserable surroundings, and in the clutches of middlemen who promise protection. The lesson clearly has been that the city's inability to deal with poverty has seriously compromised its governance. Acceptance of the services of the poor to the cities and rejection of their claim to housing have set up a contradiction that when not formally resolved have perforce found recognition outside the periphery of law. And unlawful cities cannot be sustainable.

The growth of slums has been matched by a parallel growth of informal markets, the other side of the urban informal sector, and the most visible of them are the street hawkers. In street after street, in city after city, footpaths and open spaces are cluttered with such activity. It is now universally acknowledged that like the informal settlements, informal enterprise multiplies as cities balloon in size and acquire larger consumer capacities. The informal markets and services are sought on account of their low cost, easy availability, and the inability of the formal sector to keep pace with these needs. These are very competitive outlets for goods and services. They generate employment and income for the poor and are preferred markets for a cross-section of people looking for reasonably priced convenience goods. But like the informal settlements, street vending has no place in a city's plan. Unfortunately, the street vendor cannot get into the formal market since he can never hope to buy a shop in a regular commercial centre. So the vendor sets up shop at junctions, such as bus terminuses, railway stations, hospitals, and office complexes. These are busy places where people congregate and business abounds. But just as informal settlements have been detrimental both to the city and the poor, informal enterprises on streets and open lands have brought grief in many ways to both. Such enterprises are regarded as nuisances and eyesores, making streets unhygienic and smelly. Walking on footpaths is made difficult and traffic is impeded. The poor entrepreneurs themselves survive in unease and tension, subject to threats of eviction and extortion. The attempts to throw them out of the streets have not been very successful. But wherever livelihoods have been destroyed by a stoppage of such informal activities, there has been loss of employment, rise in crime, and a compromise of the safety of citizens. Here, again, the lesson has been that the non-recognition of the sought-after services of informal enterprise works against the sustainability and 'governability' of the city.

Urban politics, on account of keeping the poor out of the formal city, has itself undergone extremely disturbing changes. There has been a virtual division of interests in what groups of citizens from the formal city want and do not want, and what residents of the informal city want and do not want. City administration increasingly seems to be slipping out of the hands of the formal city and becoming more and more representative of the informal. By taking on the role of the persecutor, and by driving the poor into the arms of 'protectors' who stand between them and eviction, the rest of the city prepares the ground for its own alienation from governance. This has left cities as houses divided against themselves. Such fractured urban centres with deep-seated animosities run the risk of turning explosive, susceptible to ignition on the flimsiest of provocation. Such growing social divides do not aid urban governance.

The cited facts amply prove that good urban governance and urban poverty are in several ways interlinked. Good urban governance, therefore, begins by recognizing that the poor by virtue of the services they provide to the cities are rightfully an integral part of the city, and planners need to plan for their needs. There has to be recognition that as the economy of a city expands, there will be more demand to fulfil roles that the expanded economy craves for, and this includes a larger number of service providers, primarily the poor. But to provide these services they need to stay in the city in decent housing, which they may not be able to buy from the formal market. They would also need to buy goods at affordable rates and need their own kinds of market. If these are not planned, they will assert their existence outside the plan. And the more unplanned the city gets, the less sustainable it becomes. The need, therefore, is to think beyond slum improvements or slum rehabilitation or hawking zones, but of strategies to integrate the needs of the poor in all city planning activities. It is because of the absence of such an approach that anti-poverty schemes of nations tie themselves up into knots, for no person can pursue an enterprise without a place to live and work, and no bank loans money to a person who has no collateral to show.

It would be a little naïve to challenge the notion that slums make for unclean cities. If by slums we mean unplanned, high density, unhygienic clusters of temporary tenements haphazardly erected out of poor material by the poor (and that is what slums are), then they do make cities unclean and unhealthy. Such slums must be prevented. But if such prevention of slums in cities means the prevention of housing for the poor through a quixotic crusade of evictions, then such a view is terribly myopic and utterly unsustainable. Demolition of structures that symbolize unauthorized commerce and undue gain is welcome. But the demolition of housing structures erected for human survival when no other outlet for survival exists needs to be seen in a different, human light. Denial of housing in some ways becomes a denial of the right to exist. The solution lies not in eviction as an a priori antidote, but in planning to adequately house the poor. This requires a new planning paradigm—the re-engineering of housing laws, policies, building codes, rules and regulations that would allow affordable housing to the poor. In their absence, slums will proliferate and their eviction will always be difficult to justify. As has been stated, 'The fundamental task before cities is not merely to rehabilitate slums, but to prevent their occurrence by adequately housing the poor' (Jha and Siddiqui 2000).

There have been arguments, and with some conviction, that select cities cannot be burdened beyond their carrying capacities either in terms of people or activities, and that these cities must be preserved as viable, salubrious, efficient units. This is an important point and deserves attention and a search for viable answers, not in the abstract, but in the specific situation of developing countries with enormous populations and heavy inter-region and intra-region population movements. Experience tells us that in such matters, cities have not entirely been in control of their own fate, and have found themselves subjected to onerous responsibilities thrust upon them on account of decisions taken by higher levels of government.

A part of the solution lies in macroeconomic and industrial policies of nations that consciously attempt to spread out industrial/commercial/service locations and opportunities of wealth creation to several areas and cities. When a limited number of cities are made to overwhelmingly concentrate such activities within their folds, quite naturally they invite a disproportionately large number of people to carry out those activities, for urbanization is substantially an outcome of economic development. Conversely, serious lack of growth and suffocation in certain areas may trigger massive migratory pressures to better-endowed centres. Care, therefore, needs to be taken that such national/regional decisions do not wreak havoc on primate cities.

That does not obviate the fact, however, that cities themselves need to make a radical reappraisal of how they serve those whose services they demand. A wholesale denial of the realities of poverty staring urban centres in the face does not serve the cause of good governance. Cities have no option but to take notice of urban poverty and their positive relationship with the city life and economy. 'If they choose to ignore these and take an anti-poor stance, they will themselves craft the destruction of their sustainability' (Jha 2001).

The second issue that merits attention is civic participation. It is of immense relevance to good urban governance. In the local context, the idea of citizens participating and sharing in city affairs has been at the heart of democratic governance from the ancient days of city-states. Indeed, the focal theme in local government functioning is the word 'self'. Several factors mandate local participation. Local administration handles issues that are vital to citizens in their daily lives, and hence they have immediate interest and stake in the performance of those services. They are also matters on which local knowledge, wisdom, and sharing have the ability to improve the quality of service delivery. And local governments have the innate capacity to mobilize community participation on these vital concerns.

This has become hugely evident in the recent disasters such as the cyclone that struck Orissa or the earthquake that devastated Gujarat. It was clearly realized after these tragic events that disaster management involves total community effort and the best way to prepare for disaster is to prepare the entire community to be in a state of informed and trained readiness for such eventualities. There is, therefore, a strong case for taking expert knowledge down to the communities and fertilizing it with community-based wisdom. It was also realized that there was a need to define the roles of different community stakeholders along with disaster-related governmental functionaries and work out coordination plans leading to the preparation of a community-based strategic plan.

Participation as an essential tool for governance also came to the fore when the UN Conference on Environment and Development held at Rio de Janeiro in 1992 discussed sustainable development and crafted the document called Agenda 21. It realized that an over-whelming percentage of implementation was within the realm of local bodies. Sustainability could not be achieved without community participation. And it was only the civic bodies that could mobilize community response. Because so many of the problems and solutions being addressed by Agenda 21 had their roots in local activities, the participation and cooperation of local authorities were regarded as a determining factor in fulfilling the objectives of Agenda 21. Rio, therefore, mandated that 'each local authority should enter into a dialogue with its citizens, local organizations, private enterprises, and through a consultative process with such key stakeholders arrive at and adopt a Local Agenda 21' (UNCED 1992: ch. 28).

But the role of participation is not merely from the point of view of the necessities of democratic polity or improvement of service delivery. It finds recommendation as it also has the ability to contribute to the feeling of community ownership, to transparency, to civic capacity building, and to empowerment. While the civic body turns into a training ground for democracy and educates citizens in public functioning, and the pros and cons of public policies, emotional commitment of the citizenry and ownership of decisions by it are equally salutary outcomes. A lot of public dissatisfaction that is noticed today about governmental decisions, and the resultant agitation and litigation that hamper the smooth implementation of programmes is on many occasions a result of misunderstandings and the lack of feeling of ownership. These can be substantially avoided if cities begin by an ab initio sharing with their people the plans they have on the anvil and develop decisions in partnership.

Additionally, participation has the knack of improving governance through the import of transparency. The very fact that the cloak of secrecy is removed from the manner a city does business reduces monopoly, discretion, arbitrariness, and the ability of individuals to indulge in malpractice. It is all these reasons that make civic participation so central to the process of governance reforms. Unfortunately, we have tried to tackle administrative wickedness through ethical rhetoric rather than address it through ways that reduce monopoly and discretion. Participation is an excellent antidote to contend with this kind of system since it has the innate capacity to limit misuse of power.

One of the best illustrations that can demonstrate this is the manner of preparation of city development plans. These have led to huge allegations of graft and nepotism with respect to demarcation of land use. The publication of plans and the seeking of public objections have been popularly regarded as mere formalities. Aggrieved individuals have, therefore, resorted to judicial interventions. Many of the ills that bedevil this process can be set right by altering the non-participatory manner of its formulation. There are many reasons that can be advanced for such a change. Since city plans are prepared once in a decade or two, and tend to freeze uses of land for such prolonged periods, it is logical that the widest possible informed consultations precede and accompany the planning process. Aspects of the plan need to be discussed by professionals, NGOs, Chambers of Commerce and Industry, slum dwellers, landowners, tenants and builders, and several such stakeholders that could contribute to city structuring. City planning is a highly complex process that tries to capture the necessities of life in all its variety. This is beyond the comprehension of a single individual or agency, and calls for the widest kind of participation. Cities have a wealth of talent and experience. Given the complexity of city life, participatory planning immediately enriches the process and quality of plans if such talent, experience, and insights are allowed to feed into them. At the same time, plans become more equitable and just because of the transparency accompanying their preparation. Additionally, it prevents the enormous discretion and monopoly that current planning methods put into a few hands, thus foreclosing possible misuse of authority, and the possibility of decisions under powerful pressures.

One of the encouraging features of urban life is the rise of multiple civil society and non-governmental organizations and their urge to increasingly participate in affairs of their cities. Non-governmental organizations can also play a healthy role in cities by lending strength to the voice and demands of the less privileged. It has been seen that such deprived communities, which are low in self-confidence and motivation, require the stimulus of external agents if they are to participate meaningfully in public life. In these circumstances, NGOs are more likely to promote participation of the poor and serve their interests than mere professional politicians who treat the urban poor essentially as vote banks.

This is not to say that participation is without its problems. Prolonged deliberations that get unfocused and fractious may lead to interminable delays. The clash of interests of different stakeholders and behind-the-scenes lobbying to promote specific agendas and the seeming inability to reconcile differing viewpoints are potent dangers that can destroy the essence of the participatory process. Given the high rates of illiteracy in many cities, public awareness at best of times is low, making meaningful participation doubly difficult. The reluctance of local bodies to devolve power to the wards and the shyness of the ward representatives to give space to citizens and their organizations have made participation an uphill task.

But a city nevertheless needs to go through this process, as this is the best way to achieve consensus. With time, difficulties get ironed out, as there is larger appreciation of each other's views and greater tolerance of dissension. A society learns then to find space for all rather than merely fight for oneself. This was witnessed in one of the Urban Management Programme (UMP) city consultations that the All India Institute of Local Self Government (AIILSG) backstopped in Mumbai. The residents' association in 'H' West Ward called the Advance Locality Management (ALM), began a contentious dialogue with the hawkers of the ward. Eventually, however, both settled to alter the lines that they had drawn for themselves and then moved towards a mutually acceptable formula in which the ALM accepted hawking in their ward but with regulatory restrictions, and the hawkers agreed to take the onus of keeping their premises and neighbourhood clean. Such a platform for participation thus became a forum for conflict management.

The third issue that this paper wishes to highlight is transparency. Quite strikingly, transparency and participation in many ways are two sides of the same coin. On the one hand, participation naturally enhances transparency. Transparency, on the other, is an essential tool for participation. Transparency signifies the conduct of public business with openness. It follows that such conduct of business will afford wide accessibility to the decision-making process. The quality of transparency is further enhanced if stakeholders are not merely informed of what business transpires, but are also given the opportunity to participate in the decision-making process and effectively influence it. This renders decisions more wholesome. In the context of urban governance, conducted at the level of urban local bodies, transparency assumes added significance. Aspects of life and services that are closest to citizens are transacted and delivered at the local level. Their quality or their absence directly and most tellingly affect the daily lives of citizens. Quite naturally, their concern with such matters is much larger than the attention they would care to give to national and global issues. Since it is also possible to foster, cement, and build close relationships among various civic actors in a city, having the advantage of a compact, circumscribed geographical area, transparency has the chance of ever greater degrees of success.

Since transparency presupposes wide access to information and comprehension of that information by an average citizen, it follows that laws, rules, and procedures need to be simplified and made comprehensible to persons of average education and intelligence. That is not the case today. While statutes may satisfy the legal luminary by their pedantic complexities, they are unintelligible to the common person. Complex rules are the very antithesis of transparency and empowerment. The less they are understood, the more they are likely to be misused. Simplifying them, therefore, is a *sine qua non* for transparency. But more importantly, in the Indian context, simplification of laws and rules also means less of them. The approach to limit misuse of authority through more control, more laws, and more bureaucracy is not the ideal approach. 'These can simply paralyze administration, and in some cases can foster new and more deeply embedded varieties of corruption' (Klitgaard *et al.* 2000).

Easy accessibility to information also has the quality of discouraging dishonesty for fear of being found out. It is a powerful tool for reducing malfeasance, for societies are also made honest by eliminating the sources of temptation and opportunities for graft. This also prevents misunderstanding of genuine decisions and prevents the conversion of fair into foul through misrepresentation and insinuation—both of which thrive in an atmosphere of ignorance and non-information.

The injection of transparency has great value in the procurement processes of municipalities. Current procurement practices have been the bane of many local bodies. Open procurement processes would help the full use of public money for purposes they are allocated. They would have the multiple impact of ridding the public coffers from the drain they suffer on account of siphoning off of public money for private gain, of improving the quality of services and infrastructure in cities, and of fostering a healthy civic life of honesty.

The opening of civic body meetings to public attendance is a further avenue of imparting transparency in cities. This will promote responsible participation by elected representatives. It will also bring larger bits of information to the people for richer citizen debate. The media itself would become more relevant to the city and could then become a powerful tool for generating meaningful debate on civic issues.

Budgets are vitally important civic documents. It is in this exercise that resources get allocated for various works and programmes. Unfortunately, this has been an exercise without reference to its citizenry. If budgets were to be opened up for wider dissemination and discussion, this would allow public examination of budgeting practices. It would be possible to see whether monies have been allocated as per planning priorities, whether they have been equitable, and whether all regions of the city have received their due share of works and assets, or whether taxes are being frittered away in unnecessary expenditures. Such transparent consultations are a certain way of making the civic body accountable to its citizens. The quality of systems would be heightened through such participation. The citizens would also repose faith in systems they have developed since they would feel full ownership. A similar control can emerge out of transparency in audits. Internal audits are susceptible to huge pressures from local functionaries and may not yield a truthful picture of how financial matters are handled in the town hall. An independent, transparent audit would encourage impartiality and would be conducted in relative freedom from influence to fix decisions.

The development of an appropriate, transparent code of conduct for elected representatives and management has also been recommended as a benchmark for public behaviour. Such a code would set the guidelines on how city officials and managers need to conduct themselves and what standards citizens should expect of their city representatives and managers. Tools such as the introduction of declaration of assets and incomes at the higher levels of city management have been found useful. Similarly, an innovative mechanism about what citizens could expect of the civic body in terms of services, by having them stated upfront in a Citizens' Charter, has caught the citizen's imagination around the world. It serves as a benchmark for the city on what to deliver and for citizens on what to expect.

It is encouraging that several city governments are attempting to open their gates wider, allow more information flow, declare charters for citizens and benchmark municipal response to citizens' demands and promote civic engagement in civic services. Citizens in some cities have also shown nascent vibrancy, and charted both partnership and adversarial courses in their attempt at holding civic bodies responsible. But the overall national impact has been limited and the principles of transparent functioning have yet to strike fertile soil.

The fourth and final issue the chapter seeks to address is the issue of security. The raison d'être of the state has been the need for ensuring peace, law and order, and a guarantee against physical violation, theft, and loot. It is evident that the other concerns of governance are central when the concerns of security are already adequately addressed. If they are not, then everything else is rendered secondary. For, as Aristotle said, 'We must live before we can live well'. The lack of security is quite certainly antithetical to stability and quality of life in cities, and to sustainable and economic development. In other words, it is fundamental to good urban governance. For insecurity leads to all-round fear, reduced interaction among people, increased distrust, restricted movement in the city after certain hours, and diversion of considerable resources to cope with such unsafe times. Thus, there is the absence of an enabling environment that promotes city life and hits at the very root of any governance, leave alone good governance. Indeed, it negates all that good governance stands for, and tends to roll back decentralization, participation, and transparency, handing back to the state extraordinary powers to deal with the exigencies of an unsettled situation. The poor are especially vulnerable because of their inability to protect themselves.

The rise of crime in cities and the quality of the criminal justice system have become a matter of increasing concern. Policing, courts, and prisons have been unable to rise to the challenges of the urban environment and have been found wanting in speed and the ability to control crime. There has been a resultant proliferation of private security companies to fill gaps in security. As things have become difficult for the crime preventing agencies, there have been reports of misuse of authority with implications on human life, limb, and freedom.

It is, therefore, evident that when we talk of good urban governance, we must perforce talk of safety in cities. Quite clearly, some of the axioms that are applied to other aspects of governance also get applied here. Participation and transparency will have their own vital roles in the way safety is administered in cities. The idea is to deal with the situation not in the traditional way, but improve the safety of cities through partnership and participation of citizens and sharing of responsibility. Clearly, security and reduction of crime in the modern urban context cannot be the concern of any single agency but a joint responsibility of everyone. New forms of community policing and justice, informal mechanisms for conflict resolution, and the mediation of elders in the community have served society well in the past and may have important lessons for handling urban crime. Several cities are also responding through the creation of Neighbourhood Watch Groups that virtually take formal control of surveillance in their neighbourhood and provide collaborative back-up to the police.

It would be apposite, therefore, in the light of factors discussed in the chapter, to pay heed to the issues of poverty, participation, transparency, and security, and treat them as issues of vital importance to good urban governance. Ignoring their weight would leave the concept of good urban governance floundering and holistic results difficult to achieve.

REFERENCES

Jha, R., *UMP Asia News: Urban Management Programme*, Mumbai: AIILSG Press, 2001.

Jha, R. and N. Siddiqui, *Towards People-friendly Cities*, Mumbai: UNICEF, 2000.

Klitgaard, R., R. Maclean-Abaroa, and H. Lindsey Parris, *Corrupt Cities*, Oakland: ICS Press, 2000.

Ministry of Urban Development & Poverty Alleviation, Government of India (MoUD&PA, GOI), *Recommendations for National Action Plan for Good Urban Governance,* New Delhi: HSMI, 2001.

UNCED, 'Local Authorities' Initiatives in Support of Agenda 21' (Section III, chapter 28), in *Rio Declaration on Environment and Development*, Rio de Janeiro, UNCED, 1992.

Contributors

RAMA V. BARU is Associate Professor, Centre of Social Medicine and Community Health, Jawaharlal Nehru University, New Delhi.

SOLOMON BENJAMIN is an independent researcher based in Bangalore.

DWAIPAYAN BHATTACHARYYA is Fellow in Political Science, Centre for Studies in Social Sciences, Kolkata.

R. BHUVANESWARI is a Ph.D. student at the London School of Economics and Political Science (LSE).

MEENA GOPAL is Associate Professor, SNDT Women's University, Mumbai.

ANWAR JAFRI is Director, Samavesh, Society for Development and Governance, Bhopal.

NIRAJA GOPAL JAYAL is Professor, Centre for the Study of Law and Governance, Jawaharlal Nehru University, New Delhi and Senior Fellow, Nehru Memorial Museum and Library, New Delhi.

RAMA NATH JHA is an Indian Administration Service officer and is presently Vice Chairman and MD, Maharashtra Road Development Corporation, Mumbai.

DILIP KARMARKAR is Adviser–Urban Sector, ICRA Management Consulting Services Limited, Mumbai.

AJIT KARNIK is Professor, College of Graduate Studies, University of Wollongong, Dubai and Professor, Department of Economics, University of Mumbai.

K.P. KRISHNAN is an Indian Administrative Service officer and is presently Joint Secretary, Ministry of Finance, Government of India.

ASHOK KUMAR is Assistant Professor, School of Planning and Architecture (SPA), New Delhi.

ABHAY PETHE is Dr Vibhooti Shukla Professor of Urban Economics and Regional Development, Department of Economics, University of Mumbai.

MARINA R. PINTO is Adjunct Professor of Public Administration, Department of Civics and Politics, University of Mumbai.

AMIT PRAKASH is Associate Professor, Centre for the Study of Law and Governance, Jawaharlal Nehru University, New Delhi.

KRIPA ANANTH PUR is Assistant Professor, Madras Institute of Development Studies, Chennai.

VIMALA RAMACHANDRAN is National Director (Education and Health) Naandi Foundation, Hyderabad.

AARTI SAIHJEE is Assistant Project Officer, Girls Education in UNICEF, New Delhi.

PRADEEP K. SHARMA is Senior Assistant Resident Representative at UNDP, Timor-Leste.

AMITA SINGH is Professor and currently Chairperson, Centre for the Study of Law and Governance, Jawaharlal Nehru University, New Delhi.

JAGPAL SINGH is Reader in Political Science, School of Social Science, Indira Gandhi National Open University, New Delhi.

VIKAS SINGH is an independent researcher and writer based in Madhya Pradesh.

RAVI S. SRIVASTAVA is Professor of Economics, Centre for the Study of Regional Development, Jawaharlal Nehru University, New Delhi. He is presently member of the National Commission for Enterprises in the Unorganised Sector, Government of India.

V. VIJAYALAKSHMI is a consultant sociologist based in Bangalore.